THE STRUGGLE OF NON-SOVEREIGN CARIBBEAN TERRITORIES

D1527533

Critical Caribbean Studies

SERIES EDITORS: YOLANDA MARTÍNEZ-SAN MIGUEL,
CARTER MATHES, AND KATHLEEN LÓPEZ

Editorial Board: Carlos U. Decena, Rutgers University, Alex Dupuy, Wesleyan University, Aisha Khan, New York University, April J. Mayes, Pomona College, Patricia Mohammed, University of West Indies, Martin Munro, Florida State University, F. Nick Nesbitt, Princeton University, Michelle Stephens, Rutgers University, Deborah Thomas, University of Pennsylvania, Lanny Thompson, University of Puerto Rico

Focused particularly in the twentieth and twenty-first centuries, although attentive to the context of earlier eras, this series encourages interdisciplinary approaches and methods and is open to scholarship in a variety of areas, including anthropology, cultural studies, diaspora and transnational studies, environmental studies, gender and sexuality studies, history, and sociology. The series pays particular attention to the four main research clusters of Critical Caribbean Studies at Rutgers University, where the coeditors serve as members of the executive board: Caribbean Critical Studies Theory and the Disciplines; Archipelagic Studies and Creolization; Caribbean Aesthetics, Poetics, and Politics; and Caribbean Colonialities.

THE STRUGGLE OF NON-SOVEREIGN CARIBBEAN TERRITORIES

Neoliberalism since the French

Antillean Uprisings of 2009

EDITED BY H. ADLAI MURDOCH

RUTGERS UNIVERSITY PRESS
New Brunswick, Camden, and Newark,
New Jersey, and London

LCCN 2020020807

A British Cataloging-in-Publication record for this book is available from the British Library.

This collection copyright © 2021 by Rutgers, The State University of New Jersey

Individual chapters copyright © 2021 in the names of their authors

All rights reserved

No part of this book may be reproduced or utilized in any form or by any means, electronic or mechanical, or by any information storage and retrieval system, without written permission from the publisher. Please contact Rutgers University Press, 106 Somerset Street, New Brunswick, NJ 08901. The only exception to this prohibition is "fair use" as defined by U.S. copyright law.

♾ The paper used in this publication meets the requirements of the American National Standard for Information Sciences—Permanence of Paper for Printed Library Materials, ANSI Z39.48-1992.

www.rutgersuniversitypress.org

Manufactured in the United States of America

Contents

THE STRUGGLE OF NON-SOVEREIGN CARIBBEAN TERRITORIES

Introduction

NON-SOVEREIGNTY AND THE
NEOLIBERAL CHALLENGE:
CONTESTING ECONOMIC
EXPLOITATION IN THE
EASTERN CARIBBEAN

H. ADLAI MURDOCH

This book is an essay collection made up of two sections. In the principal section, a group of Anglophone and Francophone scholars examine the roots, effects, and implications of the 2009 strikes and demonstrations in the territories of Guadeloupe and Martinique, emphasizing their resistance to and subversion of a hierarchical neocolonial and neoliberal praxis whose insistence on capital, profit, and their corollary of centralization reinforces the racialized patterns of socioeconomic exclusion long imposed by France on its former colonial territories. These analyses focus on a range of socio-cultural, political, and economic perspectives and practices, including the critical role played by art and media alongside politico-economic policies that generate (un)employment, labor exploitation, and unattended health risks continually made secondary to the supremacy of profit. In the second section, additional scholars provide in-depth analyses of the ways in which a politico-economic praxis of neoliberalism has instantiated broad hierar-chies of market-driven profit, capital accumulation, and economic exploita-tion upon a range of populations and territories in the non-sovereign and nominally sovereign Caribbean. Examples here range from the outsized role played by the excessive number of nongovernmental organizations (NGOs) in purportedly independent territories like Haiti; to the paradoxi-cal autonomy conferred on the former Dutch colonies of the Netherlands Antilles; to the ongoing crises of disaster, debt, and governance undergirding the "commonwealth" status accorded to Puerto Rico—all part of an exploitative history in which unidirectional trade and its corollaries of privatization and profit have long characterized neocolonial and neoliberal economies in the region.

The year 2019 marks the tenth anniversary of the social upheaval that shook Guadeloupe, Martinique, French Guiana, and Réunion—all integral parts of the French nation since 1946, and so "non-sovereign territories" in their respective regions—in February and March 2009. For forty-four days, a mass general strike protesting the elevated and inequitable cost of living in the French Caribbean DOM (*départements d'outre-mer*, or overseas departments) relative to the mainland brought the territories of Guadeloupe and Martinique to a standstill. This action was accompanied by huge demonstrations against the severe inequities of prevailing social and economic conditions, often involving as many as one hundred thousand people—one-quarter of the population of each of these territories. By February 21, these strikes and demonstrations spread to Réunion. An agreement with the French government was eventually reached on March 4 on 165 demands, including a €200 ($250) increase in the monthly minimum wage and reduced prices for public transportation, gasoline, food, housing, and water.

The strike was organized by a coalition of forty-eight organizations, including trade unions from a wide spectrum of industries (gasoline distribution, commerce, tourism, civil service, health care, education, and agriculture, to name a few), as well as environmental groups; peasant organizations, political parties, pro-independence activists, consumer rights advocates, associations for disability rights, fair housing proponents, music and dance groups, and a wide range of other political, cultural, and civic leaders. These diverse activists came together under the name Lyannaj Kont Pwofitasyon (LKP), which can be loosely translated as the Alliance Against Profiteering. In Creole, *lyannaj* refers to a coming together, or a joining of forces, for a common goal. Guadeloupean activists found themselves in *lyannaj* against the high cost of living that characterizes the French Caribbean, with its corollary of excessive profiteering and economic exploitation, locally called *pwofitasyon*. It is the extension of this analysis of the egregious effects of neoliberal economic exploitation to parallel conditions in other non-sovereign and nominally sovereign Caribbean territories that provides the enabling context for this collection of essays.

The doubleness that departmentalization inscribes operates simultaneously within several other non-sovereign Caribbean territories; indeed, the telling phrase "French and West Indian" embodies the political, psychological, and cultural patterns of this contentious postcolonial condition. At the same time, while their continuing status as French *départements d'outre-mer* is markedly at variance with the large number of independent states in the rest of the region, the ambiguity of this postcolonial existence tends to highlight their dependency; as Beverley Ormerod puts it, "the French Caribbean islands, apart from Haiti, are still owned and ruled by France. Their official status as Departments of France has not greatly altered the realities of political and cultural colonialism" (3). Be that as it may, it can also be argued that this ongoing departmentalization generates a sense of group identity that functions outside, and in spite of, the political ties to the metropole that also produce what Richard Burton has called an "unrequited longing for fusion, either by possession or by absorption, with a valorized French Other" (1992, 83). If, then, the legacy of this process, as Burton continues, is "to possess a double consciousness as both a West Indian and, since the departmentalization law of 1946, an integral citizen of France" (1992, 186), contesting the multiple and extended tensions—the benefits and deprivations—of these twin allegiances would come to be articulated in 2009 within the spheres of politics and economics as well as art, culture, and media, the very domains that had mediated the inscription of metropolitan codes of domination and hegemony.

There is a palpable history to this sense of resistance and drive for autonomy. The drive to highlight local concerns over and against those of the metropole not only is grounded in a long-standing recognition of the political and economic hierarchies, as well as the racial histories and linguistic and cultural differences, that continue to separate the DOMs from the metropole, but also marks a growing nationalist vision undergirded in turn by a drive for cultural autonomy, both of which, in effect, arose out of neocolonial empire and resistance to it and gave rise to the formulation of a specific political discourse. The importance of this conjunction of economics and politics to an assertive articulation of communal identity within a nationalist framework was outlined by Benedict Anderson; in his book *Imagined Communities*, he writes: "Nationalism has to be understood by aligning it, not with self-consciously held political ideologies, but with the large cultural systems that preceded it, out of which—as well as against which—it came into being" (1983, 19). Here, the strategic conflict is between a plurality of cultural systems, those arising out of the colonial framework imposed by the metropole, and contested first by diasporas originating on the African continent, followed by those of the Indian subcontinent, China, the Syro-Lebanese and Portuguese communities, and the various other ethnocultural groups who came together to construct the Caribbean mosaic that undergirds the strong sense of regional specificity and resistance ultimately unleashed in 2009.

Indeed, the region has long become the de facto homeland for its multitude of transplanted groups. On the one hand, as Stuart Hall has pointed out, "none of the people who now occupy the islands—black, brown, white, African, European, American, Spanish, French, East Indian, Chinese, Portuguese, Jew, Dutch—originally 'belonged' there. It is the space where the creolisations and assimilations and syncretisms were negotiated" (1990, 234). This marked ethnocultural pluralism is a key component in the generation of creolization and an activist regional identity that would catalyze the core of LKP's positions contesting non-sovereignty and articulating a vision of autonomy. At the same time, however, authors like Melanie Newton have successfully countered what she calls "the narrative of aboriginal disappearance" (2013, 108), whereby "new 'natives,' predominantly Africans and their descendants, replaced the original Antilleans and became indigenous to the Caribbean" (109). In a telling analysis, Newton confirms early patterns of colonization in the region as avatars of neoliberal exploitation, pointing out that "James's *The Black Jacobins* and Eric Williams's *Capitalism and Slavery* pioneered analysis of the Caribbean as a 'crucible' of modernity, defined by the globalization and racialization of identities; unequal inclusion into a global economy; and the intensification of human mobility, over vast distances and often under unfree conditions" (110). And so despite the eradication of indigenous populations in most of the region, given the survival of Carib communities in locations like Dominica and Saint Vincent, and the long-standing existence of as many as nine Amerindian ethnic groups—like the Arekuna, Patamona, Waiwai, Macusi, and Wapishana— in Guyana, the misperception of aboriginal absence persists. As Newton continues, "There is tacit agreement that the Caribbean is not aboriginal space. This is so despite the fact that unknown but significant numbers of people across the Caribbean know themselves to be of partly aboriginal ancestry, even if they do not seek or claim specific recognition or rights as aboriginal people" (2013, 121). Ultimately, the marginalization of these communities is integrally linked to the hierarchical insertion of other communities of color into the region's post-Columbian dreadnought of global capitalism.

In addition, in an excellent and groundbreaking analysis, Shona Jackson has recently and accurately linked the complex questions of indigeneity and creoleness not only to the articulation of creole identities, but also to issues of citizenship and labor. In *Creole Indigeneity*, she points to the marginalization of indigenous peoples while insisting on the ways in which the historical structure of exploitative labor practices in the region contributed to ongoing hierarchies of race and identity. As she writes,

> I do collectively refer to blacks and Indians as Creoles in order to make clear the ways in which their processes of becoming and belonging in the Caribbean allow them to signify on the nation in ways that maintain Indigenous Peoples as culturally and economically marginal. . . . Indigenous Peoples' own creolization processes do not allow them to signify on the nation in ways that grant them the same citizenship status of blacks and Indians, largely because of the ways in which their labor was constructed in the colonial and postcolonial state. . . . What I hope to underscore is that to the extent that labor plays a role in becoming

Creole, both Indians and blacks are able to tap into this language of
becoming to the exclusion of Indigenous Peoples. (2012, 46–47)

The extent to which such intersections of capital accumulation, neoliberal
exploitation, and cultural and political activism remain extant across the
region form the core of our explorations of patterns of profiteering in non-
sovereign Caribbean contexts. What the preceding analyses make clear is
that the issues of ethnic and racial hierarchization and marginalization
that from the beginning mediated the construction of Caribbean economies remain an integral part of neoliberal realities in the region today.

Some of these economic realities might on their face appear mislead-
ing. We should note that Guadeloupe, for example, enjoys a relatively high
standard of living, with elevated salaries compared with other Caribbean
societies given one of the highest per capita incomes in the region, with the
same minimum wage as obtains in France—the equivalent of about $1,521
euros, or $1,732 per month. But the high prices on most consumer goods
and services—anywhere from 20 percent to 170 percent higher than comparable prices in mainland France—has tended to make this equivalency a
moot point, one undermined and exacerbated by a range of other factors.
For example, Guadeloupe's unemployment rate of 23.7 percent, and Martinique's rate of 19.4 percent, should be compared with mainland France's
rate of 8.7 percent. In point of fact, since coming into force in 1946, departmentalization has produced a modernized *société de consommation*, as domestic agricultural and industrial production all but disappeared over the
ensuing decades. At present, more than 90 percent of all goods consumed
in the DOMs are imported from France; their elevated prices and the high
cost of living across the board reflect the costs of transatlantic shipping,
insurance, and the like. Merchants argue that high transportation costs,
taxes, and tariffs oblige them to charge more for imported goods. Local
political activists answer that the high prices are also the product of a larger
racial and economic history. Véronique Hélénon sums up the multiple
ramifications of this complex conundrum that emerged in 2009:

Strikers denounced the exorbitant cost of living and the economic imbalance of these societies, where the unemployment rate exceeds 20 percent against 9 percent in continental France, and the cost of food is 23 percent higher in Martinique, 28 percent higher in Guadeloupe, and 45 percent higher in Guyane than in continental France. With an overdeveloped public sphere, which occupies one-third of workers as compared to only one-fifth in continental France and which accounts for over 40 percent of salaries against 20 percent, these Caribbean societies cannot provide for their populations and therefore remain largely dependent on imports. (2011, 1)

The inequities delineated here make clear the distance and the difference between metropole and periphery, even within the presumably unitary French state. But another important point to be made here is the extent to which contemporary material conditions in the French Caribbean, particularly as regards astronomically high prices on goods and services due to the need to import the majority of consumable goods across very long distances, mirror conditions in both the sovereign and the non-sovereign Caribbean—in territories like Antigua, Jamaica, and Barbados, as well as the "Commonwealth" of Puerto Rico compared with the U.S. mainland. Ironically, most Puerto Ricans are astonished that their prices are considered cheap by Eastern Caribbean standards, and that residents of Antigua, Saint Kitts, Dominica, and so on regularly go to Puerto Rico for "bargain-basement" prices. Ramon Grosfoguel has pointed out the ironies undergirding the ongoing neocolonial and neoliberal subjugation of Puerto Rico vis-à-vis the larger capitalist structures that have overdetermined its twentieth-century history: "The prosperity of the Puerto Rican modern colony relative to Caribbean nation-states that struggled for independence constitutes a tragic historical irony. This phenomenon cannot be understood from a nationalist or colonialist perspective that assumes automatic decolonization after the formation of a nation-state, or from an approach that takes the nation-state as the unit of analysis" (2001, 5). Seen in this light, then, little differentiates the economics of departmentalization from the globalized destruction and structured dependence of nominally sovereign island economies and businesses like Puerto Rico, Jamaica, and Antigua.

In the French Antilles, local elites, like the endogamously structured, numerically minuscule *béké* group, the white descendants of the slave-era planter class, have shifted their capital advantage from the shrinking and increasingly nonviable agricultural sector to monopolize broad sections of the economy of the DOMs through their control of the import-export industry and many major retail operations, such as supermarket chains and car dealerships—promoting ineluctably neocolonial practices, drawing on patterns of capital accumulation and labor exploitation to broaden the definition of non-sovereignty in the region. Indeed, as Yarimar Bonilla has succinctly pointed out, "the fact is that in the contemporary Caribbean the *majority* of societies are non-sovereign societies" (2015, 24; emphasis in the original). Such conditions arguably turn standard economic practice on its head. Contrary to the notion that, following privatization and deregulation of the economy, when market forces determine the prices of goods and services, economies grow faster and populations enjoy higher standards of living, in reality the benefits of such growth do not trickle down to the majority of the population. Winston Griffith has analyzed these patterns well: "Proponents of neoliberal economics claim that when governments allow market forces to operate unimpeded resources will be allocated most efficiently, economies will experience faster economic growth and attain full employment, and their populations will enjoy a higher standard of living." With specific reference to Caribbean economies, however, Griffith has a diametrically opposed view; he "argues that neoliberal economics, some of the main tenets of which are privatization and deregulation of the economy, liberal trade policies, reducing government spending, pro-competitive policies, and unrestricted capital flows, will slow down their rate of economic transformation" (2010, 505). And it is but a short leap from this position to Bonilla's argument that "we can imagine the Caribbean region itself as a *non-sovereign* archipelago," wherein particular socioeconomic patterns appear to function in perpetuity (2015, 25; emphasis in the original). As we shall see, patterns of dependency across the board permeate and overdetermine the futures of sovereign and non-sovereign states.

In this Caribbean subjected to neoliberal praxes, then, almost 75 years have passed since the enactment of the 1946 law that made Guadeloupe, Martinique and French Guiana overseas departments of France; this moment also inaugurated the economic and political disaster of neocolonialism that departmentalization has come to be. With this in mind, the LKP collective pursued their broad goals of political action and social change by, not just focusing on the high cost of living, but also tackling more structural sociocultural and economic issues—calling for, among other things, the development of the local fishing industry, the promotion of local cultural initiatives, the overhaul of the educational system, sound environmental planning, and broad employment initiatives, and eventually producing a list of 120 demands.

This series of events interrogates and illuminates the telling inequities that continue to plague many areas of the post/colonial Caribbean region. Certainly, 2009 constitutes a watershed moment of confrontation, contestation, and identitarian activism and assertion for the DOM that illuminates the contradictions that undergird the neocolonially dominated postcolonial Caribbean writ large. If wide-ranging claims were made in many aspects of collective life—from living standards to the environment, cultural promotion, education, health care, and collective memory—what these claims have in common is their articulation of a sense of inequality and subjugation across the board and the desire for survival in specific terms and contexts. In other words, this moment of contestation went beyond the immediacy of a praxis of neocolonial domination to broach principles of subjectivity and agency that sought to promulgate the validity of individual and communal sovereignty even as they interrogated long-standing assumptions of autonomy and self-determination within a broad Caribbean context. What such an approach places in question, as Yolanda Martinez-San Miguel succinctly points out, are the cloaked realities of "extended colonialism and how it produces forms of colonialism without postcolonialism, as well as ideologies of emancipation without complete decolonization" (2014, 10); seen in these terms, the entire process of decolonization is ultimately at issue, especially as regards assertions of independence that often are so in name only. Martinez-San Miguel goes further, however, suggesting strongly that these attitudes and practices ultimately find their origin in the particulars and specificities of coloniality itself: "there is a particular colonial political structure that seems to be unique in the case of overseas insular possessions and that tends to circumvent the formation of sovereign national states" (10). In the event, sovereignty was effectively foreclosed through myriad means in a variety of political contexts, while concepts like independence and nationalism simultaneously emerged from the integral inequities of the colonial encounter, as the former colonizers articulated westernized models of governance that also sought to integrate what Michel-Rolph Trouillot calls North Atlantic universals into postcolonial Caribbean political systems. Trouillot defines the conundrum this way: "By North Atlantic universals, I mean words that project the North Atlantic experience on a universal scale that they themselves helped to create. North Atlantic universals are particulars that have gained a degree of universality, chunks of human history that have become historical standards. They do not describe the world; they offer visions of the world. . . . Words such as *progress, development, modernity, nation-state, and globalization* itself are among those I have in mind" (2002, 847; emphasis in the original). Read in this way, if the goal of decolonization was to insert the former colonies into a politico-temporal continuum of "progress" and "democracy" whose intrinsic principles themselves did double duty as "the terms of the dominant narratives of world history" (847), then what was simultaneously and deliberately excluded from this vision of the development of third-world nation-states was the alternative history of subjection and exploitation that had made the metropolitan profits of the colonial era possible. Winston Griffith puts it bluntly: "The laissez-faire philosophy of colonial governments resulted in a monocultural economy, the neglect of domestic food production, the absence of economic linkages and of a manufacturing class, the export of the surplus, the creation of a psychological dependent mentality and no significant material improvement in the social conditions of Caribbean peoples" (2010, 507–508). From this perspective, current policies make clear that little has changed since the colonial era.

The complex conjunction of neoliberalism, postcolonialism, and (non) sovereignty in the Caribbean region compels us first to place the efficacy of French overseas departmentalization, as well as its politico-economic corollaries, into question. And indeed, critiques of departmentalization hark back almost to the moment of its establishment in 1946. One telling analysis posits the problematic parallels that can be discerned between nineteenth-century emancipation and twentieth-century departmentalization, as the inequities governing both events are brought into sharper focus; here is Yarimar Bonilla's reading: "Like the post-emancipation colonial administrators who had to extend freedom while maintaining colonial forms of exploited labor, the twentieth-century French government was tasked with the project of extending political equality while sustaining the socio-economic inequality that conditioned the place of the Antilles in the French Republic" (2015, 31). And so if the departmentalization law theoretically bestowed the same rights and privileges on Martinicans and Guadeloupeans as on any other French citizens—as those of the Bouches-du-Rhône, for example—the law also put into practice paradoxical economic principles meant to ensure the continuing inequalities of coloniality. Indeed, if "sovereignty for the DOM, therefore, was made constitutionally impossible early on," as William F.S. Miles puts it (2005, 225), the practical implementation of departmental integration produced continuing colonial dichotomies of economy, demography, and social policy. Indeed, the egregiousness of metropolitan hypocrisy was often nothing short of mind-boggling, as Kristen Stromberg Childers writes: "On the last day of December 1947, the very night before all metropolitan laws were to go into effect in the new DOMs, the government surreptitiously passed a law codifying different salary scales for metropolitan civil servants, guaranteeing them more substantial salaries than those offered to 'indigenous' civil servants in the new departments" (88). On January 16, 1948, Aimé Césaire immediately protested this "racist sentiment that runs contrary to French traditions"[1]

(88), but unfortunately, such race-based discriminatory acts and attitudes had long been and would continue to be endemic. In other words, the pervasive racism that had historically driven the abiding sense of metropolitan superiority undergirding colonial attitudes toward France's peripheral populations of color in no way abated in the face of departmentalization's new legal strictures and assumptions.

In a telling analysis, Justin Daniel has summed up a key challenge of the stark binaries that departmentalization proposed to its population. On the one hand, the promised and implicit equalities of integration were predicated on a key selection of the universals analyzed by Michel-Rolph Trouillot and cited earlier: "Thus the implementation of departmentalization was expressed, at least in its beginning, by a complex combination of old structures, of new partially adapted structures or reinterpreted according to a past that continues to haunt the collective consciousness."[2] In this panacea of French postcolonial belonging, the hierarchies of history and race would be erased in favor of a limitless future. On the other hand, Daniel subsequently points to a sentiment of separation that went hand in hand with a conjunction of politics and culture that led to increasing assertions of cultural identity, as growing community awareness and activism produced a "phenomenon that accelerated with the decentralization process which started at the beginning of the 1980's: one can then see a real explosion of cultural activities which are so many expressions of a society's vitality."[3] In fact, one might reasonably claim that the principal struggle waged by the DOMs during the departmental era was the ongoing attempt to force the powers that be in metropolitan France to live up to the implicit claims and promises of equality of access, opportunity, and benefits embodied in the departmentalization law itself.

Simply put, on the one hand, it was argued in various quarters that departmentalization was a political chimera, one that was merely perpetuating old colonial structures and would ultimately lead to economic stagnation, as the manufacturing and agricultural production sectors were gradually wiped out in the face of economic centralization and the impossible economies of scale posed by metropolitan food imports. But on the other hand, in a telling paradox of unpredictability, political change, when it did arrive, would find its origins not just outside the DOMs, but in the heart of the metropolitan center.

In 1982, French president François Mitterrand introduced greater decentralization into the political system by creating a new level of government—the *région*—with a directly elected body, the *Conseil Régional*. Four overseas regions were established; one for each DOM. Martinique, Guadeloupe, French Guiana, and Réunion thus each became both a *département* and a *région*, giving Guadeloupe and Martinique an important "cultural right to difference" (Miles 2001, 50). This series of paradoxes, framing DOMian citizenship through both integration and difference, highlights the individual and communal tensions to be derived from participating in what has otherwise been described as a political pyramid of domination and exploitation. But it also raises a further question, that of the balance to be struck between passive acceptance of the status quo and active resistance aimed at facilitating change. One approach reads the former position as an intrinsic corollary, or extension, of the departmental experience, as Miles has argued: "If the DOM-TOM passively accept their status as overseas projections of an erstwhile European colonizer, it is because they are conditioned to do so. The educational system, the media, and consumer values all reinforce the post-colonial message of departmentalization, stressing the benefit of the current arrangement. The elevated standard of living that DOMTOM peoples enjoy, however, comes at the cost of economic and psychic dependency" (2005, 227). From this perspective, if departmentalization is at the very least a geopolitical condition rife with paradoxes and contradictions, one that, mutually constituted by its geopolitical, economic, and racial components, resembles not equality but the downside of neoliberal domination in an internationalist framework, then combating the cost to the non-sovereign constituents of the DOMs, defined principally by economic exploitation and psychic dependency, constitutes the primary goal of the contestatory actions of 2009.

If the events that form the foundation of this analysis emphasize neoliberal hegemony and its corollary of economic exploitation—and the repercussions of resistance to which it gives rise—such issues also illuminate the persistence of non-sovereign restrictions on Caribbean political and economic independence in the twentieth and twenty-first centuries. At the same time, given the ineluctable pressures created in neighboring territories by the hegemony of capital and profit, so visible recently in Haiti and again in Puerto Rico, fundamental questions of the viability of development and the advancement of indigenous and community interests in the face of global capital and money markets continue to be raised and assessed.

Among the key questions that this volume seeks to highlight and contextualize is the extent to which the decolonization model imposed on the DOMs, from an economic as well as a political perspective, is emblematic of the postcolonial paradoxes that pervade the region. Within such a context, sovereignty is beset by contradiction and limitation, as Yarimar Bonilla explains: "In the case of Guadeloupe, it is important to remember that even though its contemporary political actors are the inheritors of a previous era of anticolonial thought and struggle, they are also the product of a particular political project of decolonization through juridical integration. As such, they inhabit a privileged position from which to rethink the categories of nation, citizenship, sovereignty and authority—given that these concepts have never been successfully packaged into a (however tenuously) guaranteed bundle of rights and duties" (2015, 3). From a historical perspective, then, departmentalization was emblematic of the conundrum of Caribbean self-sufficiency in that the arc of the postcolonial experience was arguably the opposite of the traditional developmental model. On the one hand, despite a number of uprisings, broad-based political activity never quite embodied the regional spirit of regional anti-colonial resistance, and on the other, the steadily shrinking scale of local production across the board implicitly inhibited the capacity of the local economy to bring about full social and economic equality, as a recent study by Kristen Stromberg Childers makes clear:

Whereas Antilleans compared their economic and social well-being to French citizens in general, French administrators continually stressed the "particular" and "local" nature of their situations and inevitably underestimated their rights to and needs for a certain standard of living. Antilleans might merit a raise in their standard of living that would come about through state-sponsored development projects, but they could not expect to achieve parity, at least in the foreseeable future, with levels of material comfort in metropolitan France. (2016, 137)

In other words, departmentalization's paradox of postcolonial development meant that as political integration seemed to contest the legacy of colonialism, leading gradually to infrastructural development and a raised standard of living, the corollaries of economic centralization and their associated economies of scale simultaneously unleashed profit-driven economics and growing commercial dependency on the metropole as imports vastly outstripped exports. The growth of cheap credit and the consumerism that are integral to the metropolitan model of Frenchness underwrote an economy in which daily necessities were increasingly out of reach for the majority of the population, and export-oriented economic and agricultural practices, in certain circumstances, literally put the lives of the population at risk.

The strategies undertaken by LKP and others forged a new resistive path in that its terms were interactive, unpredictable, and transformational, giving rise to a new, third way toward community agency and subjectivity whose primary distinction is the alternative path taken from the binary, hierarchical framework of the departmental relation. Critically different from a response seeking simply to invert the original offending hierarchy or to negate its primary tenets, the alternative approach has been clearly explained by Benita Parry: "A reverse discourse replicating and therefore reinstalling the linguistic polarities devised by a dominant centre to exclude and act against the categorized, does not liberate the 'other' from a colonized condition. . . . To dismantle colonialist knowledge and displace the received narrative of colonialism's moment written by ruling-class historiography and perpetuated by the nationalist version, the founding concepts of the problematic must be refused" (1987, 28). In sum, then, by going beyond a simple negation of the colonialist practices emanating from the metropole—thereby implicitly validating the patterns and practices of disenfranchisement embedded in the departmental relation—the disruptive force engaged in contesting the non-sovereign status quo and its ineffective practices of inequality, exploitation, and profiteering led to the effective forging of alternate strategies for the inscription and articulation of new and assertive forms of community identity.

Taking the tensions of 2009 as a model, then, this collection of essays seeks to illuminate the predatory forces at work in a number of key sites of Caribbean neoliberal praxis, illustrating the primacy of politics, capital, and profit in the inequities of political, economic, social, and cultural domination that continue to pervade the Caribbean region. The persistent hierarchies of metropolitan capital centralization and repatriation, the adherence to neoliberalism's core principle of profiting without producing, and the widespread external political domination that flies in the face of regional claims to self-determination—which together have tended to lock France's former *vieilles colonies* turned overseas departments into a relationship of neocolonial dependency toward the metropolitan mainland—will also be seen to be the driving force in the economies of a range of non-sovereign Caribbean territories. As sovereignty itself is placed in question and under erasure, it is the struggle of these territories for autonomy and survival that drives the plural responses to this entrenched neoliberalism to be seen here, patterns that reinforce the critical importance of identitarian self-assertion for the area as a whole.

Puerto Rico

From our beginnings in the French periphery, analyzing these events leads us to broaden our focus to look at the substance, shape, and impact of similar policies in what is increasingly referred to as the contemporary "non-sovereign" Caribbean. The general consensus here is that across the region, such policies have been an abject failure in terms of achieving socioeconomic uplift within the population at large. Huber and Solt state this clearly: "In sum, on average, in the Latin American countries neoliberal reforms of trade and financial systems, tax systems, pensions, transfers to working-age families, health care systems, and education, have failed to put into place policies that firmly advance growth, stability, the reduction of poverty and inequality, and improvements of the human capital base" (2004, 162). To take a pointed example, the fact that Puerto Rico is in fact a colony of the United States in all but name—with lower wages and a lower level of living conditions in stark contrast to those of the mainland United States—remains undisputed, giving testament to the realities of the latter country's imperialist policies that target sovereign and non-sovereign countries alike. Indeed, the financial crises of debt payment and structural adjustment, compounded by massive destruction caused by Hurricanes Irma and Maria, that have paralyzed Puerto Rico over the past few years arguably have their genesis in decades of exploitative U.S. economic policy toward its wholly owned "commonwealth," as Hector Reyes points out in "Puerto Rico: The Last Colony":

> During the century of U.S. colonial rule, Puerto Rican society has changed massively. Puerto Rico ceased to be an agricultural economy in the 1950s. In 1993, more than 68 percent of workers were involved in manufacturing, services, government, or construction, and fewer than 3 percent were agricultural workers. Despite the U.S.-encouraged transformation in the economy, Puerto Rico remains a very poor country plagued by unemployment and low wages. The standard of living of the Puerto Rican working class, although among the highest in Latin America, remains significantly lower than that of the U.S. working class. In 1996, the average manufacturing wage was 60 percent of that paid in the U.S.—with many people earning the minimum wage—while in 1993, the per capita income was $6,760. GDP per capita in 1997 was $7,670. Puerto Rico's per capita income is one-third that of the United States and half that of Mississippi. Although it is difficult to compare, the cost of living has been estimated to be 25 percent higher than that

of the U.S. . . . In 1994, the unemployment rate was 16 percent, according to government figures. It has not dropped below 10 percent since 1940. Unemployment has hovered around the 15 percent mark for many years, reaching as high as 23 percent in 1983. These are the official figures, which over time tend to significantly underestimate the number of unemployed because discouraged job seekers are dropped out of the statistics. The real rate is estimated at more than 30 percent, with many towns in the central regions of the island having unemployment rates as high as 75 percent. (1997, 2)

Seen in these terms, the absolute submission of the Puerto Rican people and economy to the juggernaut of mainland U.S. profit is incontrovertible. Indeed, Reyes goes on to point out the key ways in which the exploitation embedded in the Puerto Rican experience became a model for U.S. economic policy toward the rest of the Caribbean: "U.S. capital—with help from its island-based allies—used Puerto Rico as a laboratory to test policies for economic penetration of Latin America and the Caribbean. In the first forty years of this century, Puerto Rico served primarily as a source of cheap sugar. In the 1940s and 1950s, Puerto Rico embarked on 'Operation Bootstrap,' converting the island into an export-processing zone for the assembly of finished manufactured products for U.S. firms. In many ways, 'Operation Bootstrap' represented the first application of the *maquiladora* strategy which U.S. business uses to a great extent today in Mexico, Central America and the Caribbean" (1997, 3). The trenchant truth of this analysis, positing the generation of a local service economy as a way of keeping Puerto Rican social and economic dependency on the United States in place, provides an eerie echo of the trajectory of French economic and financial policies already observed in post-departmental Guadeloupe and Martinique.

The condition of coloniality in fact effectively describes the unequal relationship between Puerto Rico and the United States since the latter territory was seized by the former during the Spanish-American War of 1898, along with Guam and the Philippines. Luis N. Rivera Pagán has described this transfer of power as "the transfer of imperial sovereignty from Madrid to Washington. . . . In early 1898 Puerto Rico was a Spanish colony; at the end of that fateful year, it had become a colony of the United States."[4] The thorny issue of citizenship quickly became central to the status of these new U.S. territories, particularly given much-vaunted American assurances of having renounced the hegemonies of imperialism that had long characterized the international agendas of other Western powers. A protracted set of legalities led in 1901 to a series of Supreme Court rulings, now known as the Insular Cases, that sought to clarify the question of how American constitutional rights applied to those in the newly acquired U.S. territories. Unsurprisingly, the Supreme Court declined to extend full constitutional rights to all places under American control, on the one hand allowing the U.S. government to exercise unilateral power over these newly acquired territories, while on the other hand establishing the doctrine of territorial incorporation, whereby the U.S. Constitution applied only partially in the unincorporated lands of Puerto Rico, Guam, and the Philippines, in contrast to the full application of the Constitution in incorporated territories, such as Alaska and Hawaii, deemed to be on a path to statehood. Arguably adding insult to the injury of the Treaty of Paris that ended the war in 1899, whereby the indigenous populations of Puerto Rico and the Philippines were made to continue as colonial subjects as well as stateless peoples (since they were denied the right to keep their Spanish citizenship as well as any right to become U.S. citizens), this moment was the inauspicious inauguration of the coloniality of Puerto Rico's "commonwealth" relationship to the United States.

Now if, as Rivera Pagan posits, "imperial power comprises at least three interrelated domains: political subordination, material appropriation, and ideological justification," the twisted legal self-rationalization outlined above certainly meets all three of these criteria.[5] And while Puerto Ricans were granted citizenship in 1917—although without the right to vote in U.S. presidential elections—this grant was quickly followed in 1920 by the egregious injustice of the Jones Act, a little-known regulation that requires that goods shipped from one American port to another be transported on a ship that is American-built, American-owned, and crewed by U.S. citizens. This century-old protectionist measure applies to all U.S. ports except the U.S. Virgin Islands, but without competitive international shipping rates, the resulting higher shipping costs for many goods are passed on to consumers. The end result is that all goods coming into Puerto Rico are unnecessarily expensive relative to goods for sale either on the U.S. mainland or other Caribbean islands, and drives up the cost of living on the island substantially. And while the Jones Act was briefly waived in the wake of Hurricane Maria, to allow the speedier delivery of disaster relief, the act was quickly restored, arguably so that economic domination and exploitation could continue unabated.

Ramon Grosfoguel uses this accumulation of inequities to point to "the obvious fact that Puerto Rico is still a colony of the United States." Indeed, he pushes this analysis of the conditions of contemporary coloniality even further, positing Puerto Rico as both paradigm and arbiter of the fabrications and deceptions undergirding our assumptions of decolonization. In other words, the ambiguities of Puerto Rico's condition, coupled with the inequities of its subjugation, "reveal the limitations of the so-called decolonization of the modern world, both in terms of the global political economy and the dominant geoculture and its imaginary. Puerto Rico . . . calls for a rethinking of the purported decolonization of the so-called independent Caribbean, republics that experience the crude exploitation of the capitalist world-system" (2001, 2). As we shall see, it is the often invisible ambiguities and dualities of decolonization and nationhood that in fact undergird the portrait of Caribbean subjection in this volume.

Even before the destruction wrought in 2017 by Hurricanes Irma and Maria, Puerto Rico had sunk into the depths of a financial crisis. Because Puerto Rico, unlike other U.S. municipalities, cannot declare bankruptcy— one striking element of its ongoing colonial legacy—and with $123 billion in debt owed by the Puerto Rican government and its corporations, the U.S. government passed the Puerto Rico Oversight, Management, and Economic Stability Act (PROMESA) in 2016, leading to the appointment of the Financial Oversight and Management Board for Puerto Rico, derisively called *la junta* by Puerto Ricans. This Washington-appointed body now overseeing the island's finances came up with a fiscal austerity plan for 2017–2026 that carved out a chasm in Puerto Rico's public service budget. The plan outlined severe cuts to health care, pensions, and education and imposed them on Puerto Rico's impoverished three million people so that mainland creditors could be repaid.

This fiscal crisis was ultimately overshadowed by a political one. Early in the summer of 2019, Puerto Rico's republican governor Ricardo Rosselló had nearly nine hundred pages of homophobic, sexist, and other pejorative messages between him and his inner circle of government officials exposed in a security leak. *Inter alia*, the messages insulted women, gay people, and the poor, and generally made fun of the suffering of everyday Puerto Ricans—even and especially the victims of Hurricane Maria. In a series of events that provide an eerie echo of the demonstrations against material day-to-day conditions organized by LKP a decade earlier, nearly half a million Puerto Ricans took to the streets each day in protest, and the chant "Ricky Renuncia" (Ricky Resign) became the cry of the movement. Well-known participants included Lin-Manuel Miranda, author and protagonist of the play *Hamilton* of Tony-award winning fame; Bad Bunny, a Puerto Rican rapper and musician; and Puerto Rican singer Ricky Martin, who was the target of several of the messages. But as the protests grew in size and fury, the pent-up public anger against Governor Rosselló, who had presided over the fiasco of mismanagement that followed the disaster of Hurricane Maria, arguably fueled the magnitude of the demonstrations.

On Monday, June 22, a demonstration in the capital city of San Juan drew an estimated one million people—almost a third of the island's total population—in protest against the governor's connivance at the mismanagement in the hurricane's aftermath and the contemporaneous economic crisis. But this was the culmination of a popular anti-government mobilization that had artfully adopted a myriad of inventive tactics to convey the people's disenchantment with the powers that be. In her *New York Times* article "Puerto Rico Protestors Got Creative: Dancing, Singing, Diving," Charo Henriquez recounts in detail the range of community-driven activities that were appropriated to rage against Rosselló; as she writes, "they did not just march and shout slogans. They applied pressure in a host of other ways, from singing and dancing to yoga and horseback riding."[6] And indeed, she goes on to recount protesters dangling from street signs; scuba diving; line dancing the Electric Slide; driving bicycles, motorcycles, and all-terrain vehicles in front of La Fortaleza, the governor's official residence; and parading, aboard kayaks and water scooters, across San Juan Bay beneath the governor's mansion. Music played a key role as well, as artists like Ricky Martin and Bad Bunny joined the protests; in addition, as Henriquez writes, "ordinary Puerto Ricans also expressed themselves in ways as diverse as the island's culture, with songs played on traditional instruments with rhythms like *plena* and *bomba*, as well as more contemporary musical genres like *urbano* and *trap*."[7] In an additional echo of the LKP anthem "La Gwadloup sé tan nou," music infused the protests with a vibrant nationalism, signaling both the cohesiveness of the community and its strong sense of cultural and territorial belonging and also division and difference from government and mainland interests, as the crowds also "broke out in spontaneous renditions of Puerto Rican standards from the 1940s and 1950s, like 'En Mi Viejo San Juan' and 'Preciosa,' considered unofficial anthems on the island."[8] But perhaps even more significant was the striking internationalization of these communal protests, as any perceived lack of mobility quickly turned a hindrance into an organized advantage; "Many Puerto Ricans have taken to emulating the *cacerolazo*, a popular South American form of protest that originated in the 1970s in Chile. People could participate wherever they were, even at home, by banging cookware and kitchen utensils at a set time, with the noise calling attention to their grievances. In Puerto Rico, people have been banging pots and pans for one minute every day at 8 p.m."[9] They even thematized their clothing and accessories; "some people have worn body paint, slogan-emblazoned shirts and even earrings depicting and mocking Mr. Rosselló."[10] Clearly, discontent was deep and pervasive, and the removal of Ricky Rosselló became the people's priority and, ultimately, their prerogative.

While Rosselló's resignation was arguably the culmination of problems that had plagued Puerto Rico for decades, the instigation of the federal oversight board and the austerity measures it imposed, along with the governor's move to privatize the publicly owned power utility, confirmed the public's conviction of its deep discontent with the island's neocolonial status quo. Indeed, there was no question that the governor's resignation announcement was driven by the voice of the people; Jose A. Del Real sums it up well: "A flurry of Puerto Rican flags flew into the air, strangers clasped arms and friends began jumping in circles, singing "¡Oé! ¡Oé! ¡Oé!" Cars from all over the city began to honk and, as people danced, fireworks erupted overhead. . . . Some cried, the emotion of recent days overcoming them as they realized something historic had happened. Their dissent mattered. 'We just changed history in Puerto Rico,' said Andrea Fanduiz, 25, a pharmacy technician who was among those celebrating."[11] Ultimately, Puerto Rico's Justice Department announced a criminal investigation into the private group chat that had set off the demonstrations, but this was just the icing on a layer cake of community subjugation and neoliberal profit that had been in place for decades, until it was upended by the very people it had been exploiting. Indeed, U.S. mainland ignorance of and prejudice against Puerto Ricans can be seen at its most egregious in a recent *New York Times* story, in which José A. Guzmán-Payano, a junior at Purdue University in West Lafayette, Indiana, went to his local CVS drugstore in October 2019 "to buy Mucinex for a cold, his mother wrote on Facebook. When an employee at the checkout saw his Puerto Rican driver's license, she asked him for a visa, and 'started confronting him about his immigration status,' Arlene Payano Burgos wrote in a post that had been shared more than 10,000 times. . . . Mr. Guzmán-Payano had to explain that, in fact, Puerto Ricans are American citizens. But the employee still would not accept the license or a United States passport that he showed her. A manager also refused to sell him the medicine. . . . Mrs. Payano, a legal secretary in Cayey, Puerto Rico . . . called the store and was also told not accepting Puerto Rican identification was store policy."[12] Such acts of othering—criminalizing

American citizens based on their appearance, skin color, or mode of speech—doubtless characterize the day-to-day realities of millions of Puerto Ricans, embodying the state of exploitative coloniality lived by the entire community.

In an important way, Puerto Rico has long functioned as the touchstone for a form of coloniality that thrives outside colonial boundaries, one that exploits the superficialities of postcolonial sovereignty in order to maintain long-standing hierarchies of exploitation in the periphery, as Ramon Grosfoguel succinctly points out: "Global coloniality, as opposed to global colonialism, is now the dominant form of core-periphery relationships in the capitalist world-economy. Core powers and transnational corporations exploit and dominate the periphery without the expense of colonial administrations" (2001, 6). Ironically, the essence of these core-periphery exploitative relationships—those that mimic the appearance of sovereignty while actually subverting and betraying it—has long been replicated in the second-oldest republic in the New World.

Haiti

In a defining irony, Haiti declared its independence on January 1, 1804, but the argument can be made that it never has really been independent, and certainly not since its acceptance of the 150-million-franc indemnity imposed on the newly independent nation by France in 1825, in an initial iteration of limited sovereignty. Payments on this debt often absorbed up to 80 percent of the nation's gross domestic product over the next century, and a looming debt crisis led to the first invasion and nineteen-year occupation of the island by U.S. forces in 1915. But our goal here is not to rehearse this aspect of Haitian (in)dependence. Rather, our focus is the current financial and political crisis, brought to a head in the scramble to capitalize on disaster following the 2010 earthquake, and highlighted by the ongoing scandal of missing millions of PetroCaribe funds. In other words, the subjugation of the population to the primacy of profit places democracy, acceptable living conditions, and independent responsible government itself in question. Amy Wilentz sums up the crisis this way:

For the Haitian people, there is almost no public education, no public sanitation, no fire safety. There is also no social security, no subsidized health care. Plus right now there's often no gas, no electricity, no water and no food. The justice system is inept, corrupt, inefficient, and unjust. The prisons are disgusting, overcrowded, and unfunded. Inflation is high. Buying power is low. Elections are corrupted by domestic money and foreign influence. . . . Thanks for all this, pure capitalism . . . extractive capitalism, a kind of racism, and the global order have conspired to undermine hope in Haiti. . . . Who's left to run the country? The grotesque, corrupt, and profoundly incompetent Moïse . . . and the corruption-creation machine that is the Haitian government. (2019, 3–4)

This scenario is the result of a capitalist order that works to extract the last scintilla of profit, enriching the few at the expense of the many; here, people and workers are just numbers, ciphers useful only insofar as they advance or diminish the profit margin. Indeed, the extent of international government involvement in—if not connivance at—neocolonial control of Haitian politics and its economy is highlighted in a recent article by Yves Engler: "President Jovenel Moïse's decision to join the Lima Group highlights the influence of another Canadian-sponsored imperial group of friends. . . . As popular discontent has grown, Moïse has become increasingly dependent on outside backing. The only reason Moïse is president is because of the so-called 'Core Group' of 'Friends of Haiti', which comprises the ambassadors of the United States, Canada, France, Brazil and Spain, as well as representatives of the EU and OAS. Core Group representatives meet regularly among themselves and with Haitian officials and periodically release collective statements on Haitian affairs."[13] Such actions and attitudes simply reinforce the clear role of puppet master played by outside businesses and, as shown here, international governments, in overdetermining the politics and positions of the simulacrum of governance operating in Haiti.

Indeed, the evidence clearly shows that this outside interference loomed ever larger as the removal of Aristide approached. And Haiti and Haitians played no role as a neoliberal plan was hatched and put into motion, with the aim of making Haiti safe, not for democracy, but rather for the continuation of policies of plunder and profit. As Engler continues, "the Core Group was spawned at the 'Ottawa initiative on Haiti.' Held at the Meech Lake Government Resort on January 31 and February 1, 2003, no Haitian officials were invited to the private gathering where U.S., French, OAS, and Canadian officials discussed overthrowing Haiti's elected government, putting the country under UN trusteeship and recreating the Haitian military."[14] It is clear, then, that in Haiti's case any claims to actual sovereignty have been strangled at birth, and even a basic infrastructure allowing for minimum conditions of economic security has been sacrificed on the altar of maximizing yield for private, often external, investment.

Haiti is known in certain circles as the "Republic of NGOs"—their number reputedly hovers around ten thousand—and a quick look at this underreported aspect of its economy explains why. Following the initial coup against President Jean-Bertrand Aristide on September 29, 1991, the beginnings of a neoliberal economic policy were put into effect at the behest of the United States following the U.S. engineering of his overthrow. Matt Kennard makes the exploitative goals and practices of this policy clear in "Haiti and the Shock Doctrine":

> From the mid-1990s through the 2000s . . . the process of opening up Haiti's economy to the predations of foreign capital was well underway. In 1996, the Haitian government had already, one diplomatic cable published by Wikileaks notes, "established legislation on the modernization of public enterprises, which allows foreign investors to participate in the management and/or ownership of state-owned enterprises." Moreover, a law of November 2002 explicitly acknowledged the "crucial role of foreign investment in assuring economic growth and aims to facilitate, liberalize, and stimulate private investment in Haiti." The law gave foreign investors exactly the same rights and protections as Haitians. A few months earlier in 2002, the Haitian parliament had voted for a new free-trade-zone law which provided "zones" with fiscal

and customs incentives for foreign enterprises—for example, a fifteen-year tax exemption. (2012, 4)

What Kennard's analysis makes clear is the extent to which U.S. government policy toward Haiti was fixated on subjecting the people and the economy of the second republic to be established in the New World to the hegemonic depredations of American capitalism. Indeed, in a telling comment on international capital's insistence on keeping the Haitian minimum wage at $1.75 a day, Jonathan Katz sums up the advantages to American businesses and their consumers this way: "For a 'Captain America Infant Toddler Boys Short-Sleeve Tee' to sell for $8 at Target—and . . . for importers and factory owners to enjoy generous margins—garment-worker wages must remain at poverty levels" (2013, 140–141). So while there is no question of improving the lot of Haitian workers in this schema, any insistence on opening up Haitian markets to foreign investment, or the "modernization of public enterprises," was a euphemism for facilitating the entry into and appropriation of key aspects of the economy—including electricity, water, and telephone services—by a range of private companies whose goal of ever-increasing wealth accumulation embodied the basic armature of U.S. capital. Further, we might well note the double irony at work here, since the prohibition on foreigners owning property in Haiti—embedded and inscribed in Haiti's constitution of 1805—was initially undone under the 1915–1934 U.S. occupation of the territory, when in 1918 that constitution was annulled and rewritten specifically to promote privatization under the aegis of none other than Franklin Delano Roosevelt, then assistant secretary of the Navy. With foreign investors now guaranteed "exactly the same rights and protections as Haitians," the obliteration of real Haitian sovereignty in favor of foreign economic manipulators was all but complete. As Kennard continues, "a good example of this greed comes from the Wikileaks cables, one of which notes that in 1996 a 'modernization commission' was set up to decide whether management contracts, long-term leases or capitalisation was the best option for each of the companies to be privatised. The commission would also set how much the Haitian government would retain of the asset, with a cap at 49%—a minority stake, stripping the Haitian people of control over their own industries. . . . It sounded like a normal sovereign country, but a sovereign country is exactly what the US and IFIs didn't want Haiti to be" (2012, 5). And this is perhaps the ultimate point to be made; if the veil of an apparent sovereignty can be maintained, there is no limit to the possibilities for capital accumulation by those holding the levers of non-sovereign power.

It is also worth noting that the case of Haiti is simultaneously unique and not unique. Despite Haiti's nominally independent status, it is important to recognize the extent to which this deliberate subversion and destabilization of an independent nation is grounded in historical hegemonic practice, one arguably aimed at delegitimizing and undoing the presumption of black agency that undergirded Haiti's assertion of a sovereignty that made history. The successive Western attempts at weakening or sidelining the political and economic independence of the burgeoning Haitian nation, starting with the imposition of the French indemnity of 150 million francs in 1825, and including the killing of more than fifteen thousand Haitians during the nineteen-year-long American occupation from 1915 to 1934, were in reality simply geopolitical penalties that shared the singular aim of undoing that model of black Caribbean sovereignty, on the one hand, while actively discouraging—if not foreclosing—the efforts of its imitators, on the other.

In the days following the January 12, 2010, earthquake that killed approximately 250,000 people, the United States quickly assumed control of Haiti's airspace; landed 6,500 soldiers on the ground, with 15,000 more troops stationed off shore; and deployed an armada of naval vessels to patrol Haitian waters. What was the point of this egregious display of military might as a response to a humanitarian disaster? An investors' conference held in Port-au-Prince in October 2009 had attracted some two hundred companies, including such transnational U.S. companies as Gap, Levi Strauss, and Citibank. They were enticed by Haiti's extremely low labor costs, as well as by claims that a revitalized garment industry could create one hundred thousand jobs. In addition, plans were announced for the privatization of the public telephone company, Téléco; the construction of a "luxury hotel complex" in the upper-crust neighborhood of Pétionville; and a $55 million investment by Royal Caribbean International at its "private Haitian beach paradise." At the same time, the United States continued to push the self-serving economic model of industrial parks filled with low-paying textile factories—or, as we know them, sweatshops—aimed at providing goods for its own populace.

And then there are the NGOs, numbering about ten thousand at last count and providing some 80 percent of the country's basic services. In 2015, ProPublica and National Public Radio (NPR) released a report on the billions of dollars that were poured into a post-earthquake reconstruction effort largely led by private nongovernmental organizations. Entitled "How the Red Cross Raised Half a Billion Dollars for Haiti and Built Six Homes,"[15] the report effectively illuminated the ratio between high overhead costs and amounts allotted for effective reconstruction. Less than one cent of each dollar of U.S. earthquake relief actually went to the Haitian government. As reported by the Associated Press, NGOs working on disaster aid received 43 cents, while 33 cents of that same dollar ended up with the U.S. military. Although apparently an extreme result, the structures and policies that made such an outcome possible are endemic to the world of NGOs and particularly to those in Haiti. Jonathan Katz explains it this way:

> Although it's a surprise to many, foreign aid isn't just handed over to foreign countries. Instead, it tends to go to domestic NGOs and contractors, ostensibly to avoid local incompetence and corruption. . . . [An NGO] might use the funds for overhead; transportation; housing; the hiring of cars, drivers, guards, and possibly a cook; and, finally, the project. Its report would go to USAID, Haitian opinions taken into account briefly, if at all. Since most of the money earmarked as aid was thus spent in the donor's country, the donor could set and judge its own priorities and take full credit for the program on the ground. (2013, 110)

Foreign aid, then, arguably exists within its own universe, as donors, recipients, and governments collaborate in the furtherance of complex arrangements that reward participants through schemes of self-perpetuating largesse. These policies were furthered by the Interim Haiti Recovery Commission (IHRC), which arguably was deliberately structured to further foreign interests, as Matt Kennard shows us: "It had twenty-six members, of which twelve were Haitian, leaving them without a voting majority. . . . The financial benefit to the American private sector of this set-up was immediately obvious. An AP investigation found that of every $100 of Haiti reconstruction contracts awarded by the American government, $98.40 returned to American companies. The focus was never on building up indigenous capacity—any work was to be outsourced to foreign companies or NGOs by the IHRC" (2012, 6). Indeed, the earthquake was to all intents and purposes a neoliberal windfall, as Kennard points out:

> As the dust was still settling in Port-au-Prince, the IFIs and various US agencies—what became the *de facto* government in the absence of a Haitian alternative—carved up the society's different sectors and doled them out amongst themselves. The Inter-American Development Bank (IADB) got education and water; the World Bank bagged energy; the United States Agency for International Development (USAID) gratefully accepted the planned new industrial parks. . . . The mass privatisation of state-run assets and the turning of Haiti into a "Caribbean sweatshop"—via an export-led garment-production and cheap-labour model—was something that the US and the IFIs had been pushing forcefully from the mid-1990s through the 2000s. Now its realisation became a distinct possibility. They could enforce it with minimal pushback from a decimated civil society and a denuded government. (2012, 2)

Cheap labor, then, was the engine driving the promise of limitless profit for local and foreign entities alike. In *Travesty in Haiti*, Timothy Schwartz has written a riveting and illuminating account of the depth and pervasiveness of corruption and mismanagement that plague the official and unofficial infrastructures, both government and NGOs. Having spent years working with foreign aid agencies on the ground, Schwartz writes at detailed length of the limitless fraud and greed that drive the claims of these agencies, creating a situation in which "the tiny agricultural country was so thoroughly inundated with surplus food from the United States and Western Europe that Port-au-Prince merchants were soon re-exporting cracked wheat to Miami retailers" (2008, 112). But the story gets worse; Schwartz describes the systematic destruction of the agricultural sector from the mid-1980s to the mid-1990s, turning Haiti, once self-sufficient in certain food staples and a net exporter of others, into a net importer as a result of the implementation of a classic neoliberal program of tariff-lowering and privatization for profit, aided and abetted by the government itself:

> The Haitian government, while perhaps never of much assistance in helping its farmers, was now brought into full cooperation in *destroying* their livelihoods and trying to push them into becoming urban factory workers. . . . The seven hundred thousand small plantations were left to wither. Meanwhile, customs taxes on industrial products had been eliminated, a low minimum wage guaranteed, labor unions suppressed, U.S. companies given the right to repatriate profits, and, guided by USAID, whose consultants were helping Haitian politicians draw up the budget, the Government invested instead in the construction of two of Port-au-Prince's four major industrial parks. (2008, 113; emphasis in original)

This is clearly nothing short of a nirvana of neoliberalism, an ongoing mutual aid pact in which the intended aid recipient in fact is made the victim. In this parody of relief that makes a mockery of sovereignty, everyone is in on the game, it seems, except for the poor, whose exploitation remains unspoken:

> Donor governments gave money in the form of food; the charities sold the food on the open market and then used the money to meet corporate overhead costs and to carry out programs that were supposed to alleviate suffering. But in the end, in the institutional struggle to survive and in an environment in which accountability did not exist, the world's largest multinational charities—CARE, CRS, World Vision,

and ADRA—executed the political will of institutions, governments, and lobbyists that had identified Haiti's comparative advantage as low wages, that is, poverty, and in doing so these charitable organizations dedicated to helping the poorest of the poor wound up working to make the people of Haiti even poorer. (Schwartz 2008, 122)

Looked at in this way, the critical triumvirate of forces that lock, say, Haiti and Puerto Rico into a never-ending cycle of economic inefficacy are critically linked through their establishment of a debilitating praxis of external political hegemony and economic exploitation that places sovereignty itself at issue, as Mark Schuller explains: "Mirroring and reproducing exaggerated inequalities within Haitian society . . . USAID-funded NGOs crafted development policies that countered the priorities set by Haiti's elected government, notably in agriculture, food security, and education. U.S.-funded NGOs promoted export-oriented agriculture . . . undermined local production by removing import tariffs, encouraged dependency by dumping U.S. agricultural surpluses . . . and funded private schools at the expense of public schools and adult literacy programs. USAID also sanitized the official human rights record, destroying documents" (Schuller 2012, 12, 23). The visible, predictable result was embodied in the foreign-oriented economic policies adopted in the wake of the massive 2010 earthquake, as foreign powers literally vied with one another to profit from the disaster.

The most recent—and perhaps the most egregious—example of Haitian corruption at the expense of the people is the 2019 PetroCaribe scandal. *PetroCaribe* refers to a Venezuelan oil-credit program extended to eighteen Caribbean nations, which allowed them to purchase millions of barrels of oil on preferential terms, with payments deferred over twenty-five years at an interest rate as low as 1 percent; recipient governments could then sell the oil and use the proceeds to pay for social programs. But by August 2019, Venezuelan oil production had dropped by almost 75 percent, forcing the indefinite suspension of fuel exports to several PetroCaribe nations, including Haiti and Jamaica. The resulting severe fuel shortages led to gas being sold on the black market for as much as $13 to $15 a gallon. This precarious state of affairs had arguably been precipitated by negotiations with the International Monetary Fund (IMF) in February 2018 to obtain $96 million in loans and grants that could be used in part to pay for fuel. But key terms of the agreement obliged the Haitian government to abandon long-standing fuel subsidies and raise prices by 38 percent for gasoline, 47 percent for diesel, and 51 percent for kerosene. This policy resulted in island-wide riots and was quickly abandoned.

These events turned the spotlight on the results of a 2017 government audit into the disbursement of the PetroCaribe funds. Edwidge Danticat puts the results this way: "A Haitian Senate report detailed how, between 2008 and 2016, funds that had been accumulated through Haiti's participation in Venezuela's oil-purchasing program, PetroCaribe, were misused, misappropriated, or embezzled by government officials and their cronies in the private sector."[16] Indeed, the sum total of missing money, which is the sum that Haiti still owes Venezuela, is $2 billion. But the blame is widespread, and the entire affair is a tragic reminder of an endemic state of affairs in which an elite circle of connections only reconfirms the prioritization of personal profit over the social welfare. In an article in the *Miami Herald*, Jacqueline Charles points out that "during the period government auditors looked into, Haiti had six governments under three different presidents—René Préval, Michel Martelly and Jocelerme Privert. . . . [An] anti-corruption commission issued its own 656-page report on the misuse of PetroCaribe funds. It concluded that charges should be filed against two former prime ministers, several ex-ministers and the owners of private firms on grounds they misappropriated and embezzled money that left post-quake Haiti with unfinished government buildings, poorly built housing and overpriced public works contracts."[17] Meanwhile, current President Jovenel Moïse—a relatively unknown former banana cultivator who, as the handpicked successor to former Haitian president Michel Martelly, won an election with turnout reported at 21 percent, and who had himself been accused of receiving millions of dollars for questionable road rehabilitation projects—was being pressed to launch an investigation into management of the PetroCaribe funds and to show results on his promise to fight corruption. But the self-styled *Neg Bannan nan*, or Banana Man, who was apparently selling water in Port-de-Paix before he magically launched a successful presidential bid, shows no signs of shedding light on millions of dollars in cost overruns, including what Jacqueline Charles cites as "a 213 percent increase in costs for grading, backfill and excavation work and a 141 percent increase on drainage-sanitation costs over the original estimates 18 months prior"—in other words, a vast array of questionable schemes in which he appeared to be at the center.[18] Ultimately, it is the people of Haiti who suffer, and whose victimization is the enabling factor grounding the extraction of profit by means public and private, foreign and local. In this interlocking mosaic of corruption, the hollow core of the twin pillars of citizenship and sovereignty redefines the parameters of the shambolic.

Dutch Antilles

The terms of this analysis of Caribbean neoliberalism and non-sovereignty do not include Suriname, a former Dutch colony on the northern coast of South America that gained independence in 1975. Rather, the name *Dutch Antilles* refers to a collection of six islands in the Eastern Caribbean. Three of the islands—Aruba, Curaçao, and Saint Martin, with a total population of some three hundred thousand people—enjoy autonomy within the Kingdom of the Netherlands, while the other three much more sparsely populated ones, Bonaire, Saint Eustatius, and Saba, have a combined population of twenty-five thousand or so and enjoy the status of "overseas municipalities" of the Netherlands, becoming politically and constitutionally integrated with the metropolis. The people of the Antilles have been Dutch citizens since the end of slavery in 1863.

As the process of Western decolonization took hold, the relationship between the kingdom and what was termed the Netherlands Antilles was proclaimed in 1954 in the *Statuut* or Charter for the Kingdom of the Netherlands. Following Surinamese independence in 1975, and the secession of Aruba as an autonomous state in 1986, the entity known as the

Netherlands Antilles came to an end when major constitutional restructuring was implemented in 2010, with Curaçao and St Maarten also acceding to internal autonomy within the kingdom. On the other hand, with regard to the three remaining territories, "the repercussions of increasingly interventionist Dutch policies since the 1990s," as Oostindie and Veenendaal put it, have resulted in "deeply ambiguous insular feelings, an ambivalence which in turn leads to urgent questions about the appropriateness of Dutch policies" (2018, 3). This ambivalence has tended to produce politico-economic confrontations with the mainland on the status of the islands themselves.

For example, on February 6, 2018, the Dutch government sought to dissolve the local authority of Saint Eustatius, following a report from the national state secretary accusing the island administration of lawlessness, financial mismanagement, and discrimination. Protests broke out over what was immediately seen as a colonial power grab aimed at undermining the island's sovereignty. But in a legal sense, that sovereignty was itself nonexistent; as an "overseas municipality" with a limited capacity for self-government, the crisis was on the verge of leading Saint Eustatius into a veritable morass of political and identitarian ambivalence. Wouter Veenendaal sums up the pitfalls of this in-betweenness this way: "The lack of complete sovereignty and full decision-making capacity can have problematic effects on the (construction of) identities, sense of nationhood, and political emancipation of the populations of overseas territories" (2016, 152). Put another way, there is certainly a degree of attractiveness and certain perceived benefits in maintaining metropolitan links, as Veenendaal continues: "It appears that economic considerations constitute a major explanation for the desire to retain the constitutional links with the Netherlands. On the southern Caribbean islands, which are located just off the Venezuelan coast, security seems to be a factor as well" (2016, 157). So it is not simply identity construction that is at issue, then; in addition, a condition of economic dependence, of subjection to the greater profit-oriented goals of the capital-driven businesses of metropolitan powers, is often the prime result of such a nonsovereign condition.

The paradoxes embedded in a recent labor report for the region provide a telling case in point. The report begins by touting an apparent increase in employment figures, only to flag an increase in part-time workers shortly thereafter as the core constituent of such an increase: "In 2018, the labour participation rate on the three islands of the Caribbean Netherlands was higher than two years previously. . . . The increase in Bonaire's net labour participation rate between 2016 and 2018 was entirely attributable to part-time workers. On the other hand, the number of full-time employees decreased. The share of people in part-time jobs grew most significantly among working young people and over-65s."[19] Clearly, here, we are also dealing with a concomitant decrease in full-time workers, as well as growth in part-time jobs concentrated at the two most vulnerable (in age-specific terms) ends of the labor spectrum, as the report clearly states. These employment patterns are well known to specialists in economics and social welfare, for the critical combination of reduced labor costs associated with part-time employment, along with the likely absence of benefit payments, makes this labor scenario literally a neoliberalist's dream.

So while such binding metropolitan ties are often presented as a panacea, they are also presented as assuring equality for residents of these "offshore municipalities" within a system that from the outset has itself been unequal. In a relative comparison, categories like social benefits and facilities infrastructure appear to assure success and advantages relative to countries that have become independent, arguably resulting in higher standards of living, better governance, and territorial integrity. But by the same token, in the face of periodic waves of desire to leave the kingdom, local traditions and values tend to be devalued, Antilleans are seen as unwanted "foreigners" on the Dutch mainland despite their legally egalitarian status, and several of the metropolitan Dutch laws that apply to these islands, like those governing euthanasia and same-sex marriage, are locally seen as anathema. Ultimately, though, the implications of non-sovereign status tend to highlight economic vulnerabilities, often showing the extent to which dependency can be exploited in the quest for profit. Veenendaal points to the problematics surrounding "local assessments of the merits and shortcomings of the non-sovereign political status. In the first place, in terms of economics and security, smallness has traditionally been associated with weakness, vulnerability, and dependence" (2016, 154).

The uniformity of these policies and practices and the pervasiveness of their results render neoliberalism an incontrovertible reality as an economic praxis across both independent and nominally autonomous Caribbean sites, putting their social and economic devastation into clear focus. Indeed, the key principles of neoliberalism have virtually come to serve as a kind of moral foundation for the contemporary world, as a recent reading by George Monbiot would have it: "Neoliberalism sees competition as the defining characteristic of human relations. . . . It maintains that "the market" delivers benefits that could never be achieved by planning. . . . Attempts to limit competition are treated as inimical to liberty. Tax and regulation should be minimised, public services should be privatised. The organisation of labour and collective bargaining by trade unions are portrayed as market distortions that impede the formation of a natural hierarchy of winners and losers" (2015, 2). Given this worldview—in which the spoils go to the victor at almost any cost, including the victimization of the most vulnerable—if human relations can be successfully reduced to "winners and losers," it comes as no surprise that market forces are marshaled to exploit the inhabitants of subjugated states, confirming their lack of sovereign agency as their natural state, fit only for plunder.

In expanding our analysis to Haiti, Puerto Rico, and the Dutch Antilles, then, it becomes clear that there are ineluctable parallels between the neocolonial practices of labor exploitation, externally driven consumerism, and overseas repatriation of profits at work in the French DOM and the neoliberal international economic forces that ultimately determine and limit the options faced by these supposedly autonomous Caribbean territories. Such parallels make it useful for us to look at Haiti, Puerto Rico, and the Dutch Antilles comparatively, even as we take the particularities of their practice as reflective of trends relevant for the greater Caribbean, sovereign or otherwise. Indeed, the scope of the 2009 protests in Guadeloupe and Martinique and the 2019 protests in Puerto Rico, and the political and

economic concerns these protests articulated, marked a thirst for transformative change that would co-opt music and media to push the boundaries of change beyond the intrinsic subordination of the commonwealth/
departmental/metropolitan relation. The spillover from the pervasive
expression of local protest aimed at the rejection of external exploitation
and the enhancement of self-definition—embodied in the popular slogan
and song "La Gwadloup sé tan nou" (Guadeloupe is ours)—into various
artistic modes of cultural expression proposed a fundamental restructuring of local economic patterns, media activity, and political and social activism. The fundamental aim here was to enhance local autonomy, meant in
its turn to lead to a reduction in the influence of metropolitan interests and
capital concerns embodied in the powerful local economic elite and an end
to price gouging and racism in hiring. In such contexts, the critical role
played by the conjunction of culture and community shapes the articulation of demands for autonomy and equality, as Stuart Hall points out:

> Popular culture, commodified and stereotyped as it often is, is not at all,
> as we sometimes think of it, the arena where we find who we really are,
> the truth of our experience. It is an arena that is profoundly mythic. It is
> a theater of popular desires, a theater of popular fantasies. It is where we
> discover and play with the identifications of ourselves, where we are imag-
> ined, where we are represented, not only to the audiences out there who
> do not get the message, but to ourselves for the first time. (1993, 113)

In this reading, the role of performance as a key arbiter in the negotiation
and representation of identity mediates the terms within which the community frames the boundaries of its being and contests its ongoing domination
through resistance. In a related way, such acts of resistance simultaneously
valorize acts of artistic expression that provoke "interventionist practices"
increasingly needed to deal with, confront, and even reorient the racialized social structures that continue to create oppressive conditions in these
territories.

The scope and urgency of these concerns, highlighting the limits of the
non-sovereign model and the need to supersede it, were given added impe-
tus and perspective by the referendum of January 24, 2010, by which Mar-

Figure I.1 Prime Minister the Hon. Gaston Browne of Antigua and Barbuda received the New Flag of the Collectivité of Martinique from President Alfred Marie-Jeanne just before the opening of the 67th meeting of the OECS Authority on June 18, 2019.

tinicans approved a new administrative structure fusing the Regional and General Councils into the Territorial Collectivity of Martinique, a political entity ratified by the French government in 2011 and giving rise to the recent groundbreaking regional initiative that saw the accession of Martinique to associate membership in the Organization of Eastern Caribbean States (OECS) in February 2015, after a unanimous all-party historical vote of the Regional Council to join the Anglophone Eastern Caribbean bloc on October 14, 2014. In its turn, Guadeloupe applied for associate membership in CARICOM, or the Caribbean Economic Community, in the same month, and was also granted associate membership in the OECS on March 14, 2019. And in a ceremonial act of mutual celebration at the sixty-seventh meeting of the OECS Authority on June 18, 2019, Alfred Marie-Jeanne, president of the Collectivité Territoriale de Martinique, presented the new flag of the Collectivity to Gaston Browne, incoming chairman of the Authority and prime minister of Antigua and Barbuda (figure I.1).

The implications and repercussions of these transformative political actions—with Martinique and Guadeloupe joining a regional political entity made up of independent Anglophone nation-states that have brought new voices and strategies of self-definition to their representation on a multiplicity of stages—constitute a recognition of regional similarities that arguably reshapes the terms and conditions of regional autonomy and integrates Martinique and Guadeloupe into a wider Caribbean zone of economic and cultural cooperation.

Similarly, the collapse of Puerto Rico's economic and political model, in a territory referred to by its longtime governing body, the United States, as a "commonwealth" or Freely Associated State, exposes the extent to which coloniality, whether viewed implicitly or explicitly, produces attitudes and codes of behavior that function through the idea of race. In this way, public pensions, public sector union contracts, and the public education system have fallen prey to the privileging of neoliberal, hedge-fund-driven economic forces on local, federal, and global levels. The source of these incongruities goes back decades; both colonial policies toward the wider Caribbean, and neocolonial policies specifically targeting Puerto Rico over decades, have been shown to have similar results. Winston Griffith sums it up well: "The historical experience of Caricom countries does not support the assertions of the proponents of neoliberal economics and the new global environment in which these countries must now operate complicates matters. . . . It has been argued that neoliberal economic policies would result in a high standard of living; but the colonial history of Caricom countries casts doubt on the validity of this assertion" (2010, 506–507). As these capital-centered policies continue to inflict incalculable economic devastation and social distress across the board, workers' wages become the ultimate arbiter of the distance between the polar opposites of profitability and poverty. Alfred Wong makes this point clear: "In the neoliberal lexicon, productivity equates low wages, regardless of their adequacy for living minimally. Just like the cruise ship business, the business model of mass land-based tourism as controlled by large trans-national corporations is based essentially on lowest cost of goods and services. . . . With each island state fighting to provide least-cost touristic services, there is an unrelenting downward pressure on local wage scale" (2015, paragraphs 12, 14). Clearly, here, providing a living wage is of secondary, even tertiary importance; workers are reduced to number equivalents, victimized a second time as their governments vie with one another for favor on the neoliberal playground.

It is increasingly clear that sovereignty for Puerto Rico in any accepted sense of the word has been constrained and foreclosed for more than a century by egregious pieces of legislation from the Jones Act to PROMESA, making sovereignty a dead letter as far as any capacity of the territory or its people for economic or political self-determination is concerned. Similarly, an analysis of the Dutch Antillean model reveals that the ambiguous advantages and disadvantages of postcolonial non-sovereignty in the Dutch Caribbean, from the secession of Aruba in 1986 to the change in the region's constitutional status in 2010, to a 2018 legislative proposal mandating that "people from Aruba, Curacao and Sint Maarten should be deported back to the Caribbean islands if they commit crimes, because Antillean youngsters are over-represented in crime figures," is embedded in an ongoing and pervasive framework of coloniality.[20] This incomprehensible insistence on expelling citizens so as to "return" them to the same country is simply one paradox of the complex, contradictory practices through which the Netherlands Antilles and the Netherlands continue to negotiate issues of power, authority, and cultural identity in the postcolonial era.

The terms and conditions of the neoliberal economic policies imposed across the wider Caribbean in recent decades have had incontrovertibly deleterious effects at the individual, island or nation, and regional levels. But, significantly, the origins of such policies are located in the absentee landlord structure of the colonial era, suggesting strongly that the contemporary persistence of colonial patterns and practices that reinscribe hegemonies of domination and submission are a paradoxical constant of the postcolonial condition. Winston Griffith makes this point clear: "The laissez-faire policies of colonial governments also deprived Caricom countries of another necessary ingredient for development, namely, the economic surplus. Colonial monetary arrangements were such that plantation owners, mainly non-residents to the region, could easily transfer their profits outside the region, thus depriving the region of much capital that could have been used for domestic capital accumulation" (2010, 507). Such policies of capital relocation are arguably a central feature of the neoliberal economic policies at work in the contemporary sovereign and non-sovereign Caribbean, and are predicated on the presumed primacy and effectiveness of external capital infusions, whose rising tide of profit will lift all boats. The proponents of these policies, as Matthew Bishop asserts, are "endowed with a rationalist's belief in the self-correcting nature of markets, the essential efficiency of global market capitalism, and they tend to emphasise the benefits available to Caribbean economies of participating if only they become competitive in market terms" (2015, 3). But the reality is that these policies are quite selective, if not exclusionary, in the segments of the economy that they benefit. Indeed, the paucity of manufacturing, for example, is balanced by the continuity of depressed wages, as Griffith continues: "The laissez-faire policies of colonial governments partly contributed to the absence of an indigenous manufacturing class in Caricom countries, as very little manufacturing developed in the monocultural economies of Caricom" (2010, 507). The result, across the board, has tended toward the promotion and valorization of systems of ownership and production that are exteriorly located and whose priority is always the repatriation of profit to the points of origin of the enabling capital.

For the Caribbean region, then, the factors outlined here have resulted in an extended and repeated pattern of economic exploitation in which external influences use local labor simply as an expendable means to a profitable end. In an illuminating study, Matthew Bishop describes these forces as "systems of economic production, distribution and consumption that are dominated by a relatively small number of disproportionately powerful multi-national corporations" (2015, 4), ineluctably characterized by "often-insidious patterns of corporate control and the fencing-off of public spaces for private enrichment" (5). This conjoining of "corporate control" and "private enrichment" result in an increasingly compromised set of sovereign states, whose independence is virtually restricted to their flag and national anthem; Bishop describes such limited and ineffective patterns of sovereignty as "insignificant in anything other than name for individual small states which are transgressed by powerful and destructive forces on a daily basis" (8), emphasizing the extent to which external capitalist forces quickly dominate the local landscape of production and dictate local economic and political policy in the furtherance of their own ends, thereby reinforcing the primacy of external profit over local development or social welfare programs.

Development is arguably the key question here, and for Bishop, what the Caribbean experience proves indisputably, from a broader perspective, is how neoliberal policies work first and foremost to fulfill and extend their own ends. In other words, the patterns and practices of the neoliberalism long at work in the Caribbean provide proof positive of the paradoxical contradiction between markets and development, of the intrinsic tendency of the former to ineluctably demonstrate that, as Bishop writes, "when left to their own devices—and skewed by the powerful and self-interested actors that inhabit them—markets will never produce development of a meaningful kind . . . they need to be shaped *strategically* to serve the purpose of development" (2015, 5–6; emphasis in the original). If, then, market forces cannot be relied on to promote the development objectives of societies, particularly those already made subject to colonial histories of exploitation and deprivation, one can only conclude that the historical experience of countries such as these makes clear the reality behind the positive assertions of the proponents of neoliberal economics, exposing it as a form of propaganda by the first world aimed at maintaining its hegemony over the third.

In the preface to his recently published *Glissant and the Middle Passage: Philosophy, Beginning, Abyss*, John E. Drabinski speaks tellingly of the compound possibilities intrinsic to the pluralities of place and self-definition. Of key importance in this schema is the Martinican philosopher's concept of Relation, wherein dynamism and unpredictability produce new patterns of nonlinear engagement, which he describes as "Glissant's second wave of decolonization . . . that re-addresses what had, in the first wave, been jettisoned in the name of self-authorization and self-authoring. . . . Paradox produces abundance, rather than paralyzing or confounding contradiction. . . . Relation is therefore dynamic, productive, dangerous, and alive with fecund engagement and appropriation" (2019, xvii). If we examine the engagement, spontaneity, and teleologies of the popular movements under consideration here, particularly those at work in Guadeloupe and Martinique in 2009 and in Puerto Rico and Haiti in 2019, it can be argued that critical tropes of creolization are actively undergirding these acts of social and cultural self-definition.

From a Glissantian perspective, creolization tends almost always to lead to unknown and unforeseeable consequences. Creolization emphasizes mobility, transformation, and flux, subverting fixed and filiative patterns of identity formation. It is to this end that Glissant supplanted the singular figure of the root by the rhizome, a pluralist spatio-cultural construct grounding the Caribbean heritage of creolization; in this way, its plural, protean properties and its insistence on displacement and doubling explode universalist and colonialist concepts of rootedness and hierarchy in favor of diversity, difference, and transformation.

If it is the random, unpredictable concatenation of cultural patterns and praxes that gives rise to a Caribbean framework of creoleness, Glissant's framework for Caribbean creolization gradually gave way to a broader articulation of global intersectionality. By scaling this vision to the "global village," this iteration of identitarian relationality, Glissant argues, already extant in the Caribbean region, more and more undergirds the multiple contacts and inflections of world cultures increasingly subject to change. Michael Dash explains Glissant's reading of the Caribbean condition this way: "The Caribbean has become exemplary in this creative global 'chaos' which proliferates everywhere" (1995, 23). In this way, he locates a creolization that actively contests metropolitan colonial models of universalist—read neocolonial—assimilation.

Glissant always stressed the role of spatiality—of place, of location—in the process that translates the composite character of the colonial trace in the periphery into a framework for transnational self-assertion, recognizing a national identitarianism that draws on borders but that also places singularities and hegemonies of history into question. These hegemonic practices, with patterns of exploitation continued into the present by economically and culturally dominant forces, generate a category that Nelson Maldonado-Torres has termed the "coloniality of Being," which he describes as fundamentally linked to race: "What is invisible about the person of color is its very humanity. . . . Invisibility and dehumanization are the primary expressions of the coloniality of Being. The coloniality of Being indicates those aspects that produce exception from the order of Being. . . . The coloniality of Being appears in historical projects and ideas of civilization which advance colonial projects of various kinds inspired or legitimized by the idea of race" (2007, 257). By contrast, any venture into the alternative epistemology of decoloniality would perforce seek to negate neocolonial and neoliberal patterns of individual and communal exploitation in favor of a fundamental transformation of the people's material conditions of existence. By expanding on this exploration of decolonial thinking, Glissant was able to relocate and reinscribe the pluralisms of division and difference of this resistive Caribbean framework as he sought to revise fixed notions of colonialism, neocolonialism, and postcolonialism using the insular Caribbean experience as a point of departure. These positional shifts would undergird the fundamentally archipelagic patterns that would ultimately enable the alternative identitarian and contestatory paths traced between 2009 and 2019.

Parry's and Glissant's positions remind us of Homi Bhabha's useful formulation of a third space, as that which "displaces the histories that constitute it, and sets up new structures of authority" (1990, 211). The new structures put into place by these strikes and protests, and demands that the material conditions of existence be set on an alternative footing, framed a new resistive positionality embraced by these non-sovereign Caribbean territories within a broader context of a global process of change and transformation. Put another way, and from a different perspective, one might claim that we have issue with what the editors of the volume *Archipelagic American Studies* define as "a push and pull between the metaphoric and the material, in which the concept of archipelago serves to mediate the phenomenology of humans' cultural relation to the solid and liquid materiality of geography" (Roberts and Stephens 2017, 7). In seeking to redefine the shaping of identities and historical processes in the Caribbean, this volume has sought to create a space for theorizing and assessing the ways in which the intersection of history, geography, economics and resistance eventuates a new rubric for Caribbean cultural studies, whereby the thought and the structure of the archipelago are relocated at the forefront of a newly nonhierarchical world.

In his last published work, *Philosophie de la relation,* Glissant insists on the importance of this link between the influence of the archipelago and a resistance to hierarchy: "The archipelago is this non-unique original reality," he claims (2009, 47), seeking to encapsulate the multiple, transformative encounters of the peoples of the Caribbean region. In other words, if here the figure of the archipelago is inscribed as both symbol and catalyst of diversity, it immediately separates itself in an important way from continental systems and their corollaries of universalism and hegemonic totality, allowing Glissant to link this archipelic thought to patterns of resistance, pluralism, and transformation: "We also come to realize that archipelic thought eventually supplants continental thought . . . and that resistance subsists in every periphery. You don't see it, and in any event you wouldn't recognize it, because you don't even recognize the existence of peripheries" (2009, 86, my translation). This new world, inscribed in and enriched by resistance, depends on the contestatory relationship between difference and colonial patterns of filiation. In asserting their intolerance of exploitation and their difference from the metropolitan center, activist groups like the *LKP* were arguably embodying Stuart Hall's formulation of the Creole as the central regional metaphor of resistance and transformation, and thus a form that is "powerfully expressive of local conditions" (2003, 28). These territories seek self-definition by demanding recognition of the historical factors linking their positionality to their place, asserting through their actions a Caribbeanness that they continue creatively to reinvent and redefine.

NOTES

1. See Centre des archives d'outre mer, Aix-en-Provence, FM AGEFOM 124/54, 16 janvier 1948.

2. Justin Daniel, "Cultural Identity and Political Identity in the French Antilles and Puerto Rico: Myths and Realities," 8, http://archives.acls.org/programs/crn/network /ebook_daniel_papers.htm (accessed January 31, 2020).

3. Daniel, "Cultural Identity and Political Identity," 12.

4. Luis N. Rivera Pagán, "The Plight of Puerto Rico: Coloniality, Diaspora, and Decolonial Resistance," *Puerto Rican Cultural Center*, May 21, 2018, https://prcc-chgo.org/2018 /05/21/the-plight-of-puerto-rico-coloniality-diaspora-and-decolonial-resistance/.

5. Rivera Pagán, "The Plight of Puerto Rico."

6. Charo Henriquez, "Puerto Rico Protestors Got Creative: Dancing, Singing, Diving," *New York Times*, July 24, 2019.

7. Henriquez, "Puerto Rico Protestors."

8. Henriquez, "Puerto Rico Protestors."

9. Henriquez, "Puerto Rico Protestors."

10. Henriquez, "Puerto Rico Protestors."

11. Jose A. Del Real, "'We Just Changed History': Cheers and Tears in San Juan," *New York Times*, July 25, 2019.

12. Karen Zraick, "He Wanted Cold Medicine, but CVS Rejected His Puerto Rican ID." *New York Times*, November 4, 2019.

13. Yves Engler, "Canada, Get Out of the Lima Group, Core Group, and OAS." *Counterpunch*, February 19, 2020.

14. Engler, "Canada, Get Out."

15. Justin Elliott and Laura Sullivan, "How the Red Cross Raised Half a Billion Dollars for Haiti and Built Six Homes," *ProPublica*, June 3, 2015, https://www.propublica .org/article/how-the-red-cross-raised-half-a-billion-dollars-for-haiti-and-built-6-homes.

16. Edwidge Danticat, "Haitians Want to Know What the Government Has Done with Missing Oil Money," *New Yorker*, October 19, 2018.

17. Jacqueline Charles, "Haiti President Accused of Embezzlement Scheme in Government Audit of Venezuela Aid Money," *Miami Herald*, June 4, 2019.

18. Jacqueline Charles, "Haiti President Accused," *Miami Herald*, June 4, 2019.

19. "More Caribbean Dutch in Employment in 2018," Saba-News.com, April 26, 2019, https://www.saba-news.com/more-caribbean-dutch-in-employment-in-2018/.

20. "PVV Calls for Deportation of Antilleans with a Criminal Conviction." Dutch-News.nl, June 7, 2018, https://www.dutchnews.nl/news/2018/06/pvv-calls-for-deportation -of-antilleans-with-a-criminal-conviction/.

REFERENCES

Anderson, Benedict. 1983. *Imagined Communities: Reflections on the Origin and Spread of Nationalism*. London: Verso.

Bhabha, Homi K. 1990. "The Third Space: An Interview with Homi Bhabha." In *Identity, Community, Culture, Difference*, edited by Jonathan Rutherford, 201–213. London: Lawrence and Wishert.

Bishop, Matthew. 2015. "Caribbean Development in the Midst of New Regional and Global Dynamics." Presented at the Forum on the Future of the Caribbean, "Situating the Caribbean within the New Global Political Economy of Development," UWI St. Augustine, Trinidad, and Tobago, May 5–7.

Bonilla, Yarimar. 2015. *Non-sovereign Futures: French Caribbean Politics in the Wake of Disenchantment*. Chicago: University of Chicago Press.

Burton, Richard D. E. 1992. "Between the Particular and the Universal: Dilemmas of the Martinican Intellectual." *Intellectuals in the Twentieth-Century Caribbean*, edited by Alistair Hennessy, 186–210. London: Macmillan Caribbean.

Childers, Kristen Stromberg. 2016. *Seeking Imperialism's Embrace: National Identity, Decolonization, and Assimilation in the French Caribbean*. New York: Oxford University Press.

Dash, J. Michael. 1995. *Edouard Glissant*. New York: Cambridge.

Drabinski, John E. 2019. *Glissant and the Middle Passage: Philosophy, Beginning, Abyss*. Minneapolis: University of Minnesota Press.

Engler, Yves. 2020. "Canada, Get Out of the Lima Group, Core Group, and OAS." *Counterpunch*, February 19.

Glissant, Edouard. 2009. *Philosophie de la relation*. Paris: Gallimard.

Griffith, Winston H. 2010. "Neoliberal Economics and Caribbean Economies." *Journal of Economic Issues* xliv, no. 2: 505–511.

Grosfoguel, Ramon. 2001. *Colonial Subjects: Puerto Ricans in Global Perspective*. Berkeley: University of California Press.

Hall, Stuart. 1990. "Cultural Identity and Diaspora." In *Identity: Community, Culture, Difference*, edited by Jonathan Rutherford, 222–237. London: Lawrence and Wishart.

———. 1993. "What Is This 'Black' in Black Popular Culture?" *Social Justice* 20, no. 1–2: 104–114.

———. 2003. "Créolité and the Process of Creolization." *Créolité and Creolization: Documenta 11, Platform 3*, edited by Okwui Enwezor et al., 27–41. Hatje Cantz: Ostfildern-Ruit, Germany.

Hélénon, Véronique. 2011. *French Caribbeans in Africa: Diasporic Connections and Colonial Administration 1880–1939*. New York: Palgrave Macmillan.

Huber, Evelyne, and Fredrick Solt. 2004. "Successes and Failures of Neoliberalism." *Latin American Research Review* 39, no. 3: 150–164.

Jackson, Shona N. 2012. *Creole Indigeneity: Between Myth and Nation in the Caribbean*. Minneapolis: University of Minnesota Press.

Katz, Jonathan M. 2013. *The Big Truck That Went By: How the World Came to Save Haiti and Left Behind a Disaster*. New York: Palgrave Macmillan.

Kennard, Matt. 2012. "Haiti and the Shock Doctrine." *openDemocracy*, August 14, https://www.opendemocracy.net/en/haiti-and-shock-doctrine/.

Maldonado-Torres, Nelson. 2007. "On the Coloniality of Being." *Cultural Studies* 21, no. 2–3: 240–270.

Martinez-San Miguel, Yolanda. 2014. *Coloniality of Diasporas: Rethinking Intra-colonial Migrations in a Pan-Caribbean Context*. New York: Palgrave Macmillan.

Miles, William F. S. 2001. "Fifty Years of Assimilation: Assessing France's Experience of Caribbean Decolonisation through Administrative Reform." In *Islands at the Crossroads: Politics in the Non-independent Caribbean*, edited by Aarón Gamaliel Ramos and Angel Israel Rivera, 45–60. Kingston, Jamaica: Ian Randle Publishers.

————. 2005. "Democracy without Sovereignty: France's Postcolonial Paradox." *Brown Journal of World Affairs* xi, no. 2: 223–234.

Monbiot, George. 2015. "Neoliberalism: The Ideology at the Root of All Our Problems." *Guardian*, April 15.

Newton, Melanie J. 2013. "Returns to a Native Land: Indigeneity and Decolonization in the Anglophone Caribbean." *Small Axe* 17, no. 2 [41]: 108–122.

Oostindie, Gert, and Wouter Veenendaal. 2018. "Head versus Heart: The Ambiguities of Non-sovereignty in the Dutch Caribbean." *Regional and Federal Studies* 28, no. 1: 25–45.

Ormerod, Beverley. 1985. *An Introduction to the French Caribbean Novel.* London: Heinemann.

Parry, Benita. 1987. "Problems in Current Theories of Colonial Discourse." *Oxford Literary Review* 9, no. 1: 27–58.

Reyes, Hector. 1997. "Puerto Rico: The Last Colony." *International Socialist Review*, no. 3.

Roberts, Brian Russell, and Michelle Ann Stephens. 2017. "Introduction: Archipelagic American Studies—Decontinentalizing the Study of American Culture." In *Archipelagic American Studies*, edited by Brian Russell Roberts and Michelle Ann Stephens, 1–54. Durham, NC: Duke University Press.

Schuller, Mark. 2012. *Killing with Kindness: Haiti, International Aid, and NGOs.* New Brunswick: Rutgers University Press.

Schwartz, Timothy T. 2008. *Travesty in Haiti: A True Account of Christian Missions, Orphanages, Food Aid, Fraud and Drug Trafficking.* BookSurge Publishing.

Trouillot, Michel-Rolph. 2002. "North Atlantic Universals: Analytical Fictions 1492–1945." *South Atlantic Quarterly* 101, no. 4: 839–858.

Veenendaal, Wouter. 2016. "Smallness and Status Debates in Overseas Territories: Evidence from the Dutch Caribbean." *Geopolitics* 21, no. 1: 148–170.

Wilentz, Amy. 2019. "Haiti Is in the Streets." *Nation*, October 24.

Wong, Alfred. 2015. "Caribbean Island Tourism: Pathway to Continued Colonial Servitude." *Études caribbénnes*, August–December, 31–32.

PART I

NEOLIBERALISM, IDENTITY, AND RESISTANCE IN THE *DÉPARTEMENTS D'OUTRE-MER*

1

Bridging the Divide to Face the Plantationocene

THE CHLORDECONE
CONTAMINATION AND THE 2009
SOCIAL EVENTS IN MARTINIQUE
AND GUADELOUPE

MALCOM FERDINAND

Five centuries of a socially unequal and capitalistic globalization led to such important ecological destructions that geologists redefined our era as the Anthropocene: an era in which human activities are a significant geological force leaving their traces in Earth's crust (Crutzen et al. 2011; Bonneuil and Fressoz 2016). Such traces include persistent toxic chemicals left over by an expanding chemical industry and the development of intensive farming (Cicolella 2017; Steiner et al. 2012). Scientifically, it is no longer valid to separate the conflicts and tensions of human affairs from global ecological changes. To that end, in emphasizing the part played by the social inequalities, injustices, and dominations of capitalist developments and plantation economies in the changes induced in Earth's ecosystems, social scientists have given different names to this era, such as Capitolocene and Plantationocene (Haraway 2015). An entry point to the seemingly daunting task of bringing together sociopolitical issues and ecological changes globally can be found at the local level, as shown here in the case of the French Caribbean islands of Martinique and Guadeloupe.

Martinique and Guadeloupe are facing the challenges brought by the Plantationocene, while still being embedded in a social and ecological divide. This divide is particularly salient in the disconnect between the 2009 social events and the chemical pollution of these islands. The 2009 events of Guadeloupe and Martinique brought to light the chronic social crisis endured by the *outre-mer*, the overseas departments of France (Lurel 2016). Higher levels of unemployment and poverty, higher social inequalities, and lower levels of transport and medical infrastructures compared with mainland France constitute the social landscape of Martinique and Guadeloupe (William et al. 2012). Less visible at the time was the concerning ecological state of these Caribbean islands. Because they are in tropical latitudes, Martinique and Guadeloupe are particularly exposed to the impacts of climate change and experience acutely the negative effects of intensive monocultures of export crops, heavily reliant on toxic chemicals. Indeed, the 2009 events took place in the very same period during which inhabitants learned of the dire consequences of a long-lasting chemical pollution of their islands resulting from the use of a pesticide in banana plantations called chlordecone (CLD). What were then the connections between the chronic social crisis and the toxic chemical pollution in these postcolonial and post-slavery societies? Despite their concomitance, the apparent rift between these two issues points to the characteristic divide of modernity between nature and culture, environment and society, ecology and politics (Latour 1997; Descola 2005). In an attempt to bridge this divide, this chapter investigates the connections between the ecological crisis at the heart of the CLD pollution and the social crisis that burst onto the French national political scene in 2009.

Such an endeavor requires an interdisciplinary approach bringing the results of toxicology, epidemiology, agronomy, and environmental research into dialogue with an empirically based sociological investigation, and with the analytical tools of political sociology and the sociology of risk as well as science and technologies studies. The social analysis relies on numerous research field trips to Martinique and Guadeloupe from 2011 to 2018, during which I conducted interviews with activists, state and local authorities, and scientists involved in social protests or local ecological conflicts (or both). To begin, the first part of this chapter presents the environmental and medical characteristics of the CLD contamination in Martinique and Guadeloupe within the socioeconomic context of the local banana production. The second part highlights the resulting criticism, anxiety, and environmental justice demands on the part of numerous local ecological nongovernmental organizations (NGOs). The third part details how this contamination has been politically framed solely as an environmental and public health problem, leaving aside its social underpinnings. The fourth part starts bridging the ecological-social divide by bringing to the fore the little acknowledged and yet very tangible connections between the CLD contamination and the 2009 social events. Finally, I contend that these two issues, far from being separate, are intricate parts of the same structural problems associated with plantation economies. Bridging this divide might be a way to collectively and courageously face the Plantationocene.

Chlordecone Contamination: Long-Lasting, Generalized Harm

With the backdrop a chronic social crisis, the first decade of the millennia has shed light on the contamination of Martinique and Guadeloupe by toxic chemicals used in banana plantations. Following the decline of the sugar cane market at the end of the nineteenth century, challenged by the beetroot, the Antillean planters turned their gaze toward banana plantations. The emerging markets of the beginning of the twentieth century, as well as technological advances in transport ships that allowed bananas to be sold across the world, facilitated the change in crop production. Although the declining sugar cane production is still in place, bananas became the main export crop in the second half of the twentieth century. Today, this industry accounts for around ten thousand jobs on both islands and produces 270,000 tons of bananas yearly (BGM 2019). Ninety-five percent of the production is exported to mainland France and other parts of Europe, amounting to 2 percent of the global exportation market (Laurent 2011). As part of the development of this production, the use of toxic chemicals such as CLD became common practice.

CLD is an organochlorine molecule (of the same chemical family as DDT) produced in the United States until 1975, which was used worldwide as a pesticide for domestic and agricultural purposes. Under the commercial names Kepone and Curlone, CLD was officially used in the banana plantations of Martinique and Guadeloupe from 1972 to 1993. A white powder was spread at the root of banana plants by agricultural workers to eradicate a banana weevil that threatened the yield of the production. In twenty-one years, one-sixth of world CLD production was spread on twenty thousand hectares of land on two densely populated islands, causing a long-lasting, generalized, and harmful ecological contamination (Ferdinand 2015).

First, because of its particular cage-like structure, the CLD molecule is very persistent. Models predict that the CLD contamination of the land may last from sixty years to seven centuries depending on the type of soils (Cabidoche 2009). Although progress has been made in the search for depollution techniques, a viable method of land decontamination has yet to be found (Chaussonerie et al. 2016). Second, this contamination of the land has spread to all parts of the ecosystems. This molecule is now found in soils, in inland aquifers and coastal waters, in animal and vegetable foods, in human blood, in umbilical cords and breastfeeding milk (AFSSA 2007, 67–68; Guldner et al. 2011). According to a 2018 study, over 90 percent of the inhabitants have CLD in their blood, with an average concentration of 0,14μg/L and 0,13μg/L, respectively, in Martinique and Guadeloupe (Santé Publique France and ANSES 2018). Third, being both an endocrine disruptor and a carcinogenic agent, CLD is extremely harmful. The health risks from acute exposure to CLD were already known in the United States, where a leak at the factory of Hopewell in 1975 caused severe physical damage to workers. They developed symptoms known as the "Kepone syndrome," including weight loss, reduced quality of sperm, and anarchic global eye movements (EPA 2009). Medical research has proved that chronic exposure to CLD in Martinique and Guadeloupe delays the cognitive development of infants, may induce premature birth, and increases the chance of prostate cancer (Kadhel et al. 2014; Dallaire et al. 2012; Multigner et al. 2010). Although no single factor can be held responsible for prostate cancer, it is important to bear in mind that, with 163 and 161 cases of prostate cancer respectively per one hundred thousand inhabitants for the 2010 to 2014 period, Martinique and Guadeloupe have some of the highest rates of prostate cancer in the world (Sante Publique France and ANSES 2018, 5).

Additional research is currently being conducted to assess the impact of CLD on the development of children and the occurrence of pathologies including breast cancer and chronic hepatitis (IRSET 2018). The harm caused by this molecule points to a kind of *slow violence* impacting both humans and nonhumans, one that, although unseen, exerts itself over a long period of time (Nixon 2011). This corporeal burden, the act of carrying unwillingly all of these toxic molecules in one's body, not only induces bodily harm but also infringes upon the conception of masculinity in these societies, particularly with respect to prostate cancer (Agard-Jones 2013; Mitman et al. 2004; Murphy 2006).

This contamination has also caused a number of social and economic difficulties with regard to state interventions. It was only in 1999 that CLD contamination was made into a public health problem (Godard and Bellec 2002). From then on, the French state implemented a number of measures to protect its citizens. In 2000, charcoal filters were introduced to water catchment areas (Bonan and Prime 2001, 45). In 2003, it was made compulsory to test the arable land for CLD before cultivating root vegetables. Heavily contaminated lands could no longer legally produce root vegetables. Since 2008, fishing has been forbidden in inland rivers and parts of coastal waters. As a result, many agricultural workers, inland fish farmers, and coastal fishermen, most of whom had never used CLD, had to move to other areas when possible or stop their traditional activities. Some either went early into retirement or changed their profession completely. Besides the loss of activities and financial consequences, these measures alienated people from their own milieu and ecosystems. Mr. Casius, a fisherman with more than forty years of experience, had to stop fishing in the Genipa Bay of Martinique. He describes the subsequent loss of landmarks: "Mr. Casius—I have my marks here [in Genipa]! Even with this foggy weather, I can find my way. But other there, I am not sure I can earn my bread. Other there it is not the same thing."[1]

Similarly, Mr. Pierce is a vegetable farmer in the town of Lamentin in Martinique. Mr. Pierce was part of a Martinican organization called ORGAPEYI

("Organic country" in Creole) that promotes organic agricultural practices without pesticides. Although he had not used CLD, when he found out his land was contaminated, he had to stop his agricultural work:

> Mr. Pierce—In 2006, when I found out my land was contaminated, I had to stop all the basic crops such as yams and sweet potatoes. Because of the Maximum Residues Level allowed, I could still do tomatoes and cucumbers. But when you listen to the researchers, they tell you that the more often you ingest little doses, the more you poison yourself. I was authorized to produce crops with small doses of toxicity. Since I eat what I produce, I could not poison myself. So, I stopped altogether. In good consciousness, I could not poison people. . . . I had to go look for work elsewhere, I worked as a security agent. . . . You become poorer and poorer, your aspirations become smaller. Me, I had the desire to live! Now I don't live, I survive.[2]

Today, many subsistence farmers endure the stigmatization of consumers fearing they might be selling contaminated products. When produce from one product in one town is found to exceed the authorized CLD residue level, all farmers of that town are affected, as was the case in the Martinican town of Morne-Rouge in October 2018. Many consumers, and particularly soon-to-be parents, no longer trust local products, favoring imports. This doubt in the very nurturing nature of these islands for inhabitants is one of the most concerning consequences of the CLD contamination.

Demands for Environmental Justice

Points of Conflict

The CLD contamination has generated anger and resentment directed both at the banana industry owned by Béké members and the services of the French state in charge of health and agriculture. The Békés are a socio-ethnic group of Martinique and Guadeloupe composed mostly of white people who identify themselves as being direct descendants of the first colonists and slave owners (Cabort-Masson 1992). Three aspects of the CLD case concentrate the indignation of civil society. First, the criticism concerns the very authorization of a molecule that was known by the authorities to be persistent and harmful since the late 1960s. Indeed, the first request for the authorization of CLD by banana production owners to the Toxic Committee (in charge of such authorization in France) was refused because of the close similarity of CLD to DDT. Yet, four years later, in 1972, the same request was granted with alleged bribery from banana planters (Joly 2010). The strong belief within the population that this contamination is the continuation of a colonial attitude to these postcolonial societies by the French state was also stirred up by the way the use of CLD was eventually stopped. In 1990, an EU regulation banned CLD while still allowing the banana producers to use their remaining stock for two more years, until 1992. Although this two-year period is a common regulatory practice to allow producers to find alternative methods and products, this grace period was perceived to be wholly illegitimate. Moreover, from 1992 to 1993, two illegal extensions were given by the ministry of agriculture, encapsulating in the eyes of the public a state-level disdain for the inhabitants of Martinique and Guadeloupe (Beaugendre 2005, 25). This criticism is all the more scathing since the United States had banned the production of CLD since 1976, and the International Agency for Research on Cancer classified CLD as a possible carcinogen (2b) in 1979. The civil population does not understand why the use of this molecule was continued until 1993 while the authorities knew it was dangerous long before.

Political criticism of a contemptuous state was followed by social ire against some Béké members for their role in this contamination. Not only is banana production controlled by Béké members, but one particular banana company, Les Etablissements de Laguarrigue, played an even more active part in the contamination. As production in the United States was stopped in 1975, this Martinican company bought the patent for the manufacture of CLD and organized French production of CLD with a factory based in Bezier in the South of mainland France. This CLD was then sold under the name Curlone (Beaugendre 2005, 20). The very fact that the legal and illegal authorizations were granted by the French state to members of the Békés to produce, to sell and to use CLD in Martinique and Guadeloupe, fueled anew criticism of the continuation of a colonial treatment of these populations (Verdol 2014). Furthermore, a 2018 article in the newspaper *Le Monde* revealed that during the two-year period from 1990 to 1992, granted officially to allow the company to empty out the remaining stock, the company actually produced even more CLD (Vincent 2018).

Second, the social criticism points to the French authorities' delay in enacting measures to protect the civilian population. In contrast to the 1975 stoppage after the leak at the United States Hopewell factory, it was not until the 2000s that state authorities took this contamination seriously and the inhabitants became publicly aware of it (Torny 2009). Although three official reports in 1979, 1980, and in 1993 had emphasized the presence of CLD in the Martinique and Guadeloupe ecosystem, it took almost thirty years to start protecting the population (Snegarrof 1977; Kermarrec 1980, 149; Beaugendre 2005, 39).

Third, the way the contamination of the CLD is dealt with is criticized. Since the (re)discovery of the CLD contamination in 1999, the philosophical stance of the French state's approach rests on a tolerable daily intake of quantities of CLD known as the maximum residues level (MLR) (Godard and Bellec 2002). Based on the estimated diet of the inhabitants, residual limits of CLD in water, vegetables, meat, and fishery products have been determined by ANSES at the demand of the French state; below these limits, the product is considered safe. A number of ecological and medical organizations challenge this approach with two main arguments. First, as expressed by Dr. Jos Pelage, the president of a Martinican doctors association (AMSES), since CLD is an endocrine disruptor, its mere presence is sufficient to possibly create major harm (Toussay 2018). Second, as highlighted by the NGO Ecology Urbaine, headed by Louis Boutrin and Raphael Confiant, CLD is just one of the many molecules used in banana plantations to which the population is exposed. Deriving a quantitative limit for just one molecule does not take into account the combined effects of multiple exposures to multiple toxic molecules (Boutrin and Confiant 2007).

History of the CLD Protest

CLD contamination was first directly criticized in 2006 and 2007 in two activist book publications denouncing the scandal (Boutrin and Confiant 2007; Nicolino and Veillerette 2007) as well as in a report done by an independent medical research organization called ARTAC, presided over by the oncologist Dominique Belpomme (Belpomme et al. 2007). In 2006 in Guadeloupe, a collective group comprising local syndicates and ecological NGOs filed a complaint "against X", so that the responsible agent of this contamination could be identified (Durimel 2009). At the same time, a doctor living in Guadeloupe, Dominique Denivet, who had to stop his work because of severe health problems that he attributed to CLD, filed a complaint (Verdol 2009, 115). Similarly, in Martinique, the ecological organizations Assaupamar and Ecology Urbaine in Martinique also filed a complaint accusing the French state of the crime of poisoning in 2007. Although Denivet's complaint was dismissed in 2016, both collective complaints were delocalized to the administrative tribunal of Paris and conjoined into one single case. The result is still pending. The length of this trial is also a subject of criticism, particularly given how swift this process was in the United States. Less than a year after the stoppage of production, the company Allied Chemicals had already undergone congressional hearings and was tried and condemned in 1976 (Reich and Spong 1983), while the contaminated nearby Saint-James River was being closely monitored.

Criticism in Martinique took the form of demonstrations by fishermen in December 2012. Organized by the fishermen's syndicate SAPEM, headed by Bertrand Cambussy, and assisted by the lawyer and founder of the NGO "non au CLD" (No to CLD), Mr. Germany, as well as Assaupamar, fishermen blocked the port of Fort-de-France for eleven days to demand justice for their loss of activities. In December 2013, fishermen from the town of Sainte-Marie in Guadeloupe did the same thing, blocking a regional road to demand justice. From 2012 to 2014, CLD resurfaced in demonstrations as part of a different pesticide problem. Since 1958, the banana industry on these islands had used aerial spraying to fight off diseases of banana plants.

Martinique and Guadeloupe were by far the most intensely sprayed departments in all the territories of France (Allain and Grivault 2010). Spraying toxic chemicals from above, including endocrine disruptors, on small and densely populated islands presented a significant health risk for banana workers and inhabitants, schools, and shops in the vicinity of banana plantations. Recognizing the health risks to both agricultural workers and surrounding inhabitants, the European Union banned aerial spraying and enjoined its state members to do so nationally, including in the *Outre-mer* in 2010. In 2011, France enacted a law that did forbid aerial spraying, tolerating however some exceptions where there was supposedly no alternative. From 2011 to 2014, a legal and political conflict took place in Martinique and Guadeloupe between local ecological collectives wanting to see this practice effectively end and owners of the banana industry wanting to use this legal exception to pursue this dangerous practice (Ferdinand 2018). As a consequence of three years of demonstrations and legal battles against aerial spraying, the contamination of CLD was widely publicized, becoming an argument not to further the use of dangerous pesticides.

Protests against CLD took a drastic turn at the end of 2017, particularly in Martinique. A technical and regulatory change in 2013 by the European Commission regarding the measurements of liposoluble residues in meat products resulted in a five- to tenfold increase in the residue level of CLD (EU 2013). However, this new authorized level was effectively applied in France only at the end of 2017, following a scientific validation by ANSES (the French agency in charge of work, food, and environment safety) that found no significant risk associated with that increased level of exposure (ANSES 2017). The effective increase in exposure of the population intensified the feeling of being unjustly treated by the government. Ecological collectives already in place against aerial spraying were reactivated. At the end of 2017, Martine Ducteil and Guillaume Lerebour, two students pursuing agricultural studies in Martinique, started an online petition to stop this exposure entitled "je suis chlordeconé" (I am "chlordeconed"), that mimicked the esthetics of the popular online slogan "Je suis Charlie" following the 2015 terrorist attacks in Paris against *Charlie Hebdo*. This petition has been signed by more than 167,000 people. Demonstrations were held by the collective "Zero chlordecone" on March 25 and April 14, 2018, in the streets of Lamentin and Fort-de France in Martinique. Aside from established ecological and medical organizations such as Assaupamar and AMSES, a younger generation of demonstrators emerged. These include Santé Environnement Sans Derogations (Health and Environment without Exceptions), the grassroots movement called "Moun" ("people" or "person" in Creole) headed by Olivier Berisson, and the singular and powerful voice of Anicia Berton. Miss Berton is now undergoing treatment for her second cancer. Making a direct connection between her own medical situation and the pollution of the island, she questions the actions of the French state. As part of the collective demonstration, her story has captivated the public as she was elected as the "personality of the year 2018" in Martinique.

The long time taken by the judicial investigation combined with the population's existing mistrust of the French state has led some to question France's ability to be objective in this matter. In Guadeloupe, the ecological NGO ENVIE-Santé headed by Philippe and Joelle Verdol, which had already called on the European Union and the World Health Organization in 2014, also initiated a crowdfunding platform in 2018 to finance legal action against the French state for allowing the continued exposure of the Antillean people to CLD (Verdol 2014, 2018). Likewise, during the 2018 demonstrations in Martinique, workshops were held encouraging local inhabitants to file a new collective complaint against the state.

Antillean anger was echoed at both the national and international levels. In June 2018, European deputies Michel Rivasi and Younous Omarjee criticized the lack of transparency of the French state in this affair (Outremer 360 2018). European deputies Eric Andrieu and Louis-Joseph Manscour demanded that the European Union lower the maximum residue level for CLD in meat products and that it undertake an international investigation (Andrieu 2018). These demonstrations have shaken the government to the point where President Macron came to Martinique in September 2018. In the agricultural town of Morne-Rouge in Martinique, on September 27, Emmanuel Macron did assert that the French state should face up to its responsibilities and that the government should aim for "Zéro Chlordecone" (No CLD). However, he made sure to frame the CLD contamination as merely an "environmental scandal" and even challenged its relation to the development of prostate cancers despite scientific evidence showing otherwise. Confusingly, while opening the door for CLD to be recognized as a professional disease for agricultural workers, he refused to discuss demands for compensation from a population with a 92 to 95 percent contamination rate (Martinique 1ère 2017). In effect, Macron recognized the responsibility of the French state while diminishing the extent of the wrong caused. In response to this speech, the opposition party in France, La France insoumise, headed by Jean-Luc Melenchon, requested a new parliamentary investigation that, unlike the two previous ones of 2004 and 2009, would have juridical power to indict people (Franceinfo 2018). Following this 2019 parliamentary investigation of CLD, in which even more state malpractices were uncovered, activists in Martinique led more confrontational protests, regularly blocking some commercial centers whose owners are believed to be linked to the affair. Seven of these activists were arrested for their "disturbance" and were set to go to trial on January 13, 2020. The anti-CLD movement denounced the double standard whereby activists are put on trial because of their protests but polluters can still go about their business undisturbed. On January 13, violent confrontations between protesters and the police erupted, causing many bloody injuries and forcing the trial to be postponed.

CLD contamination has thus become a classic case of environmental justice, as seen across the world, where a part of population that is unequally exposed to dangerous environmental pollution denounces this injustice and advocates through protest and juridical means the right to live in a healthy environment (Schlosberg 2007; Bullard 2000). The specificity of this case lies in the colonial and slavery history of Martinique and Guadeloupe, in their relation to the French state and in their ethnic composition. Criticism of the CLD contamination is exacerbated by the historical mistrust of the French postcolonial state (Larcher 2014; Dumont 2010). By following racial lines to some extent, this conflict reenacts the ancestral opposition between former masters and former slaves. The right to live in a safe environment is thus intrinsically associated with demands to be treated equally by the postcolonial French state, taking the form of a *decolonial environmental justice* (Ferdinand 2017).

Chlordecone and the Forgotten Social Question

The fields of science and technology studies and pragmatic sociology have shown that there are different ways that an invisible pollution, such as the CLD contamination, can be made a public issue (Gusfield 1984; Akrich et al. 2010; Callon et al. 2014). Social inequalities and relations of power are equally prominent in the processes leading to a pollution becoming a societal issue and being effectively tackled by relevant state agencies or remaining purposefully hidden, as demonstrated by the recent field of agnotology (Frickel 2014; Proctor 2011). Up to now, despite their differences, both local activists and the French state have framed the CLD case as an environmental and public health issue, relegating to the background the socioeconomic inequalities at the heart of the use of pesticides on banana plantations. This iteration of the modern divide is first symbolized by how little attention was paid to the first victims of this contamination: agricultural workers. Although chemical pollutions disregard land borders and social class frontiers (Beck 2008), agricultural workers represent a particularly exposed group within the population. They were the ones manipulating toxic products, at times with their bare hands, and spending more time than the rest of the population in contact with the polluted soil of the banana plantations. Being exposed to dangerous products has become the condition of their professional activities: a *toxic condition*. Yet, despite being at the center of the CLD contamination, their voices remain relatively absent from the political scene.

In fact, the very first people who protested against the use of CLD were the agricultural workers themselves. The cumulative effects of unequal exposure to toxic products and social inequality were poignant in the last great workers' strike in Martinique in 1974, commonly known as Chalvet. Denouncing difficult working conditions, and the lack of a minimum wage or job security with a regular salary, agricultural workers went on a month-long strike in February 1974. This strike was subjected to a strong state police repression that caused three deaths and numerous injuries. During this strike, the Comité des Travailleurs (Workers Committee) established a list of eleven points detailing their demands. Among the claims for better working conditions, a pay raise, and regular hours, there is a demand for the "complete removal of toxic products," including the commercial formulation of CLD, "Kepone," and for access to appropriate protective gear (aprons and gloves) (De Lépine 2014, 333). In other words, more than twenty-five years before the French state made any efforts to mitigate CLD pollution, these workers were already petitioning against it. However, the final accords between the workers and the owners explicitly removed these two demands. The workers' demand for and attainment of more social equality came at the expense of their ecological and health concerns.

Another instance of the cumulative effect of social inequality and acute toxic exposure to pesticide is found in the struggle to ban aerial spraying on banana plantations from 2011 to 2014. Very few agricultural workers openly took part in this conflict. Ms. Meru, an agricultural worker with more than thirty years of experience in the banana industry, and also a member of a union in Martinique, explains her stance regarding this issue:

Ms. Meru—Regarding aerial spray, we fought. We fought to stop the helicopter from spraying while there were workers in the fields, even while they were eating. When we go out on the field, we stay there to eat during lunch and after 3 P.M. we go back. However, most of the time it fell on us during the lunch break. We were sprayed upon with oil, and sometimes were forced to throw away our meal soaked with oil. By the 1990s, we had had enough. We demanded to stop this. But we were not heard. When we criticized the owners, when we threatened to go on strikes, they simply replied, "you will be fired," or "go home." They used to say "you can just go." We fought and in the late 1990s and early 2000s, we negotiated for the helicopter to spray only in the afternoon, and no longer in the morning.[3]

Criticizing their exposure to dangerous pesticides, these workers were again turned away on the basis of their social position. The workers were then faced with this terrible alternative: either they faced the difficulty and at times misery of unemployment, or they accepted this toxic condition. This strangling situation impeded the willingness of agricultural workers to take center stage in making pesticide a public issue. Despite being at the center of both uses and exposure to toxic chemicals, every single time questions of pesticide use became a public issue and a matter of controversy, agricultural workers and members of unions have been either almost absent or silent. No collective justice action has been taken by workers, in contrast to other similar cases in South America (Soluri 2005).

This testifies to the failure of the French state and local authorities to recognize the health concerns of agricultural workers with respect to CLD for the better part of four decades. As in other cases, such as asbestos pollution in France, CLD contamination became a public issue only when the state and the Antillean societies realized that this contamination had also spread to the water systems and had affected not just the agricultural workers but the rest of the inhabitants as well (Henry 2007). Despite explicitly calling for CLD removal as early as 1974, it was not until 1999 that authorities started to take effective measures to mitigate the impact of the resulting pollution. The suffering of agricultural workers was not valued on an equal basis with that of the rest of the society.

In tackling this contamination, state authorities have thus far implemented three interministerial plans that aim to protect the citizens from this pollution and to research the sanitary and environmental impacts, with spending amounting to one hundred million euros. However, one of the most telling examples of the former disregard for agricultural workers' health concerns is the inability to find an exhaustive list of the names of those who worked in banana plantations from 1972 to 1993. While some paper archives were lost or deteriorated, workers who were employed on a day-to-day basis had left no trace through official records. Efforts to find workers have yielded only the names of the intendants—or administrators—of the plantations and those who had a more permanent employment status

(Barrau et al. 2012). Literally and literarily, the more precarious agricultural workers have been forgotten—and with them, the social question as well. While emphasizing the concerning issues of environmental pollutions, public health, and the demand for reparation, activists and the state have contributed to framing the CLD contamination only as an environmental problem whose health consequences are still put into doubt by elected officials, including the president of France. The chronic social crisis and the concerning issue of food security have been overlooked. All these issues were raised in the 2009 social movements in Martinique and Guadeloupe.

The 2009 Social Movement and the Chlordecone Contamination

The 2009 social events in Martinique and Guadeloupe had at their core the concerns of French citizens regarding their living conditions and their dignity as equal French citizens. In their demonstration both the Liyannaj Kont Pwofitasyon (LKP; Alliance against Profiteering) in Guadeloupe and the K5F (Collective of the 5th of February) in Martinique denounced the social inequalities within their creole societies as well as the inequalities with mainland France. Ecological issues, though not at the center of the demands and claims, were nonetheless present, albeit feebly. Three instances illustrate the small yet remarkable presence of these issues before, during, and after the 2009 events. First, in the weeks preceding the social movement on both islands, a telling TV documentary by Roman Bolzinger, *Les derniers maîtres de la Martinique* (The Last Masters of Martinique), contributed to lighting the match to a sensitive social crisis. This documentary focused essentially on the economic privilege enjoyed by a few Béké families of Martinique. Besides the description of their privileged relations with the French state, the families' economic dominance, and the racist comments of one of them in particular, a major point of this documentary was the very issue of CLD contamination. Detailing the part played by some Béké owners of banana plantations, and the allegedly criminal actions of two ministers of agriculture, the very story of CLD seems by itself to encapsulate the anger and feeling of injustice felt by the inhabitants in 2009.

Second, the CLD contamination was explicitly emphasized in demands made by both movements in Martinique and Guadeloupe. The demands platform of the LKP in Guadeloupe was organized thematically in ten themes ranked in the following order: living conditions; education; professional training; employment; union rights and freedom; public services; production; planning and infrastructure; culture; "stop profiteering." Under the "living conditions" theme was included the following subsection on the environment: "Contamination of land by chlordecone: adoption of measures to protect the inhabitants of contaminated areas; reparation for professional and civil victims." Similarly, in Martinique, among the 236 points of agreement as part of the deal to end the general strike, a number of points specifically targeted ecological issues, including "21. Immediate forbidding of any sort of aerial spraying by adapting the European Law to the French law, without any possibility of derogation"; "24. A specific fund to be created to help farmers in difficulty because of chlordecone."[4] Although secondary, the right to live in an ecologically safe environment and have better living conditions was articulated into a similar set of demands to the state.

Third, a practice that was born from the movement exemplifies a significant ecological action: that of reconnecting farmers with consumers via local markets. Indeed, one of the major ecological criticisms of modern societies describes the ever-expanding circuits of production, where local inhabitants do not eat what is produced locally, and inversely local products are not sold locally. Not only do such economic circuits imply a heavy carbon dioxide emission because of transportation, but they also create a disconnect between local inhabitants and the ecosystem they inhabit. Such is the case in Martinique and Guadeloupe. Although root vegetables are major components of a traditional food regimen, most come from imports. Between 1981 and 2007, the production of root vegetables in Guadeloupe decreased by 60 percent (Agreste Guadeloupe 2009). From 1995 to 2015, Guadeloupe imported thirty-three times more root vegetables than it was able to export (Agreste Guadeloupe 2017). Similarly, from 2010 to 2018, Martinique could produce less than a third of the root vegetables it needed (DAAF 2018).

Though driven by necessity, the markets born out of the 2009 movement symbolize one way to re-establish small economic circuits, to reduce the carbon footprint, and to renew a direct relation between producers and consumers. In Guadeloupe, this practice is still in place today; every day of the week, a local market is held in one of the towns of Guadeloupe, where one can greet local famers and buy their products directly.

In any case, social movements usually include a collection of heterogeneous components. It is noteworthy nonetheless that these ecological and public health issues found their place. However, these ecological bread crumbs are not nodal elements of a well-structured social ecology as developed elsewhere (Bookchin 1995; Foster 2009). Indeed, despite the mutual sympathy between unions and ecological organizations, and despite the common anger felt both by ecological and social activists toward an allegedly faulty postcolonial state, there still persists a social and ecological divide. Apart from an exception made for the recent field of postcolonial ecocriticism, this divide is also prominent within scholarship focusing on postcolonial and post-slavery societies (Graham and Tiffin 2009; DeLoughrey and Handley 2011). While ecological issues are investigated by academics in the fields of life and earth sciences, social and political movements are researched by academics in the humanities and social sciences. As a result, for individuals from activists to state authorities and academics, ecological issues and social issues in postcolonial and post-slavery societies appear to be two different realities. Chlordecone remains an environmental issue, while the 2009 protests remain a social one. While both social and ecological issues are recognized to be important on each side, there seems to be no clear articulation of the way these two fields constitute a common problem: that of inhabiting Earth and living together.

Bridging the Divide: Facing the Plantationocene

The social-ecological divide finds one of its roots in a history of the environmental movement in western society since the late nineteenth century that has focused primarily on the conservation and preservation of asocial, apolitical, and ahistorical environments. From the preservation of the wilderness in the United States, to the fight against pollution, ecology has commonly been associated with postmaterial concerns for nature and the planet that are quite distinct from the social question (Guha and Martinez-Allier 1997). This theoretical construction of ecological issues gave rise to a sociological divide within the cohort of activists themselves. In the 1960s, particularly in the United States, ecological organizations were (and still are) dominated by middle-class, college-educated white men with almost no experience of the racial discrimination and poverty endured by contemporary African Americans and people of color (Taylor 2016). Such an apolitical and asocial understanding of ecology has created a number of misguided ideas that poor people do not really care about the environment. Such would seem to be the case in some Caribbean islands (Jaffe 2016).

However, different activists and academic movements, such as social ecology, political ecology, ecofeminism, environmental justice, and postcolonial ecocriticism and environmental history, have all made significant contributions to elaborate a social and political understanding of past and current ecological issues (DeLoughrey and Handley 2011; Gorz 2008; Hache 2016; Merchant 1989; Davis 2007). Such an attempt to bridge the divide has been made in Martinique (Baver and Lynch 2006), much as in Puerto Rico. Since the mid-1970s, Martinique has had a strong and popular ecological movement centered on patriotic groups. In particular, an NGO called Assaupamar (Organization of the Preservation of the Martinican Heritage), created in 1980, has been a major ecological actor, being both popular and successful against many industrial and commercial projects that threatened local ecosystems, particularly the coastal mangroves. Alongside Assaupamar, other ecological organizations were created, including PUMA, led by Florent Grabin, and Ecologie Urbaine, led by renowned writer Raphael Confiant and Louis Boutrin. In 1992, former members of Assaupamar also created a political party, MODEMAS (Mouvement des democrats et écologistes pour une Martinique souveraine), that has been very successful in local elections. Garcin Malsa, cofounder of the party, occupied the position of mayor in the southern town of Sainte-Anne for twenty-five years (1989–2014). In 2012, a second ecological political party was founded by Confiant and

Boutrin called Martinique Ecologie. This movement has managed to articulate the concern for the preservation of nature and a cultural heritage with the demand for more equality within the French republic (Ferdinand 2016). For the past thirty-five years, the resourceful and tenacious team of Assaupamar, including among others Henri Louis Regis, Pascal Tourbillon, and Marie-Jeanne Toulon, have held a central place regarding ecological issues and still do in the case of the CLD contamination. Yet, despite these efforts, this ecological movement did not manage to build lasting alliances with social movements and thus maintained the social-ecological divide.

Guadeloupe also has a solid ecological movement that held central stage in the aerial spraying conflict from 2011 to 2014. Ecological NGOs such as AMAZONA, ENVIE-Santé, and ASFA, headed by Béatrice Ibéné, and the political party Caraïbe Ecologie Les Verts, have been important actors. However, the social-ecological divide still persists.

The term *Plantationocene* becomes useful to understand the living conditions and realities of the inhabitants of Martinique and Guadeloupe. It invites us to focus on the environmental, socioeconomic, and political units that are plantations: the very units that were and still are at the roots of the way these islands (and much of the rest of Earth) are inhabited. In doing so, one can realize that plantation units constitute the very important connection between the 2009 events and more generally the chronic social crisis on one side, and the dire CLD contamination and the ecological state of these islands on the other side.

On the one hand, the high cost of living denounced in the 2009 strike in Martinique and Guadeloupe is directly linked to an economic model that has as one of its core principles the preservation of plantation units. Those plantations that are located on the most fertile lands of the islands are geared toward exporting monoculture crops to the other side of the Atlantic Ocean. Behind the high prices of imported products, there remains the economic constitution of the islands, which is centered on plantations. This plantation economy is one of the drivers of the structural and social inequalities in Martinique and Guadeloupe with regard to mainland France.

On the other hand, the CLD contamination is the direct result of the techniques used to maintain these plantations and to ensure their continued profit, regardless of the environmental and public health price. CLD is but one of the molecules used in banana plantations. At least until 2015, banana workers were still exposed to fourteen other active substance molecules that are suspected to be carcinogens, endocrine disruptors, or reprotoxins (Santé publique France and ANSES 2018, 4). Moreover, in 2018, another toxic and potentially carcinogenic molecule used on sugar plantations, called Azilox, made headlines. This herbicide was officially forbidden by France in 2012 because of the lack of sufficient research establishing its safety. However, yearly exceptions are made for the sugar cane industry in Martinique (DAAF 2015). Although they provide employment for about ten thousand people out of eight hundred thousand, these plantations are not geared to provide food security (MOM 2016; BGM 2019). Regardless of the clichés, inhabitants of Martinique and Guadeloupe do not live off rum and bananas. Yet, it is because of rum and bananas that these people have been and still are exposed to toxic chemicals.

In this light, one can note that the outcome of the 2009 social movements and the CLD contamination consisted of technical solutions that neither change nor challenge the economic model of these islands. On the one hand, an agreement was made for a list of one hundred products of first necessity to be made cheaper. On the other hand, provisions were made for the economy to continue as before, by simply changing the chemicals used, while the population ingests toxic molecules daily. In other words, technical solutions that maintain the plantation economy, and protect the position of plantation owners, further social inequalities and continue food insecurity.

Maintaining this social/ecological divide, whether willingly or not, is counterproductive. It is aporetic to tackle the social crisis at play while disregarding the destruction of the ecosystems that is the condition of the designated economy. Inversely, it is also aporetic to tackle environmental pollution while disregarding the social inequalities at the heart of the economic model that led to the pollution in the first place. If, as noted by Yarimar Bonilla,

Antilleans have creatively demonstrated an understanding of freedom and emancipation that bypasses independence and sovereignty, the challenge of envisioning a future on ecologically safe islands still stands (Bonilla 2015). Bringing together the relentless voices on either side of the social-ecological divide might be a way to take up this challenge and lay the foundation for a geological era defined by justice and equality.

NOTES

1. Interview conducted with Mr. Casius in May 2012.

2. Interview conducted with Mr. Pierce in October 2018

3. Interview with Ms. Meru, Martinique, Fort-de-France, 2014.

4. "Accord sur le cadre de travail sur les revendications du Collectif du 5 février sur l'agriculture et l'environnment," March 10, 2009, http://www.cgt-martinique.fr/iso_album /agriculture_et_environnement.pdf, translated by the author.

REFERENCES

AFSSA. 2007. *Actualisation de l'exposition alimentaire au chlordécone de la population antillaise, évaluation de l'impact de mesures de maîtrises des risques.* Document technique AQR/FH/2007-219 (September).

Agard-Jones, Vanessa. 2013. "Sovereign Intimacies: Scaling Sexual Politics in Martinique." Dissertation, New York University, New York.

Agreste Guadeloupe. 2017. "1995–2015: Vingt-ans d'échanges." *Agreste Guadeloupe,* no. 3 (September).

Akrich, Madeleine, Barthe Yannick, and Rémy Catherine, eds. 2010. *Sur la piste environnementale: Menaces sanitaires et mobilisations profanes.* Paris: ParisTech–Presses des Mines.

Allain, Yves-Marie, and Gilbert Grivault. 2010. *Rapport: Interdiction des épandages aériens de produits phytopharmaceutiques sauf dérogations, situation actuelle proposition de mise en œuvre des dérogations.* Ministère de l'Écologie, de l'Énergie, du Développement durable et de la Mer & Ministère de l'Alimentation, de l'Agriculture et de la Pêche (February).

Andrieu, Eric. 2018. "Chlordécone: le scandale d'Etat continue." *Eric-Andrieu,* September 28. http://www.eric-andrieu.eu/chloredecone-le-scandale-detat-continue/.

ANSES. 2017. *Exposition des consommateurs des Antilles au chlordécone, résultats de l'étude Kannari, avis de l'Anses: Rapport d'expertise collective* (December).

Balland, P., R. Mestre, and M. Fagot. 1998. *Rapport sur l'évaluation des risques liés à l'utilisation de produits phytosanitaires en Guadeloupe et en Martinique.* Ministère de l'Aménagement du territoire et de l'Environnement—ministère de l'Agriculture et de la Pêche, affaire no. 1998-0054-01, Paris.

Barrau, M., M. Ledrans, J. Spinosi, and J.-L. Marchand. 2012. *Étude de faisabilité de reconstitution de la cohorte des travailleurs agricoles exposés au chlordécone en Martinique et Guadeloupe—Plan national chlordécone 1 et 2.* Saint-Maurice: Institut de veille sanitaire.

Baver, S., and B. Lynch, eds. 2006. *Beyond Sand and Sun: Caribbean Environmentalisms.* New Brunswick, NJ: Rutgers University Press.

Beaugendre, J. 2005. *Rapport d'information sur l'utilisation du chlordécone et des autres pesticides dans l'agriculture martiniquaise et guadeloupéenne,* Assemblée nationale, commission des Affaires économiques, de l'Environnement et du Territoire.

Beck, Ulrich. 2008. *La société du risque: Sur la voie d'une autre modernité,* translated by Laure Bernardi. Paris: Flammarion.

Belpomme, D., et al. 2007. *Rapport d'expertise et d'audit externe concernant la pollution par les pesticides en Martinique. Conséquences agrobiologiques, alimentaires et sanitaires et proposition d'un plan de sauvegarde en cinq points.* Association pour la recherche thérapeutique anti-cancéreuse (ARTAC).

BGM (Bananes de Guadeloupe et de Martinique). 2019. *BGM,* February 9. http://www.bananeguadeloupemartinique.com/notre-filiere/.

Bonan, Henri, and Jean-Louis Prime. 2001. *Rapport sur la présence de pesticides dans les eaux de consommation humaine en Guadeloupe.* Inspection générale des affaires sociales (Ministère de l'Emploi et de la Solidarité) et Inspection générale de l'environnement (Ministère de l'Aménagement du Territoire et de l'Environnement).

Bonilla, Y. 2015. *Non-sovereign Futures: French Caribbean Politics in the Wake of Disenchantment.* Chicago: University of Chicago Press.

Bonneuil, Christophe, and Jean-Baptiste Fressoz. 2016. *L'événement anthropocène: La Terre, l'histoire et nous.* Paris: Editions Points.

Bookchin, Murray. 1995. *Ecology of Freedom: The Emergence and Dissolution of Hierarchy.* New York: Blackrose Books.

Boutrin, L., and R. Confiant. 2007. *Chronique d'un empoisonnement annoncé: le scandale du chlordécone aux Antilles françaises 1972–2002.* Paris: L'Harmattan.

Bullard, Robert. 2000. *Dumping in Dixie: Race, Class and Environmental Quality.* Boulder, CO: Westview Press.

Cabidoche, Y.-M., et al. 2009. "Long-Term Pollution by Chlordecone of Tropical Volcanic Soils in the French West Indies: A Simple Leaching Model Accounts for Current Residue." *Environmental Pollution* 157 (June): 1697–1705.

Cabort-Masson, Guy. 1992. *Les puissances d'argent en Martinique.* Saint-Joseph, Martinique: Edition de la V.d.P.

Callon, Michel, Pierre Lascoumes, and Yannick Barthe. 2014. *Agir dans un monde incertain: Essai sur la démocratie technique.* Paris: Points (éditions révisée).

Chaussonnerie, S., P-L. Saaidi, E. Ugarte, et al. 2016. "Microbial Degradation of a Recalcitrant Pesticide: Chlordecone." *Frontiers in Microbiology* 7, no. 2025.

Cicolella, André. 2017. *Planète Toxique: Le scandale invisible des maladies chroniques,* Paris: Editions Points.

Croissant, Jennifer. 2014. "Agnotology: Ignorance and Absence or Towards a Sociology of Things That Aren't There." *Social Epistemology* 28, no. 1: 4–25.

Crutzen, Paul, Will Steffen, Jacques Grinewald, and John McNeill. 2011. "The Anthropocene: Conceptual and Historical Perspectives." *Philosophical Transactions of the Royal Society A: Mathematical, Physical and Engineering Sciences* 369: 842–867.

DAAF (Direction de l'alimentation, de l'agriculture et de la forêt Martinique). 2015. Dérogation pour l'Asulox. *Phytosanitairement Votre,* no. 2.

———. 2018. "Mémento agricole 2018." http://daaf.martinique.agriculture.gouv.fr/Memento-agricole-2018.

Dallaire, R., G. Muckle, F. Rouget, P. Kadhel, H. Bataille, L. Guldner, S. Seurin, V. Chajès, C. Monfort, O. Boucher, J. P. Thomé, S. W. Jacobson, L. Multigner, and S. Cordier.

2012. "Cognitive, Visual, and Motor Development of 7-Month-Old Guadeloupean Infants Exposed to Chlordecone." *Environmental Research* 118: 79–85.

Davis, Mike. 2007. *Le pire des mondes possible: De l'explosion urbaine au bidonville global.* Paris: La Découverte.

De Lépine, Edouard. 2014. *Chalvet février 1974, suivi de 102 documents pour servir à l'histoire des luttes ouvrières de janvier-février 1974 à la Martinique.* Fort-de-France: Le Teneur.

DeLoughrey, Elizabeth, and George Handley, eds. 2011. *Postcolonial Ecologies: Literatures of the Environment.* New York: Oxford University Press.

Descola, Philippe. 2005. *Par-delà nature et culture.* Paris: Editions Gallimard.

Dumont, J. 2010. *L'amère patrie: Histoire des Antilles françaises au XXe siècle.* Paris: Fayard.

Durimel, Harry. 2009. "Bilan sur la mobilisation au chlordécone." *Potomitan*, September. http://www.potomitan.info/gwadloup/chlordecone.php.

Environmental Protection Agency (EPA). 2009. *Toxicological Review of Chlordecone (Kepone): In Support of Summary on the Integrated Risk Information System (IRIS).* Washington, DC: EPA.

Epstein, Samuel. 1978. "Kepone-Hazard Evaluation," *Science of the Total Environment* 9–1 (January).

EU (European Union). 2013. Règlement (UE) no. 212/2013 du 11 mars 2013 remplaçant l'annexe I du règlement (CE) no. 396/2005 du Parlement européen et du Conseil aux fins d'ajouts et de modifications relatifs aux produits concernés par ladite annexe.

Ferdinand, Malcom. 2015. "De l'usage du Chlordécone aux Antilles: L'égalité en question." In *Revue française des affaires sociales: Enjeux environnementaux, protection sociale et inégalités sociales,* edited by F. Augagneur and J. Fagnani, 163–183. Paris: La documentation française.

———. 2016. "Ecology, Identity, and Colonialism in Martinique: The Discourse of an Ecological NGO (1980–2011)." In *The Caribbean: Aesthetics, World-Ecology, Politics,* edited by C. Campbell and M. Niblett, 174–188. Liverpool: Liverpool University Press.

———. 2017. "Living in Contaminated Land: Struggle for a Decolonial Environmental Justice in Contemporary Martinique and Guadeloupe." In *Heritage and Rights of Indigenous Peoples,* edited by M. Castillo, 95–107. Leiden: Leiden University Press.

———. 2018. "L'interdiction de l'épandage aérien en France: Des contestations locales aux Antilles à l'interdiction nationale (2009–2014)." In *Contestations, résistances et négociations environnementales,* edited by A. Ambroisine-Rendu, A. Vrignon, and A. Trespeush Berthelot, 207–222. Limoges: Presses Universitaires de Limoges.

Fintz, M. 2009. *Éléments historiques sur l'arrivée du chlordécone en France entre 1968 et 1981.* Paris: AFSSET.

Foster, John Bellamy. 2009. *The Ecological Revolution: Making Peace with the Planet.* New York: Monthly Review Press.

Franceinfo. 2018. "Chlordécone: les députés de La France Insoumise pour une commission d'enquête." *la 1ère francetvinfo,* October 4.

Frickel, Scott. 2014. "Absences: Methodological Note About Nothing in Particular." *Social Epistemology* 28, no. 1: 86–95.

Godard, E., and S. Bellec. 2002. *Contamination par les produits phytosanitaires organochlorés en Martinique: Caractérisation de l'exposition des populations.* Ministère de l'Emploi et de la Solidarité, Direction de la santé et du développement social (DSDS) de la Martinique.

Gorz, André. 2008. *Ecologica.* Paris: Editions Galilée.

Graham, Huggan, and Helen Tiffin. 2009. *Postcolonial Ecocriticism: Literature, Animals, Environments.* London: Routledge.

Guha, Ramachandra, and Juan Martinez-Allier. 1997. *Varieties of Environmentalism.* London: Earthscan.

Guldner, L., et al. 2011. "Exposition de la population antillaise au chlordécone. Numéro thématique. Chlordécone aux Antilles: bilan actualisé des risques sanitaires." *Bulletin épidémiologique hebdomadaire,* no. 3-4-5.

Gusfield, Joseph. 1984. *The Culture of Public Problems: Drinking-Driving and the Symbolic Order.* Chicago: University of Chicago Press.

Hache, Emilie, ed. 2016. *Recueil de textes écoféministes.* Paris: Camboukris.

Haraway, Donna. 2015. "Anthropocene, Capitalocene, Plantationocene, Chthulucene: Making Kin." *Environmental Humanities* 6: 159–165.

Henry, Emmanuel. 2007. *Amiante: Un scandale improbable, sociologie d'un problème public.* Rennes: Presses Universitaires de Rennes.

IRSET (Institut de Recherche en Santé, Environnement et Travail). 2018. *Etudes destinées à identifier les dangers et risques sanitaires associés à l'exposition au chlordécone* (September 13).

Jaffe, Rivke. 2016. *Concrete Jungles: Urban Pollution and the Politics of Difference in the Caribbean.* New York: Oxford University Press.

Joly, P.-B. 2010. *La saga du chlordécone aux Antilles françaises. Reconstruction chronologique 1968–2008.* Paris: INRA Sciences en Société.

Kadhel, P., et al. 2012. "Cognitive, Visual, and Motor Development of 7-Month-Old Guadeloupean Infants Exposed to Chlordecone." *Environmental Research,* no. 118: 79–85.

Kadhel, P., C. Monfort, N. Costet, F. Rouget, J. P. Thomé, L. Multigner, and S. Cordier. 2014. "Chlordecone Exposure, Length of Gestation, and Risk of Preterm Birth." *American Journal of Epidemiology* 179: 536–544.

Kermarrec, A. 1980. *Niveau actuel de la contamination des chaînes biologiques en Guadeloupe: Pesticides et métaux lourds.* Petit-Bourg, Guadeloupe: INRA.

Larcher, S. 2014. *L'autre citoyen, l'idéal républicain et les Antilles après l'esclavage.* Paris: Armand Colin.

Latour, Bruno. 1997. *Nous n'avons jamais été modernes: essai d'anthropologie symétrique.* Paris: La Découverte.

Laurent, Didier. 2011. "La banane en Guadeloupe et en Martinique." *Agreste Primeur,* no. 262 (June): 1–4.

Le Déaut, J., and C. Procaccia. 2009. *Rapport sur les impacts de l'utilisation de la chlordécone et des pesticides aux Antilles: bilan et perspectives d'évolution.* Office parlementaire d'évaluation des choix scientifiques et technologiques.

Lurel, Victorin. 2016. *Égalité réelle Outre-mer: Rapport au premier ministre.* Assemblée nationale, March.

Martinique 1ère. 2017. "Chlordécone aux Antilles: Macron parle scandale environnemental et réparation." *Martinique 1ère,* September 27. https://la1ere.francetvinfo.fr/martinique/chlordecone-aux-antilles-emmanuel-macron-parle-environnemental-reparation-632186.html.

Merchant, Carolyn. 1989. *Ecological Revolutions: Nature, Gender, and Science in New England.* Chapel Hill: University of North Carolina Press.

Mitman, Gregg, Michelle Murphy, and Christopher Sellers, eds. 2004. *Osiris Volume 19: Landscapes of Exposure; Knowledge and Illness in Modern Environments*. Chicago: University of Chicago Press.

MOM (Ministère des Outre-mer). 2016. "Accompagenement de la filière canne / sucre / rhum. Ministère des Outre-mer," November 17. http://www.outre-mer.gouv.fr/accompagenement-de-la-filiere-canne-sucre-rhum.

Multigner, L., et al. 2010. "Chlordecone Exposure and Risk of Prostate Cancer." *Journal of Clinical Oncology* 28, no. 21: 3457–3462.

Murphy, Michelle. 2006. *Sick Building Syndrome and the Problem of Uncertainty: Environmental Politics, Technoscience, and Women Workers*. Durham: Duke University Press.

Nicolino, F., and F. Veillerette. 2007. *Pesticides, révélations sur un scandale français*. Paris: Fayard.

Nixon, Rob. 2011. *Slow Violence and the Environmentalism of the Poor*. Cambridge, MA: Harvard University Press.

Outre-mer 360. 2018. "Pollution au chlordécone aux Antilles," June 30. http://outremers360.com/societe/pollution-au-chlordecone-aux-antilles-les-deputes-europeens-younous-omarjee-et-michele-rivasi-denoncent-un-scandale-detat-et-reclament-une-enquete-parlementaire/.

Proctor, Robert. 2011. *Origins of the Cigarette Catastrophe and the Case for Abolition*. Berkeley: University of California Press.

Reich, M. R., and J. K. Spong. 1983. "Kepone: A Chemical Disaster in Hopewell, Virginia." *International Journal of Health Services* 13, no. 2: 227–246.

Santé publique France and ANSES. 2018. *Martinique / Guadeloupe. Évaluation des expositions à la chlordécone et aux autres pesticides. Surveillance du cancer de la prostate. Les résultats des études récentes de Santé publique France et de l'ANSES*. Saint-Maurice: Santé publique France, September.

Schlosberg, David. 2007. *Defining Environmental Justice: Theories, Movements, Nature*. Oxford: Oxford University Press, 2007.

Snégaroff, J. 1977. "Résidus d'insecticides organochlorés dans la région bananière de Guadeloupe." *Phytiatrie-phytopharmacie* 26: 251–268.

Soluri, John. 2005. *Banana Cultures: Agriculture, Consumption, and Environmental Change in Honduras and the United States*. Austin: University of Texas Press.

Steiner, Achim, et al. 2012. *Global Chemical Outlook, vers une gestion rationnelle des produits chimiques*, rapport de synthèse, PNUE.

Taylor, Dorceyta. 2016. *The Rise of the American Conservation Movement: Power, Privilege, and Environmental Protection*. Durham, NC: Duke University Press.

Torny, D. 2009. "De la découverte de la pollution à la construction de la crise sanitaire." In *Impacts sanitaires de l'utilisation de la chlordécone aux Antilles françaises, recommandations pour les recherches et actions de santé publique*, INSERM et INVS.

———. 2010. "Gérer une pollution durable, le cas du chlordécone aux Antilles françaises." *Courrier de l'environnement de l'INRA*, no. 59 (October).

Toussay, Jade. 2018. "Le chlordécone, ce pesticide 'bombe à retardement' de la Martinique pour 20 générations." *Huffington Post*, February 13. https://www.huffingtonpost.fr/2018/02/13/le-chlordecone-ce-pesticide-bombe-a-retardement-de-la-martinique-pour-20-generations_a_23354147/.

Verdol, Philippe. 2009. *L'île-monde dans l'œil des pesticides*. Matoury, French Guiana: Ibis Rouge.

————. 2014. *Du chlordécone comme arme chimique française en Guadeloupe et en Martinique et de ses effets en Europe et dans le monde, plainte et demande de réparations.* Paris: L'Harmattan.

————. 2018. "Guadeloupe et Martinique: Une surexposition aux pesticides unique au monde." *Kisskissbankbank*, February 2. https://www.kisskissbankbank.com/fr/projects /guadeloupe-et-martinique-une-surexposition-aux-pesticides-unique-au-monde/tabs /description.

Vincent, Faustine. 2018. "Chlordécone: Les Antilles empoisonnées pour des générations." *LeMonde*, 7 June. https://abonnes.lemonde.fr/planete/article/2018/06/06/chlordecone -les-antilles-empoisonnees-pour-sept-siecles_5310192_3244.html.

William, Jean-Claude, Fred Reno, and Fabienne Alvarez, eds. 2012. *Mobilisations sociales aux Antilles: les événements de 2009 dans tous leurs sens.* Paris: Karthala.

2

From the Film *Nèg maron* (2004) to the *Manifeste pour les "produits" de haute nécessité* (2009)

YOUTH DISPOSSESSION,
GENERAL STRIKES, AND
ALTERNATIVE ECONOMIES
IN THE FRENCH CARIBBEAN

LOUISE HARDWICK

The 2009 general strikes in the overseas French Caribbean departments of Guadeloupe, Martinique, and French Guiana brought economic concerns to the fore. Strikers railed against "la vie chère" (the high cost of living), and numerous reports highlighted the economic disparities between the metropolitan center and the overseas departments. Of the 120 demands made by the newly formed Liyannaj Kont Pwofitasyon (LKP), the call for a pay rise of 200€ for the lowest-income earners became emblematic of the struggle. The strikes turned violent, with outbreaks of rioting and looting. The death of trade unionist Jacques Bino, who was shot during riots on February 18, 2009, underscored the dangers of this sustained period of unrest. On February 26, the 200€ salary increase known as "L'Accord Bino" was agreed on.[1]

The Guadeloupean archipelago has known a history of strikes, of which the most serious occurred in May 1967 when construction workers went on strike, demanding a 2 percent salary increase. Negotiations failed, leading to demonstrations in Pointe-à-Pitre and the surrounding suburbs. The CRS opened fire on the crowds, reportedly killing eight people and injuring numerous others, many of whom were innocent bystanders. The actual number of dead is contested and believed to be higher: this is an ongoing *travail de mémoire* in Guadeloupe.[2] For the current generation of

young Guadeloupeans, however, the events of 2009 represent the most significant internal political action to have occurred in their lifetime.

This chapter turns to recent cultural works to examine the socioeconomic concerns highlighted by the strikes. The analysis first focuses on
filmmaker Jean-Claude Flamand-Barny's film *Nèg maron* and puts forward
the argument that the very concerns raised by the strikes were already
finding urgent expression in Guadeloupean cultural output prior to 2009.
Examination of the film's DVD box gives the year of release as 2004, although
several online sources, including Barny's official website, state that this is
2005, the year when it was released in metropolitan France (Flamand-Barny
2004). The film offers a critique of social dispossession among adolescents
and young people in their early twenties, raising pressing questions about
contemporary society, consumer culture, crime, race, history, intergenerational communication, and individual responsibility and autonomy. *Nèg
maron* predated, and anticipated, the events of early 2009, and emerges as
highly significant in sustaining an intense and urgent debate on questions
of youth dispossession in Guadeloupe in particular and in the *départements
d'outre-mer* (DOMs) more generally.

The analysis then moves to consider another perspective on social and
cultural dispossession that emerges from the *Manifeste pour les "produits" de
haute nécessité*, published during the 2009 strikes in *Le Monde* by a group of
leading cultural figures based in Martinique. The discussion highlights the
authors' problematic position, poised between a radical future rethinking
of economy and consumer culture, on the one hand, and a nostalgic evocation of a bygone era on the other. To overcome these divides, and reconcile
consumerism with creativity, the authors of the *Manifeste* introduce the
concept of *créaconsommation*, examined in the present study for both its
philosophical and political potential.

These two neglected cultural works make incisive contributions to
contemporary debates on economics, the environment, history, and politics in the DOMs, and emerge as important instances of cross-fertilization
between culture and politics in their desire to envisage and give rise to
alternative social and economic models for the future.

French Caribbean Economics

In 2010, general unemployment in Guadeloupe rose to 23.8 percent. Within this overall figure, the most disadvantaged subgroup was young people under the age of thirty, with an unemployment rate of 44.2 percent.[3] The economic dispossession of a generation of young Guadeloupeans was discussed in media coverage of the strike, but was somewhat eclipsed by the tumultuous clamor generated and sustained by a handful of controversial personalities. These included Elie Domota, leader of Liyannaj Kont Pwofitasyon, known as LKP, the group that represented a "collectif d'organisations syndicales, associatives, politiques et culturelles de Guadeloupe"[4] (collective group bringing together trade unions, affiliates, political and cultural organizations) and Yves Jégo, the French secretary of state for overseas at the time, whose belated arrival in Guadeloupe on February 1 and sudden departure seven days later provoked intense anger. Jégo was subsequently replaced by Marie-Luce Penchard on June 23, 2009, and did not receive another ministerial portfolio.

In the specific case of the French Caribbean, the economic history of the DOM-ROMs (*départements et régions d'outre-mer*) has been characterized by dependency on France. Rather than operating as independent markets, these islands and regions were developed as what the French colonial historians Aldrich and Connell term "transfer economies or consumer colonies."[5] From their creation, the early colonies existed in order to benefit the *mère-patrie* (mother country), and were developed following the logic of mercantilism, which dominated European thought between the sixteenth and eighteenth centuries and dictated that maximizing net exports was the best way to ensure and enhance national prosperity. It was therefore decided that "each nation must carve out its own sphere of economic domination and exclusive profit. . . . The colonies . . . had to be complementary to the mother country, producing only those commodities not available in Europe."[6] In the French sphere of influence, the Edict of Fontainebleau of 1727 formally inaugurated the "Exclusif," the economic policy that ensured that France retained monopoly rights over all colonial production. This decree underwent several modifications, but the so-called *pacte colonial* preserved France's monopoly on trade within the empire through the upheavals of the French Revolution to the era of free trade in the 1860s and even beyond, as France still maintains firm administrative (and by extension, political and economic) control of the overseas domains.

The neoliberal phase of global capitalism has served to further exacerbate economic dispossession in the Antilles. The 2009 strikes drew attention to the fact that a small number of companies control the prices at which commodities are imported to the DOMs, thereby holding the power to dictate consumer prices. This is illustrated by the prelude to the strike action, when in December 2008 the SARA, the only gasoline supplier to the French Antilles, announced a further rise in prices. The SARA is known to all Antilleans; the abbreviation stands for La Société Anonyme de la Raffinerie des Antilles. Created in 1969, it was a joint initiative of five petrol companies: Total, Elf, Shell, Esso, and Texaco. The SARA has a gasoline refinery in Martinique, as well as a depot in Jarry in Guadeloupe, built in 1970, and two depots in French Guiana, constructed in 1982. It was the SARA gas price hike that provided the catalyst for the creation of LKP and the forty-four-day strike action in Guadeloupe.

LKP aimed to alter metropolitan perspectives of Guadeloupe and the other DOMs by disproving the common metropolitan belief that Guadeloupe benefited unfairly from "l'assistanat" (government subsidies) and therefore represented nothing but a constant drain on metropolitan French budgets. To challenge this dominant perception, Domota and LKP drew attention to the unfavorable trading circumstances in which the DOMs find themselves locked, identifying these structures as remnants of the colonial system that have never been adequately addressed or revised. The movement's Creole name, Liyannaj Kont Pwofitasyon, captured metropolitan attention; one possible English translation would be "together against profiteering." The very term *pwofitasyon*, or profiteering, demands a revision of contemporary French attitudes toward the islands and their inhabitants. Far from being seen as economic drains on France, *pwofitasyon* recasts Antilleans as a group who, rather than exploiting metropolitan state financial assistance, are themselves perpetually condemned to be economically exploited by metropolitan markets.

Nèg maron

The issue of economic exploitation comes to the fore in *Nèg maron*, a film directed by Jean-Claude Flamand-Barny (who now works under the name Jean-Claude Barny), and produced by Mathieu Kassovitz. Barny and Kassovitz have known each other since adolescence, and Barny worked as a casting director on Kassovitz's global hit *La Haine*.[7] Barny began working on *Nèg maron* in 1999 and moved back to Guadeloupe, where he had spent his childhood, to complete the project. Skillfully blending the present with references to the slave past—with the title alone forging this connection, as the term *nèg maron* originated to refer to a runaway, escaped slave (and has ambiguous connotations in the current era)—the film raises difficult questions about the future of Guadeloupean society. Barny does not shy away from acknowledging young Guadeloupeans' complicity in antisocial behavior, and he undertakes to examine spirals of violence in a nuanced manner, careful to maintain that these are not inevitable, but can be understood as a direct consequence of a combination of difficult personal circumstances and misguided choices. This entails a perceptive, and ultimately critical, evaluation of the rhetoric of victimization. Although set in the contemporary era, the film is particularly remarkable for its desire to trace the historical circumstances—political and economic—that still provide the framework for contemporary Guadeloupean society. In this manner, it directly anticipates key themes raised during the general strike concerning the tension between an individual and the wider community, and the role of indigenous Creole culture for such communities, mapping areas that would become central to political debate in 2009.

Central to the film is the tension between black Guadeloupeans and the *békés*. The békés are the descendants of the white plantocracy in the French Antilles, and *Nèg maron* anticipates many of the accusations that would be leveled at the békés during 2009. At the film's opening, best friends Josua and Silex arrive late for a meeting, held at the beach, with Marcus, a béké.

Marcus quickly gets down to business and asks (or rather, tells) the youths to break into a house that belongs to one of his relatives, in order to retrieve some papers he regrets having signed, suggesting some kind of financial transaction is at stake. He addresses the pair of youths in a casual, offhand manner as he orders them to do his dirty work. His sports car cuts a stark contrast with the moped on which the young men arrive, while in the background, white tourists emerge from the sea with their surfboards, further underscoring the contrast between the black Guadeloupeans' lives and the lives of the white people around them.

In this early scene, there is already discernible tension between Marcus and Silex, as Marcus jangles the keys to his sports car in front of Silex, then taunts him, calling him "Rastaman." The scene quickly turns sour. Infuriated, Silex draws a knife, while Marcus simultaneously draws a gun—the choice of weapons again highlighting socioeconomic differences between the men. The editing is fast-paced and the scene at the beach deteriorates so rapidly that the viewer barely has time to register what has happened. For a moment, Silex stands with his blade poised a few inches from Marcus's face, while Marcus's gun is angled at his stomach. Horrified, Josua tries to keep the two men apart and tells Marcus, "C'est pas dans la plantation de tes ancêtres ici! Tout ça c'est fini!" (You're not on your ancestors' plantation anymore! All that is over and done with!).[8] In so doing, Josua unwittingly voices the painful, unspoken truth evident in all the differences in status apparent in the scene: in spite of Josua's words to the contrary, their unequal relationship with Marcus is still very much shaped by the slave past.

The next scene takes place in a large, luxurious villa with a stylish, modern kitchen and living room. The youths are making themselves at home; Silex casually calls out to ask whether Josua is hungry, while Josua flicks through an endless selection of television channels. Significantly, one of the channels is showing a strike, although it does not hold Josua's attention: this scene anticipates the union meeting the young men attend later in the film, but fail to become engaged in.[9] It becomes apparent that this is not their house, and they have entered illegally. Crucially, the audience does not see the actual break-in, allowing the illusion to be created that Guadeloupeans live in comfortable modern surroundings, with the obligatory swimming pool in the back garden. Their escape route over the high back wall serves to further underline the physical divides between the well-off and the poor in contemporary Guadeloupe.

To the young men, prosperity appears to be inextricably connected with race. When they join up with a group of friends to hang out, despite the lethargy and lack of purpose that characterizes the group, they nonetheless voice their opinions about the circuits of power in their country. None of them appears to have any kind of job or regular occupation, apart from Patte-Cochie, who is a small-time drug dealer. Patte enlightens one of their friends, Pedro, who has recently returned from the *metropole* and is therefore regarded by the other youths as a *negropolitan* (a term commonly used to designate a black person who has returned to the islands from mainland France): "Vous allez voir qui contrôle l'univers. . . . De quoi je parle? Tu vas au casino, c'est chez eux, tu vas au cinéma, super-hyper-marché, acheter une voiture neuve, partout, c'est chez eux." (Now you're gonna see who controls the universe. . . . What am I talking about? You go to the casino, it's theirs, the super-hyper-market, the car salesroom, everywhere, it's all theirs.) Approximately thirty minutes into the film, the break-in commissioned by Marcus at the film's opening is committed, in a climactic scene central to the film's development. As the young men search for the documents in an old, colonial house, Silex's attention is drawn to images hanging on the walls. These clearly date from the colonial era: the camera focuses on the image of a steam train in the cane fields, and we then follow Silex's horrified gaze to a plan of a slave ship, every available space crammed with Africans. It is particularly noticeable that this image is one that shows slaves in even more ramped conditions than other plans of slave ships: their bodies are rammed in, and shown in bent, contorted poses.[10] As Meredith Robinson comments, the use of camera angles and sound distortion in this scene is highly suggestive of the experience of being on a slave ship: "the soundtrack . . . seems to place Silex in the belly of the ship, completely immersed in the picture. The creaking continues as [the youths] both take a step back from the picture. In doing so, they appear to show the unsteady footing felt on board a ship" (Robinson 2014, 148).

The scene is didactic, guiding the spectator's view, and might be considered to be a heavy-handed, unsubtle reference to the trauma of the slave past. However, by including it in the context of a break-in performed by young black Guadeloupean men at the command of a béké, and by reminding the audience that the colonial house in question belongs to Marcus's own family, the evocative image of the inhumanity of the slave ship is rendered multilayered and all the more powerful. It raises two critical questions: first, if abolition occurred in 1848, then *what kind of family* would still choose to display such images of domination and subjugation in their personal space, and second, why *in the current era* are the two black youths employed in illegal activity as the béké's lackeys? The scene thus passes critical comment on the power structures of contemporary Guadeloupe, from their origins under plantation slavery, to their failure to evolve in the modern era.

When Josua and Silex arrive for a second meeting with Marcus, this time with the aim of handing over the dossier, they find him slumped in his car, killed by a gunshot to the head. Worried that their presence will incriminate them, they speed off, but in his haste, Josua mistakenly leaves the stolen dossier on Marcus's dashboard. The next section of the film documents Josua's steady decline. Convinced that his fingerprints will be discovered on the dossier and lead to his arrest, he lies low and sinks into depression.

The film's climactic resolution is set at a sublimely beautiful Guadeloupean location, la Pointe des Châteaux, an expanse of rocky coastline overlooked by a large, foreboding cross, which lies at the easternmost tip of the island of Grande-Terre. Here, Silex and Josua have a final confrontation. Silex confesses to Marcus's murder, an act he explains as an accident, claiming that he was provoked by the other man's constant goading: "C'était un accident. . . . Il n'arrêtait pas, il n'arrêtait pas. Il a ressorti son gun. Il a avancé. Puis ché rien. Le coup est parti." (It was an accident. . . . He wouldn't stop, he wouldn't stop. He got his gun out again. And walked toward me. Then, well, I dunno. The shot went off.) Josua, who had begun to suspect the truth, experiences this admission as the ultimate act of betrayal by his best friend. Leaving a distraught Josua framed against the huge white cross of la Pointe des Châteaux, Silex speeds off on his moped to hand himself in to the police, in order to absolve Josua of any blame, only to be killed in a road accident of the kind that the film's exhilarating opening sequence, where the two youths ride wildly through the countryside on Silex's moped, subtly anticipated.

The film's prevailing mood is of oppression; characters feel trapped in Guadeloupe and trapped in their dead-end lives. The settings used constantly underscore the insularity of their world, as characters are either static and trapped indoors, or shown traveling through the island landscape in a series of misguided journeys, by moped, car, or coach. Significant scenes occur at the island's extremities, by the shore, when the violent emotions being expressed contrast with and subvert the backdrop of a tropical paradise; indeed, the DVD case includes a critique taken from *Le Parisien*, underscoring the film's deliberate subversion of the "tropical paradise" image of the Caribbean DOMs: "Loin des clichés plages-rhum-cocotiers, ce film donne une vision peu commune des tropiques" (Far from the clichés of beaches-rum-and-coconut-trees, this film shows a less familiar side to the tropics). *Nèg maron* is certainly closer to a work such as Euzhan Palcy's *Rue Cases-Nègres* (1983) than to Pascal Legitimus's *Antilles sur Seine* (2000), a TF1 attempt at a Caribbean-inflected comedy with the tagline "le film qui va vous tropicaliser!" (the film that will tropicalize you!). In contrast, Barny's film contrives to undertake a sustained exploration of the themes of freedom of choice and responsibility among young men (and, to a lesser extent, and more problematically, young women): to what extent can people control their own destinies, even when they are all too aware of being born into disadvantageous economic circumstances?

Nèg maron advocates a "prise de conscience" (new awareness), which entails balancing an educated awareness of financial exploitation in Guadeloupe, both past and present, with a mental outlook that goes beyond post-slavery victimhood. This is illustrated and explored in a deliberately nondirect manner in a scene when Josua recounts the cryptic tale of an African sage during one of the youths' dope-fueled afternoons. The youths settle down in Silex's shack, admiring the poster of a motorbike on his wall and also observing that his fridge is empty. After these two subtle clues as to the implicit contradiction in Silex's situation—on the one hand, he covets expensive goods such as motorcycles; on the other, he cannot even afford sufficient food to feed himself—the young men's thoughts take on a more philosophical direction, led by Josua, under the influence of a shared joint. Josua recounts a riddle: In a village in Africa, a sage is called upon to resolve a dispute between two hunters. After the first hunter has spoken and given his version of events, the sage says, "Tu as raison" (you are right). He then listens to the second hunter, whose account is different, and afterward the sage says, "Tu as raison." The head of the village is at a loss to understand, and says to the sage, "Maître, je ne comprends pas, il y a forcément l'un des deux qui a tort." (Master, I don't understand. One of them must be wrong.) The sage once more responds: "Tu as raison." This cyclic narrative highlights the film's major theme: the need to take responsibility for one's own actions and seek to resolve disputes autonomously. The sage listens and passes the judgment that is required of him, but leaves it to the hunters and village chief to recognize their differences and decide how to reconcile them. It appears in this tangential yet pivotal scene that Josua is now on his own path to understanding: he has evidently memorized the riddle, even if he has yet to fully grasp its significance and begin to apply its lessons to his own life.

This episode can be compared to an equally unexpected scene that takes place in a public toilet in Kassowitz's La Haine, in which a stranger tells the principal characters (again, all youths trying to find their way in life) a poignant story about the Gulag. In Kassowitz's film, the stranger, an implied Holocaust survivor, tells the story of a friend of his who climbed down from a train full of Jewish deportees in Siberia to relieve himself, but in his quest for privacy went too far away from the wagon. The train then began to move off again. The tale hinges on the tragicomic repetitive image of the man running to catch up with the train as it departed. When he runs holding his trousers up, he keeps up with the train but is unable to haul himself onto it, but when he holds out his arms and lets his trousers fall down, they catch around his ankles and he is unable to run fast enough. Eventually, he abandons the struggle and resigns himself to his fate, left to freeze to death.

Structurally, both segments are self-contained, develop their own, repetitive narrative, and go off at a tangent from the main plot, yet their message sums up the essence of each film: how to move forward in life, despite constant challenges. The situation of deadlock represented in the African sage's tale also recalls the "situation bloquée" (blocked situation) famously evoked by Edouard Glissant at the beginning of Le Discours antillais,[11] and suggests it is up to the individual parties concerned, that is to say all Antilleans— black, mixed race, and béké—to recognize their situations and work to find a resolution. The prevailing message in Nèg maron would seem to be that looking for external answers will not help matters advance, and the real solutions must come from within the Antillean community: a position that is also very evident in the Manifeste pour les "produits" de haute nécessité published in 2009.

Manifeste pour les "produits" de haute nécessité

On February 16, 2009, as Guadeloupe was about to enter a second month of strikes, and as Martinique neared the end of its second week of strikes, Le Monde published the Manifeste pour les "produits" de haute nécessité, which was coauthored by a collective of nine leading cultural figures and academics from or based in Martinique: Ernest Breleur, Patrick Chamoiseau, Serge Domi, Gérard Delver, Edouard Glissant, Guillaume Pigeard de Gurbert, Olivier Portecop, Olivier Pulvar, and Jean-Claude William.[12] The manifesto is both a reflection on a specific moment in modern Antillean history and a wider discussion of the development of Antillean society and culture.

Through its title alone the publication directly engages with the lexicon of the 2009 strikes, which focused on "la vie chère" (the high cost of living) and "le panier de la ménagère" (the housewife's shopping basket).

The group LKP, which coordinated strike action in Guadeloupe, placed the issue of the cost of living at the very top of the group's famous list of 120 demands, calling for a "baisse significative de toutes les taxes et marges sur les produits de première nécessité" (significant drop in all taxes and margins on basic necessities);[13] the alternative term "les denrées de première nécessité" (basic goods) was also frequently used.[14] The *Manifeste* spans questions of a pragmatic but also philosophical and ideological nature, from "food security" to environmental issues, and even gives rise to debates on the very nature of work, in an attempt to think through an alternative to the consumer-driven direction contemporary Caribbean society appears to have taken—a direction, as the above analysis has shown, that is only too evident in *Nèg maron*.

As the anthropologist Yarimar Bonilla has observed, in a challenge to these deeply embedded Western consumer patterns, the physical isolation caused by the 2009 strikes, when shipping containers could not reach the islands, forced a certain return to traditional food practices and creole gardens (Bonilla 2010, 126). It is precisely this reawakening to what can be produced locally—both in terms of foodstuffs, and in terms of cultural production and personal fulfillment—that the authors of the manifesto explore. For what are the "'produits' de haute nécessité" to which the title alludes? According to the *Manifeste*, these "produits" are abstract concepts and values, rather than material ones. They include taking responsibility for one's own existence, understanding that *la vie chère* stems from an unfettered global free-market system, and ultimately turning away from France in order to develop greater self-sufficiency and a more Caribbean-focused market.

Le prosaïque *and* le poétique

As the authors work through their understanding of "'produits' de haute nécessité," they jubilantly proclaim that the poetic ideal to which we should all aspire consists of "vivre sa vie, et la vie, dans toute l'ampleur du poétique" (Breleur et al. 2009, 5; live your life, and life in general, in the bountiful plenitude of the poetic). Indeed, the *Manifeste* is structured around two dichotomies: it denounces the rise of le prosaïque over le poétique, under-stood as the prosaic, or the mundane, over the poetic; that is to say, the rise of the globalizing hegemonizing forces of late capitalism, which promote unreflective consumerism and exclude any possibility that processes of production and consumerism might be linked with self-fulfillment and cre-ativity. This domination, they argue, in turn reduces all human beings to a role as either consommateur or producteur (consumers or producers), minus-cule and ultimately disposable cogs in an enormous economic totalizing machine: again, this is reminiscent of the consumer-conscious, direction-less, frustrated lives of the young people in Nèg maron.

The poétique denotes everything that brings a "sens à l'existence" (Bre-leur et al. 2009, 2; meaning to existence), such as music, dance and sport, as well as more abstract concepts such as those "d'honneur . . . , de philoso-phie, de spiritualité, d'amour, de temps libre affecté à l'accomplissement du grand désir intime" (Breleur et al. 2009, 2; of honor . . . , philosophy, spiri-tuality, love, and free time spent in the pursuit of accomplishing some great intimate desire). The poétique, then, is unmistakably grounded in the personal sphere of everyday life and specifically creole culture. It is juxta-posed with the prosaïque, the mundane essentials needed for physical sur-vival: "les nécessités immédiates du boire-survivre-manger" (Breleur et al. 2009, 2; the immediate necessities of drinking-surviving-eating). The mun-dane or prosaïque, according to the Manifeste, describes the life that a person chooses when he or she subscribes to the dogma of consumerism, as dic-tated by the West.

Neoliberalism is portrayed as an unstoppable menace, which reigns throughout the world: "il pèse sur la totalité des peoples" (Breleur et al. 2009, 2; it weighs upon all peoples, everywhere). The manifesto denounces the fact that those who follow it do so with an unquestioning obedience as the system is now "étendu à l'ensemble de la planète avec la force aveugle d'une religion" (Breleur et al. 2009, 4; spread across the entire planet with the strength, blind and unquestioning, of a religion). Neoliberalism has turned the average human into an insatiable, unthinking consumerist monster, deftly and damningly figured as "ce Frankenstein consommateur

qui se réduit à son panier de nécessités" (Breleur et al. 2009, 5; this Frankenstein consumer, who can be reduced to his basic shopping basket).

The manifesto also includes a discussion of the two Creole terms that
captivated audiences across the Francophone world during the strikes: *liyannaj* and *pwofitasyon*, which were at the very heart of the LKP movement,
constituting as they do the L and the P of its name. *Pwofitasyon*, or profiteering, denounces the exploitation and abuse inflicted on the Antillean population, inviting a series of readjustments to the way the DOMs are perceived
externally. The term turns the common preconception—that the DOMs are
economic drains—on its head, arguing that, rather than exploiting French
subsidies, the citizens of the DOMs are themselves being exploited, because
they are locked into unfavorable trade deals with metropolitan France,
which leads to higher living costs: *la vie chère*. To counteract this situation,
a dynamic of *Liyannaj* was advocated by the strikers, a term that evokes the
ideas of collectivity and connectivity as catalysts of social change; the manifesto engages with and celebrates this term, and argues that it represents
the only viable method with which to effect real change in the DOMs:

> Mais le plus important est que par la dynamique du *Lyannaj* [*sic*]—qui
> est d'allier et de rallier, de lier, relier et relayer tout ce qui se trouvait
> désolidarisé—la souffrance réelle du plus grand nombre (confrontée à
> un délire de concentrations économiques, d'ententes et de profits) rejoint
> des aspirations diffuses, encore inexprimables mais bien réelles, chez
> les jeunes, les grandes personnes, oubliés, invisibles et autres souffrants
> indéchiffrables de nos sociétés. La plupart de ceux qui y défilent en
> masse découvrent (ou recommencent à se souvenir) que l'on peut saisir
> l'impossible au collet, ou enlever le trône à notre renoncement à la
> fatalité. (Breleur et al. 2009, 2)

> Yet the most important goal is, through the dynamic of *Lyannaj*—
> which means alliances and grouping together, connecting, linking,
> and joining up all that which has been weakened—the very real suf-
> fering of the many (confounded by delirious economic conundrums,
> arrangements, and profits) is chiming with the diffuse aspirations, as

yet unexplainable but very real, held by young people, and older people, and by the forgotten, invisible, and other concealed people who are suffering in our societies. Most of those who are out there demonstrating en masse are discovering (or beginning to remember once again) that it is possible to seize the impossible by the throat, or dethrone our abiding acceptance of fatality.

The authors of the *Manifeste* envisage that *lyannaj* will promote a process whereby the energy of a damaged and suffering society can be transformed into "aspirations," permitting the DOMs to move toward a situation of greater autonomy.

The *Manifeste* also scathingly broaches the issue of the islands' dependence on food imports from metropolitan France. Food security is a contentious issue in the Caribbean, as islands generate little of their own produce, relying largely on imports from mainland France. As McCusker argues in a study of Patrick Chamoiseau that predates the strikes, in his literature, Chamoiseau has long been drawing attention to the fact that "the Antillean people are now feeding on over-priced metropolitan food, mainly purchased in French-owned supermarkets, and have forgotten local traditions of cooking and sourcing food."[15] It is claimed that consumer goods and services in the French Antilles cost anything between 20 and 170 percent more than on the mainland (Bonilla 2010, 130). According to an article published during the 2009 strikes in *Le Monde*, in December 2008, a kilo of carrots in Paris cost 1.29 €, whereas in Guadeloupe, they cost 4.12 €—almost four times as much.[16]

Freedom of Choice and Increased Responsibility

Both *Nèg maron* and the *Manifeste* point to economic structures that were imposed under colonialism and are still in place today. These structures, to an extent, replicate the patterns of colonialism and slavery by maintaining a white, plantocratic elite in control of the Antillean economy.[17] The film, and to a lesser extent the manifesto, sets out this extremely sensitive contemporary issue. Yet both works argue that contemporary Antilleans are in danger of being held hostage by anger if, rather than pouring their energies into the sustained interrogation of the complexities of their own situation and working together to attempt to generate possible solutions, they instead focus on nurturing a sense of rage, and violence.

In early March 2009, as the general strike was about to enter its seventh week, the television channel France 2 devoted part of an episode of the current affairs program *Mots croisés* to the Antilles. Presented by Yves Calvi, the panel was composed of prominent figures: Christiane Taubira (at the time, the French elected representative for French Guiana and architect of the *loi Taubira*, which recognized slavery as a crime against humanity), Jacques Marseille (an economic historian at the Sorbonne), Michel Giraud (sociologist at the leading French research organization, the Centre National pour la Recherche Scientifique), Marijosé Alié (a presenter for France Ô), and Yves Thréard (deputy managing editor of *Le Figaro*). The program included a satellite link with Willy Angèle, the president of the MEDEF (the *Mouvement des Entreprises de France*, the largest employers' organization in France) in Guadeloupe. The program also included a segment entitled "Les Jeunes Martiniquais" which further demonstrated the relevance of the arguments presented by Flamand-Barny:

> First Youth: On est quatre cent mille. Il n'y a que 2000 blancs, qui ont des postes importants, alors qu'il y a des Martiniquais de souche comme moi qui ont des capacités ou les diplômes pour être à la tête de cette collectivité ou administration. C'est ça qu'on dénonce ici. Il n'y a pas assez d'égalité en Martinique.
>
> Young Woman: Avec mon bac +5 on m'a proposée caissière, hôtesse d'accueil, standardiste. Je regarde autour de moi et je vois simplement que la dame qui répond au téléphone c'est une Martiniquaise, et celle qui est dans le bureau climatisé c'est une blanche.
>
> Second Youth: Je suis dans le domaine du terrassement, et je regarde la plupart des terrassements réalisés sur les autoroutes et ce sont les békés qui les ont faits. Nous les noirs, nous sommes pas dedans; nous sommes obligés d'attendre et de récupérer les miettes. (my transcript)

First Youth: There are four hundred thousand of us. There are only 2000 white people, who hold important jobs, whereas there are Martinicans born and bred, like myself, who have the abilities or the qualifications to be leading this collectivity [the term in French denotes a political status] or government. That's what we're denouncing right here and now. There's not enough equality in Martinique.

Young Woman: I hold the baccalaureate qualification and five additional years of university study [to French viewers, this indicates she is qualified to master's level]. The kind of jobs I'm offered are supermarket checkout assistant, receptionist, switchboard operator. I look around, and I see quite clearly that the woman answering the telephone is a [black] Martinican, and the one in the air-conditioned office is white.

Second Youth: I work in highway maintenance, and when I look at most of the jobs being carried out, I see that it's the békés who are doing it. We black people, we're not on the inside; we are forced to wait our turn, and then pick up whatever crumbs we can.

These vox pops create a direct echo with the words of Patte in *Nèg maron*, and once again depict the residual resentment toward the békés in the Antillean population—a resentment which shows no sign of diminishing among the younger generations. Indeed, during the 2009 strike, Domota's rhetoric directly harnessed these existing racial tensions, through comments such as "Soit ils appliqueront l'accord, soit ils quitteront la Guadeloupe" (Either they apply the accord, or they leave Guadeloupe) and "Nous ne laisserons pas une bande de békés rétablir l'esclavage" (We will not allow a bunch of békés to reintroduce slavery).[18]

Taking a clear and explicit distance from Domota's approach, during *Mots croisés*, Angèle reproached the LKP for using "des pratiques de violence" (violent practices) and for operating "sur un registre qui est de la revendication musclée" (adopting a tone of thuggish threats). In contrast, he argued that it was imperative to bring about change through consistent, methodical, and strategic political activism, and warned that rapid changes in response to LKP demands would only produce "des réponses partielles, temporaires" (short-term, temporary answers). For example, according to Angèle, the MEDEF had already carried out lengthy research into the SARA, producing a dossier setting out the problems they had with the organization. Angèle added that a sustained framework for change must also tackle "le problème de l'insertion" (the problems faced by young people entering the workplace), commenting that the MEDEF was committed to finding work placements for young people and had plans to create an MBA degree in Guadeloupe.[19] Fully aware of the racial rhetoric being mobilized during the riots, he urged his compatriots to channel their energy, not into anger, but into long-term initiatives: "Il faut qu'on dépasse le ressentiment, il faut qu'on dépasse la stratégie du bouc émissaire. . . . C'est facile de dire que c'est X ou Y qui est responsable de notre passé, de notre destin, des soixante années de départementalisation: nous sommes tous responsables. . . . Ce que nous disons c'est qu'on ne bâtit pas dans la colère, dans la précipitation, dans le ressentiment, et en mettant une partie de la communauté antillaise quelle qu'elle soit en bouc émissaire" (my transcript) (We need to move beyond resentment, we need to move beyond the strategy of scapegoats. . . . It's all too easy to say that it's X or Y that is responsible for our past, for our future, for sixty years of departmentalization: we are all responsible. . . . Our message is that you cannot build anything meaningful in anger, in resentment, without due reflection, and by designating one section of the Antillean community—whichever section that might be—as a scapegoat). This move toward greater individual responsibility is echoed during the program by Michel Giraud, who paraphrases the author and political activist Daniel Maximin and highlights his efforts to bring about just such a reversal of agency, in a shift from victimization to action: "Nous ne sommes pas les enfants de l'esclavage. Nous sommes les enfants de la *résistance* à l'esclavage."[20] (We are not the children of slavery, but the children of the resistance to slavery.) In the years preceding the strike, Barny had homed in on these very questions of responsibility toward oneself and toward society, questions that must result in a vigorous interrogation of social, economic and political structures in the Antilles.

A similar shift can be observed in the rhetoric used by the Martinican authors of the 2009 *Manifeste*. The manifesto argues that the problems identified on a daily basis—the békés' enduring economic power, youth delinquency, drugs and the environment—can be resolved only if Antilleans assume responsibility for their actions and devise future development strategies that work in their own favor. Market forces have contributed to the acculturation of Antilleans, by alienating them from indigenous culture—as argued in *Eloge de la créolité*—and even encouraging them to abandon creole culture altogether. The result is that young Antilleans are conditioned to take up their role as passive—and therefore vulnerable—consumers in a globalized market: "[Ces prix] sont aussi enchâssés dans une absurdité coloniale qui nous a détournés de notre manger-pays, de notre environnement proche et de nos réalités culturelles, pour nous livrer sans pantalon et sans jardins-bokay [sic] aux modes alimentaires européens"[21] ([These prices] are also entrenched in a colonial absurdity that has made us turn our backs on our own local food, our local environment, and our cultural realities, only to hand us straight over, without so much as breeches or creole gardens [in the original, this is wordplay and evokes a popular creole song, *Sans chemise, sans pantalon*], to be promptly devoured by European alimentary trends). The dilemma remains as to *how* such a process toward greater autonomy and self-determination may be achieved. Is it realistic to encourage contemporary Antilleans to wean themselves off metropolitan diets in favor of locally grown produce? What further infrastructure changes might need to be implemented to make this goal more achievable? The issue is pertinent across the Caribbean. The U.N. initiative "Promoting CARICOM/CARIFORUM Food Security" was created to address just this kind of endemic problem in the Caribbean, and identified the major issues of "low agricultural productivity and production; decreased earnings from traditional crops; inadequate trade policy; high dependence on imported food; increasing poverty and growing food-related diseases such as obesity, hypertension, cancer and diabetes."[22] In the French Antilles (which are not currently part of CARICOM) the problem has been compounded by the kepone (chlordecone) pesticide scandal exposed in 2008, which resulted in the long-term pollution of Caribbean DOM soils, years after the chemical was banned in metropolitan France. Will it be possible to overhaul French Antillean economies, establishing networks with new trading partners and negotiating more beneficial terms? Moreover, will it be possible to recognize and address in any meaningful and sustained manner the wider social problems of youth disenfranchisement and unemployment, which were identified by Barny years before the strike occurred?

The 2009 strike has largely been characterized as a prelude to change, rather than a decisive moment of change in itself. Bonilla in particular reads it as an experimental time that "served as a pre-figurative movement in which alternative economic, social and political configurations could be both imagined and experienced" (Bonilla 2010, 127). The legacy of 2009 appears to reside in a creative outpouring that gave rise to new—but transitory—political structures and slogans, and that emphasized potentiality, rather than providing a basis for sustainable, clearly defined development. Indeed, while the principles put forward by the *Manifeste* are admirable in their ambition, the text is not without flaws. The dichotomy created between *poétique* and *prosaïque* is reductive, offering no compromise or middle ground for readers. Despite purporting to offer advice on how to move to a fairer, "post-capitaliste" society (Breleur et al. 2009, 9), the text fails to offer any concrete, specific advice. The *Manifeste* suggests overcoming the major problem of food security simply by eating "sain et autrement" (Breleur et al. 2009, 6; healthily and differently), yet does not expand on how this might be achieved. It is notable that the serious ecological issues raised by the kepone (chlordecone) pollution scandal go completely unaddressed.

Nonetheless, the debates and philosophical reflections around the significance of the strikes of 2009 do emphasize the potential for change. This process of change is sketched out at the *Manifesto*'s close, borrowing an environmental metaphor for a rethinking of the "ecology" of how French Caribbean citizens live their lives: "Le plein emploi ne sera pas du prosaïque productiviste, mais il s'envisagera dans ce qu'il peut créer en socialisation,

en autoproduction, en temps libre, en temps mort, en ce qu'il pourra per-
mettre de solidarités, de partages, de soutiens aux plus démantelés, de
revitalisations écologiques de notre environnement" (Breleur et al. 2009, 7;
Full employment will not just result in prosaic productivism, but it will set
its sights on what can be created in terms of socialization, self-productivity,
in our free time, in our down time, in terms of what it can lead to in solidarity, exchange, support for the most needy, and the ecological reinvigo-
ration of our environment).

Human beings, then, should be considered as connected parts of a wider
ecological network—rather than as some kind of center around which everything gravitates. In order to better apprehend this wider ecology, it will
become essential to reconceptualize the meaning of work itself. Here, the
thinkers of the manifesto give a direct nod to the philosopher André Gorz's
writing on redefining the nature of work. In a passage that seems to
respond directly to the rapid growth of the tertiary sector and the stifling
administrative apparatuses it has put in place, they themselves propose
that a new paradigm should and must be introduced: "Il y aura du travail et
des revenues de citoyenneté dans ce qui stimule, qui aide à rêver, qui mène
à méditer ou qui ouvre aux délices de l'ennui, qui installe en musique, qui
oriente en randonnée dans le pays des livres, des arts, du chant, de la philosophie, de l'étude ou de la consommation de haute nécessité qui ouvre à
création—créaconsommation" (Breleur et al. 2009, 7; There will be work
and income generated by all that which stimulates, all that which helps us
dream, all that which leads us to meditate or indeed to the delights of bore-
dom, all that which expresses itself through music, which wends its way
through the land of books, art, singing, philosophy, study, or even consumerism, if it is basic, necessary consumerism that opens the way for true
creation—crea-consumerism). The neologism *créaconsommation* conveys
the new order to which the authors aspire: they are not so naive as to demand
that consumerism ceases altogether, but they plead for a revised consumerism which allows for and is driven by creativity and self-fulfillment. Capitalism's overbearing and frenetic dominance, the authors contend, can only be
challenged by "un épanouissement humain qui s'inscrit dans l'horizontale

plenitude du vivant" (Breleur et al. 2009, 9; a human blossoming that becomes inscribed in the bountiful horizon of the living). Indeed, this phrase itself evokes a rhizomatic spreading out, and further connects the manifesto to its authors' wider literary works; in particular, the "vivant," or the living, is a term that assumed increasing importance in the late work of the philosopher and coauthor of the manifesto, Edouard Glissant.[23] This closing phrase, while lofty, poetic, and enigmatic, captures the rethinking of human interactions—with each other, and with the natural world—for which the authors strive.[24] The manifesto develops its own innovative lexicon and environmental agenda, and looks likely to become one of the earliest and most concise expressions of an important new philosophical direction for French Caribbean culture. Through these important works, authors and filmmakers emphasize the power of art and culture to alter consciousnesses and effect change. In such a way, these small islands, peripheries, are placing themselves as a counterbalance to the might of European and westernized hegemonic structures.

Acknowledgments

I would like to thank the organizers of three international conferences, all held in 2014, where I presented earlier versions of this work and benefited from constructive feedback from interdisciplinary audiences: conferences held at New York University (20th and 21st Century French and Francophone Studies Colloquium, "Money"), the University of Oxford ("Language and Identity in Francophone Worlds") and the University of Birmingham (UK) ("Future Caribbean Spaces": Race in the Americas—R.I.T.A. Network).

NOTES

Some of the material discussed in this chapter builds on an earlier article that responded to the 2009 strikes (Hardwick 2012). This material is reproduced and revisited here with the permission of Oxford University Press.

1. See https://www.journal-officiel.gouv.fr/publications/bocc/pdf/2009/0011/CCO_20090011_0011_0011.pdf (accessed June 11, 2020).

2. The only published written account of events is by Jean-Pierre Sainton and Raymond Gama, Mé 67 (Guadeloupe: Société Guadeloupéenne d'édition et de diffusion [Sogéd], 1985).

3. "L'enquête emploi en Guadeloupe deuxième trimestre 2010: Progression du chômage en 2010," Institut national de la statistique et des études économiques (Insee), http://www .insee.fr/fr/themes/document.asp?reg_id=26&ref_id=16987 (accessed June 21, 2011).

4. According to the home page of the official LKP website: http://www.lkp-gwa.org/ (accessed April 19, 2010).

5. Robert Aldrich and John Connell, *France's Overseas Frontier: Départements et Terri-toires d'Outre-mer* (Cambridge: Cambridge University Press, 1992), 7.

6. Aldrich and Connell, *France's Overseas Frontier*, 16.

7. Mathieu Kassovitz, *La Haine* (France: Canal+, 1995).

8. All translations are my own unless otherwise stated.

9. I explore the significance of unions in the film further in an earlier article (Hard-wick 2012).

10. The disturbing image is similar to the drawing of a slave ship named *Marie-Séraphique*. See www.slaveryandremembrance.org/collections/object/index.cfm?id=OB0026&lang =fra (accessed June 17, 2020).

11. Edouard Glissant, *Le Discours antillais* (Paris: Editions Gallimard, 1997 [1981]), 13.

12. It is notable that the authors are exclusively male, whereas other written outputs from Martinique responding to the 2009 crisis included female contributors. See Suzanne Dracius, Ernest Pépin, Patrick-Mathelié-Guinlet, Hector Poullet, José Pento-scrope, Lisa David, Alain Caprice, and LKP, *Guadeloupe & Martinique en grève générale contre l'exploitation outrancière et contre la vie chère* (Martinique: Editions Desnel, 2009).

13. Quoted in Michel Maurhein, *La Guadeloupe du 20 janvier au 04 mars 2009* (Auteurs Indépendants, 2009), 46.

14. Guy Numa, "Les départements d'outre-mer: des économies sous tutelle," in *La révolution antillaise: Quelle place pour l'outre-mer dans la république?*, edited by Luc Laven-ture, 29–47 (Paris: Eyrolles/France ô, 2009), 29.

15. Maeve McCusker, *Patrick Chamoiseau: Recovering Memory* (Liverpool: Liverpool University Press, 2007), 24.

16. "Un coût de vie nettement plus élevé qu'en métropole," in "Focus/Décryptage: Les DOM, des départements à l'économie sinistrée," *Le Monde*, February 20, 2009, 17.

17. For an expanded anthropological account of the events immediately leading up to the strike, which includes a fuller discussion of racial and socioeconomic tensions, see a second publication by Yarimar Bonilla, *Non-sovereign Futures: French Caribbean Politics in the Wake of Disenchantment* (Chicago: Chicago University Press, 2015). Interestingly, in this monograph, Bonilla describes attending a workshop on *Nèg maron* organized by union activists, during which the workshop leader criticized the film for its representa-tion of maroons, and appeared to interpret the film as a perversion of history and a youth-centered glorification of violence (57–60). Such a reading is quite at odds with the present analysis of *Nèg maron*'s engagement with questions of individual and collective responsibility.

18. These comments were reportedly made during an interview with TV Guadeloupe. See http://www.lepoint.fr/actualites-societe/2009-03-07/guadeloupe-domota-menace -les-chefs-d-entreprise/920/0/323275 (accessed April 21, 2010).

19. As of 2020, online searches for an MBA in Guadeloupe locate one course, in the discipline of sports management. It has not been possible to ascertain whether this MBA has any link to Angèle: https://www.mba-esg.com/actus/mba-management-du -sport-en-guadeloupe-premiere-reussie (accessed June 17, 2020).

20. Maximin makes this statement in several different forms, most recently: "Il apparaît clairement dans ce concentré d'histoires blessées que l'on ne peut les définir que par ce qu'elles ont créé: des sociétés et des cultures issues non directement de l'esclavage, mais essentiellement de la résistance à l'esclavage et des combats pour son abolition" (What appears most clearly from examining these many fractured histories is that they can best be defined by what they have created: societies and cultures that arose not directly from slavery, but rather from the essence of sheer resistance to slavery and struggles to bring about its abolition) (*Les Fruits du cyclone: Une géopoétique de la Caraïbe* [Paris: Seuil, 2006], 15). The statement recalls Fanon's "Je ne suis pas esclave de l'Esclavage qui déshumanisa mes pères" (I am not the slave of the Slavery that dehumanized my forefathers) (*Peau noire, masques blancs* [Paris: Seuil, 1952], 186). It was a central motif of Maximin's interventions in public debates on slavery during the 150th anniversary of abolition in 1998 and informed his contributions to the Année des outré-mer in 2011: http://www.outre-mer.gouv.fr/?2011-annee-des-outre-mer-une-manifestation-pour-aller-au-dela-des.html (accessed July 12, 2011).

21. Maximin, *Les Fruits du cyclone*, 6.

22. Food and Agriculture Organization of the United Nations (FAO) Project, "Promoting CARICOM/ CARIFORUM Food Security" (GTFS/RLA/141/ITA). Adapted from http://www.rlc.fao.org/progesp/pesa/caricom2/what.htm (accessed June 24, 2010).

23. For a reading of "le vivant" (the living) in late Glissant, see two articles in a special issue of *Callaloo: A Journal of African Diaspora Arts and Letters* in memory of Edouard Glissant, edited by Celia Britton: Alessandro Corio, "The Living and the Poetic Intention: Glissant's Biopolitics of Literature," *Callaloo* 36, no. 4 (2013): 916–931; and Valérie Loichot, "Edouard Glissant's Graves," *Callaloo* 36, no. 4 (2013): 1014–1032.

24. I explore the environmental dimension of the *Manifeste* in a separate journal article. See Hardwick 2016.

REFERENCES

Bonilla, Yarimar. 2010. "Guadeloupe Is Ours: The Prefigurative Politics of the Mass Strike in the French Antilles," *Interventions* 12: 125–37.

Breleur, Patrick Chamoiseau, Serge Domi, Gérard Delver, Edouard Glissant, Guillaume Pigeard de Gurbert, Olivier Portecop, Olivier Pulvar, and Jean-Claude William. 2009. *Manifeste pour les "produits" de haute nécessité*. Paris: Editions Galaade, Institut de Tout-Monde.

Flamand-Barny, Jean-Claude, dir. 2004. *Nèg maron*. France: Mat Films, Kasso Inc. Productions, and France 2 Cinéma.

Hardwick, Louise. 2012. "Depicting Social Dispossession in Guadeloupe: *Nèg Maron*, *Lettre ouverte à la jeunesse* and the General Strike of 2009." *Forum for Modern Language Studies* 48, no. 3: 288–305.

———. 2016. "Towards Biopolitical Ecocriticism: The Example of the *Manifeste pour les 'produits' de haute nécessité*." *French Studies* 70, no. 3 (July): 362–382.

Robinson, Meredith. 2014. "No Chains on Feet or Mind: Jean-Claude Flamand Barny's Neg Maron (2005)." In *Postcolonial Film: History, Empire Resistance*, edited by Rebecca Weaver-Hightower and Peter Hulme, 137–153. New York: Routledge.

3 Artists against Exploitation

THE L'HERMINIER MUSEUM SQUAT AS A DEMONSTRATION AGAINST "LA VIE CHÈRE"

ALIX PIERRE

Most analyses of social movements published to date consider protest from a politico-economic or social point of view. The very name of the coalition at the origin of the massive strike movement in Guadeloupe, Liyannaj Kont Pwofitasyon (LKP; Alliance against Profiteering), imposes this type of approach. This popular movement protested "la vie chère" (the costly life) in which the trade system between France and Guadeloupe was seen as responsible for an increase in prices that had exacerbated the situation of a population already suffering from the fall-out of the global economic crisis. Michel Desse's article nicely summarizes the approach that views the economic crisis and its effects on island economies as the source of the 2009 strikes in Guadeloupe and Martinique. The author highlights a decline in agriculture due to unfavorable negotiations with the World Trade Organization (WTO) and a downturn in the tourism industry. Desse also mentions unemployment and underemployment, direct consequences of the downturn in both the sectors already mentioned and also of the 2007 oil crisis. The author states: "It's in this context exacerbated by the global crisis, which tends to marginalize the Caribbean islands, that the Guadeloupean collective 'Liyannaj Kont Pwofitasyon' (LKP) . . . issued a platform of 146 demands" (Desse 2010, 2). Desse emphasizes his economic approach by going over these demands with a fine-toothed comb: "They reflect the economic sectors in crisis as 25 demands concern employment, the integration of the unemployed, and training; 17 address reducing prices and taxes; 19 target public utilities; 14 focus on the agricultural sector and 1 on tourism.

These demands take into account current problems illustrating the damaged economic sectors. In spite of numerous assistance programs, unemployment remains endemic and increasing, revealing the crises affecting different economic sectors and development perspectives" (Desse 2010, 2).

Desse goes on to demonstrate the causal relationship between the unequal trade balance in Guadeloupe and Martinique and the sharp rise in costs of ocean freight, air transport, and fuel that led to an excessive increase in consumer prices beginning in 2007. Among researchers, the conflict is seen as an indicator of the broader juridico-political crisis, in the constitutional sense, facing the overseas departments and regions (DROM). The relationship between France and the DROM is being reevaluated, and more specifically the statutory future of the DROM. In the case of Guadeloupe, Martinique, and French Guiana, which all joined the movement, the departmentalization system itself is being contested. On this point, Michel Desse and Mario Selise assert: "These social movements have been very active in Reunion Island, French Guiana, and Guadeloupe as well as in Martinique. They have led to political and institutional crises demonstrating the incompatibility of the departmentalization system, marred by a certain maldevelopment that does not prevent "Pwofitasyon," and the political and economic frustrations of overseas citizens" (2010, 3).

The day following the signing of an agreement in Guadeloupe after forty-four days of strikes, Nicolas Sarkozy recommended the formation of an "Overseas Estates-General" to the political representatives of the DOM, their social partners, the management representatives, and the rest of their fellow citizens. Such a recommendation, with the goal of recasting a specific status for each within the framework of a "Plural Republic," demonstrates the soundness of the analyses. The absence of LKP and the principal trade union confederations from the assemblies in April and July 2009, with the state having decided everything ahead of time, shows that the prevailing unease has still not disappeared.

In the scholarly studies that have appeared, emphasis is often placed on an examination of the power struggle between *léta fransé* (the French state) and the Guadeloupean people, in a politico-historical approach. Syliane

Larcher notes that the directors of the movement come from the social sector. They are union leaders, ANPE (National Employment Agency) agents, social workers, and educators, joined by small businesspersons. Additionally, it is well documented that the main spokespersons are separatists affiliated with the movement. Labor demands and, accordingly, local organizations including Eli Domota's, occupy a justifiably prominent place. The economic approach, with its many variations, takes precedence among scholars.

However, the list of 120 demands drawn up by LKP on December 16, 2009, at the very beginning of the conflict, includes grievances such as land management, culture, language, and history, which primarily concern the local artistic community. The collective demands media programming that fully integrates Guadeloupean language and culture through consultation with cultural players and their inclusion on administrative boards. The development of businesses and nonprofits for cultural integration is another demand. The restoration of popular historical sites (*lieux de mémoire*) and the creation of a cultural institute in a municipality of northern Basse-Terre are also proposed.

LKP's complex list of grievances, in this particular passage, reveals something that seems to be missing from most of the published work on the social movement: that the political, the economic, and the cultural are intrinsically linked. The demands show the role of culture as an integral part of the affirmation of nationalism and of the self. Across different time periods and schools of thought, from Negritude to Antillanité and Créolité, regardless of political tendencies, from departmentalization to autonomy, Antillean thinkers and activists have always been conscious of the central role of culture in the search for identity and self-actualization. The Antillean's feeling of being torn between being French and European and being Caribbean, Antillean, and Creole expresses itself more in the cultural domain than elsewhere. In the 1980s, theorists talked about the "mal antillais" (Antillean affliction). Edouard Glissant made it the theme of *Le Discours antillais* (Caribbean Discourse, 1981). The Guadeloupean sociolinguist Dany Bébel-Gisler articulates the issue nicely: "The central cultural question is to figure out how to bring to fruition the 'cultural heritage,' the collective force bequeathed to us by our different ancestors" (1989, 93).

The separatist artist Joël Nankin takes up this point when he states in an interview: "I am Guadeloupean, deeply Guadeloupean and Caribbean. I'm someone with a history, and I'm trying to find my place in the world because it's always difficult for the colonial subject to situate themself, and I consider myself a colonial subject, someone living under the heel of others, which is to say France. . . . The hardest thing is living in a country where alienation and acculturation are complete. It's like a permanent wound."[1]

Patrick Chamoiseau expands on this question in *Ecrire en pays dominé* (Writing in a Dominated Land, 1997). The national struggle is always accompanied by cultural demands. In the 1980s, this was key to the autonomist movement, which devised the political slogan "Palé kréyòl, jouwé gwoka" (Speak Creole, play the gwoka [traditional drum]). Similarly, LKP has called into question the lack of an autochthonous cultural policy that would make room for the local rather than simply imitating and enforcing a framework imported from France. Chamoiseau raises the same question: "How can you write when from dawn to dusk your imagination soaks up images, thoughts, values that are not your own? How can you write when what you are vegetates outside the flows that determine your life? How can you write in a dominated land?" (2002, 17). This article focuses precisely on a social segment of this subgroup of players driven by the same questions, and whose role in the movement has not yet been considered in research and publications.

From the very beginning, artists joined the association of forty-eight professional, political, cultural, civic, and social organizations orchestrating the social movement against *la vie chère* in Guadeloupe. The organizations Akiyo, Voukoum, and Mas ka klé, well-known carnival groups seen as cultural movements, were shoulder to shoulder with demonstrators. Jean-Luc Bonniol explains, from a historical, political, and social point of view, how the ideological significance of these groups goes beyond mere entertainment:

Carnival associations multiplied in Guadeloupe during the 80s and 90s, in a context where the nationalist movement had fertilized the cultural movement. . . . These cultural players now saw themselves as "patriots," the term replacing that of nationalist. . . . One group seems particularly emblematic: Voukoum in Basse-Terre (we could also mention Akiyo in Pointe-à-Pitre). Proclaiming themselves a *mouvman kiltirel Gwadloup* (Guadeloupe cultural movement), the group, rooted in activist causes and engagement, is clearly situated within the question of cultural resistance: the goal is to go against the establishment, to "showcase our ways and customs so that our misguided youth can rediscover our cultural references," to promote street culture, the popular aspects of Guadeloupean cultural heritage (the idea of heritage is explicitly deployed). . . . We must allow "the men and women of this region to be agents participating in the development of their own culture. . . . For us, the lovers of Guadeloupean cultural heritage, only abnegation can allow us to carry higher still the *chaltouné* [torch] of defense and safeguard of our *fondal-natal* heritage. (2004, 150)

This extract shows the close link between policy, labor, and culture for the activist sector of the population. Political conscientization does not exclude culture, and cultural and syndicalist conscientization are politicized. Popular culture (its practice) is considered a tool of resistance. This is unsurprising given that many founding members of the aforementioned organizations are partisans of the nationalist current engaged in all-out community action. The three groups mentioned here do significant work in raising awareness among youth and attract hundreds of supporters who parade during the carnival period. The associations are regularly invited to perform in France and the West, thus exporting Guadeloupean culture. More precisely, in 2009, artists' engagement within the general social movement took various forms. Some, following the example of freelance entertainers (*intermittents du spectacle*), marched under the banner of "Awtis Kont Pwofitasyon." Others, sometimes the same people, transformed for example the parking lot of the Palais de la Mutualité—the site of daily *gran kozé* (parley) with the people—into an outdoor performance space.[2]

Concerned with representing all social currents, Elie Domota and the LKP board met with the artists in order to consider their grievances and communicate them to the governing bodies during negotiations. The movement allows us to note that the crisis in Guadeloupean society was not only politico-economic but also identitary. In his analysis, Rosan Monza outlines the bases for the concerns of local cultural and artistic players, affirming that

> the presence, among the directors of LKP, of no fewer than five of the island's most influential cultural associations demonstrates the importance of the question of cultural identity in Guadeloupe. Departmentalization did not afford a halt to the depersonalization process or the fracturing of creole identity between the aspiration for greater equality and recognition and assimilation to French culture. . . . The primary reason [for local politicians' being overwhelmed and discredited by the popular movement] according to [Senator Lucette Michaux-Chevry] stems from the insufficient investment of public policy in cultural projects that would have had the power to promote and to reconcile Guadeloupe with a complex history and culture branded by colonial antagonism. (2009, 12)

After a bitter fight, over the years, in the context of departmentalization local representatives demanded and obtained from the French government increased decision-making power. While there was undeniable progress in certain areas (education, parity of social benefits, property, and facilities), with regard to cultural policy, officials do not seem to have had a coherent vision built on collaboration with the public. Initiatives were considered only in the short term and for cronyistic electoral purposes. In this respect, despite the liberalization of the audiovisual landscape, the press, media, and cultural venues, remain instruments or affiliates of the state, which dictates the main themes. Consequently, with very few exceptions, the status quo remains intact in terms of programming and content.

In our conception, culture is understood as artistic, aesthetic, and intellectual creativity. It is considered from the perspective of artistic creation, production, performance, and dissemination. Specifically, on the island, confronted by these generalized deleterious conditions, at the very heart of the protest movement a collective of artists, Awtis 4 chimen, decided to "occupy" without authorization an abandoned building, part of the state's real estate holdings, in order to adapt it for their needs. This analysis aims to be both investigative and evaluative. How does squatting an abandoned administrative building contribute to the protest movement against *la vie chère*? Do we have the right to equate the squatters with other protesters? Would this occupation not be more likely to discredit the work of the forty-eight organizations that, throughout the crisis, successfully endeavored to contain outbursts, the violence of the crowd, and confrontations with law enforcement? Which aspects of this illicit operation affirm that it indicates some level of success? What motivates us to draw such a conclusion?

These questions are all the more relevant given that when one asks the man on the street, the average Guadeloupean, about the results of the pro-test movement against *la vie chère*, the changes it brought about, the assess-ments are generally negative.[3] The masses have adopted a dominant alarmist discourse (circulated by employers and political and legal authori-ties) that emphasizes the breakdown of social and economic structures that followed the return to normalcy. They mention the series of (mostly small) business closures and the attendant layoffs at the end of the conflict. Per-sonally, we hope to produce a more nuanced evaluation. We want to show that the power struggle with *léta* (employers and the government) did not have exclusively negative repercussions. It fostered or went hand in hand with a cultural renaissance or, better, conscientization at the heart of the art world. The occupation of the L'Herminier Museum (*Skwat 4chimen*) is the acting out, on an artistic level, of LKP's logic. It constitutes the practi-cal application of a manifesto written by the group's artists, which itself echoed LKP's demands. In the document from January 20, 2009, that includes the list of demands we read: "People of Guadeloupe, workers, peasants, artisans, retirees, unemployed, businesspeople, youth, *LIYANNAJ KONT PWOFITASYON* is our construction, our idea, our tool, our con-sciousness. *Liyannaj kont pwofitasyon* is us!!! *An nou bay lanmen pou ba'y sans é pouvwa* [Help us to give it meaning and power]. So that everywhere in the towns, in the cities, in the countryside, the people take to the streets." We read here a clear call to action, to collective engagement. The street is the privileged site where the protesters will make themselves heard. In the words of Pierre Favre, LKP "leverages public space through collective action" (2007, 135). In the artist collective's text from May 27, 2009, two statements of intent sum up their position: "TAKE POSSESSION of performance and display spaces in order to make our work VISIBLE. . . . INITIATE RELEVANT ACTS of protest in public spaces out of respect for the citizenry and Democracy." The two statements echo each other, speak to each other. The idea of participatory democracy is suggested here. The role of civil society in the exercise of democracy and community management is evoked. On this point, Cécile Blatrix asserts: "It's essentially at the local level that the 'right to participation' is most established, particularly in certain sectors of state action: environment, urban planning, living conditions, and land use seem to constitute particularly fertile ground for the flourishing of participatory democracy" (2009, 99).

Now, as we will see, the occupation of this site derives precisely from (the management of) urban planning, living conditions, and land use. We thus argue that the squat is a revolutionary form of action on the island. One of the artists who participated, Nikki Elisé, writes on her website: "Awtis 4Chimen, the 4 paths artists created the first Guadeloupean artists' squat by occupying the L'Herminier Museum in Point-à-Pitre since May of 2009. The group is made up of visual artists, photographers, sculptors, metalworkers, engravers, etc. We strive for the visibility of art in Guadeloupe, high-quality artwork in high-quality, specialized venues for our exhibitions."[4]

We maintain that the subversive nature—in the sense of an innovative process—of the squat is borne out on three specific fronts that we will discuss. First, as a form of protest, the squat is unique inasmuch as it is a fundamentally participatory "bottom-up" approach. This is an initiative of the masses in response to specific social problems (juvenile delinquency, prostitution, drug dealing and use, substandard housing, and a lack of appropriate studio and exhibition space for artists) and the lack of political will among local elected officials. Second, the "colonization" of the site and its transformation into creation, exhibition, and living space has profound ecological significance. By recycling an unoccupied building, the artists resolved an alarming socioeconomic and environmental problem (the housing crisis) in the artistic and cultural sector. Third, through its exhibitory process, the museum helped improve the staging and the legitimacy of LKP in the eyes of the Guadeloupean people. Indeed, in November 2010, the first photography exhibition, dedicated to the movement and entitled "44 days," was organized there. We will conclude by showing how the social movement coincided with the democratization of the art world, particularly visual arts. The act of occupation allowed for the positioning of art squats[5] as a new artistic territory.

The Squat as a Mode of Collective Action

The action of Awtis 4 chimen was completely new to the island. It was the first time that an artist collective had squatted in a building. They understood this action as a civic, public-spirited process. Before going further, it is appropriate to first come to an understanding of the term *squat* and to place it in the broader French context to which Guadeloupe belongs. Colonized since 1635, Guadeloupe became a department in 1946. Today, like the rest of the French population, its inhabitants are not only French but also hold European passports. The list of terms used (overseas department/ DOM, French department in America, overseas department and region/ DROM, overseas territory, outermost region), which has fluctuated over time, shows the mother country's difficulty in naming and thus being unified with Guadeloupe and the other islands. Aimé Césaire said it best when he told the National Assembly, "we are not citizens in our own right but entirely on our own."

The invention of the squat can be traced to the end of the nineteenth century, to the end of World War II, according to Cécile Péchu, a leading scholar of this question. And for purposes of our argument we follow the interpretation she suggests: "It's the first meaning of the word squat, defined as 'the act of illegally occupying a locale for housing or collective use' [and not the second definition, which refers to the building itself], that interests us here" (2010, 9). For scholars of the question,[6] squatting is understood as a weapon in the arsenal of collective action.

Drawing on existing studies and her own investigation of the subject, Péchu sees two logics of public use of the squat: a "class" logic and a "counter-culture" logic. In the first case, the ultimate goal of the action is to obtain the right to housing for workers and the poor. This movement developed between 1946 and 1970 and aligns with the political ideology of the Left. The "counter-culture" logic "aims to change the lives of the inhabitants of the occupied site or of the surrounding area and is often accompanied by a thematics of 'liberated spaces' (Péchu 2010, 19). This context prioritizes the right to space in which to live or create differently. This vision has roots in the utopian communitarian movement. Péchu situates it within the field of protest as well as resistance in the sense that "it's about taking rather than asking" (2010, 19).

If we look at the origin of the movement, the occupation of buildings arose from the late nineteenth-century anarchist practice of "doing a moonlight flit," which apparently consisted of moving out while avoiding paying the rent. From this clandestine and individual form of resistance that appeared in the 1880s, the squat gradually became a collective mode of protest. According to Péchu, chronologically the "class" logic was first to be implemented. The goal was to obtain from authorities the right to housing for the many families of limited means. This trend was predominant in France and Europe until the 1970s, lost ground to the "countercultural" logic, and then regained momentum in the 1980s, particularly through the work of the organization Right to Housing (*Droit au logement*).

Countercultural squats appeared in Europe following the events of 1968. Péchu states that "they are committed to utopian communitarianism, the idea of head-on opposition to the system, and a desire to rethink life in the cities and urban neighborhoods by offering cultural spaces and alternative social events. It's no longer about the right to housing, but about the right to a space to live differently. In this light, the squat is an end in itself" (2010, 88). Globally, we identify three currents of countercultural squat in France. The first, which spanned the 1960s to the 1980s, expressed utopian communitarianism, counterculture, and opposition to the system. The second united these three aspects around the idea of the alternative. The last, which began in the 1980s, distinguished political squats from art squats.

We thus arrive at the art squats with which we associate *skwat 4 chimen*. These appeared in Paris at the end of the 1980s. To better understand the situation, we must examine the socioeconomic context facing the artists at the time. Studios were becoming rare. Artists lived on miniscule incomes, often the minimum income benefit (*revenu minimum d'insertion*). This status prevented them from accessing the few public studios that existed but were highly inadequate. Péchu notes that at the same time, some artists— particularly the younger generation—saw the squat as a marketing strategy, that would afford them a degree of artistic reputation from the margins. From 1989 to 1992, the number of squats in the capital grew. They were located primarily in the working-class neighborhoods to the east of Paris. Péchu writes: "Art squats of this period are characterized by the 'interlinking of the artistic and the political.' They are often critical of the mainstream art market and of consumerist and sanctified aspects of culture. They insist on the nomadic nature of the squat and its creation of a temporary autonomous zone. For these artists, the squat is often an end in itself" (2010, 109).

How does the L'Herminier museum squat fit into this long western tradition? We must take a close look at statements made by the collective's members. We draw once again on Nikki Elisé. She writes on her site: "The 4chimen artists, organized as a nonprofit per the 1901 law, authors of the first Guadeloupean art squat (visual arts) we claim the occupation of the L'Herminier Museum Pointe-à-Pitre a magnificent building tied to the city's cultural history, closed and abandoned to the homeless, dealers, petty criminal and other ladies of the night for more than 15 years. We demand effective and dedicated exhibition spaces for the visual arts and a real cultural policy in Guadeloupe."[7]

Emphasis is immediately placed on the organization's legitimacy from a legal standpoint. This is not an illegal group, but an organization registered with the Prefecture. The artists place their association directly under the auspices of the law of July 1, 1901, related to partnership agreements. This law guarantees one of the major republican freedoms. Thanks to the legislative fight let by Pierre Waldeck-Rousseau, all citizens have to right to associate without prior authorization. The government site pertaining to nonprofit associations notes:

> The law of 1901 establishes the right to association on entirely new grounds. It preserves the freedoms and rights of individuals while allowing for their collective action. It ends the restrictive regime and preventative prohibition order of the "le chapelier" law, from the article of the penal code, of the law of 1804. It does not restore any aspect of the bygone corporate law and establishes the right of association on the principles of the revolution of 1789: primacy of the individual, of their rights and freedoms, freedom to join or leave an association, limitation of the purpose of an association to a defined objective, equality of members of an association, administration by free deliberation among members.[8]

Thus benefiting from the gains of the common-law regime, the collective strives to explain the nature of its actions. Its chief concern is the preservation of the island's cultural heritage. There is a clearly stated cultural project: the preservation of real estate and of a historic site. This characteristic appears in the five configurations of squat established by Hans Pruijit: the conservation squat that aims to preserve the city and the landscape. The occupied structure has a rich past that the artists do not discuss in detail but evoke symbolically. What is, then, the importance of this building? It has multiple advantages. The first relates to location: the address. The building is situated in the center of the capital city Pointe-à-Pitre. It is on the corner of two major streets, rue Sadie and rue Jean Jaurès. At the time of its construction, the Grand Hôtel des Antilles was nearby. The second attractive feature is architectonic. The house belongs to an architectural style common not only in Guadeloupe but throughout the region. It is described in the following terms on the Guadeloupean cultural heritage website: "a lovely brick house in a colonial style, its metallic structure embellished with cast iron columns and balconies with ironwork filigree. The house can be accessed via a small staircase of volcanic stones." The site culture.gouv.fr offers additional information: the house has a second story, a tile roof, and zinc filigree crowning and vergeboard. The floor of the gallery is made up of decorative cement tiles. The balustrade of the balconies boasts elegant geometric patterns: rinceaux, interlace. The front gate, decorated with wrought iron rinceaux, bears the inscription "CHAMBER OF AGRICULTURE L'HERMINIER MUSEUM." The third interesting feature relates to the original function of the premises, which subsequently fell into disuse. Designed by the Parisian engineer Suffit, erected in 1873 by the Guadeloupe Chamber of Agriculture, the house became the L'Herminier Museum in the twentieth century and was finally listed as a historical monument in 2008. Built on the lands of the L'Herminier family (the pharmacist Félix Louis L'Herminier and his son, the botanist Ferdinand Joseph L'Herminier), the building housed from the beginning the Guadeloupe Chamber of Agriculture, which held its meetings there, and the botanical and zoological collections of the L'Herminier family.

Felix Louis L'Herminier and his son Ferdinand Joseph were two of the pioneers of Guadeloupean naturalism. Holding degrees in botany, chemistry, and pharmacy, the father arrived in Guadeloupe in 1798. Over time, motivated by his passion for zoology and herpetology, he collected plants, pieces of fossilized lava, insects, and birds from the island, its dependencies, and the rest of the Caribbean, including in the United States. He sent his discoveries to the Natural History Museum in Paris, which succeeded the Jardin du Roi founded in 1635. His encyclopedic work earned him the roles of *Naturaliste du Roi* (the king's herbalist) and director of the Guadeloupe botanical garden in 1819. Herbalist and medical doctor, working at the Saint Jules hospital, the son shared his father's interest in ornithology and botany. He collected many varieties of fern. He received the Légion d'Honneur in 1866 for his courage and dedication during the earthquake of 1843 and the cholera epidemic of 1865. He was also a member of the Pointe-à-Pitre town council.

The L'Herminier collections were displayed in the Guadeloupe Museum of Natural History until 1960. The museum also housed other miscellaneous specimens including a large whalebone, numerous fossils, insects, sawfish rostrums, and taxidermied animals including birds, lizards, and a crocodile. On the walls hung Native American axes in oval or circular designs, and relief carvings. Since then, the establishment has been separated from its collections, and some of the pieces are now in the Victor Schoelcher Museum. Today, one can find online the postcards showing the museum's interior and its rich collection. Thus, by occupying the building, the artists seek to symbolically celebrate this legacy. And if the original content cannot be resurrected, the building itself can.

Nonetheless, beyond conservationist action, through its process the collective makes it their mission to raise public awareness of a glaring social ill: precarity. In a report submitted to the Economic and Social Council in 1987 and which remains a key reference on the subject, father Joseph Wresinski, founder of the human rights movement ATD Fourth World, defines precarity as "the absence of one or more of the securities that allow families to fulfill their basic responsibilities and to exercise their fundamental rights. The insecurity that results from this can be more or less extensive and have more or less serious and irrevocable consequences. It leads to extreme poverty when it affects multiple aspects of life, when it becomes persistent, when it jeopardizes the chances of reassuming responsibilities and reclaiming rights for oneself in a foreseeable future" (1987, 6).

The citation from Awtis 4 chimen mentions those most affected, with the homeless at the top of the list. A measure enacted by the Elysée one month before the museum occupation confirms the significance that public authorities ascribe to the problem. Indeed, on April 6, 2009, the government[9] sent a mission letter to Serge Letchimy, deputy mayor of Fort-de-France, member of the socialist group, and urban planner by training, requesting that he draw up a report of the substandard and unfit housing in the DROM. The report, which first focused on Guadeloupe, Martinique, French Guiana, and Reunion Island and was subsequently extended to include Mayotte and Saint Martin, was given to the prime minister in September 2009 and presented to the Economic Affairs Committee in October 2009.

The bill suggested[10] by commissioner Letchimy raised, in his assessment, three issues: the right to housing in the overseas territories, which itself reflects a glaring national problem (France had three million inadequately housed residents in 2009); the problem of unfit housing; and finally the problem of social equity and justice. To that end, the report says "once housing becomes a problem of this scope, the consequences impact human life, in education, health, etc." The numbers given in the report are striking:

> We noted between 50,000 and 60,000 homes that fall into the category of informal and precarious housing in Guadeloupe, Martinique, French Guiana, and Reunion, of which a large number can considered totally unfit. This represents between 10 and 12% of the existing structures in each department—and even 20% in French Guiana where the growth of shanty towns has accelerated due to immigration from neighboring Brazil and Suriname. In Mayotte, the situation is graver still: 40% of housing is considered precarious, which is to say 23,000 dwellings. If we include that Overseas collectivity, we can thus estimate the number of unfit dwellings at 83,000, housing around 200,000 people, the equivalent of the population of French Guiana. A large portion—80 to 90%— of precarious housing is made up of informal housing, which is built by individuals without a permit, and in 85% of cases on other people's land. (Assemblée nationale 2011)

The thread between the Chamber of Agriculture building and social precarity is insalubrity. With regard to housing, when sanitation is poorly or not at all managed, in a snowball effect, it fuels related, equally pernicious calamities: juvenile delinquency, prostitution, and trafficking of contraband. Local authorities, governed by public health code, are responsible for reducing substandard housing. The law stipulates that "when a building endangers the health or safety of its occupants, the prefect may file a suit for unsafe conditions against the owner of a dwelling or the property management firm if the building is co-owned." A building abandoned for fifteen years and inhabited by a criminal population would not seem to be a priority for its owner or for those charged with managing the city and its residential and commercial properties.

Faced with the deficiency and the vacuum created by local decision makers, the artists, who are citizens above all, took action. In taking the reins, they echoed the concerns of LKP, who between December 2008 and January 2009 stated: "Given the incompetence of those who have the power and responsibility to raise these issues and provide solutions, labor organizations, cultural movements and associations, political organizations and parties have decided by way of a massive popular movement to raise them, to propose alternatives, and to demand negotiations to make them happen."[11]

The L'Herminier Museum is situated near a prestigious school, the foremost of the island: Carnot High School. Founded in 1883, thanks to the efforts of administrator, politician, and Point-à-Pitre native Alexandre Isaac, it was thus the first high school in the city. Many of the island's renowned political, literary, and judicial figures studied there. At the time of the squat, a bookstore heavily patronized by the general public sat across from the institution. In the immediate area, there is a motley assortment of businesses including pharmacies, clothing stores, bars, restaurants, bakeries, and butcheries. It is a commercial neighborhood. The presence of the homeless, dealers, resellers, drug users, and sex workers is thus detrimental to the healthy functioning of the neighborhood.

The situation is all the more grave given that we know academic failure to be one of the causes of juvenile crime[12] (Boulogne 2010, 12). The Carnot students constitute a prime target for dealers and prostitutes, who in all likelihood themselves suffered academic failure. In a statement on the specifics of delinquency in the Antilles, Gaëlle Compper-Durand asserts that in Guadeloupe, criminality—in this case, theft and violent crime—increased by 112 percent between 1990 and 2000.

The report states: "In 2008, the number of physical assaults was twice the national level (13.8 confirmed incidents per 1,000 residents versus 7.3 at the national level). They increased markedly in 2009: 15.4 confirmed incidents per 1,000 residents versus 7.5 at the national level" (Compper-Durand 2010, 27). This situation earned Guadeloupe the unfortunate title of first French department for physical violence in 2008. In addition to the substantial increase in violence and child abuse, sexual assault, harassment, and

assault against youth and adults, Compper-Durand notes another phenomenon: the development of narcotics use and trafficking. The rate of growth
was more than 40 percent between 1990 and 2000. She also mentions a shift
in formal prostitution. She states: "Due to the effects of the reduction in
substandard housing, prostitution has spread throughout the department,
while prostitutes are no longer only full-time sex workers, but also occa-
sional workers (students, employees of the service sector, single parents)
who use this means to round out the end of the month" (2010, 28).

During the period in which we are interested, as Compper-Durand
explains, professional precarity (the general economic slump pushing
people to informal work), a lack of qualifications, unemployment (more
than 23 percent), and exclusion from consumer society pushed the young
(and the less young) toward the informal and then criminal economy (the
potential for significant income is attractive). She shows that public authorities' responses,[13] commendable as they were, remained largely insufficient
because of a lack of sufficient funding and of adequate manpower and
expertise. One component of the measures enacted by local communities
addressed the quasi-public sector. Compper-Durand notes: "Nonprofits
spearheaded city policy and were all the more in demand given their direct
involvement in the daily lives of people. In the Antilles, their advantages
include dynamism, adaptability, and a wide reach" (2010, 40).

4 chimen's approach fits precisely into this context, as their statement
of intent suggests. The difference here stems from the fact that the usual
model for managing policy in the city and/or the region is reversed. The
initiative does not belong to the city, which in general opts for a top-down
logic, but to the people organizing nonprofits, whose logic of prevention
and eradication of economic and social poverty and criminality seems better suited to the situation. Lauren Andres argues that "while the local public players distance themselves [from the squats], players from civil society,
on the other hand, take symbolic and material possession of these spaces"
(2006, 10). For Maria Gravari-Barbas, their actions can be characterized as
"initiatives from below . . . hence their distinction from major urban planning operations, public or private" (2004, 217). Compper-Durand views the

flexibility in how such associations operate, their ability to be both reactive and proactive, as important assets. They contrast with bureaucratic red tape and political games, by which we mean vote-seeking, which often dictates the behavior of local officials.

In the final analysis, we are witnessing the replacement of "destitution" squats by art squats. Thus, on a certain level we are correct to think that the art squat plays an essential role, at least symbolically, as a catalyst for the gentrification of a neighborhood. Elsa Vivant and Eric Charmes point out that artists' role in rehabilitating working-class areas has been extensively studied. They argue that the arrival of artists tends to reverse the negative image of industrial wasteland, presenting it instead as an asset for residents, owners, and developers. They discuss the example of the Bas-Montreuil neighborhood of Paris: "This neighborhood of small workshops and working-class housing was taken over by audiovisual and entertainment industry professionals living on limited and unstable incomes. It was subsequently transformed into a resource site for professionals in these fields, finally becoming a desirable residential neighborhood for the middle class" (2008, 1).

Skwat 4 chimen tackles generalized criminality. In choosing to reside on site, the artists provide security, whereas it would be expensive to hire professionals. They kill two birds with one stone: they breathe life back into the space by living there, and they ward off delinquents. The artists foster a quality of life more in keeping with the cornerstones that are the school and the bookstore, prime spaces of knowledge and culture. In advocating for a better way of living (together), the squat also advances a highly ecological practice to which we now turn our attention.

The Squat as an Ecological Practice

One month after registering with the prefecture, having considered several structures, Awtis 4 chimen decided to take over a state-owned building that had been closed for nearly two decades. The artists cleaned it up and immediately began renovating it, with the intention of living there and using it collectively. As we have shown, this act partakes fully of an established

Western and French tradition. This practice has two ecological consequences. Lauren Andres states that "for the cultural and artistic players,
taking possession of these unclaimed spaces [brownfields] is a response to
the absence of other available space. The brownfields are sources of inspiration directly related to the architecture of the site" (2006, 5). Our ecological argument will be articulated around these two poles.

The artists take possession of the space, confronting the public authorities' inability to provide them with appropriate studio and performance
spaces. In choosing their site, the artists reflect on their existence (as living
beings and artists), on the interactions and relationships between them (living beings), and on the interactions between them (living beings) and their
milieu (ecosystem). The approach of Awtis 4 chimen is ecological for several reasons. First, they opt for renovation rather than for new construction.
In this sense, they are doing recycling work, thus limiting their carbon
footprint. Second, the building is at the intersection of two busy streets. It
is situated at the heart of the urban conglomeration of Pointe-à-Pitre, and
therefore close to existing infrastructure. The city center is well served by
public transit. Third, this type of creole construction incorporates many
elements that support energy efficiency and environmental protection. The
building is oriented in the direction of the rising sun, which helps keeps the
house sunny. The roof height was designed to maximize ventilation and to
keep the air warm. The roof has four pitches that allow for better airflow.
Finally, the windows' wooden shutters and the blinds have two functions:
to allow free airflow and to foster a natural cooling of the building's interior. Thus, one achieves a strong energy performance while also optimizing
the health and comfort of inhabitants and visitors. From the beginning, the
architect, Suffit, designed a house adapted to the tropical climate.

We are now suggesting that given the concerns of the era, the *skwat 4
chimen* can be viewed as an eco-squat or as an artistic eco-laboratory. Hugues
de Varine, a local and community development consultant and former
director of the International Council of Museums, suggests the following
definition of the ecomuseum: "The ecomuseum is first and foremost a community and an objective: the development of that community" (1989, 30).

The guiding idea is to reinforce the link between the institution, its social milieu, and its environment. Public participation in its activities is a priority. Integration into the ecosystem and development are critical. According to Varine, "an ecomuseum showcases the entirety of the culture and heritage tied to its geographical area and its sphere of influence" (23).

The association's manifesto and its members' posts online reinforce this analogy. The collective innovates and turns its members into "transformers." The group seeks to spark new momentum and invites a rethinking of artistic practice on the island with regard to questions that have not necessarily been discussed previously: the status of the Guadeloupean contemporary artist, the relationship between the artist, the civic arena, and the economy of culture and art. The manifesto offers a nuanced portrait of the artist on the island. Aware that race is a social construct heavily impacted by the historical, social, economic, and political context in which the individual evolves, Awtis 4 chimen characterizes the individual as "Toucouleur, tout moun" (every color, every person). National identity is established in the presence of ecology as a subject addressed in the works. Thus, we read, "*Awtis 4 chimen* is rooted, anchored in the reality of the country of Guadeloupe and the region of the Caribbean, which is to say that creation is based in the cultural, societal, economic, ethnic, geographic environment." The artists' daily lived experience informs their work. It is incumbent upon them to craft the idiom best suited to the translation of their ideas ("freely offer their thoughts with new codes and references").

To thoroughly emphasize this prerogative, Awtis 4 chimen proposes a revealing, endogenous lexical field. The artist is related to the *gadèdzafè* (seer) and the *maco* (nosy person). Both cases center on the handling of esoteric knowledge. The first term refers to a principle of knowledge inherited from Africa: the Ifa system of divination based on a large corpus of texts and mathematical formulas. It is used in Yoruba communities and the African diaspora, including Guadeloupe. The *babalawo* (or *gadèdzafè* in Guadeloupean Creole) or priest possesses the key to interpreting the code.

With time, artists, as understood by Awtis 4 chimen, have their consciousness awakened. They are not satisfied with reproducing the externally

imposed models ("exoticist [*doudouiste*], folklorist, backward") that make
the artists, their culture, and their works desiderata for the West, perpetually in search of exoticism and eroticism. We can refer here to Edward Said,
who has shown how the West created and orientalized the East for its own
purposes: "The Orient is an integral part of European material civilization
and culture. . . . The Orient was almost a European invention, and had
been since antiquity a place of romance, exotic beings, haunting memories
and landscapes, remarkable experiences" (1995, 1–2). Said characterizes Orientalism as a way of dealing with the East based on its place in Western
European experience. The same is true of exoticism (*doudouisme*) in the
French and francophone context.

The 4 chimen artist rejects this objectifying alienation that renders the
artist a stranger to their own culture and milieu. On the contrary, they are
aware of their place in the universe. This is an example *conscientizacao* as
discussed by Paulo Freire, that act of knowledge, that realization of reality,
that reading of the world (which comes before the reading of the word)
(1984, 36). Thus, armed with this critical awareness of reality, individuals can
write their own (artistic) history. This conscientization births several stances.

Seen in this way, art and artist no longer live in isolation, as the manifesto affirms: "4 chimen is a space of creation, experimentation, encounter,
confrontation." The artist's workspace and methods are radically reconsidered here. The squat affords a proximity that generates ideas. Within the
group and in the new setting, photographers, engravers, sculptors, painters, videographers, and musicians rub shoulders and exchange ideas. Based
in decompartmentalization, these discussions nurture their thinking and,
in time, their creations. The goal is to both move beyond and interrogate
existing frameworks. Nicolas Aubouin pinpoints the question when he
states that "the artistic projects from art squats are born foremost from a
desire to move outside of institutional frameworks and escape from the
formatting that cultural institutions like the theater, the opera, or museums prescribe for aesthetic norms (size of works, monodisciplinarity), the
working conditions for creation and dissemination (length of rehearsals
and performances), interaction with the audience. Indeed, by moving away
from traditional spaces for artistic creation and dissemination, these play-

ers develop projects that break down the boundaries between artists from different disciplines, between artists and the audience, between the audience and the people" (2009, 16).

Interdisciplinarity and collaboration are privileged by such a context. Proximity also impacts the relationship with the audience. The artists live, work, and exhibit their work on site. Inasmuch as studios are more accessible, the people participate to a certain extent in the creative process. Once again, through its process, the squat rethinks art from top to bottom, particularly its functions and professions. Aubouin explains: "The direct relationship between the artists and their audience challenges the role of some art world middlemen, such as gallery owners or art market agents, as well as some intermediaries from cultural institutions (docents, studio organizers, etc.)" (2009, 18). The *Skwat 4 chimen* was formed to be not only a reliable workspace, but also an "effective and dedicated exhibition space for the visual arts"; the act of occupation seems to us to have also laid the groundwork for a "real cultural policy in Guadeloupe."

We would now like to further discuss the place of art in society. By this we mean any process that involves seeking out populations that do not have access to artistic works and do not patronize the spaces devoted thereto. In this context, art is seen as a critical indicator that brings questions to light. What is art's place in society outside of performance or exhibition spaces? How do cultural programming and the places where art is created structure space in order to bring people together and create social harmony or collective inspiration? What essential things does art provide to the people? In other words, how do we evaluate the squat's role in education, exhibition, and dissemination, in conjunction with its social and community functions? We suggest that the *Skwat 4 chimen* experiment must be understood a "new artistic territory." The question raised here concerns art and its ability to recreate social ties and revamp the civic arena.

The Squat as a New Artistic Territory

The activities developed in the newly inhabited space affect creation, the technical production of projects, and the dissemination of works (open studios, exhibitions). These activities are accompanied by various social actions in the forms of youth workshops (through partnerships with schools and other nonprofits) and events held on the premises of the squat. The artists also hope to dismantle the boundaries between artists and audience, studio and exhibition spaces, by opening creative spaces and by fostering ties between artists and spectators, professionals and amateurs.

In his analysis of squats as sites of experimentation and innovation, Nicolas Aubouin identifies four founding principles. We see these implemented by the *Skwat 4 chimen*. For the occupiers, the goal is to create a space open to artists from different disciplines, to foster interdisciplinary artistic collaborations; to develop a culture of proximity through no-cost access to exhibitions and studios; to make the creative process visible through the artists' involvement in receiving the public, or in some cases even involving the public in the creative process. The squatters have criticized the lack of a coherent local cultural policy. The supervisory institutions, the Regional Council and the Cultural Affairs Board, have readily acknowledged the shortcomings.

The artists seek to fill this void, as their manifesto shows: "Guide the public in understanding our process (conference-debates, publishing . . .). Protect creation and preserve heritage"; "Export our works and become known throughout the world!"[14] The squat has become a crossroads, a point of encounter between artists and the general public. This is a new blueprint for the cohabitation of art and the city. The artists charted a new geography of art and culture. Art ended up at the heart of the city rather than to the side, in the periphery. The reconstruction of the city and the management of culture were called into question. The act of occupation contained several messages.

We can see a dynamization of the neighborhood from a socioeconomic point of view. After the end of the school day (5 P.M.), the closing of shops (7 P.M.) and the last run of public transit, the area, like everywhere else on the island, was emptied of its consumer population and transformed into a bedroom community, only coming back to life the following day. The debates, the open studios, and the exhibitions have brought a richer (cultural) nightlife. Residents who did not live in the city center once again had a reason to come back there after business hours, or to linger in the streets late into the evening. The shortage of foodstuffs and staple goods resulting from the lengthy strikes forced Guadeloupeans to return to a conviviality that rampant consumerism had eliminated. Residents engaged in carpooling and bartering, for example. The squat, in its own way, participated in this art of togetherness.

Awtis 4 chimen also called expography[15] into question, and in this particular way aligned completely with the 2009 social movement. We see the photography exhibition entitled "44 Jou, Rétwoskpèktiv" (44 Days, Retrospective) as the closest overlap between the L'Herminier Museum occupation and Liyannaj Kont Pwofitasyon. The exhibit, which lasted from January 29 to February 27, 2010, is in our view the most successful form of the Awtis Kont Pwofitasyon movement. As the title indicates, the exhibition sought to revisit the media coverage of the forty-four days of the strike through the work of eight photographers from the island, one year later. Indeed, the project simultaneously had significant social and professional implications.

The exhibition invited dialogue, or *bokantaj*,[16] between the artists and the people. As such, given its subject matter, it led to controversy. Frantz Succab, a playwright, and Joëlle Ferly, a video and installation artist, each wrote a preface for the "44 Jou" catalog designed by the National Theater, which hosted the exhibition a year later. Ferly's commentary, in particular, allow us to appreciate the complexity of the task Awtis 4 chimen tackled in putting together the exhibition. Some artists, fearing for their careers, didn't want to participate. Others broke with the collective. On this point, Ferly discusses censorship and self-censorship. She mentions the team's difficulty in finding an exhibition space, and institutional representatives' lack of cooperation in making a suitable space available. In her text "Are There Engaged Photographers in Guadeloupe?" Ferly writes:

> For the "44 Jou" exhibition isn't only a "new photo exhibition;" it's above first and foremost the active decision of these authors . . . to share with us the realities of their profession . . . to make us aware that

there are representations, and then there are representations! Now
we must ask ourselves about those imposed by outside authorities
that often simply perpetuate clichés that are ever so harmful to our
people. . . . Why not acknowledge that the A4 association is on its way
to becoming the only alternative art promotion space in Guadeloupe,
without censorship, without interests other than that of transmitting
the true intentions of the artists? 44 Jou would then not just be an exhibition that lets us relive the events of January 2009, but only and above
all, the only way to discover, through its authors, who we really are.
(Galvani 2010)

The last sentence of this quotation is crucial, and all the more so given
that in the foreword, Ferly questions the necessity of having photographers
"sent from France to come represent US: as though our photographs didn't
know how." The exhibition questions art and culture's place in society, particularly as concerns historiography. In becoming expographers, the artists
democratized the museum process and raised questions: Who decides
what should be displayed? Who chooses the place where the works should
be displayed? Who decides how the creations should be installed? Who
chooses the expographic writing? Who says what, and in whose name?

By producing the exhibition in the squat, through its process, the federation translated expographically the LKP social movement, including its
cultural and artistic demands. The authors deployed a full-scale protest, and
it was successful, as they spontaneously squatted the abandoned brownfield. Whereas other protesters marched through the streets chanting
"la Gwadloup sé tan nou" (Guadeloupe belongs to us), they served themselves by squatting, declaring in their own way "L'Herminier sé tan nou"
(L'Herminier belongs to us). They created an archival space in which the
people were able to "revisit" the event through the eyes, not of the foreign
press, but of local photographers. The exhibition helped to show that the
movement, controversial though it may be, deserves to be valued, put on
display. The originality of this approach lies in the fact that its creators did
not wait for the validation of public authorities.

As representatives of civil society, they acted outside the state and established powers. The expography was staunchly participatory. Initially, the viewpoint and vision of the Guadeloupean citizen photographers was emphasized. Subsequently, public participation was solicited through responses to this "local" reading and staging of the conflict. In both cases, the goal was to elicit the expression of a specific memory. We see a parallel between this process and one that took place in the United States in the 1960s, which Jean-Claude Duclos discusses:

> By taking over the museum to recognize one's own history, reclaim one's dignity, and fully exercise one's civic rights, John Kinard and the Black population of a Washington neighborhood gave the museum as an institution, at the start of the 1960s, an identitary, social, and cultural mission that it had not previously held. The National Museum of the American Indian, opened in Washington in 2004, testifies to this same objective. At the entrance, guides—all American citizens of Indian [Native American] origin, offer to escort visitors. Based in the memory of their group of origin (Navajo, Comanche, Sioux . . .), presenting the museum quickly becomes an emotional experience of which the visitors will retain a lasting memory. Described as "communal," these museums show how the museum as an institution allows populations that have experienced segregation, stigmatization, spoliation, or even extermination, to access the right of free expression, separate from mainstream thinking, and to obtain the recognition they lack. (2012, 45–49)

Conclusion

The 2009 social movement against *la vie chère* saw an unprecedented mobilization of the Guadeloupean people. Its strength came precisely from the fact that all segments of society were represented in forty-eight professional, political, cultural, civic, and social organizations. Artists joined with the protesters. Analysts agree on recognizing that this movement was a denial of local political power challenged by a civil society sick of waiting for long-term initiatives appropriate to the context. Murielle Vairac explains: "Social malaise exacerbated by the economic crisis contributed to the discrediting of political authorities while also bringing to light the complex functioning of a society in which the mechanisms inherited from the plantation era still exist" (2010, 3). In our analysis, we have paid particular attention to a process that went unnoticed and thus has not yet been reported in scholarly research: the squatting of the L'Herminier Museum, home of the Chamber of Agriculture, by an artist collective. We maintain that this act of illegally occupying a building belonging to the state, in order to inhabit and collectively use it, participates fully in the movement against *la vie chère* or Liyannaj Kont Pwofitasyon, as it came to be known. We have attempted to show that it can be considered an innovative initiative. To this end, we emphasized three specific characteristics: the squat as a mode of collective action, the squat as an ecological practice, and the squat as a new artistic territory.

We consider the squat as a supplementary tool in the arsenal available to Guadeloupean protesters. The act of occupation displaced the conversation onto the cultural and artistic domain. In short, Awtis 4 chimen highlighted an issue raised in LKP's list of demands, which were also concerned with culture. Occupying a building belonging to the state simultaneously addressed cultural/artistic politics and the culture/art of politics. The legitimacy of those in power was called into question. We refer once again to Vairac, who indicates that "this discrediting of legitimacy was an emerging effect of the economic crisis, which revealed the vulnerability of the authorities. Over the course of movement, the competence of elected officials was weakened, as they had been unable, according to the Collective, to provide responses to their questions and lacked sufficient power to act" (2010, 3).

Thus, confronting the failure of the top-down logic of local politics, the artist collective suggested a bottom-up approach to the glaring problems facing certain populations. First, they saw their actions as participating in the process of conserving cultural heritage. The L'Herminier Museum is considered a building of incalculable worth in terms of natural history, the arts, and the sciences, particularly architecture, construction, and housing in Guadeloupe. Second, the artists tackled head-on the problem of precarity and its effects, including substandard housing, juvenile delinquency, drug use, petty crime, and prostitution. In so doing, as a registered nonprofit, the artists demonstrated that—as experts have suggested—the nonprofit sector is the driving political force in the city (Compper-Durand 2010; Vairac 2010). Third, as the result of a lack of studio and exhibit space, they replaced a poverty squat with an experimental squat, a creative laboratory.

We next showed the highly ecological nature of the occupation of the building. Facing a shortage of artist studios, rather than planning to build new spaces, the artists renovated an existing structure. They thus limited their carbon footprint. Their choice of building proved to be strategic on two levels. First of all, it is located in an area with suitable infrastructure, especially with regard to public transit, the water supply, and the electrical grid. Second, with regard to its construction, the building conforms to sustainability standards for the tropical climate. These include natural light, thorough ventilation, and rainwater management. We have demonstrated the ecological dimension of the squat in terms of how it reinforces the collective's ties to their social milieu and immediate environment. An in-depth analysis of Awtis 4 chimen's manifesto highlighted civic participation by members of the urban conglomeration, whether artists or residents, and their grounding in local socioeconomic and political geographies. This underscored the fact that, for Awtis 4 chimen, the very status of the artist, the relationship between the artist, the civic arena, and the art and cultural economy relate to the celebration of Guadeloupean, or even Caribbean, culture and heritage.

Finally, we demonstrated how the 4 chimen squat functions as a new artistic territory of the type imagined by Fabrice Lextrait and his disciples. Their experimentations impacted every aspect of artistic practice. The boundary between living space and work space was eliminated because the artists lived on site. The partitioning of genres was also called into question. The squat favored interdisciplinarity in the conception of its projects. Photographers, painters, videographers, sculptors, and musicians collaborated on diverse programming. Interactions with the public were less formal, and the public took part in the creative process through debates, workshops, and open studios.

Facing a vacuum left by the public authorities, the artists laid the groundwork for a viable cultural policy that reevaluated the geography of culture and art. The artistic community established itself at the heart of the civic arena rather than in its periphery. The organization of the city and cultural and artistic management were also reconsidered. Ultimately, all professions closely or tangentially related to art and culture were called into question. The exhibition dedicated to the 2009 social movement and entitled "44 Jou, Rétwospèktiv" undoubtedly crystallized this reassessment. By becoming their own expographers, the artists from the collective democratized museum practice, which had previously been compartmentalized, and thus raised relevant questions: Who decides what is displayed? Who chooses the exhibit space? Who decides how the works are installed? Who chooses the expographic writing? Who says what in whose name, and with what intentions?

In producing the exhibit, Awtis 4 chimen established its role as a social mediator and simultaneously became, if not the best mouthpiece for the LKP movement, at least the entity that offered the broadest platform on the island for its dissemination and discussion. In the preface to the exhibition catalog written at the time, Joëlle Ferly asked, "Why not acknowledge that the A4 association is on its way to becoming the only alternative art promotion space in Guadeloupe, without censorship, without interests other than that of transmitting the true intentions of the artists?" She thus confirms the gap that existed in the artistic landscape before the arrival of Awtis 4 chimen. Fabrice Lextrait underscores the innovative aspect of new artistic territories:

> These spaces aim to accommodate debates of social issues, and to provoke human interactions and encounters. It's not a question of mobilizing artists to reduce social divisions, but of inventing what Bernard Lubat calls "the space of the poelitical," a space in which *"les paroles qui*

portent ont remplacé les porte-parole."[17] New visions of the artist, the intellectual, and the citizen are at work in the squats, in society's "interstitial spaces." Since we can no longer drop bombs, we raise questions. The artist is in the scrum, like in rugby. A game of combat requiring solidarity, power, selflessness, finesse, strength, generosity, excessiveness, brutality, an individual game within the collective. (2001, 6)

It must be noted here that, in the case of the Guadeloupean artists, their protest was immediately successful—which is characteristic of the art squat. They did not have to wait for negotiations to achieve their goal. By occupying the building, they instantly satisfied their need for work and exhibition space. The occupation gave them the opportunity to experiment and to propose alternatives to existing problems. In time, they helped to reinvigorate the social life of the area by thinking, and encouraging others to think, about the relationships between the individual and the community.

Additionally, beyond sociopolitical rifts, they recognized the importance of Liyannaj Kont Pwofitasyon and the opportunity to benefit from the larger platform it represented. LKP's unificatory breadth, as a movement in which different segments of the population recognized their mutual commitment to similar goals, does not go unnoticed. Rather than letting civil society organize in disconnected groups and fight independently for differing projects and goals, or in parallel though differing structures and activities, LKP chose a third organizational model. It united various groups around interconnected tasks and structures in order to attain objectives aimed at creating social change. The strength and success of this approach are specifically linked to the fact that LKP was able to integrate its diverse members and offer them a platform for free and collaborative expression. The successful collaboration of a cross section of Guadeloupean civil society organizations was in their view important enough to be made the subject of its own exhibition. The originality of this approach derives from the fact that these initiatives, which grew out of a local context, were the work of citizen artists, while the state and its local representatives played no role whatsoever.

NOTES

1. Mélina Seymour Gradel, "Joel Nankin artiste 'patriote,'" http://vimeo.com/2246648 (accessed April 24, 2017).

2. An event noteworthy for its symbolic value: in 2005, following the closure of the health insurance company MGEN, the organizations Akiyo, Copagua (Guadeloupean Patriots' Collective), Mouvman Nonm, and UGTG returned the premises of the Palais de la Mutualité to the Guadeloupean people. The site was located near the UGTG headquarters, which would become the headquarters of LKP in December of that year.

3. During the annual conference of the Association for Caribbean Studies, held in Guadeloupe in 2012, we interviewed a diverse panel of residents. We also attended two sessions on LKP that led to heated exchanges among panelists, and between speakers and the audience, which confirmed our thesis.

4. Nikki Elisé, "Awtis 4 chimen 3 oeuvres," https://www.artmajeur.com/fr/nikkielise/artworks/galleries/1307608/awtis-4-chimen (accessed April 24, 2017).

5. Translator's note: While the author uses both *squat* and *friche* to describe the *4 chimen* residential art collective, there exists no good English equivalent for *friche* in this context. As such, *squat* is maintained throughout. The reader is advised to consider the ecological implications of *friche* (that is, brownfield or industrial wasteland) that *squat* does not capture.

6. Charles Tilly, James Scott, Nathalie Duclos, Mounia Bennani-Chraïbi, Olivier Fillieule, and Cécile Péchu.

7. Nikki Elisé, "Awtis 4 chimen 3 oeuvres."

8. "La loi du 1er juillet 1901 et la liberté d'association," www.associations.gouv.fr (accessed April 24, 2017).

9. The minister of health, housing, and overseas territories.

10. The bill, submitted to the Assemblée Nationale, was unanimously passed. The Letchimy Law went into effect on June 23, 2011.

11. Union Générale des Travailleurs de Guadeloupe, "20 janvier 2009: Gwadloupéyen doubout kont profitasyon!," http://ugtg.org/article_687.html.

12. In 2009–2010, 30 percent of students entering sixth grade in the Guadeloupean school system did not know how to properly use French; 20 percent had significant reading deficiencies, and 40 percent were limited readers. This generalized academic failure contributed to minors' dropping out of school and to their falling into delinquency, living on the margins of societal rules.

13. These include structural responses, such as situational prevention, urban development, geographic priority zones, and the creation of both a local and an intermunicipal Safety and Delinquency Prevention Council; partnership-based responses, such as the fight against crime, the prevention of recidivism, and victim services; and quasi-public responses.

14. Awtis4chimen, "Préambule," Awtis4chimen.blogspot.com (accessed April 24, 2017).

15. This term, coined by André Desvallées, refers to the group of techniques developed for exhibition production. It differs from museology, which includes museum layout, conservation, restoration, and security, as well as exhibition.

16. Creole translation of the word. It is the more commonly used term in this sociocultural context.

17. Translator's note: This untranslatable word play essentially means that, in this space of the "poelitical," reverberant, artistic language has replaced the vacuous language of the political spokesperson.

REFERENCES

Andres, Lauren. 2006. "Temps de veille de la friche urbaine et diversité des processus d'appropriation: la Belle de Mai (Marseille), et le Flon (Lausanne)." *Géocarrefour* 81, no. 2: 159–166.

Assemblée nationale. 2011. No. 3084 de M. Serge Letchimy député sur la proposition de loi de M. Jean-Marc Ayrault et plusieurs de ses collègues portant dispositions particulières relatives à l'habitat informel et la lutte contre l'habitat indigne dans les départements et régions d'outre-mer (3043).

Aubouin, Nicolas. 2009. "L'art ancré sur les territoires: Les politiques publiques à la renverse." *Pyramides* 18: 13–36.

Bagchi, Alaknanda. 1996. "Conflicting Nationalisms: The Voice of the Subaltern in Mahasweta Devi's Bashai Tudu." *Tulsa Studies in Women's Literature* 15, no. 1: 41–50.

Bébel-Gisler, Dany. 1989. *Le défi culturel guadeloupéen: devenir ce que nous sommes*. Paris: Editions Caribéennes.

Bennani-Chraïbi, Mounia, and Olivier Fillieule. 2002. "Exit, Voice, Loyalty et bien d'autres choses encore." In *Résistances et protestations dans les sociétés musulmanes*, edited by Mounia Bennani-Chraïbi and Olivier Fillieule, 43–126. Paris: Presses de Sciences Po.

Blatrix, Cécile. 2009. "La démocratie participative en représentation." *Sociétés contemporaines* 2, no. 74: 97–119. *Cairn*, doi:10.3917/soco.074.0097.

Bonniol, Jean-Luc. 2004. "La tradition dans tous ses états: Illustration antillaise." *Fabrication des traditions inventions des modernités*, edited by Dejean Dimitrijevic, 149–161. Paris: Edition de la Maison des sciences de l'homme.

Boulogne, Edouard. 2010. "La violence des jeunes en Guadeloupe." *Le Scrutateur*, August 11. lescrutateur.com/article-la-violence-des-jeunes-en-guadeloupe-55225708.html (accessed April 24, 2017).

Césaire, Aimé. 1955. *Discours sur le colonialisme*. Paris: Présence Africaine.

Chamoiseau, Patrick. 2002. *Écrire en pays dominé*. Paris: Editions Gallimard.

Compper-Durand, Gaëlle. 2010. "Les caractéristiques de la délinquance dans les Antilles." *La prévention de la délinquance dans les Antilles et la Guyane: Un réseau d'acteurs entre prévention sociale et prévention situationnelle*. Actes du séminaire, May 27 and 28.

Desse, Michel. 2010. "Guadeloupe, Martinique, LKP crise de 2009, crise économique, déclin économique: de crises en crises: la Guadeloupe et la Martinique." *Études caribéennes* 17, (December). doi:10.4000/etudescaribeennes.4880.

Desse, Michel, and Mario Selise. 2010. "Crise et conflits dans les territoires insulaires de la Caraïbe et de l'Océan Indien (2009–2010)." *Études caribéennes* 17 (December). doi: 10.4000/etudescaribeennes.5013.

Desvallées, André, and François Mairesse. 2011. *Dictionnaire encyclopédique de muséologie*. Paris: Armand Colin.

de Varine, Hugues. 1989. "L'écomusée." *Gazette* 11 (Spring): 29–40.

Duclos, Jean-Claude. 2012. "De la muséographie participative." *L'Observatoire*, no. 40.

Favre, Pierre. 2007. "Les manifestations de rue entre espace privé et espaces publics." In *L'Atelier du populiste*, edited by Pierre Favre, Olivier Fillieule, and Fabien Jobard, 193–213. Paris: La Découverte, 2007.

Freire, Paulo. 1984. *L'importance de lire et le processus de libération*. Buenos Aires: Siglo Veintiuno Editores.

Galvani, Celia. 2010. Le livre 44 Jou Rétwospèktiv. Catalog of photo exhibition, January 29–February 27. https://en.calameo.com/read/003289608b676d976ab12.

Gravari-Barbas, Maria. 2004. "Les friches culturelles: Jeu d'acteurs et inscription spatial d'un anti-équipement culturel." *Métropolisation et grands équipements structurants*, edited by C. Siino, F. Laumière, and F. Leriche, 217–234. Toulouse: Presses Universitaires du Mirail.

Larcher, Syliane. 2009. "Les Antilles françaises ou les vestiges de l'Empire? Les aléas d'une citoyenneté sociale outre-mer." *La Vie des idées*, February 20. http://laviedesidees .fr/Les-Antilles-françaises-ou-les.html.

Lextrait, Fabrice. 2001. "Friches, laboratoires, fabriques, squat, projets pluridisciplinaires . . . Une nouvelle époque de l'action culturelle." Paris: La documentation française. Maisonscreole.net/patrimoine-guadeloupe/musee-de-lherminier.

Monza, Rosan. 2009. "Géopolitique de la crise guadeloupéenne: Crise sociale et/ou postcoloniale?" *Hérodote* 4, no. 135: 170–197. doi: 10.3917/her.135.0170.

Péchu, Cécile. 2010. *Les squats*. Paris: Presses de Sciences Po.

Said, Edward. 1995. *Orientalism: Western Conceptions of the Orient*. New York: Penguin Books.

Scott, C. James. 1985. *Weapons of the Weak: Everyday Forms of Peasant Resistance*. Hartford, CT: Yale University Press.

Tilly, Charles. 1995. "Contentious Repertoires in Great Britain, 1758–1834." In *Repertories and Cycles of Collective Action*, edited by Mark Traugott, 15–42. Durham, NC: Duke University Press.

Vairac, Murielle. 2010. "Les ressorts de l'essor de la société civile en Guadeloupe." *Études caribéennes* 17 (December). doi: 10.4000/etudescaribeennes.5013.

Vivant, Elsa, and Eric Charmes. 2008. "La gentrification et ses pionniers: Le rôle des artistes off en question." *Métropoles* 3. metropoles.revues.rg/1972.

Wresinski, Joseph. 1987. "Grande pauvreté et précarité sociale." Report given to the Conseil économique et social français, February 10–11, 1987. *Journal Officiel*, no. 6 (February 28).

4   # Martinique, or the Greatness and Weakness of Spontaneity

A VIEW OF FEBRUARY 2009

HANÉTHA VÉTÉ-CONGOLO

The form of decolonization chosen by the people of Martinique in 1946 (before India in 1947) did not impose a structure free of colonial modes of conceptualization and operation. The system that was put into place favored social and economic inequalities reminiscent of the former colonial order and springing, to a large extent, from structural mechanisms. The 2009 general strike (Févriyé 2009), which threw together Martinicans of all professional, civilian, social and economic backgrounds for five weeks, unveiled and raised issues encompassing critical political considerations that compel a Fanonian decryption to try to make its productions intelligible, despite the fact that its focus primarily targeted the social constraints and realities experienced by the majority of the population. This strike was far from being a "lutte de libération nationale" in its plainest sense but was nonetheless carried out with the aim of a social transformation that would entail liberation from impeding economic and structural mechanisms.[1] However, the spontaneous effervescence, dynamism, voluntarism, and optimism observed, and the meaningful "paroles" or speech abundantly uttered, mark an amplitude giving the impression that some of the long-standing and articulated concerns could be solved "here and now." Indeed, the space and praxis of the *grève* was a critical production evoking Fanon's proposition on the greatness of spontaneity, the whole stemming directly from intrinsic conceptual and pragmatic Martinican properties anchored in traditional practices. Within the scope of the spontaneity paradigm, it is one of my aims here to point to the manifestation of such traditional Martinican properties during the grève and offer an explication of their critical signification from a Fanonian perspective. Among the productions within the space of the grève was a creation, Télé Otonòm Mawon, arguably among the primary crystalizing achievements of the movement. Shedding light on questions relating to democratic and deontological speech, Télé Otonòm Mawon reflects its foundation in the contemporaneous and the modern, underscoring issues beyond simple mediatic concerns to reach more aesthetic and axiological considerations pertaining to questions of visual representation and self-representation, power and empowerment, and strategies of struggle promising long-lasting transformation. However, the same praxis of the grève and creation accentuate limits and complexities themselves apparent to Fanon's stance on the weakness of spontaneity.

Using Fanon's conceptual framework and drawing on a series of interviews I conducted in Martinique during the summers of 2009, 2010, 2011, 2012, 2015, 2016, and 2017, in relation to Févriyé 2009, I want, first of all, to shed light on those aspects of the production-creation of the grève that are seldom brought to light, even as their importance in understanding certain Martinican modes of thought and action is critical. Second, I want to stress some of the limits and complexities that the said modes may reveal and that intervene in a critical way in initiatives aimed at socioeconomic and political transformation.

Martinique's Audiovisual Landscape: A Structure, an Ideology

A recent survey shows that 89 percent of Martinicans watch TV and that they listen to the radio for about five hours daily.[2] Although people are well equipped with the more newly invented technological devices, television and radios remain their preferred means for keeping themselves informed. The audiovisual landscape comprises Martinique Première (formally RFO), a state and public utility system; Antilles Télévision (ATV), a private television network; and Canal satellite, a subscription television and cable service (Bambridge et al. 2002, 41–46). In 1964, the first TV programs came to Martinique, and with the advent of the left in political power in the 1980s, the Conseil Supérieur d'Audiovisuel (CSA) was created to ensure mediatic deontology and freedom of speech but, even more importantly, the diffusion of French culture and language.[3]

Because of the traces they left in the collective memory during the post-colonial period, up to and including the 1980s when local media, exclusively controlled by France, were essentially based on colonial parameters and censorship, Martinicans have a long history of distrust toward the (official) media which they convey through eloquent epithets. The collective memory regarding the media that still pervades society today has retained the fact that Aimé Césaire was "interdit d'antenne" (was banned from appearing in the media) in the 1970s when France decided to implant ORTF (Office de radiodiffusion-télévision française), an official organ of the state media, in the country. This contributes to sustaining an overt expression of general defiance. For instance, the main local newspaper, *France-Antilles*, is constantly subjected to a *jeu de mot* (play on words) that conveys the people's perception and counter-reaction to what they consider to be a primary tool for misinformation. The newspaper is ironically but revealingly labeled "France-Manti" which means "France-liar." RFO (Radio France Outre Mer),[4] the main national and public network, could also be renamed "FRo" (France Radio Zero). This general spirit of distrust, particularly as it is expressed against the visual media, is also triggered by the fact that television programs seldom broadcast shows and images that draw directly on the Martinican experience; instead shows originating from the national French channels are rebroadcast. The fact of the matter is that, since the inception of television in Martinique in 1964, there has been no audiovisual project thought out carefully enough to align its concept and programs to Martinique's local and regional reality. Further, if, today, efforts have been made regarding the main media that now include in their programming some of Martinique's local particularities, it remains a complex matter to achieve such a goal fully and regionally, for a myriad of linguistic, institutional, structural, technical, and political reasons (Alie-Monthieux 2002, 251–253). This causes the bewildering situation journalist Patrice Louis describes in "Radios périphériques et régions ultra-périphériques" whereby, daily, Martinicans listen to minute details of mainland French daily life, including information about the weather or short area-specific news items (Louis 2002, 247–249). Even though many express indifference to such a state of affairs, one realizes that what drives the renaming of the main media outlets is a level of awareness of the incongruity. This is why it is far from rare to hear popular verbal defiance toward the media, characterizing them as "colonial." In any case, Kanal Martinique Télévision (KMT) and ZoukTV were created in the 2000s and although less powerful than the established national networks, they serve as "télé de proximité" (community television), offering "émissions de proximité," or local programs.

During Févriyé 2009, *France-Antilles* was not officially on grève but many of its journalists were, just as at RFO some journalists were on grève on the first day.[5] Most of them returned to work on February 6, with only a few clearly displaying support for the grève by demonstrating until the end. In any case, the broadcast of the media programs was impeded, and *France-Antilles* and RFO were among the main media covering the grève in addition to national networks dispatched for the occasion.

The Local and National Media: Covering the Grève

In "Conflictualité et conflit social à la Martinique: Paroles d'acteurs," Philippe Auvergnon and Patrick Le Moal report words and phrases they collected from Martinicans conveying verbally their view of the local media. The authors go on to conclude that "because the press has no crusty piece of news to write about . . . it plays a non-negligible role in relationship and social conflicts management" (2000, 13). The factors generating such a general outlook on the press could be witnessed during Févriyé 2009. On February 12, in the local RFO Martinique news section, a K5F (Kolèktif 5 févriyé; February 5 Collective) representative was challenged by a journalist who was insistently questioning the Kolèktif's negotiating methodology, which was, according to him, unnecessarily prolonging the demonstration. Insignificant *form* was apparently a concern to this journalist, and through his tendentious question, "Est-ce que ça peut durer des mois?" (Could this last for months?), he insinuated the Kolèktif's culpability in the escalation of the situation. The representative refuted this insinuation, reaffirming the *fond*—the kernel point and reason—of their claims: "Going on strike is no pleasurable activity. This is not a game, we are not having fun here. Contrariwise, we have a responsibility vis-à-vis the Martinican population to succeed, that is to obtain a significant decrease of the goods' cost, we cannot content ourselves with inappropriate solutions. . . . There are many things to change within the system."[6] In a written communiqué published on their blog, the K5F publicly denounced the damaging treatment they thought the local media were inflicting on them, accusing the latter of irresponsibility and of seeking to provoke a feeling of fear among the people, by systematically using terms such as "chaos," "hysteria," "hunger," and "shortage."[7]

The fact that ATV started a series of shows and interviews on the grève, giving the floor to detractors and inviting the K5F to express themselves only after a few shows in which much damage had been done in terms of the perception of many vis-à-vis the K5F and the grève, reveals a bias that calls for deontological questioning.

On February 13 and from a broader perspective, by showing that the Guadeloupe movement was likely to affect the perception of Martinican "non-grévistes" (those who are not on strike), the "20 heures," the main evening news broadcast of the French public national television channel, France 2, showed members of the Guadeloupean Union CGT asking business owners to close their shops. Comments of the shop owners were emphasized, lamenting that the police claimed to have ministerial instructions to "not do anything." This clearly portrayed the Liyannaj Kont Pwofitasyon (LKP), the union collective on strike in Guadeloupe, in a bad light, which Yves Jégo, the Overseas Department State Secretary, aggravated peremptorily by asserting that "this is a terror climate where pressures are exerted. [Guadeloupe] is a torn society that deals with its conflicts only through violence and where social dialogue relies solely on historical conflicts."[8]

The rendition of the events in the national press was no less prejudicial. On February 6, *Libération*, the leftist French newspaper founded by Jean-Paul Sartre, had already written that the February 5 march in Martinique had taken place "in a carnival ambiance."[9] In an attempt to decrypt the Martinique and Guadeloupe events in the Édito Politique of Radio Europe 1, the journalist reminds the listeners of the general perspective of continental French people, according to whom Martinicans and Guadeloupeans are "these people" who are in simplistic need of "du soleil et d'un peu de carnaval."[10] Apparently, the form of expression for discontent seemed strange to the *Libération* commentator but it is worth underlining the fact that this mode of perception and comprehension of the Martinican form of expression reveals clearly the commentator's estrangement regarding the Martinican *manière d'être* (way of being) and its cultural and societal values. The continuity of perception that joins the way in which the French have apprehended African-descended Martinicans from the period of enslavement to contemporary times is clearly manifest, and indeed the origins of this thought and perception paradigm can be traced back to the aforementioned period. One notes a deep incapacity to go beyond one's framework of precepts to grasp critical referents and meaning that may support and make intelligible a particular reaction or action different from one's own individual *manière d'être*. In his *Histoire générale des Antilles habitée par les Francois*, du Tertre explains how the enslaved Africans embody the fact that God purposely bestowed only limited intelligence on the servile for, contrary to the Jews who would not fail to adopt an attitude compatible with their plight, the Africans paradoxically sing, dance, and divert themselves much more than the enslavers (1667, 526). This relegation to incoherence and irrationality, and the concomitant condemnation of African spontaneity vis-à-vis this particular mode of expression in a context of extreme hardship, resemble that of the 2009 *Libération* journalists who labeled the way the Martinique strikers expressed their discontentment as "carnival," with the most pejorative emphasis placed on the term *carnival*, equating it here to incoherence and anarchy.

Martinicans are aware of the dual aspects of carnival since they resort to terminology to distinguish them, with the apparently superficial dimension being called *bakannal* and a more meaningful and deep one termed *kannaval* (*carnaval*). As the historical Saint-Pierre carnival but also current carnival manifestations show, carnival carries a deeper and significant anthropological, political, and social significance, its space being used to deliver political and aesthetic perspectives as well as critical interpretations of social events often rendered through songs or other artistic performances. It is also the singular annual moment when the masses converge explicitly and actively around shared values and a binding way of articulating the latter. Carnival is a public space of personal and collective expression and production. One of the complexities of carnival is that it offers and invites one to explore infinite possibilities at the same time as it compels one to think, produce, and deliver them within the limits of operative conventions. It is only to the neophyte that carnival appears disordered; its structure is rigidly set, and its codes, which invoke coherence and cohesion, are collectively respected. Carnival is a place where the confluence between the personal and the collective, the private and the public, is best expressed and captured and, in its intimate relation with creativity and creation as well as its capacity to gather masses together, carnival also informs on a critical manner of expression for deep collective values. It is therefore meaningful that this particular form of articulation and rendition of thought and views, which can support personal and collective creative production and critical ideological and political stances, was performed and used as a procedure during the strike. An intrinsic aspect of the Martinique carnival that singularizes it is that it is not a "spectacle," in that it is not meant to be watched although there can be spectators. It is meant to be lived, as any person watching the carnival can join in the "vidé" (collective carnival procession) in situ and impromptu, even those who are not members of any particular carnival band, thus becoming a contributor to the mass's creative expression. Here, the popular characteristic of carnival—that is, the fact that it concerns the people and is made by and with the people—is given full meaning. But carnival is also, together with the "fêtes patronales," the sole collective space and time during which what I will call here "restitution" takes place; that is, it is the time of the year when the entire country can witness the creative results of the cultural and civic work done all year long by grassroots and cultural, educative and social integration associations. These facts provide significant and pertinent meaning to the spontaneous form of the reaction and action of the "peuple" on strike. However, this complex position, practice, and signification of carnival was ignored by the French commentators, and carnival, and syllogistically the people's manner of expression, were considered solely from their surface appearance and portrayed by the national press in an elliptical and pejorative way that exclusively connotes festive frivolity and appalling incoherence.

To the journalists' condescending relegation, the "grévistes" correctively and witheringly answered, singing, "désann an lari-a sé pa an kannaval"[11] (being in the streets fighting for justice is no carnival), thus challenging the reductive approach to their movement and carnival itself on the one hand and, on the other, setting forth the notion of seriousness, sacrifice, and efforts their action entailed, notions that augmented its ethical validity. Here, the strikers showed that they owned fully the multifaceted dimensions of carnival and that they were able to assess the dimension to use to qualify their method of expressing dissatisfaction. It is important to note that the "grève générale" compelled the cancellation of the carnival ordinarily scheduled at this time of the year; no prioritizing of a general desire to make merry was manifested.[12] In any case, this connoted use of the term *carnival* by the national press in this context of massive, serious, and consensual local protest and demands for more socioeconomic justice, strikingly articulates the dismissal of the *manière d'être* of Martinicans and the complexity and form of the Martinican response to their socioeconomic and political situation. For, indeed, music and songs played a meaningful role during the strike and they were eloquently performed according to the traditional *bèlè* codes and rhythm with denunciating and galvanizing lyrics such as "Matinik lévé" (stand up Martinique), "tjè-nou blendé" (our heart is made of iron[13]; or we are courageous, we will resist till the end), "Matinik sé péyi nou sé li ki ta nou"[14] (Martinique belongs to us, she is our country), or "wouj pou la viktwa, sé pou la viktwa nou ka alé"[15] (red for victory, we will win).

The Aesthetic of Struggle

The least that one can say is that the media's gaze at and representation of the strike and the strikers is at critical variance with the motivated choices made by the latter to represent their own views on the strike and their claims. This reliance on traditional mores was generally spontaneous but also largely impelled and sustained intentionally by the numerous cultural associations determined to support the strike sensibly through their competences. They certainly procured the political discourse held by the majority an aesthetic destined to reinforce and manifest clearly and visually its intended axiology. The question of "showing" eloquently, or projecting and mirroring in a concrete and univocal way, one that everyone could identify and recognize as authentic, the ambitions and political positioning appears as an important factor to consider. Some of the Martinicans' most significant culturo-political emblems were consequently used to such an extent that they constituted an "esthétique de lutte" (aesthetic of struggle) also standing as a sort of "méthode de lutte" or fighting method. The fighting method itself consisted in drawing upon deep, intrinsic, collectively acknowledged, and unifying cultural Martinican referents. Therefore, traditional dances were equally meaningful and were performed: *bèlè*[16] but also *ladja* and *danmyé*, the fight dances[17] that appropriately rendered the general sentiment and discourse. The metaphysical and political scope of the drum and fight dancing is to be seen in the fact that, springing from the enslaved Africans' cultures, which were performed on the plantation, these dances and drumming provoked fear among colonial authorities, who banned their practice. During the grève, therefore, the choice of this form of expression did not gesture toward any festive intemperance but suggested an intent to magnify the aspiration for socioeconomic transformation. These songs and dances were performed during the march but also on the outside steps of the Maison des syndicats, the gathering place where the crowd waited for the results of the negotiations between the Kolèktif, the authorities, and the "patronat." The songs and dances were also performed outside of the Préfecture where the negotiations took place.

A recurring perspective on the part of my informants underlined the fact that, to them, the playing of the drum during this wait was not only a necessity, a strategy, but also a powerful bearer of significant meaning, just like the traditional chants and dances: "Le tambour parlait là sur eux. On était déterminé." (The drum was speaking upon them I tell you. We were determined.) Another, founder of a cultural association in the town of Lamentin affirms how, to him, the drum was a means of communication with the Kolèktif to which it gave the requisite strength to negotiate radically because, while inside with the authorities, they could understand that the crowd outside was still highly mobilized. He stresses that their intention was to "help" with "koutmen," an important operating paradigm regulating the interactions and mental disposition within the grève: "On donnait un koutmen aux gars. On leur faisait savoir comme ça, avec le tambour, qu'ils ne devaient pas mollir. On est là." (With the drum, we let them know that they should be unswerving negotiators. We were with them.) It is to be mentioned that, revealingly, this same interviewee went on to expatiate on the fact that, while the negotiations had led to an agreement to reduce the cost of goods per category, the agri-food business corporation unexpectedly recanted and sought to negotiate reductions on goods per item. To sum up the situation, he exclaimed: "Se mésyé sé de kotjen, yo té lé fè nou manjé kaka" (These sharks are tricksters. They wanted to lead us astray). This ill-intentioned disposition of the adverse party made the presence and use of the drum even more compelling, according to him. If the drum could stimulate and indicate the crowd's unfailing commitment to the Kolèktif and in turn ensure the latter's vigorous constancy, the drum could also convey to the other party the seriousness of the consensual resolution of the population: "Sans ça, ces messieurs auraient cru qu'on faisait la fête. Il fallait qu'on leur fasse savoir qu'on était là." (Without the drum, these sharks would have thought we were joking. We needed to let them know that we were serious.) Another interviewee additionally explains that the negotiations were so long, lasting until the evening, when many of the strikers returned home, that there needed to be a strong message articulating their vigilance to the authorities: "We needed to let these sharks know that, maybe there were many less of us but the drum was there. We needed to support our people. They were inside fighting for us. These power people are crooks. They exaggerate. They have a long tradition of abuse against us. Under circumstances like this one, if you do not remain vigilant and do not find a way to show them that you are determined, they do not respect you. We have the drum."[18]

Unapologetically symbolic in nature, the concrete presence and playing of the drum exerted an intentional impact that aspired to sustain this action aimed at determining more equitable and constructive social values for the majority. The chants, dances, and drumming contributed to confirming, strengthening, and even to helping materialize the ethic of the action. This form of expression was, so to speak, setting the record straight. It is apparent, therefore, that the crowd had elaborated its ways and forms of communication in intimate and informed relation to the axiological substance it was promoting.

This form of communication chosen to express a specific discourse eloquently supported the political foundation underlying the strikers' action. However, mediatic communication itself was still a point of concern, as one of the leaders of the Kolèktif affirmed when addressing the crowd: "In the fight, the information issue is fundamental. It is true that we communicate with the radio and TV stations but they broadcast whatever they feel like. So we must circulate the information to you ourselves."[19] A guest of the first show of Télé Otonòm Mawon, leader of an anti-capitalist and nationalist political party, Conseil national des comités populaires (CNCP), explicitly accused RFO of lying and misinforming the public about the K5F's work.[20] That is why, at Télé Otonòm Mawon, one of the Kolèktif's leaders was systematically assigned the task of reporting the strike-related facts directly to the crowd gathered at La Maison des syndicats and the Préfecture. Needless to say, the established media perspective on the grève and the K5F bore the traits of moral violence.

Télé Otonòm Mawon, or the Greatness of Spontaneity

Fanon insists that spontaneity attains a greatness in its ability to mediate achievements. It is here that his expression, "technique de lutte," can be drawn upon to specify the "méthode de lutte" paradigm as the following involves a technical approach regarding the way to respond to the realities of the phenomena being displayed during the strike. Days after the latter started, a group of journalists, audiovisual professionals, technicians, and other members of the civilian society, all of them "grévistes," met at the Téyat Otonòm Mawon, a cultural center in Fort-de-France, to discuss the events. Many members of the audiovisual professional group gathered there castigated the tendentious coverage they felt the local and national media were proffering of the strike. They deplored the possible negative effect this journalistic coverage could provoke among some of the viewers not on strike and unable to directly witness the reality exposed in the streets. Nevertheless, the group, whose members supported the grève, felt that while the local and national media were offering a distorted image of the facts of the strike and failing to capture and inform precisely on the productive and meaningful vitality unfolding, the Kolèktif itself was overwhelmed by the unprecedented response of the people. The Kolèktif too failed to capture the scope and intricacies of the expressive popular dynamic and utilized an ineffective communication strategy. In fact, one of the most notable aspects of the strike is based on the fact that eloquent and multilayered words and discourses, which I call "parole," were widely held by the people. This "parole" was so broadly articulated that it constituted a true phenomenon within the grève. It captured the people's profound, most preoccupying malaise and grievances as well as their ideological perspective, one that escaped the simple realm of material considerations. Several journalists whom I interviewed and who contributed to Télé Otonòm Mawon manifested the frustration they felt with the K5F's strategies and even castigated what some termed their inability to "get it" and acknowledge the complexity of the situation. One of them declared: "These guys [the K5F] were way off beam. They really were shortsighted. They were missing the point. We were in the streets. We were hearing what people were saying, we discussed with them. They were talking about many important things but the K5F was pathetic."[21] The problem being raised, therefore, concerned information content, dissemination, and scope as much as journalistic ideology and deontology. Seen in this way, it becomes evident that the axiological issues posed here constituted the principal subject of these journalists' awareness.

This is when Jocelyn Vautor, a private TV producer and "petit patron," suggested that they create their own TV apparatus to counter these identified biases and gaps. Again, "showing," as a way to project what is authentic, appears to be a strong motivation grounding such action. For Vautor, "it was important to show everyone what was happening in the streets and let everyone know what the people were talking about. People talked a lot about many things and the rest of the country did not know it. At the same time, it was important to know what the rest of the country thought of the strike, of everything."[22] Vautor was nonetheless dumbfounded when the next day, his professional colleagues, all from the various public and private media outlets of the country, supplied their own personal material with a determination to create the TV outlet. With a more impactful form of communication commensurate with the substance sustaining the legitimacy of the grève, Télé Otonòm Mawon—TOM—was then physically created the next day. This is so much so that one can also claim that, while the Guadeloupe "grève générale" concomitantly taking place gave rise to the unescapable visibility of one individual, Élie Domota, a charismatic leader who will probably find permanent valorization in the historical memory, the Martinique grève, which benefited from no such individual leadership, gave way to Télé Otonòm Mawon, a collective action that is similarly worthy of memorable imprint. This said, one should not fail to underline the fact that while the Guadeloupe strikers were led by a charismatic leader, the outcome of their collective action for social justice did not differ from that of Martinique. Through this enterprise led by these journalists and their displayed state of mind arises the question of power, for indeed, their reaction answers the question: What power do we have and how can it serve the community and its cause?

What this group actually demonstrated was a display of power yoking together the question of means—material, technical, structural, conceptual, and intellectual—and that of ownership for, indeed, through their creative action, they changed the course and impact of information diffusion and treatment and offered the people an anchorage point to rally around apart from the Maison des syndicats, the K5F, and the mainstream media. Télé Otonòm Mawon became, after the K5F, which benefited from the adhesion of the strikers, the undeniable second force of the grève. In Fanon's terminology, such a group in a colonial society corresponds to the bourgeois proletariat, and they formulate power through action and through supporting the "peuple" with their "intellectual and technical capital" (Fanon 2002, 147). It is undeniable that, through their action-creation, these audiovisual professionals and amateurs appear as actors and leaders of a revolution in the audiovisual and media sphere, one that is critical in mass movement with a social justice agenda and drawing upon a democratic ideology. This exercise of power through action presents them as leading a "politic of responsible people, of leaders inserted in history embracing, with their muscles and brain, the leadership of the fight for liberation" (Fanon 2002, 141).[23]

Let us consider here the notion of *koutmen* for what it teaches us about some of the values supporting this group of journalists' action and about the strikers' comportment that also reinforces the question of (self-)power, one's awareness of it, and its application and signification. It is true that strikers blocked the port of Fort-de-France, the entrance gate for basic goods in a Martinique that relies heavily on imports. Strikers also affected the capacity of supermarkets to remain open. This created a shortage of basic goods that impaired Martinicans' day-to-day activities and placed them in a situation where autarkic gestures gained a larger-than-life significance. Resorting to old and dormant ways of inducing a level of self-reliance, ingenious creativity and genuine production became imperial.

Koutmen then appeared as the prime reasonable and effective response permitting immediate and reliable sustenance. From the French *coup de main*, which means "help," the Creole *koutmen*, while aimed at the material level in that its application implies a concrete context, carries an epistemological and philosophical resonance that points to one of the core principles shared by the majority. Koutmen is a practice of mutual and systematic assistance that was formerly highly enforced. It is subtended by critical modes of thought and is supported by the founding principles of solidarity and perspective on both the individual and the collective levels whereby their interdependency and trans-categorical rapport are vital and inescapable constituents. The moral outlook on the individual and the community brings about a praxis and behavior that consist in voluntarily and altruistically contributing one's skills, thoughts, time, and energy to the advancement of a person or a cause. The primary motive of koutmen is benevolent, in the sense that its application serves to remedy a shortfall, but the motive is also creation-production, since koutmen aims at bringing into positive existence an element that is necessary to a person's or the community's well-being but that does not yet exist. The pervasive observance of this principle and praxis was not simply the result of dire socioeconomic position the people of Martinique were plunged into up to the 1970s. This observance also relied on a deep philosophical position entailing the notions of "merit" and of "rights," as koutmen was, more often than not, propelled by the conviction that not only did its beneficiary deserve the latter but that the product or creation spawning from koutmen also constituted an inalienable right. Koutmen was predominantly exercised in areas of human life generally regarded as basic or primary, hence its intimate relation with the very notion of dignity. In this way, the construction of a house usually relied on koutmen in the same way as the cultivation of ground provisions and the capacity to lodge and feed oneself and one's family did, thereby guaranteeing one's dignity. Koutmen also requires a developed sense of responsibility as, through it, community members declare, individually and collectively, their ability to take charge of their own fate when facing the authorities' deficiency.

Koutmen epitomizes the application of moral and practical support at once at the same time as it points to an ethic of life. It is also a practice that unveils an approach regarding the individual and the collective, two coordinates that koutmen shows to be mutually inclusive and worthwhile. Individuals know their worth and place in the collective, to which they can give shape, significance, and meaning. Given its focus on concrete production and creation—in that, after koutmen that which did not exist materially now exists in the life of the beneficiary and participates to the beneficiary's uplift, material and moral—one can understand its exalted standing as a social force. But for the same reasons koutmen is also a tool for empowerment. The heavy consumerism paradigm by which the people of Martinique have been determined, and that gave the impression that the contribution of one's neighbor to one's development is derisory and unnecessary, has had a severe impact on the fluid practice of koutmen. The aspect of koutmen that places the individual at the center of social actions and social gain seems to have been granted precedence over that which sees the collective as fundamental thanks to the common work of individuals. During the grève, however, the buried axiology carried by this practice resurfaced, and Martinicans applied it in a way that testifies to its complex epistemological meaning. Manifestations of koutmen took multiple forms, which enhanced the new wave of ambient optimism and the feeling that the country was in a new mode. An interviewee articulated it this way: "Yes, it was different! I had never experienced this in Martinique in this way. We used to do this but before. We were together, we shared everything. People helped one another."[24] It is to be expected that it became a general resource in this time of crisis, amid demands for social balance and justice, as well as the specific koutmen relied upon by the Télé Otonòm Mawon's actors.

When asked, Vautor recognizes that "TOM is the fruit of koutmen." However, although he deplores the K5F's poor handling of communication, he denies that his original idea of creating TOM was expressly in order to support the Kolèktif: "No, I never meant to help the K5F directly. We did this for the people."[25] Nevertheless, many of the TOM crew members I interviewed affirmed that the goal of TOM was to "donner un kout-men au K5F" (give a hand to the K5F). This contradiction already indicates a level of complexity and even of ambiguity that is understandably appended to movements that arise out of urgency and spontaneity. One cannot account with certainty for the exact number of members in the TOM crew since an overflow of spontaneous contributions was proposed by many of those in the media sphere, as was pointed out by Vautor who officiated as the editor in chief.[26] Some members worked permanently from beginning to end, while others came intermittently to reinforce the crew. Interestingly, some RFO journalists who were not "en grève" but reported to work daily also came by TOM at the end of their work day to consolidate aspects of the set, technically and materially. TOM was certainly ephemeral, but it was no low-technology or stealth endeavor. It is indeed striking to capture the seriousness and arresting professional standards with which the *télé* (television station), circumstantially based and short-lived as it was, was structured and executed. Structurally, TOM was organized according to the conventions of the profession, with an editorial board, a newsroom, photo and investigative journalists, camera operators, presenters, a makeup artist, and a main coordinator. Koutmen was as extensive as it was expansive and emerged from the very heart of the strike, so much so that one can assert that TOM was truly the people's télé. Indeed, first, its set was organized and decorated by the Moun lakilti (artists) group while the demonstrators themselves procured financial contributions to feed the crew members and make the T-shirt uniforms and banners meant to identify TOM. Several established small businesses also contributed banners and T-shirts even though the businesses refrained from making this information public lest they antagonize their influential clients who opposed the grève. The emphasis that the TOM members I interviewed placed on the crowd's generosity toward and adhesion to the télé is striking: "People donated a lot. Without that, we could not have created TOM. It was amazing."[27] Secondly, the director of the private Kanal Martinique Télévision (KMT) offered a time slot of his communication channel, which allowed the technical and legal functioning of TOM to take place. To raise awareness about

TOM's broadcast, the crew members themselves held a sign as the march passed by their location. Thus, TOM could come on air with a first broadcast on February 16 and a final one on March 14, 2009. It is difficult to measure the audience that TOM benefited from since no survey was conducted. However, its popular impact was formidable, and for the duration of the grève it became an incontestable countrywide communication factor.

TOM was hosted in the Téyat Otonòm Mawon, located in Fort-de-France, hence its eponymic appellation.[28] Téyat Otonòm Mawon was created in 2005 to replace the Petit Théâtre de la Croix Mission, a branch of the state-subsidized Centre Dramatique Régional—CDR—that had been closed by the Regional Council and whose original goal had been to produce popular theater. Significantly, Téyat Otonòm Mawon's motto is inspired by a phrase commonly attributed to Dr. Pierre Aliker—Aimé Césaire's most faithful political companion—"La chance de la Martinique, c'est le travail des Martiniquais."[29] It is managed by Joël Reschid,[30] a theater producer who, influenced by Martinican writer Vincent Placoly, believes in "la révolution permanente" (permanent revolution), the "théâtre d'intervention sociale" (social theater) and a "théâtre d'interrogation historique" (a theater that poses a critical outlook on history) that tackles iconoclastic subject matter challenging established ideas, the imposed supremacy of the formalized Western aesthetic and theatrical modes. According to Reschid, his paramount dramaturgic intention is to affirm intrinsic Caribbean particularities and to meaningfully relate to the Martinican society so as to foster coherent social and cultural development. This is the reason why in their theatrical productions, Téyat Otonòm Mawon strongly relies on Caribbean orality and the techniques of the traditional Martinican conteur to develop an iconoclastic sense of aesthetics that appeals to the public. Reschid stresses that, not being financially subsidized, although the town authorities graciously lend the space and defray the cost of electricity and water, Téyat Otonòm Mawon was built on "autonomie et beaucoup de solidarité" (autonomy and a lot of koutmen). Unfunded therefore, Téyat Otonòm Mawon is supported by koutmen and, in 2005, was refurbished by its members, who also periodically donate financial or material aid or provide needed technical assistance. In its aspiration to create a popular theater, without formal restrictions or social hierarchy and to offer both an alternative and opportunity to explore and practice new and other ways, the Téyat makes its space and its human and material resources available to any member of the Martinican society with a manageable dramaturgy. This state of affairs, in addition to Reschid's and his team's political outlook on theater, led them to rename the space in accordance with its current nomenclature that bears both a descriptive and qualitative component. While indeed "Otonòm," which means "se débrouiller par soi-même" (to manage by one's own means) evokes freedom, the word also refers to self-reliance and largely insinuates that the creations produced through the Téyat result from genuine and ingenious craft as much as tenacity and laborious efforts. "Mawon" translates their ideological stance alluding to emancipatory defiance and disputing restrictive norms in that it conveys, "pas de théâtre béni oui-oui" (no yes-massa theater) that critically reproduces imposed and inappropriate European dramaturgic values.[31] Of course, "mawon" echoes the historical response of enslaved Africans faced with the anti-human living conditions of the plantation, a response through which they succeeded in leaving the oppressive site to erect the *mornes*, with new and jarring paradigms. Derived from this historical fact, the term *mawon* has come to be associated with an ideological and political posture, "marronnage," which figures engaging the opposition and the circumvention and over-coming of obstacles, especially those jeopardizing human integrity. Its use generally conveys a strong political claim. With its political objective and highly symbolic name, Téyat Otonòm Mawon was appropriately indicated to serve as a host for Télé Otonòm Mawon. Given the particularities of the latter television station, one cannot fail to decipher a marronnage dimension onto the people's action in that they authoritatively circumvent the official and established system of communication to erect a new one whose intention is to proffer increased ethical and liberating principles and mechanisms.

Indeed, a priori, one cannot bypass the marronnage dimensions of Télé Otonòm Mawon and the impression of a deeply concerted and thought-out political perspective governing the materialization of the action-creation. The very *raison d'être* and primordial principles of TOM were born of several convictions, by means of which one can ascertain that the response was, at least to a certain extent, supported by a political position. The first is that the socioeconomic fight was just. The second conviction was that the broadcasting media were biased and, consequently, producers of injustice. TOM was thus also impelled by a professional conscience, a will to safeguard an ethic whose foundation was understood as a possible support for new social values and different ways of treating and disseminating information and facts. This perspective is to be highly prized in the predominantly technological age of social upheavals, false and ephemeral news, and a fast and less deep treatment and reception of information. To the professional conscience that guided its occurrence can also be added the implications of a moral conscience aimed at benefiting a just cause whose promoters were enduring despicable moral violence. TOM also shed light on some of the ideological attributes shared by its founders. Addressing the population and to posit the legitimacy and political distinction of TOM vis-à-vis the established media in the very first aired shows, Vautor asserts that, in Martinique, "we all know the media are not free"—hence the responsibility of the TOM journalists to place their competences at the service of the popular movement that concerns the emancipation of all.[32] This daring statement is of capital importance as it relates to crucial aspects of the people's life, freedom of speech, and the deontology, democratic nature, and trustworthiness of official communication apparatuses. What Vautor expresses here is a general concern ("we all know") internal to and about the media circle, which amplifies the experience of general malaise urging the people to demonstrate in the street. Vautor's statement implies that the creation of TOM is not simply a consequence of the phenomenon emerging from the grève, but that it also reveals a broader and deeper societal and political question concerning the Martinican media and society more generally. The grève therefore offers the opportunity to address it, making TOM, in this context, a tool established for the people but "against" the mainstream and restricting establishment—hence the dissident character one can perceive with regard to TOM. Through his statement, then, Vautor elaborates a discourse on the relation of the individual and the group to mechanisms defining their fate, which, in turn, mediate their power, responsibility, and freedom to engage in a praxis capable of evading the confining paradigm and redefining not only their relation to that paradigm but, in addition, their individual or collective fate.

As a counterproposition to the established media, therefore, TOM embraces a corrective, oppositional, and circumventive perspective. Interestingly, the color red became the identifying mark of the strike once its participants donned a red T-shirt, one that symbolized CGTM, the most popular and toughest union. This is the reason why the phrase used to refer to TOM was "Red Action," projecting TOM as embodying an ethics through which its founders assumed their individual (their subgroup's) part and expressed their commitment to and solidarity with the meaningful collective moment facing the larger group and the power relations that drive and enable inequalities. In a country where "assistanat" (the practice of state handouts) is denounced and Martinicans are portrayed as relinquishing their responsibilities in favor of the authorities from whom state handouts are expected, the groups displayed a reasonable sense of resourceful responsibility and independence. In these types of actions the political character of their position can be seen. Together with the strike itself, this localized *prise de position* on the part of Red Action suggests that its initiators took to heart Césaire's self-injunction to not remain "en l'attitude stérile du spectateur" (1983, 22; in the sterile position of the spectator). As a matter of fact, Césaire was called upon, as a witness and inspiring father whose pride his children were soliciting. Protestors held signs on which could be read, "Césaire, regarde ton peuple" (Césaire, look at your people) as if to suggest that his exhortation was, at long last, implemented and could elicit pride. The mere evocation of Césaire points to the political substratum guiding some of the thoughts held and discourses proffered, and embodies the will to demonstrate the power and the authentic nature of the personality that contest impressions of inertia and unconsciousness.

The third conviction suggesting that, in spite of everything, TOM was also propelled by a political outlook, was their thinking that the people's "parole" held a paramount significance not grasped by the K5F or the authorities and that as a result, it was an entity that needed to be shored up. Here, by seeking to create an awareness of this critical category, another aspect of the reparative justice established as a principal goal by TOM is revealed. Vautor, as well as the other TOM members who were interviewed, largely expounded on their objective to "give the floor to the people, let people speak, show the events" (donner la parole aux gens, laisser les gens parler, montrer) and to "let the country be aware of what was happening" (faire le pays savoir ce qui se passait), thus underlining the goal of communication in its simplest form. Here can be seen the intention of empowering people through giving them the possibility of not only speaking but also seeing their action reflected back to them and to those not in the march. The initiative that, when known, understood, and mobilized, could exercise influence by empowering people is revealed as enabling possible transformation in and for the future. It is through this ideological stance—deviating as it does from the directives and direction set by powerful agents within the strike—that we can locate one of the principal "mawon" dimensions of TOM.

TOM was created as the result of a committed stance shared by all of those initiating it. Indeed, the audiovisual professionals supported the strike and its founding principles and committed to put forth fundamental aspects of the events they believed were unjustly ignored or distorted by the established media. This paradigm is inscribed in a principle of autonomy from the established media, the politicians, and the K5F, a position reiterated by the presenter during the second broadcast of TOM. The freedom of expression, operation, and orientation advocated by TOM points to that aspect of its characteristics that underlines its "otonòm" identity: "TOM belongs to all Martinicans. It bears no mediatic allegiance. It is a television created by presenters, journalists, technical staffs of all of the media in the country. It is your television."[33] One of its objectives was to ensure the visibility of the truth through the visibility of the people.

Although Vautor maintains that TOM was never meant to serve the Kolèktif communication system, a seat was specifically reserved for a K5F representative who was present during each show to inform the people. Similarly, during the second show, the presenter holds that "TOM, c'est BOM," "Blog otonòm mawon,"[34] thus univocally equating the télé to the K5F and "BOM, blog du Collectif février 2009"[35] that was created specifically to facilitate the public relations of the "intersyndicale." Additionally, as already underlined, on the TOM set signs could be seen labeled "Red Action," a symbol of the grève and of the K5F itself. Nathalie Jos, an RFO journalist working for TOM, also asserts that "TOM was a communication vector for the movement. The media were not reporting on what we saw in the streets. . . . Our relations with the K5F were cordial and we were converging with them . . . at first, we wanted the K5F to be heard."[36] Whether TOM was or was not at the service of the K5F per se, the fact of the matter is that Vautor strictly tied its life duration to that of the grève as he announced this important factor on the first broadcast: "What is Télévision Otonòm Mawon? It is a télé to inform people so that the people of Martinique know what is currently happening in the country. . . . This télé starts today and will end the same day the strike ends."[37] In his ontological definition of TOM, a statement about the purpose of the télé and its close attachment to the grève, Vautor clearly enunciates a position that reminisces of "la lutte" through civic action and a clear militancy bordering on the social and political claims of the Kolèktif. Nathalie Jos also emphasizes that, at first, TOM's intention was to broadcast information from the K5F. However, very soon, they realized the deontological risks of such a stance and so extended the floor to all protagonists including the *Békés*, the Prefect, and the "patronnat" (employers) so as to anchor their contribution in journalism and not propaganda.[38] This is the reason that, when declaring TOM's identity on the first broadcast, Vautor makes a key point by signaling that TOM is not propaganda television and that both the télé and its journalists are free of established ideologies. Here, of course, we should note the capacity for professional and deontological distance but also for corrective and constructive self-introspection. It remains true that TOM was driven by conviction and was largely heard as the voice of the K5F that prevailed among the majority. During the second show, therefore, the first sequence featured guests such as a K5F representative, a representative of the LKP who had come from Guadeloupe,[39] a politician, and a representative of the kolèktif of lawyers who had volunteered to accompany the K5F to the negotiations with the authorities. TOM's otonòm identity is reflected in the will to propose an ideological alternative and in the capacity of its members to proffer a nuanced and balanced approach to information treatment and dissemination despite its apparent ideological convictions. An additional aim was to allow the people not on strike to obtain accurate information leading to an informed understanding of the situation, which leads to the fourth objective of contradicting an established mediatic practice seen as pernicious.

TOM's productive if iconoclastic method as well as its assured sense of adaptation and innovation are well known. Its foundational structure may have aligned on the universal and fixed conventions of the profession but its operating principles evinced a perspective contradicting some of the constraining aspects of the said conventions thereby illuminating TOM's otonòm character on four levels. The first is the absence of formal and administrative constraints in the perspective and format of the shows proposed. This transpired through the democratic, equitable, and free speech granted to all sides including the public that constantly interjected and interacted with the guests. In fact, in contradistinction to ordinary visual broadcasts, the local people and their intrinsic concerns were at the center of all of the shows, hence giving credible meaning to the notion of "télé de proximité." TOM aimed at being a tool at the exclusive service of "informing," "showing" and "speaking," a principle Vautor makes explicit in the first broadcast: "This is all about bringing an exceptional answer to an exceptional event. We created this télé with all of our brothers and sisters who volunteered to help. This is not a propaganda télé. This is a télé to inform the Martinican population of what is happening in the country, so that the people can be informed of what is going on. . . . The télé will end on the day the strike ends. Everyone will have the floor to speak, the politicians, the unions, the planters, people . . . everyone. We all know why we are in the streets we all know that our society is ill."[40] Guests were invited due to their expertise or their embodying a level of authority and power in a particular domain. Therefore, their "parole" could be construed as authoritative. Yet, they were systematically interrupted, challenged, or corrected by members of the public whose practical experience of the subject matters discussed also produced a perspective presenting itself as very authoritative. The members of the audience then underscored the dichotomy between the theoretical approach of the experts and their lived experience of the subject matter that granted them plain credibility in their statements. Through the flow of speech and the exchanges it permitted between the parties, the shows exposed the dichotomy between the governed and the governing, unveiling the conscience of the former built on direct empiricism and the unawareness of the latter owing to their abstract approach to situations others live concretely. Through their authoritative interventions during the show's discussions and during which they proved to be the educators of those standing as the embodiment of authority, the people reframed established authority and authenticated their own legitimacy. This reversal of authority and of the power dynamic through which the truth is reestablished or the "records are set straight" by those most qualified and experienced is what makes of the audience's "parole" an instrument for possible transformation.

Vautor underlined how important it was for people to feel that, in such an unprecedented moment of protest, they were free to speak their minds with neither tacit pressure, orientation, nor preset directive from the media. He makes a point to stress that, given the trends in the streets whereby "la parole fusait. Il se passait tellement de choses, c'était tellement important et on ne voyait rien à la télé" ("la parole" streamed forth, and so many important things were happening but we saw none of that on TV) and the lack of acknowledgement by the "système," TOM aimed at two targets. It was an outlet created for the people at home to be deontologically informed, to see and understand the movements in the streets, on the one hand, and for the "parole" of those in the streets to be heard, on the other. In other words, some of TOM's principles simply concerned, respectively, "truth" and "facts," acknowledgement, validation, and civic action. TOM was a sort of "caisse centrale de résonnance de la parole" (central soundboard for what people say). Indeed, the instruction given to the journalists was: "Donnez de l'information sans la détourner. Donnez la parole aux gens. Laissez les gens parler."[41] (Inform people without altering the information. Give the floor to people. Let the people speak.) Speaking, freedom, and democratic dissemination of speech were indeed particularities denoting the ethical core of TOM. It can be said that TOM gave voice to the street in that it showed how critical was the notion of discourse and pervasive the discourses themselves. It also showed how the "parole" in the streets corroborated that held in many households whose members were not necessarily demonstrating—hence its prolongation or extension. It expanded the communication and interconnection among the people on strike in the streets as much as it created a multifaceted bridge between them and those at home. When asked what she thought of TOM's reports, a seventy-five-year-old woman from the town of Gros-Morne, who said that she was too old to march but also did not have any means of transportation to Fort-de-France, exclaimed: "I agreed with all they were saying. Do you think that the government likes us? The béké and the French practice the same exploitation."[42] And so it can be said that, even though there were discordant voices against the "grève," TOM contributed to uncovering the extent and the homogeneity of thoughts concerning the K5F's "revendications" and other cultural and political preoccupations. The action consequently remained focused on materiality as the intent was also to demonstrate that "what was happening in the country" manifested *deep meaning*. On the one hand, those at home were directly briefed on many intricate details and could watch the unfolding of the events pertaining to the strike. On the other hand, TOM brought the voices of the nonstrikers at home into the discussion by sending reporters to the "communes" to interview people of different generations and social backgrounds. Besides, certain sections of the population who seldom appeared on TV or were typically portrayed in an unflattering light as social outcasts were offered the possibility of taking part in the kind of popular debate from which they were generally excluded, thereby projecting their vision of the country and of their situation onto the future. In this way, TOM proffered "la désexclusion." Many of these social outcasts could demonstrate an incisive critical analysis of global, regional, and local worlds, their stake within them contributing to their understanding of their personal plight and to their contestation of the common perception held of them.[43] Consequently, TOM was instrumental in making it clear that, regardless of any personal circumstances, a common analytical approach and general understanding of the common situation endured by the majority in fact existed.

If this substantive content of the people's thoughts was expounded and largely broadcast "comme c'est," that is, "as is," and the philosophical modus operandi promoted was "laissez parler les gens" (let the people speak), it is worth considering the third property that crystallizes TOM's form and otonòm trait. It is found in the internal dynamic and methodological perspective on the practice of journalism. The traditional journalistic practice compartmentalizes skills, establishes unilateral categories and expertise, and operates within rigid visual and time formats. For example, any particular program must be developed within a set length of time, which is usually very limited. Although TOM replicated the conventional structure of most TV networks, it broke away from this traditional practice. Indeed, tasks were distributed according to needs and not according to technical and hierarchical specialization: "Everybody did everything. It was out of the question for someone to tell me, 'I do news coverage not photos.' We all were versatile. The photographers could do news coverage and vice versa. Many topics were covered by cameramen. And it was all good. They did a great job."[44] The format of the shows was also unconventional with regard to length and visual rendition, since subjects were not necessarily strictly timed to the conventional minute and thirty seconds and viewers could view "as is" the interactions and movements on the set exactly as they were developing. In the television world, this is not shown to the viewers as it is thought to manifest a lack of professionalism and seriousness and is seen as crediting disorder while being aesthetically unappealing. At TOM, this nonetheless gave the shows a humane and inviting tonality since they appeared as "spectacles vivants" (live performances) that projected the idea of authenticity and credibility, with people acting meaningfully instead of being mere viewers. This unconventionality also projected a sense of authenticity and transparency jarring with the opacity and distortion of information the local media were accused of perpetrating. Subjects were shown in the way they had been filmed and not as illustrations of the journalists' personalized comments. For Vautor, these clips of people's "paroles," thoughts, impressions and analysis of their personal situation as well as the broader one, were authoritatively powerful since "le sujet, il parle tout seul" (the subject matter is explicit). Vautor assures us that this method ensured that the information was given with no distortion inasmuch as it helped his team not waste time. Journalists were invited on the shows later on to report, describe, and discuss what they had seen and heard in the streets. At first, some protested this unconventional way of "faire du journalism" (doing journalism), being reluctant to adhere to the principle of versatility and defy some of the set codes of their profession. Nevertheless, consensus regarding this method was ultimately achieved, and they adapted and committed to the innovation in the face of the quality of the work accomplished. Many learned new skills and could impressively execute their tasks. This different way of "faire du journalisme" also stimulated and transformed some established journalists who, having escaped censorship, could speak much more candidly. "Why are you not like that all the time? Why don't you do this in this way all the time?" were the questions members of the public as well as the crew addressed to Nathalie Jos, who distinguished herself incisively during the shows. To these questions, she answered in one of the shows: "Ici, je suis libre" (Here, I am free). This echoes Vautor's statement on the first broadcast of TOM and frames it as credible. In the third show, one can hear Jos remind the public of the censorship in journalism and the limited power journalists have in the decision-making process about the topics being broadcast and the manner in which they are broadcast.[45] This is why Jos's conclusive perspective on their work within TOM is rather appreciative: "We achieved something spectacular. We have been able to show what the other media did not show. We produced a more just vision of what was happening. There was a true emancipation of 'parole' this has been a kind of pressure releasing outlet. . . . Many of us discovered new skills. . . . We truly accomplished something."[46]

Finally, it is important to highlight the fourth "otonòm" characteristic of TOM embodied in the creative technique chosen to ensure the public's attention and its connection to the shows; TOM also resorted to a visual aesthetic that conveyed its ideology and demonstrated what was at stake. The set decor featured symbols germane with "la lutte" and could be seen in the "kòn lanbi" (conch shell), an object embodying music as well as being a symbol of resistance and protest. It could also be visualized through placards with denunciatory phrases featuring expressive words such as "solidarité" "lyannaj," "Lavi artis rèd,"[47] or "Code noir." The most striking backdrop displays a roadblock made of unappealing road symbols compactly piled up together that jar with the bright and distinct references that reminisce on art as if to signify that all that is on the other side of the barricade will be kept at bay lest it tarnish the creative and significant meaning of the plastic order. But TOM also employed a less material aesthetic principle that is as symbolic as it is political. According to Joël Reschid, the "stratégie du conteur" (storyteller's strategy) and especially the phase consisting in entertaining the audience with "Timtim" (riddles) to arouse but also to assess and ensure their interest, was deliberately used to stimulate the said audience. The members of the latter were encouraged to speak to one another and to express their thoughts openly. When the TOM crew sensed they were ready and "la parole était la plus fructueuse, la plus convaincante" (what they were saying was the most fruitful and convincing),[48] they started cameras and the show. In light of that practice, one can recognize the focused intention of proposing a striking "parole porteuse de sens" (meaningful "parole") thus outlining their social and political motivation and quest for authenticity and credibility.

The Weakness of Spontaneity

Despite the a priori impressions, however, one realizes a fortiori that, although the télé is a fitting response to a clearly identified vacuum and its intention is to selflessly serve and to propose more balance and justice, which in its turn introduces an axiological perspective, its establishment corresponds to a "concours de circonstances," or combination of factors: the unveiling of immediate and pressing needs that, in their turn, give rise to a fitting but spontaneous reaction. The density of the grève was a social galvanizing force that grew out of intuition and enthusiasm and also led to the emergence of Télé Otonòm Mawon. Nathalie Jos recounts her state of mind: "Euphoria was at its peak. La parole was freely expressed. There was an incredible turbulence, an effervescence and a sort of emulation. So, when Jocelyn told me that he was creating this TV to give the floor to people and asked whether I wanted to join them, I did not even think. I was intimately convinced that we needed our TV. The media were not going to do this."[49]

Given that achievements impelled by spontaneity can be short-lived, Fanon has also considered the reverse side of this equation by also reminding us that "voluntarist impetuosity" is sustained with a "doctrine of instantanism" (2002, 129), a contradiction that could be found in a change in the "technique de combat," or struggle strategy, grounding long-term projections and planning. Ultimately, achievement and true progress associated with knowledge require a proper and necessary transition based on the authenticity and depth of one's awareness (Fanon 2002, 133). If it is true that the Guadeloupe movement benefited from a charismatic leader, one whose presence still did not prevent an outcome different from that of Martinique, it is nevertheless true that Févriyé 2009 was characterized by many serious limits of leadership. The first one could be seen in the K5F refusing to acknowledge that the people's "paroles" did not convey solely material concerns but were also, to a large extent, complementarily and genuinely political, manifesting unsettled but preoccupying issues borne by many. These "paroles" actually corroborated many K5F claims such as the demand for the Creole language to be taught at all grade levels or for preference to be given to Martinicans in job offers since a growing trend indicated that continental French people were hired more and more often while the local unemployment rate remained alarmingly high. More and more continental French schoolteachers were transferred to the Martinique "académie" while Martinicans were stuck in France or simply obtained no appointment, which caused a raft of social and family disruptions. Although these items were included in the K5F platform of claims, its strong political nature was neutralized.

I have shown how critical the collective TOM production team was in taking charge of this popular "parole," thus revealing their civilian power and bringing values, creativity, and productivity to the surface. Through this act of reparation, TOM became the best "porte-parole" (spokesperson) for the people's "paroles" that it worked to legitimize. At the same time, while on the one hand it univocally embodied possibilities and methods for future development as well as Téyat Otonòm Mawon's motto, "La chance de la Martinique est le travail des Martiniquais" (What is going to make Martinique great is the labor of Martinicans), on the other hand, it activated Césaire's injunction. This is why, globally, the prime achievement of the Martinique general strike of 2009 can be seen in the effective creation of this "télé de proximité" whose role, along with its supportive ethics, testified to what Martinicans can produce in the domain of developing an efficient collectivity. This is of paramount importance from both a concrete and an abstract perspective, converging through a social, economic, political, cultural, and moral prism. Nevertheless, it is important to underline the fact that this same collective effort helps capture some of the ambiguities that, perhaps, characterize Martinique most effectively. As forceful as it may have been, TOM was not construed to endure beyond the short term. Scheduled to end on the same day as the social movement, it nevertheless continued to broadcast past March 14. The members deemed it useful to show the multiple reporting they possessed featuring grassroots Martinique and wished to offer a more lasting and effective mediatic tool enlarging the media landscape and offering alternatives to the people.

However, interpersonal discord and internal issues concerning the direction the télé was to adopt provoked an irreparable scission. We should not forget that TOM was made up of independent professionals and members of the established media, the latter being a body "against" which Vautor unambiguously positioned himself ("we all know the media is not free"). Even though Vautor announced clearly that the existence and context of operation of TOM were the delimited space of the grève, which here does not suggest that the action had been thought out on a larger scale and in the context of the global development of the country, one notes that, at its core, the direction of Vautor's ideology may not have been so much for the people and for a redefinition of the relation with the media but rather against the mainstream media. This, of course, limits severely the possibilities and scope of the enterprise. And so, if it is true that the Red Action was governed by a voluntarist political stance concerning the treatment and diffusion of information, it remains that one must question the depth and firmness of these political convictions and ethics. One can already discern an arresting symptom in the appellation Télé Otonòm Mawon, as its critically powerful meaning creates a priori the impression of a clearly thought-out revolutionary name bestowed by an active, conscious, and established political ideology. The readiness and apposite nature of the name, and the fact that the group of audiovisual professionals was meeting in Téyat Otonòm Mawon to debrief after they had marched, also conveniently compelled the revolutionary name of the télé. This in turn compels a Fanonian analysis of revolutionary leaders in a colonial context. The question as regards Martinique is not whether there is a conscience and awareness of the mechanisms and ideologies impeding personal and collective emancipation. Nor is it whether means and power are owned by those who might aspire to radical change. During the strike, the people's profuse "parole" about ethno-structures; political status; the relationship with France; neocolonialism; and social, economic, and racial inequalities—in a word, their intrinsic reality—pointed to the existence of such a conscience and awareness. The question rather concerns the texture, the firmness, the depth, and reliability of this awareness that allows for a projection beyond the immediacy of experience. It is to be said though that, in the context of Martinique, in contrast to West and North Africa, which Fanon uses as examples and which are differently construed from Martinique, the "faiblesse idéologique" (the ideological weakness) concerns the *lumpen-proletariat* as much as the bourgeoisie. Any observer of Martinican society would have thought that, given the unprecedented and galvanized energy at work, the slogans and especially the unprecedentedly massive and force-ful reaction of the people, even the creation of TOM that subsumed this fertile and political energy, unmistakably signaled a thrust signifying a determination to solve many of the issues raised. But it is Fanon who points out to us that given the euphoria and "voluntarist impetuosity," because of the multiple difficulties and the instinct of survival, since their action was born out of a "doctrine of instantaneism," "the group [who] literally behaves as if the fate of the country could be determined here and now"[50] (2002, 129) is destined for self-negation. When, as a leader, Vautor affirmed that, "we all know" that the local media "are not free," he posited an ines-capable and grave issue crucially related to freedom of expression and democracy. The end of the TOM enterprise signals a return to the status quo and (dominance of the) very structure and apparatus that were being virulently denounced, hence the appearance of a compromise of principles and persistent, unsettled axiological questions. The patent display of force that itself articulates a discourse on power and empowerment, individual and collective freedom and responsibility, now compels the key question of the individual and the leading bourgeois group vis-à-vis this power, respon-siveness, and freedom. What are they doing with the power they demon-strated they had and knew how to use for effective personal and collective transformation?

It is, in this light, interesting to pay attention to the general outcome and aftermaths of the grève. All voices tend to concur, concluding that the Martinique general strike that took place in 2009 was a failure. Since the end of the grève générale, *France-Antilles* has made it a point to publish every three months a study comparing prices in Martinique and France. The May 2017 comparison indicates that, for basic goods, prices in Martinique are 28 percent higher than in France.[51] Much like many of the interviewees, Reschid asserts that the grève was a failure because, to him, "on s'est fait avoir" (we have been conned). He laments that "les syndicalistes ont une organisation anti-patron et non une volonté d'organiser les ouvriers pour leur bien-être" (the unions work against the employers and not for the well-being of workers).

When, in 2015, I asked them about their conclusive analysis of the grève, many of my interviewees strikingly but revealingly answered: "Ça n'a servi a rien" (It was useless). Referring to the agro-industrial powers, some asserted that "We can do nothing against these people" or "What can we do against this system!" When I asked her whether she would contribute to a strike again, a hairdresser from Saint-Joseph who marched in Fort-de-France during the first days of the strike but was later on impeded by the lack of transportation to the capital city told me: "We demonstrated in the streets for 38 days. All of this, for nothing."[52] Others answered: "Janmen pa!" (Never again!) or "We did all of this for nothing. The situation is unchanged."[53] An informant astonishingly echoed Fanon's stress on the realism that takes over the ardent illusion for change (2002 129) when she emphasized the "sacrifices" made to no avail: "Les enfants ne sont pas allés en classe pendant un mois! J'ai tout laissé tombé pour faire la grève. Men lé pli gwo toujou pli gwo! Pwofitasyon pa fini!" (Our kids did not go to school for a month! I dropped everything to partake in the strike! But the privileged are still enjoying their privileges! Exploitation is intact!) A general impression expressed is that "nou ka tounen an ron ron ron" (we are turning around and around), an illustration of the lived reality articulated in a Guadeloupean song that one of my informants sang. The frustration, resignation, and disillusion persisting among the people were plainly expressed when they failed to respond to a call for a general strike against "la vie chère" on October 26, 2010, from both the Guadeloupean LKP and the Martinique K5F. The latter had already called for a mobilization on October 3, 2009, because the "salary increase was not effective, the BCba goods are rarely found in supermarkets . . . and six months after [Févriyé 2009] the price for gas is starting to rise again,"[54] but the call was only partly successful.

The people's spontaneity, arising from their expectation of the immediate reabsorption of the socioeconomic disparity, was therefore challenged by the "Réalisme le plus quotidien" (routine realism) and "la leçon des faits" (Fanon 2002, 129; teaching from the facts) that distanced them from any (future and massive) militant action. Such a discouragement may seem disquieting because, since the abolition of enslavement, no collective movement of this magnitude for questions pertaining to the people's social and economic well-being had been experienced. This first attempt in the twenty-first century did last, within the Martinican context, for a substantial time, but nevertheless is far from equivalent to either the 2004–2005 Ukrainian Orange Revolution or the 2010–2012 Arab Spring. Here a key principle of Fanon's thought resonates, whereby any fight not responding to the crucial condition of organization and strong leadership results merely in "carnaval et flonflons" (carnival and oompahs) and "movement perpétuel" (perpetual movements), with the term *carnaval* here plainly signifying *bakannal*. Indeed, the outcome of the grève is apparent in the Fanonian warning regarding the adversary's strategy that proposes: "a minimum of readaptation, some reforms at the top of the ladder, a flag and at the very bottom, the divisive mass, still in its "medieval" character, that continues its perpetual movement" (2002, 141).[55] It is interesting to note how, although referring to the béké cast (the descendants of the enslavers) in an article published in March 2009, journalists of *Le Monde* covering the grève in Martinique and Guadeloupe could sum up the general circular pattern of the "vèglé"[56] phenomenon that typifies the way authorities deal with Martinican and Guadeloupean grievances: "Since the beginning of colonization, the owner families of the Antilles have known many revolts of the enslaved, many peasant revolts, strikes of factory workers and the blockade of commercial zones. Each time, they have let the cyclones quieten down, negotiated or summoned the 'moun bleus,' the law enforcement officers. There have been many deaths and salary raises. Then, everything went back to their order. Theirs of course."[57]

The manifest lassitude of the people is certainly based on the complex intersection of many factors. This precludes neither the acknowledgment of their historically proven resilience nor the questioning of their understanding of the fight for a core transformation of the means of their dignified existence, an understanding that does not take into account Fanon's warning about the methodologies of the colonized, the ambivalence of their leadership, and the subterfuges of the adversary. The emphasis the interviewees place on the length of the movement (thirty-eight days) and the extent of the efforts ("tout ça") made to maintain it enlighten us as to the strikers' perception, according to which their sacrifices were articulated in terms of longitude and latitude, which determines their expectation for true change. This view jars with Fanon's perspective holding that "neither the courageous tenacity nor the beauty of slogans suffice" (2002, 131) to attain radical change. If therefore, in the case of Martinique, the existence of awareness is not in question, it is also true that the issue of the firming up and consolidation of both the lumpen and bourgeois proletariat alike does exist. As shown by the facts of the grève, in the fragmented K5F leadership as well as the disconcerted reaction of the politicians and the discontinuation of the power-empowerment and responsibility-freedom exercise via TOM, one can see how, contrary to Fanon's advocacy, "management" is not in a position to propose an enlightened organization capable of bringing the "peuple" to a quick and lasting transformation (Fanon 2002, 141).

Considering the "Action Psychologique"

The people's discouragement and resignation are so pronounced that they have been sustained by an "action psychologique" (Fanon 2002, 131), comprising propaganda against the grève led by the media immediately after its conclusion; this contributed to the creation, among the people, of a feeling of guilt, resentment, lassitude, and bitterness. This also left little space for a distanced analysis bringing to the fore the critical meaning of the collective enterprise. The tactic of the business world proved its seriousness and efficiency in its chosen moment to launch its offensive—that is, after the strike, at a time when the guarantee of audibility was ensured. One notes a crude displacement of the paradigm of concern from the popular claim for social decency to one that concentrates purely on economic performance, interest, and gain. Perhaps the general bitterness of the business-men's group toward the grève is best symbolized by the written words of Guillaume de Reynald, a businessman and the only béké who was a UMP municipal counselor from 2014 to 2015, who labeled the "grévistes" via their leaders as "diggers of Martinique, extremists, independentists, racists and assassins."[58] De Reynald amalgamates the people's action for social justice to a claim for independence that in turn, he equates to an act of terrorism.

On May 31, 2010, in a published text, Cyril Comte, the president of the MEDEF (Mouvement des enterprises de France), the "patronat" union, directly accused the K5F of having seriously endangered the economic fabric and "dialogue social," or social dialogue, of Martinique that they had been building in tandem with the unions since the memorable 1999 Toyota strike, one that had opposed employees of a car dealership and provoked much turmoil (Auvergnon 2004). Comte's strategy to incriminate the K5F relies on an explicit pejorative discourse and the use of a chosen lexical field encompassing words and phrases such as "incongruous and ambiguous creation of the Collectif du 5 février," "failure of the social dialogue," "death-like," and "deviance." Comte makes a point in sparing the "Martiniquais" (Martinicans) of any reproach since he suggests they were "de bonne foi" (of good faith). He therefore portrays the K5F as a manipulative force that misled the people: "We have seen that the February 2009 crisis led to more adverse results than those Martinicans had imagined in all good faith, weakening the small business ecosystem and especially those that had just been created."[59] At this point, one has to stress the fact that, just as the K5F did not receive the more profound popular "paroles" carrying the people's concerns, the post-strike offensive of the "patronats" reveals that their objective is not to address the people's perspective and claims but rather to oppose the "syndicats," which raises questions about leadership and power vis-à-vis the people in times of struggle.

The leaders of the economic sector took the floor after Févriyé 2009 and, in this context, conferences and talks reporting formal studies led by experts were organized, setting the tone for an impression of seriousness, rigor, structure, and objectivity contrary to the spontaneity of the people's massive participation in the strike. In 2012 and 2015, the Martinique CCI (Chambre de commerce et d'industrie) organized talks to take stock of the economic situation after the strike. Although Manuel Baudouin, president of the CCI, concluded the 2015 talk, "La Martinique est-elle sortie de la crise de 2009?,"[60] in a way that suggested that perhaps the Martinique "machine économique" had not been proved to have made the best strategic and pertinent economic and business decisions to circumvent the economic aftermath of the grève, and that they might need to be less timid and transgress certain established paradigms to arrive at the growth for which they have a real potential, he nevertheless affirmed that the "inquiétudes" (concerns) expressed in the preceding 2012 talk were well founded. The economist Olivier Sudrie, who also ultimately insists on the rebounding capacity of the Martinique economic fabric, starts his analysis using terms and phrases such as "panne de croissance" (growth stall), "inquiétant" (worrisome), and "la résilience économique est faible" (the economic resilience is weak), and finally infers: "The situation is rather dismal. . . . Since 2009, the performance of the Martinique economy is the lowest of all of the Overseas Departments."[61] The tension between the optimistic conclusion and the "constat sombre" (dismal report) does not lessen the lasting pessimism enforcing a negative image of Févriyé 2009, all the more so since one also realizes that the economic world appears as the ultimate redress of a vast disorder caused by irresponsible thoughtlessness. This gives a dimension to the sense of responsibility and consciousness that encompasses long-term anticipation and projection and that certainly jars with what was expressed, say, through TOM action. Similarly, as a means of indicating the impact of the strike on the economy, the deployment of financial reports, graphs, and figures also stands in contrast with "paroles," the mode through which the strikers articulated the disastrous effects of socioeconomic disequilibrium onto their reality.

It is worth underlining that, just as the paroles of the béké were heard at the very beginning of the strike with Alain Huygues Despointes, an agro-industry businessman, claiming that enslavement bore positive aspects and racial admixture was an unharmonious abomination he deemed regrettable,[62] Béké speech was also largely articulated after the grève. In an interview given in early March 2009 to the French radio network BFM, Jean-Louis de Lucy de Fossarieu,[63] a béké businessman, affirms that the group of businessmen he traveled with from Martinique and Guadeloupe to France, did so expressly to "explain to the French public, political and media interlocutors [they] are going to meet with, that, what happened in the Antilles is not a social crisis. It is purely a political movement with one clear objective, the independence of the islands [and that] these movements were led by a handful of State civil servants . . . who have but one sole goal, . . . independence, at all costs including violence."[64]

De Lucy too uses a terminology reminiscent of death. Like Cyril Comte, he patronizes the "people," denying their will and capacity for perception and implying a childish innocence about them that made it easy for the K5F to exert its predatory nature against them: "When you tell people that you are going to obtain substantial salary raises of 200 to 300 euros . . . and lower prices on a series of goods, it is of course normal that they believe you. . . . Progressively people realized that they were being manipulated and now . . . we are going to count the dead regarding the number of businesses that collapsed and people who will not be unemployed. . . . I will fight because if the islands become independent, we are all dead."[65]

It is clear that, on the one hand, de Lucy expresses a fear also found among enslavers during the enslavement period, while, on the other hand, his going to France to discuss the case of the Antilles testifies to his belief that, in the context of potential independence and as the owner of Martinique, France's decision was the only admissible one. The fear of independence expressed by this Béké's voice is contradicted by Raphaël Confiant's point of view, according to which the February 2009 crisis in Martinique was one that marked a desire for more assimilation, since what it claimed was equal social treatment with the French from continental France. Indeed, in his "Attaquer les Békés . . . en paroles," Confiant labels the grève as the "grève assimilationiste de février 2009."[66] And indeed, Confiant expresses his disagreement with the Békés, accusing them of having been unable to be true Caribbean Creoles leading Martinique to independence, as did other white American Creoles like George Washington, Simon Bolivar, José Martí, and Pedro II of Brazil. Besides, the interpretation by the management class of the social claims that they view as a mask for a hidden statutory political agenda carried out by politicians and the unions also crudely conflicts with the politicians' inertia and their plight of being overwhelmed during the grève. In any case, the anti-Févriyé 2009 propaganda of the "gros patronat," targeting the K5F and focusing on economic regression, did prove to leave an imprint in people's minds, as evinced by the interviews I carried out in Martinique from 2015 to 2017. Many of the informants I interviewed in the period of 2009–2012 thought, when I interviewed them again in 2015–2017, that, the grève was responsible for the deterioration of the economic texture of Martinique. While many continued to support the motivations and actions of 2009, they never failed to end by pointing out to me that "ça a fait beaucoup de dégats. Il y a eu tellement d'entreprises qui ont fermé" (but [the grève] caused much damage. So many businesses closed down). Even a quick search on the Internet leads to information likely to generate the reader's skepticism about the movement. Initial information erroneously assures that the outcome was satisfying to the strikers while another sets forth the image of a strike that impeded in a prolonged way the vital agencies of the country: "For a month, the strike paralyzed all sectors, private and public, namely gas stations, small and large businesses, hotels and tourism related industries, schools and public transportation."[67]

Finally, it goes without saying that, in the development of Martinican social history, Févriyé 2009 will remain memorable for the formidable hope it generated in the majority and the way the phenomena it triggered allowed one to elicit certain particularities constitutive of the Martinican *manière d'être*. However, contradictorily, the axiological point of view allows us to identify questionable and unsettled limitations to the said action. This illuminates a complexity that cautions against taking lightly, or taking for granted, any sociopolitical phenomenon emanating from the Martinican context. It appears that as a leading force formed of groups with sundry political and ideological foundations, the K5F was not able to bypass implicit political divergences to present a firm front offering a holistic approach to the people's demands. Similarly, TOM became a leading force but was ultimately unable to reconcile the disparate stances of its members and transcend the limitations of the initial short-term project to lead to a longer-termed agenda aiming at lasting transformation in Martinique's audiovisual sphere. It is the third set of leaders made up of the "management" that actually demonstrates not only ideological and political coherence but, more particularly, a firm resolve to maintain the socioeconomic status quo.

NOTES

1. See the "principaux axes de la plateforme revendicative du collectif du 5 février 2009 contre la vie chère et pour l'emploi" (the K5F's claims against the high cost of living and for employment), which encompass claims beyond the material such as the adaptation of schoolbooks to the reality of the Martinican culture and history, the creation of a conservatory for traditional art, the generalization of the Creole language teaching, the validation of diplomas from other Caribbean countries, the right to live and work in Martinique, the right to give preference to Martinicans in hiring processes: http://www.cgt-martinique.fr/iso_album/plate_forme_revendicative_v4_(1).pdf.

2. Jade Toussay, "Radio et télévision sont les média préférés des Ultramarins," *Mediaphore.com*, April 18, 2016, https://www.mediaphore.com/2016/04/radio-et-television-sont -les-medias-preferes-des-ultramarins/.

3. *CSA, Conseil Supérieur de l'Audiovisuel, République française*, http://www.csa.fr/Le -CSA/Presentation-du-Conseil.

4. In 2010, "RFO" was renamed "Martinique première."

5. Actually, many of the RFO journalists participated in the strike on February 5 to such an extent that the "journal télévisé" was affected. The reporting of the grève was done "tout en images" (only with images) because of the lack of journalists: see Peggy Pinel-Fereol, "Grève du 5 février 2009 . . . On s'en souvient!," *Martinique 1*, February 5, 207, http://la1ere.francetvinfo.fr/martinique/greve-du-5-fevrier-2009-on-s-souvient-440451 .html.

6. "Extrait Journal RFO Martinique," February 13, 2009, https://www.youtube.com /watch?v=EaW40Haboto. "Faire la grève ce n'est pas un Plaisir, ce n'est pas un jeu, on s'amuse pas là, par contre nous avons une grande responsabilité face à la population martiniquaise c'est de réussir ce mouvement, c'est-à-dire d'obtenir une baisse significative du cout de la vie on ne peut pas se contenter de saupoudrage, . . . il y a des choses à changer dans le système lui-même." All translations from French and Creole to English are my own unless otherwise stated.

7. "Communiqué de presse du 16/02/2009, à 07H00: Information importante," *Blog Otonom Mawon du Collectif 5 Février 2009*, February 16, 2009, http://collectif5fevrier .blogspot.com/2009_02_16_archive.html.

8. "20 heures: [émission du 13 février 2009]," July 23, 2012, https://www.youtube.com /watch?v=F-PJNesCfc8. "C'est un climat de terreur, climat de pression . . . c'est une

société déchirée qui ne règle ses conflits que par la violence où le dialogue social est un dialogue qui repose sur des conflits historiques."

9. *Libération*, " La Martinique bloquée à son tour," February 6, 2009, http://www .liberation.fr/societe/2009/02/06/la-martinique-bloquee-a-son-tour_308188: "Hier, les transports étaient complètement à l'arrêt dans l'île, et les rideaux de fer de la plupart des commerces de Fort-de-France baissés pendant le défilé, qui s'est déroulé dans une ambiance de carnaval et sans aucun incident." (Yesterday, there was no transportation on the island and most shops were closed in Fort-de-France during the strike that took place in a carnival-like ambiance without any incident.)

10. *Blog Otonom Mawon du Collectif 5 fevrier 2009*, http://collectif5fevrier.blogspot.com /2009/03/entendu-sur-europe1.html#comment-form.

11. Jo Manicou, "TOM émission 01 partie 03," February 18, 2009, https://vimeo.com /3266816.

12. "Carnaval annulé en Martinique," *Le Figaro*, February 20, 2009, http://www .lefigaro.fr/flash-actu/2009/02/20/01011-20090220FILWWW00479-carnaval-annule-en -martinique.php.

13. "Grève Générale en MARTINIQUE 'Tchè Nou Blendé,' TAMBOU BO KAN-NAL," March 15, 2009, https://www.youtube.com/watch?v=YsTzF8N6-E0.

14. "Grève générale Martinique, Lundi 09 Février 2009 047," February 13, 2009, https://www.youtube.com/watch?v=vM7lB9d0tr0.

15. "WOUJ POU LA VIKTWA," March 16, 2009, https://www.youtube.com/watch?v =IRQvFIZIN7A.

16. Jo Manicou, "TOM émission 03," February 19, 2009, https://vimeo.com/3289112.

17. "Ladja 5 février 2009," August 29, 2009, https://www.youtube.com/watch?v=TNyIqi Y6TZk.

18. "On avait besoin de faire à ces messieurs comprendre que les gens n'étaient peut-être plus là mais le tambour était là. On devait donner aux gars du courage. Ils se battaient à l'intérieur pour nous. Ces messieurs sont filous. Yo ka fouté bon fè. Yo za las fè nou manjé kaka. Dans des cas comme ça, si tu n'es pas véyatif et tu trouves pas un moyen pour leur faire savoir que tu es là, ils se foutent de toi. Nous, on a le tambour."

19. "Grève Générale 2009: Martinique, ils ont gagné aussi!," March 15, 2009, https:// www.youtube.com/watch?v=-oLVEjiAksg.

20. Jo Manicou, "TOM emission 01 partie 01," February 17, 2009, https://vimeo.com /3261300.

21. "Ces gars-là étaient à côté de la plaque. Ils étaient vraiment obtus. Ils ne comprenaient rien du tout. Nous, on était dans toutes les rues. On entendait les gens, on discutait avec eux. Ils disaient beaucoup de choses mais le K5F c'était des pieds."

22. "Il fallait montrer ce qui se passait dans les rues, faire entendre ce que disaient les gens. Les gens parlaient beaucoup, de beaucoup de choses et le reste du pays ne le savait pas. En même temps, il fallait savoir ce que le reste du pays pensait de la grève, de tout."

23. "Politique de responsables, de dirigeants insérés dans l'histoire qui assument avec leurs muscles et avec leurs cerveaux la direction de la lutte de libération."

24. "Oui, c'était différent! Moi, j'avais jamais vécu ça en Martinique comme ça. On faisait ça avant. On était ensemble, on partageait tout. On s'occupait les uns des autres. Il y avait beaucoup de coups de main."

25. "Non, je n'ai jamais fait ça pour aider le K5F. C'était les gens" (Jocelyn Vautor).

26. "Je ne peux pas dire combien de gars il y avait dans la TOM. Les gars sont venus. Tous ceux qui avaient un équipement sont venus avec. Les gars étaient là et ça n'arrêtait pas."

27. "Les gens ont donné. Sans ça, on n'aurait pas pu. C'était incroyable." Interview conducted on July 6, 2016, Fort-de-France.

28. Jo Manicou, "TOM emission 01 partie 03," February 18, 2009, https://vimeo.com /3266816.

29. "Only the work of Martinicans can develop and emancipate Martinique."

30. All of the quotations from Reschid are from an interview he gave me on July 20, 2015, at the Théâtre Otonòm Mawon, Fort-de-France.

31. "No yes-massah theater."

32. Jo Manicou, "TOM émission 01partie 03."

33. Jo Manicou, "TOM emission 02," February 18, 2009, https://vimeo.com/3275158.

34. *Blog Otonom Mawon du Collectif 5 février 2009,* http://collectif5fevrier.blogspot .com/ (accessed May 1, 2017).

35. *Blog Otonom Mawon du Collectif 5 février 2009.*

36. "La TOM a été un vecteur de communication pour le mouvement. Les media ne rapportaient pas ce que nous on voyait dans la rue. Les journalistes étaient frileux. . . . Nous avions des rapports cordiaux avec le K5F. Nous étions en grande convergence avec eux car au départ, nous voulions que le K5F soit entendu."

37. An Télévision Otonòm Mawon sé ki sa . . . Télévision d'information . . . porter l'information pour ce qui se passe actuellement en Martinique pour que le peuple martiniquais soit au courant . . . télé ta-la ka koumansé jòdi-a, i ké fini lèmouvman-an ké arété." "Tele Otonom Mawon 1ere.m4v," February 24, 2010, https://www.youtube .com/watch?v=0191aZHvimc.

38. Phone interview with Natalie Jos, May 12, 2017.

39. Members of the LKP and K5F were dispatched respectively to Martinique and Guadeloupe directly to take stock, and TOM had several live contacts with LKP.

40. "Tele Otonom Mawon 1ere.m4v," February 24, 2010, https://www.youtube.com /watch?v=0191aZHvimc.

41. Interview with Jocelyn Vautor, July 6, 2016.

42. Interview conducted on July 25, 2016, Gros-Morne. "Tou sa yo té ka di-la-a fout vré. Ou ka di gouvènman enmen-nou? Ki bétjé ki Fransé sémenm profitasyon."

43. "Télé Otonom Mawon du 25 Février 2009," February 25, 2009, https://www .youtube.com/watch?v=gfyEoaoeOro.

44. Interview with Jocelyn Vautor, July 6, 2016. "Tout le monde faisait tout. Il n'était pas question qu'un journaliste me dise, 'je suis reporter je ne prends pas d'images.' On était tous polyvalents. Les JRI pouvaient être journalistes et vice versa. Beaucoup de sujets étaient faits par des cameramen. Et tout était bien. Ils ont bien fait leur boulot."

45. Jo Manicou, "TOM emission 03," February 19, 2009, https://vimeo.com/3289112.

46. Phone interview with Natalie Jos, May 12, 2017. "Nous avons réussi quelque chose de formidable, nous avons pu montrer ce que les autres media ne montraient pas et montrer une vision beaucoup plus juste de ce qui se passait, il y a eu véritablement une libération de la parole. . . . Cela a été un exutoire. . . . Beaucoup de gens ont appris à faire de l'animation, beaucoup de gens ont découvert des compétences. . . . Il y a un vrai travail de fait."

47. "The life of artists is difficult."

48. Interview with Raschid, August 8, 2015.

49. Phone interview with Natalie Jos, May 12, 2017. "L'euphorie était à son comble. La parole était libre. Il y avait un grand bouillonnement. Il a eu une certaine émulation. Donc quand Jocelyn m'a dit qu'il faisait la tv pour donner la parole aux gens et demandé si je voulais les rejoindre, je n'ai même pas réfléchi. J'étais intimement persuadée qu'il nous fallait notre tv car les médias étaient frileux."

50. "Le groupe . . . se comporte littéralement comme si le sort du pays se jouait ici et maintenant."

51. Peggy Pinel-Fereol, "Les prix sont toujours plus élevés en Martinique," *Martinique 1*, June 5, 2017, http://la1ere.francetvinfo.fr/martinique/prix-sont-toujours-plus-eleves-mar tinique-480745.html.

52. "Nous sommes restés 38 jours dans les rues. Tout ça, pour rien!" Saint-Joseph, July 2, 2015.

53. "On a fait tout ça pour rien. La situation n'a pas changé." Saint-Joseph, July 2, 2015.

54. La CGTM, "Mobilisons-nous massivement pour la manifestation," http://www.cgt -martinique.fr/syndicat-cgt-martinique-cgtm-archives-greve-generale-declarations.asp.

55. "Un minimum de réadaptation, quelques reformes au sommet, un drapeau et, tout en bas, la masse divisive, toujours 'moyenâgeuse,' qui continue son mouvement perpétuel."

56. For an explanation of "vèglé," see Hanétha Vété-Congolo, *L'interoralité caribéenne: le mot conté de l'identité (Vers un trait d'esthétique caribéenne)* (Paris: Connaissances et Savoirs, 2016).

57. Béatrice Gurrey and Benoît Hopquin, "Békés: Une affaire d'héritage," *Le Monde*, March 5, 2009, http://www.lemonde.fr/societe/article/2009/02/28/bekes-une-affaire-d -heritage_1161662_3224.html#meter_toaster.

58. "Guillaume de Reynal, le béké en phase avec ses ancêtres," *Bondamanjak*, June 21, 2016, http://www.bondamanjak.com/guillaume-de-reynal-beke-phase-ancetres/.

59. "Après le dialogue social, la nécessité du dialogue syndical," May 31, 2020, http:// www.medef-martinique.fr/Apres-le-dialogue-social-la: "création hétéroclite et ambigüe du Collectif du 5 février," "échec du dialogue syndical," "mortifère," "dérive," "on a vu que la crise de février 2009 aura produit les effets inverses de ceux imaginés par de nombreux Martiniquais de bonne foi en fragilisant plus que tout l'écosystème des petites entre prises, et en particulier les entreprises de créations récentes."

60. *La Martinique est-elle sortie de la crise de 2009?* "Etude comparative des dynamiques de croissance Martinique-Guadeloupe," February 6, 2015, https://www.youtube.com /watch?v=3J6_bY6bSFI Accessed on February 2017.

61. "Le constat est assez sombre . . . les performances de l'économie martiniquaise sont, sur la longue période depuis 2009, vraiment les plus faibles de l'ensemble des departements d'Outre Mer." Olivier Sudrie, "La Martinique est-elle sortie de la crise de 2009? Etude comparative des dynamiques de croissance Martinique-Guadeloupe," Feb ruary 8, 2015, https://www.youtube.com/watch?v=3J6_bY6bSFI.

62. "Les derniers maitres de la Martinique," January 8, 2016, https://www.youtube .com/watch?v=4NoOS2f4xVg.

63. "Jean-Louis de Lucy, 'ITW BFM du 6/3/09' (Béké Martiniquais)," March 17, 2009, https://www.youtube.com/watch?v=PgBGPGE65QY.

64. "Pour expliquer aux interlocuteurs publics, politiques et médiatiques que nous rencontrons, que ce qui s'est passé aux Antilles n'est pas une crise sociale c'est un mouvement purement politique qui a un objectif clair l'indépendance des iles. . . . Ces mouvements ont été menés par un groupe minoritaire de fonctionnaires de l'État . . . qui n'ont qu'un but, l'indépendance des îles par toute voie, y compris la violence."

65. "Quand vous dites à une population que vous allez obtenir une augmentation de salaires substantielles, de 200 à 300 euros . . . les baisses de prix sur tout un ensemble de produits, . . . c'est normal que les populations vous croient . . . au fur et à mesure . . . les populations se sont rendu compte qu'elles étaient manipulées, . . . et aujourd'hui on va compter les morts, sur le plan des entreprises et sur le plan des milliers de chômeurs . . . et moi je me battrai parce que si ces îles sont indépendantes, elles sont foutues."

66. Raphaël Confiant, "Attaquer les Békés . . . en paroles," *Potomitan*, May 18, 2016, http://www.potomitan.info/confiant/beke.php.

67. Wikipédia, "Grève générale en Guyane et aux Antilles françaises en 2009," last updated February 28, 2020, https://fr.wikipedia.org/wiki/Gr%C3%A8ve_g%C3%A9n %C3%A9rale_aux_Antilles_fran%C3%A7aises_en_2009.

REFERENCES

Alie-Monthieux, Marie-Josée. 2002. "RFO, le pari caribéen." *Hermès, La Revue* 32–33, no. 1: 251–253.

Auvergnon, Philippe. 2004. "Conflictualité et dialogue social à la Martinique." *Travail et emploi* 98 (April): 109–123.

Auvergnon, Philippe, and Patrick Le Moal. 2000. *Conflictualité et dialogue social à la Martinique: paroles d'acteurs.* https://halshs.archives-ouvertes.fr/halshs-00126635/document.

Bambridge, Tamatoa, Doumengue Jean-Pierre, Ollivier Bruno, and Simonin Jacky. 2002. "Les médias Outre-Mer." *Hermès, La Revue* 32–33: 41–46.

Césaire, Aimé. 1983. *Cahier d'un retour au pays natal.* Paris: Présence Africaine.

du Tertre, Jean-Baptiste. 1667. *Histoire des Antilles habitées par les François,* Tome II. Paris: T. Jolly.

Fanon, Frantz. 2002. *Les damnés de la terre.* Paris: La Découverte.

Louis, Patrice. 2002. "Radios périphériques et régions ultra-périphériques." *Hermès, La Revue* 32–33: 247–249.

5 Neoliberalism and Caribbean Economies

MARTINIQUE, GUADELOUPE, AND
THE EXPLOITATIVE STRATEGIES
OF METROPOLITAN CAPITAL

H. ADLAI MURDOCH

PAGET HENRY

In this essay, we will attempt to put into a more comprehensive perspective the interpretations surrounding the Liyannaj Kont Pwofitasyon (LKP)–led uprisings in Martinique and Guadeloupe offered by the authors of this volume. This task is important given the ambivalent and contradictory nature of the responses and solutions proffered. In spite of the clear roots of these uprisings in real socioeconomic pain, the responses don't fall easily along left-right, nationalist-semicolonial, or progressive-conservative lines. Further, the themes that emerged from these uprisings were very diverse. They included unemployment, the high cost of living, racial discrimination and inequality, and ecological pollution. In other words, although sharing definite lines of continuity with previous uprisings, the LKP-led uprisings are indeed unique and thus in need of special commentary.

In putting these uprisings in a broader perspective, we need to connect to earlier revolts such as the 1802 uprising in Guadeloupe in response to Napoleon's attempt to reestablish slavery, those that led to departmentalization, and to revolts they inspired such as the Haitian Revolution and the recent *gilets jaunes* or Yellow Vests revolts in France. The revolt of 1802 was clearly a militarized, nationalist, and anti-slavery uprising with definite revolutionary potential. Hence we can understand Dessalines's tribute to its leaders, which included the very pregnant heroine, Solitude. Its rallying cry was "freedom or death." The insurrectionary activities around departmentalization were of a different nature. They were significantly less militarized, less determined to take power and expel the French, but also very nationalistic. Watching the revolts of the Yellow Vests unfold across France, one could not avoid thinking of the earlier uprisings led by the LKP in Guadeloupe and Martinique. The name and rallying cry of this uprising, "together against profiteering," pointed to both its differences from the 1802 insurrection and the socialist and communist struggles that led to departmentalization and also to similarities with the Yellow Vests revolts. The correspondences between the LKP and the Yellow Vests' modes of self-organizing and making of demands were quite striking. The LKP revolts in two French overseas departments inspiring revolts in France can only make us think of the case of the French Revolution inspiring revolutionary action in the colony of Haiti. With the help of C.L.R. James and the Créolité school, these are some of the connections that we will have to make if we are to put these important uprisings in their proper perspective.

While it is more or less a given that there are a variety of forms, histories, and discourses of postcoloniality, one might also reasonably claim that postcolonial theory can in principle be applied to a number of different political and cultural contexts, analyzing a variety of cultural forms and economic practices that have emerged from colonial relations of domination and subordination as they came to exist during the heyday of modern European imperialism, particularly in the New World of Anglophone and Francophone Caribbean territories. In a key way, such relations of domination, submission and exploitation continue to exist in our neocolonial era between nations and their concentrations of ethnic groups and cultures. Such theories actively engage with and are enabled by a set of racially grounded perspectives and practices that continue to fuel both commercial and political policies of capital accumulation and economic exploitation on a more or less global scale. As a result, discourses of identity and nationalism came to dominate the Anglophone postcolonial debate, even as their corollaries of migration and diaspora reflected the increasing inequalities that served to ground the continuing imperial-colonial economic relation, impelling the relocation of populations from the periphery toward the metropole.

For the French Antilles, this trajectory of capital, profit, and migrant movement would differ from that of their independent Anglophone counterparts, but this was arguably a difference of degree rather than one of kind; following the advent of overseas departmentalization or political integration into the former colonial mainland of France's four *vieilles colonies* in 1946—the only instance in colonial history of the subjects and territory of the formerly colonized becoming a legal part of their former colonizers— and despite successive impositions of autonomy that made the three Caribbean *départements d'outre-mer* into a *region monodépartementale* in 1982 and a DOM-ROM, or *region d'outre-mer*, in 2003, these peripheral territories— integral parts of France—are marked by a tangible series of ongoing economic disadvantages in comparison with the French mainland. For example, unemployment hovers at around 30 percent, as compared with about 8 percent for the metropole. Departmentalization has also led to a modernized consumer society, as more than 90 percent of all goods consumed in the DOMs are imported from France, and their elevated prices reflect the cost of transportation across the Atlantic even as the principle of diminishing returns renders the cost of local production prohibitive. Meanwhile, migration to the metropole—and its attendant social, cultural, and linguistic corollaries—has probably been the most visible consequence of 1946; in point of fact, *domien* population movement into France was actively catalyzed by the creation of the state agency BUMIDOM, whose aim was the creation of a safety valve alleviating rampant regional unemployment. Between its inauguration in April 1963 and its dissolution eighteen years later, BUMIDOM funneled more than 160,000 workers from Guadeloupe, Martinique, French Guiana, and Réunion onto the French mainland, many of whom sought to escape rising unemployment in their own territories even as BUMIDOM attempted to assuage France's postwar labor shortage.[1] As a result, the rapidly changing demographics of contemporary France show that there are almost eight hundred thousand persons of French Caribbean birth or descent living on the French mainland today; this is more than

1 percent of the total French population, and as many as make up the entire population of Guadeloupe and Martinique combined, with more than 80 percent of this population residing in Paris—now known in certain quarters as the "third island."[2]

The paradox of political independence among the Anglophone former colonies of the Eastern Caribbean was not accompanied by parallel patterns of economic self-sufficiency. Indeed, the reduction and virtual elimination of domestic agricultural and industrial production that has pervaded the region in the wake of the collapse of sugar cane cultivation—engendering an environment in which the majority of food staples like meat and vegetables are imported along with durable goods like refrigerators and motor cars—encountered an eerie parallel in the French Antilles, where the agricultural and plantation economies all but disappeared beginning with the first postdepartmental decade. Interestingly enough, such patterns parallel almost exactly the rationale for the extremely elevated retail prices in the Anglophone Caribbean, where by contrast most consumer goods are imported from North America. It is clear, then, that contemporary material conditions in the French Caribbean, particularly as regards astronomically high prices on goods and services resulting from the need to import the majority of consumable goods across very long distances, mirror conditions in the independent Anglophone Caribbean—territories like Saint Lucia, Jamaica, and Barbados—as well as non-sovereign territories like the "Commonwealth" of Puerto Rico. One indicator of this cost is contained in a recent statement by Didacus Jules, director general of the Organization of Eastern Caribbean States (OECS) during a conference with the Inter-American Institute for Cooperation on Agriculture (IICA) in July 2018, pointing out that "our food import bill has reached almost one billion dollars, and we must lower this cost."[3] But given that they address only OECS conditions, these figures reflect only a partial picture. Taking CARICOM as a whole, the situation is indeed grim:

CARICOM countries currently import in excess of US$4 billion in food annually, an increase of 50 percent since 2000. Food imports are projected to increase to US $8–10 billion by 2020 if current efforts are not successful in addressing this problem. Almost all CARICOM countries import more than 60 percent of the food they consume, with half of them importing more than 80 percent of the food they consume. Only three countries (Belize, Guyana, and Haiti) produce more than 50 percent of their consumption. Processed foods, grains (wheat and corn), and livestock products (meat and dairy) are among the top five food import categories, accounting for over US $1 billion or approximately 25 percent of annual food imports regionally.[4]

This CARICOM conundrum is emblematic of the paradox of regional consumption, in which territories historically associated with exporting agricultural produce are now compelled through a concatenation of global forces to import the majority of their consumer goods. From a historical perspective, agricultural production in the region was long dominated by the sugar and banana industries, but although these continue to survive in some form, they are largely oriented toward export markets. With the disappearance of preferential marketing prices under the Lomé Convention— a trade and aid agreement between the European Economic Community (EEC) and seventy-one African, Caribbean, and Pacific (ACP) countries, first signed in February 1975 in Lomé, Togo—the emergence of the single European market at the end of 1992 restricted ACP preferential access to EU markets. Ultimately the WTO Dispute Settlement Body effectively ended the cross-subsidies that had benefited ACP countries for many years, leading to greater competition from Latin America and Africa. Put another way, the advent of globalized competition and markets led inexorably to the shrinking of Caribbean agricultural production, which led in its turn to a steady increase in the importation of internationally sourced food products:

> With the loss of preferential access to international markets, regional governments have opted to pursue economic diversification strategies that are more focused on service-oriented industries such as financial services and tourism. Consequently, agriculture's contribution to GDP

has steadily declined over time. Coupled with constraints on productivity due to small scale operations, limited public and private investment and natural disasters, the agricultural sector has performed relatively weakly in many countries. . . . Domestic food production has consistently been inadequate to satisfy domestic demand and, as such, Caribbean countries have grown increasingly dependent on food imports over time. Most countries are net food importers and in some food categories—staples in particular—the gap between domestic consumption and domestic production is quite significant, with consumption two to nearly four times greater than production.[5]

These patterns dominated and overdetermined the economic picture in the postcolonial Caribbean from the initial independence of Jamaica and Trinidad and Tobago in 1962. Abandoned to their capital-free futures, populated by communities that historically had been capital themselves, the independent Anglophone Caribbean territories turned increasingly to tourism as a source of foreign currency and job creation, even as the viability of local mineral resources like bauxite was progressively eroded by first-world financial and political interests. But while the end result in these independent territories was the decimation of local agricultural production and light industry, and the concomitant elevated price structure and distorted balance of payments regime that stem from the unbounded scale of importations, it is even more surprising that similar scenarios befell French Antillean island economies supposedly integrated into their metropole.

The Crisis of French Capitalism and Its Peripheries

Just as the connections between French Revolution and the Haitian Revolution pointed to a shared crisis of French capitalism and the sugar empire on which it was based, so the revolts of workers in Guadeloupe and Martinique and those of the Yellow Vests point to a shared crisis of the French social market economy, as it struggles to respond to the Anglo-American project of neoliberal globalization. Thus we will have to look at the nature of this crisis and the changes that it has brought to the economy of the

French imperial center and to the departmentalized but still peripheralized economies of Martinique and Guadeloupe.

One of our major suggestions here is that the common factor underlying the LKP and Yellow Vests uprisings was the arrival of a new crisis phase in the history of French capitalism. This crisis is the result of the unraveling of the neoliberal solutions to the economic crises of the 1970s. The crises of the 1970s had their origins in the collapse of Keynesian solutions to the problems of the Great Depression and World War II. These solutions all increased the role of the state in the management of advanced central economies as a result of pressures from workers organized in socialist and communist parties.

These internal pressures from the Western working classes were reinforced by external ones, coming from the colonies, which challenged the imperial foundations of the empires of Western capitalism. These still formally and substantively colonized areas were as devastated, if not more so, by the economic hurricanes released by the Great Depression. These storms revived with renewed intensity the nationalist push for formal decolonization and programs of economic development. It was in this high pressured, post-Depression context that the distinct French version of the social market economy came into being, along with that in West Germany and the welfare states in Britain and the United States. These economic formations all marked different points of mixture or compromise between earlier ideas of pure capitalism or pure socialism. The New Deal in the United States was the least influenced by socialist policies, with France being one of the more socialist-influenced of these postwar, post-Depression economic formations.

By the early 1970s, these mixed economic formations began to break down, as supporting conditions began to deteriorate. First, there was the collapse in 1971 of the gold dollar standard as the United States could no longer back its currency with gold and thus also serve as a world reserve currency. This profoundly disturbed the postwar order of international trading. Second, there was the growing bargaining power of trade unions, increasing the cost of labor and of goods produced in the West. Third, the

1970s was a period of stagflation, the unusual combination of inflation and rising unemployment. Fourth, this was a period of rising Asian competition, particularly from Japan. Fifth, there were the 1973 and subsequent oil shocks, as Arab countries, organized into the Organization of the Petroleum Exporting Countries (OPEC), increased the price of petroleum in part for political reasons. This price increase, together with the collapse of the gold standard, would dramatically increase the debt burdens of many developing countries, including the Caribbean. Sixth and finally, we had the economic revolt of the now formally decolonized periphery, as it called for a New International Economic Order (NIEO). This economic movement came out of Latin America and the Caribbean. In 1974, the proposal was brought before a special session of the U.N. General Assembly by the Argentinian economist Raul Prebisch and former Jamaican prime minister Michael Manley. There it was overwhelmingly supported by the periphery and vetoed by the center.

As Gérard Duménil and Dominique Lévy pointed out in their well-known work *Capital Resurgent: Roots of the Neoliberal Revolution*, the upshot of these increasingly adverse trends was that "in the 1970s the rate of capital profitability had significantly declined" (2004, 9). In other words, in the West, the first element to really feel the impact of these adverse trends and to respond in an organized fashion was the financial sector—banks, insurance companies, shareholders, bondholders, and hedge funds. The resulting revolt was primarily a shareholders' revolt, and the rallying cry of this movement was "shareholder value." In the United States, takeover entrepreneurs engineered the hostile takeover of major companies that were not delivering the desired levels of shareholder value, effectively putting corporate managers on notice that shareholder value had to be increased.

This new emphasis on maximizing shareholder value would be just one of the many changes that would usher in the neoliberal phase of Western capitalism, including that of France. First, there were significant changes in patterns of corporate governance. The most important of these made the CEOs and chief financial officers of major corporations into stockholders. This move broke with earlier patterns of governance and gave to top management a personal stake in increasing shareholder value. These activist shareholders also pushed for and got from their central banks policies of high interest rates aimed at combating the effects of inflation. These were the opening shots fired on behalf of the neoliberal revolution.

Along with these opening rounds, these stockholders and their growing band of corporate allies pushed for and got the deregulation of banking systems, which had been very carefully regulated after the experiences of the Great Depression. Banks would now be more directly exposed to the ups and downs of the markets, even though they were the holders of the savings of private citizens. This emerging financial oligarchy started pushing Western corporations to get bigger through mergers and acquisitions, making billions of dollars in profits. They simultaneously pushed to liberalize and globalize financial and later other commodity markets, so that even the tiny Eastern Caribbean region had to create its own stock market on which less than ten companies trade stocks per day—all part of the grand strategy to restore shareholder value and thus "the rate of capital profitability." By 1980, all of these piecemeal policies came together as an integrated package that was called neoliberal globalization and was put into place primarily by the United States and Britain.

Also important from the perspective of Martinique and Guadeloupe, the push to liberalize and globalize both financial and commodity markets represented a restructuring of the global economic order, which was not the more Keynesian NIEO of the global South. Indeed it was a finance-dominated and market-driven alternative to the proposals of Prebisch and Manley. We have called this Western alternative to the NIEO the Neoliberal Global Economic Order, or NGEO. As we will see, it was in the context of the NGEO's forced liberalization and globalization of banana and sugar markets, and the inability of France to resist, that Guadeloupe and Martinique abandoned long-established agricultural sectors—a pattern of productivity marking an insistent independence—and turned to tourism, a sector defined by the nonproduction of material goods.

As Duménil and Lévy have pointed out, this neoliberal revolt on the part of shareholders made them the dominant factors in financial sectors in

Western countries like the United States, Britain, and to a lesser degree France by the mid-1980s. Shareholders were now what Duménil and Lévy call "the center of the center" (2004, 9). As such, shareholders had displaced the leadership of major industrial corporations, while rearranging the hierarchical relations between them. Further, shareholders pushed aside the Keynesian framework of economic thinking and policy making and replaced it with the frameworks of Friedrich Hayek and Milton Friedman. These neoliberal shifts have greatly affected the role of the state in the advanced economies, as well as the extent to which socialist ideals and pressures can still be incorporated into policies of economic planning and management.

For social market economies like France, the success of this neoliberal revolt ushered in a period of difficult adjustment. Given the stronger socialist elements in France's postwar *dirigisme*, neoliberal policies of state downsizing, private sector upsizing and financial dominance, and increased market competition all proved very challenging. The resistance of trade unions, workers, and the socialist and communist parties has been much stronger than in the United States or Britain. But, in spite of this significant difference, the direction of change in France and other social market economies has been in the direction of these neoliberal reforms and away from the socialist elements of the post-Depression dirigisme. These trends have been evident in the policies of socialist presidents that have come to power in France, and in the cooperation of the French Communist Party with the French bourgeoisie and other national parties. This distinct relation to a tradition of socialist organized resistance must also be the context within which we view the LKP and Yellow Vests revolts.

Before going on to look at the concatenation of economic and political factors that would ultimately tip the neoliberal balance in the French Caribbean, it is striking to note the structural and political similarities that obtain between the interests of the *gilets jaunes* in 2018–2019 and those of the LKP in Guadeloupe and Martinique a decade earlier. Etienne Balibar has recently articulated the pervasive neoliberal framework undergirding the former movement so that its parallels with LKP are pellucidly clear. He speaks tellingly of

the massive trends of contemporary capitalism. . . . Without unnecessarily complicating matters, I would say that they embody and denounce
the generalized precariousness of activity and livelihoods that today
affects millions of French people and immigrants of every educational
level and geographical location . . . because they are caught between two
major trends characteristic of neo-liberalism, both based on the application of "free and undistorted competition."

On the one hand, the new iron law of wage compression, both direct
and indirect (including pensions, of course), to which globalization and
deregulated technological change contribute, as well as the weakening of trade-union organizations; on the other hand, the accelerated
uberization of "manual" or "intellectual" jobs that do not depend on
companies with a fixed location but rather on digital platforms, creating a competition "to the death" between individuals (called "self-
entrepreneurs") whom their masters control by intermittent demand
and by debt.

The two tendencies converge, and workers or employees from cities,
suburbs and countryside who have not yet reached the bottom see that
they cannot stop it. (Balibar 2018, 8)

In other words, it is this sacrifice of wages and workers' rights on the altar
of profits that made their explosion in the periphery of the French Antilles
in 2009 the harbinger of a parallel trajectory of concerns on the French
mainland ten years later. Adhering to this economic model, then, creates a
system of stratified wealth literally on the backs of those working to create
it, as Christophe Guilluy suggests: "From the 1980s onwards, it was clear
there was a price to be paid for western societies adapting to a new economic model and that price was sacrificing the European and American
working class. . . . The paradox is this is not a result of the failure of the
globalised economic model but of its *success*" (2018; emphasis in original). It
is in this context that policies like the NGEO eventually took root.

In spite of the high visibility of the growing inequities and hardships
associated with the NGEO, it was not until the onset of the Great Recession

of 2008 that the house of mortgaged cards upon which the dominance of finance was built came crashing down and gave rise to economic earthquakes, tsunamis, hurricanes, typhoons, and storms. It was not the private sector or the markets that organized the rescue and cleanup from the debris of these powerful explosions. Rather it was the state. Governments and their central banks have been at the helm of the central economies ever since this destructive economic collapse. Banks have been bailed out to the tune of trillions of dollars, while innocent homeowners were left to sink with mortgages that were deeply underwater. This collapse of the neoliberal order was global with banks and other corporations collapsing in both center and periphery. The common epicenter of these eruptions and dramatic collapses was exposed for all to see, coming as it did from the center of the center. If Duménil and Lévy gave us the classic French account of the rise of the neoliberal order, then it is Thomas Piketty's *Capital in the 21st Century* that has given us the classic French account of its decline and still unresolved state.

Martinique, Guadeloupe, and French Dirigisme

The colonial history of Guadeloupe and Martinique was shaped by the reorganization of their indigenous economies around French financial and merchant investments in the plantation production of sugar, for export to France, with the use of enslaved Africans as the primary labor force. This was the incorporation that made these two island economies subject to the crises that have interrupted capital accumulation in France. At the same time, it also made capital accumulation in France subject to the insurrectionary projects of enslaved Africans and their post-slavery descendants, who have consistently demonstrated their deep dissatisfaction with this socioeconomic order. In addition to the major investors being French, the sugar planters on the islands were largely the descendants of white French colonizers, constituting an intermediary class, the *békés*, between the investors in the center and the enslaved Africans. These were early features of the economies of Guadeloupe and Martinique that have persisted into the present, in spite of African projects of revolt and major disruptions in

French projects of capital accumulation. To put the LKP revolts in their proper perspective, we must keep this history of black revolt in mind at the same time that we examine in detail the impact of the Great Depression, the rise of French dirigisme and its neoliberal reforms on Martinique and Guadeloupe, the responses of both the békés and the Afro-Caribbean population.

As a country, France has one hundred and one departments, ninety-six of which are on the mainland; most of this latter category do very well. It has only five external or overseas departments: Martinique, Guadeloupe, French Guiana, Réunion, and Mayotte, none of which has been doing really well. While Mayotte became a department only in 2011, it shares the economic deprivation of the other DOMs; overall, the departmentalization of these territories, which were former French colonies, can be seen as the result of a compromise between the opposing historic forces and projects of black resistance and those of imperial France, which included the economic interest of the intermediary béké class. In Martinique and Guadeloupe, black resistance entered a new phase around the turn of the twentieth century. It moved out of a Republican and Schoelcherite period, as rising Pan African and Negritude discourses of race began taking on more explicit class dimensions by embracing socialist ideas. As the strikes and other mass actions of the black laboring class began to mushroom in the 1920s and 1930s, the workers began organizing themselves into independent socialist and communist parties. Ultimately, these island parties would later become integral parts of the French Socialist Party (PSF) and the French Communist Party (PCF).

This deep integration of the island parties into their counterparts in France, we think, had important implications for the compromise that resulted in departmentalization. The importance of this factor can be seen from a quick contrast with cases of the Anglophone Caribbean. Starting three decades later than their French counterparts, the insurrectionary protests of the 1930s found their organizational model in the British Labour Party. Many influential regional figures, such as Sir Arthur Lewis, were members of the British Labour Party, and local parties like the Antigua

Labour Party and the St. Kitts Labour Party had what was called corresponding relations with the British Labour Party. But in spite of this early paternal relationship, these bonds were broken very quickly, with island labor parties becoming independent parties, and making decisions on their own.

The significance of this greater independence of parties in the Anglophone Caribbean increased with the rise of Stalinism in the Soviet Union and the policy of socialism in one country. This policy argued for the consolidation of socialism in the Soviet Union as the number one goal of all communist parties and became the basis for the rigid control of all communist parties by Moscow. The French Communist Party adopted this line and was extremely loyal to Moscow. Through this centralizing of control, Stalinism came to Martinique and Guadeloupe, subjecting the specific interests of blacks, who had originally formed these parties, to the interests of the PCF and to those of Moscow. Decision making in the Antigua Labour Party, for example, was thus very different from that in the Martinican Communist Party (PCM) or the Guadeloupean Communist Party (PCG).

Also quite different in the case of the Anglophone Caribbean was the British cultural policy of limited assimilation, as compared with the French policy of *assimilation*. The extent to which Francophone Caribbean people were convinced or wished they could assimilate and become as genuinely French as citizens born in France had no counterpart in the Anglophone Caribbean with regard to Britain. There were certainly individuals who aspired to be British, and indeed many who migrated to Britain in the 1940s and 1950s, but with so little encouragement from this imperial center and with widespread racism spawned by migration, it never became a serious decolonization policy option as in the Francophone Caribbean. Thus French paternalism, mediated by this distinct policy of assimilation, became an important factor in the decision to opt for departmentalization.

A third important factor in the complex of forces that produced this outcome was the greater strength of the planter class after the insurrectionary communist activities, in large part a result of the more consistent support they got from the French state. With the rise of the textile industry in Britain, cheaper sugar from outside of the empire, and the production of sugar from the sugar beet, the dominant influence that the planters and their merchant allies had on the British government really began to weaken significantly after 1842. Compared to the much more innovative and competitive leaders of the textile industry, the planters in Jamaica, Barbados, and Antigua appeared to British political elites as a stagnant and receding class that was unable to reinvent itself for the emerging liberal and competitive phase of British capitalism. Thus the nationalist leaders of the decolonization movement in the Anglophone Caribbean skillfully manipulated these ambivalent attitudes of British political elites toward the planter class. In the case of Antigua and Barbuda, the planter class was roundly defeated in the course of the nationalist struggle.

In sum, whereas in the Anglophone Caribbean we had a version of the British welfare state that was much more independent of British party politics, in Martinique and Guadeloupe we had a version of French dirigisme that was much more integrated into and dependent upon French party politics. Thus dirigisme in Martinique and Guadeloupe meant a comparatively firm alliance with the French state and an equally firm alliance between French capitalists and shareholders with béké capitalists, along with the PCM and the PCG playing a supporting role as a result of their integration into the PCF. As a governing politico-economic structure, it would be even more vulnerable to the impact of the NGEO than French dirigisme.

However, the crisis of the dirigisme-driven economies of Martinique and Guadeloupe began before the adverse trends of the 1970s noted earlier. Rather it began with the unfolding of the crisis of Stalinism and the revelations about the inner workings of the regime, which included labor camps; in spite of this, the PCF remained loyal to Moscow. However, the crisis of Stalinism produced many splits and breaks that severely weakened the communist movement, including Aimé Césaire's historic resignation from the party as a declaration of independence and restoration of initiative for the black subject. In his well-known letter of resignation, Césaire wrote: "usurping bureaucrats that are cut off from the people have achieved the pitiable wonder of transforming into a nightmare what humanity has for so long cherished as a dream—socialism" (146). In short, Stalinism, via the

PCF, dealt a deadly blow to the socialist flank of dirigisme in Guadeloupe and Martinique.

Already in a profound state of crisis, the onset of the adverse trends of the 1970s—collapse of the gold dollar standard, oil shocks from OPEC, rising inflation, and so on—delivered a set of consecutive blows to the capitalist flank of the dirigisme economies of Martinique and Guadeloupe. The disrupting of this flank only further weakened a system that had been disequilibrated by the disrupting of its socialist flank. Thus the implementing of the neoliberal reforms by the United States and Britain amounted to the laying of the tracks along which the economies of Guadeloupe and Martinique would make their downward slide. As markets were liberalized, the protected markets in France for sugar and banana producers in Martinique and Guadeloupe became a site of struggle between the United States and the European Union (EU), particularly regarding the ways in which these protections excluded Latin American bananas. The United States won this particular battle, forcing the entry of Latin American bananas into the British and French markets from which they had been excluded under the previous system. It was primarily the self-interested manner in which the central countries implemented many of the neoliberal rules that enabled the West to subsidize its agriculture and save sugar and banana production in both islands. But, in spite of these subsidizing countermoves by France, the disequilibrating impact of the reforms on incomes, prices, and the redistributive mechanisms of the island economies were more than those at the bottom could bear. Fred Constant makes this point well: "While the French Caribbean was not exempt from any European economic constraints, such as the European Common External Tariff or the European Common Levy, the DOMs did not benefit, on an equal footing, from the European Regional development packages or the European Agricultural Common policy or from most of the European funds" (2001, 82). Simply put, one can arguably propose that prejudice and hierarchical advantages and disadvantages toward the periphery had been built into a system that claimed to have been founded and to operate on principles of openness and egalitarianism. As time passed, a breaking point would be reached, bringing to explosive levels the insurrectionary tendencies and projects of workers and others who were marginalized and discarded by the neoliberal order of things.

The Impact of Neoliberal Reforms on Agriculture in Martinique and Guadeloupe

Now the metropolitan integration of these territories and their economies illuminates a key paradox with regard to such regional factors as per capita income, wage and price structures, and the general cost of living. Indeed, despite the presumed parity implicit in the departmental condition, numerous exploitative inequities between metropole and periphery remained stubbornly in place; for example, it took forty years from the act of departmentalization in 1946 for equivalence in the minimum wage to be enacted. William F. S. Miles points to the "symbolic and financially important parity finally established on New Year's 1996 between the minimum wage prevailing in the overseas departments and in the metropole. For many workers and politicians overseas, the disparity in the minimum wage remained a longstanding irritant and a contradiction to the equality implicit in departmentalisation" (2001, 52). But such inequalities persisted despite the presumed benefits of metropolitan integration, their instantiation of an implicit coloniality forcing the inhabitants of these communities literally to turn to metropolitan handouts to survive, as Norman Girvan points out: "Martinique, Guadeloupe and French Guiana benefit from transfer payments from France to support social services and a bureaucracy equivalent to those on the French mainland" (2012, 9). Now when Caribbean independent territories turn to entities like the International Monetary Fund (IMF) for relief, the resulting performance criteria and reporting requirements appear eerily similar to historical patterns and practices of colonial domination, as Girvan emphasizes: "On the face of it, this degree of control is similar to that exercised by a colonial power over the finances and economic policies of a dependent territory. Financial dependency in conjunction with overall economic dependency can therefore become a source of control over a nominally independent state" (2012, 12). Put another way, the advent of neocolonial and neoliberal policies and their imposition of global free trade rules on the historically deprived and undersourced capital framework of the Caribbean exposed independence as a sham, resulting in markets, consumers and workers being increasingly caught up in externally driven strategies of capital accumulation, profit, and exploitation that literally made competition by local firms virtually impossible. Girvan explains this phenomenon well: "The effect of these provisions of 'Free Trade Agreements' is to further strengthen the position of U.S. and EU corporations in exploiting the markets, labour and natural resources of Caribbean countries; placing local firms at a considerable disadvantage. There is further erosion of national state sovereignty by means of regulatory restrictions and on binding extra-national arbitration in investor-state disputes" (2012, 13–14).

If the key elements undergirding neocolonial exploitation in these independent Caribbean territories operates by placing capital in an advantageous position in order to erode state sovereignty and restrict and subvert the viability of local firms, then the irony of these practices will consist in uncovering how they succeeded in overdetermining the economies of the French DOMs in the same way. For the high prices on most consumer goods and services—anywhere from 20 to 170 percent higher than comparable prices in mainland France—has tended to make their equivalency a moot point, one undermined and exacerbated by other factors.

In *Seeking Imperialism's Embrace*, Kristin Stromberg Childers surveys the key documents of this period, revealing clearly that the pervasive racism that had historically driven the abiding sense of metropolitan superiority undergirding colonial attitudes toward France's peripheral populations of color in no way abated in the face of departmentalization's new legal strictures and assumptions. Indeed, what we witness repeatedly is that, starting in December 1946, "administrative parity" is "almost immediately blocked." Further, these convictions of peripheral underdevelopment "implied a number of substantial differences in political culture, standards of living, economic productivity, and family structure," all of which "came to stand in for considerations of race" (2016, 124). As a result, the economic predominance in this racialized neocolonial economy of the béké descendants of the white planter class—a group who numbered fewer than 5 percent of the population of the islands—continued to expand, maintaining a monopolistic economic stranglehold on the Antillean economy, and, as metropolitan neoliberal policies took hold, branching out from agriculture into such key areas as supermarkets, shopping malls, and car dealerships. Disappointment with departmentalization set in quickly, however, as the promised parity in salaries, social benefits, and economic infrastructure that was meant to flow from the 1946 law seemed elusive, if not invisible, and indeed the ongoing disparities showed that many assumptions, patterns, and practices with regard to labor, income, and "productivity" seemed even more glaringly race-based than before, if that were possible. On the other hand, departmentalization ultimately brought infrastructural development, island-wide electricity and pipe-borne water, European-quality roads and four-lane highways, unemployment and health insurance, and the French minimum wage along with it, while simultaneously the plantation and agricultural economies were steadily eradicated.

This analytical perspective highlights the paradoxical character of the departmental condition as a double-edged sword. Viewed in one way, the parity with the metropole instantiated in the French Antilles, although it took decades for its promise to be fulfilled, brought with it the corollary of an elevated standard of living by comparison with these islands' Anglophone counterparts. In a key way, then, this was arguably the primary trade-off for their condition of non-sovereignty. William F. S. Miles has long done sterling research and writing on the complexities of this condition, and deserves to be quoted at length:

> *Départementalisation* entailed the extension of the same rights and privileges applying in the Metropolitan French *départements* to the overseas ones. Although it took decades before they reached the same monetary levels, these *droits acquis* included social security, minimum wage, child allowance, health insurance, unemployment compensation, and all other components of the French welfare state . . . That "dependence"

still made for a relatively high standard of living, at least by regional standards. By the time of the 2002 campaign, Martinique enjoyed the second highest per capita income in the Caribbean, second only to the Bahamas, and the highest of all four French overseas states. . . . But GNP per capita was still only 58 percent of that prevailing in the French Metropole. (2003, 223, 229–230)

Perhaps the key point to be made here is the link between "dependence," on the one hand, and the relative measure of per capita income by comparison with the metropole, on the other; seen in this way, the discrimination that Childers has described as characterizing the metropolitan relationship to the DOMs/colonies of the periphery comes clearly into focus. Ultimately, the shrinking agricultural component had to be weighed against the provision of social services and the burgeoning civil service sector; in other words, advantages and disadvantages that exist side by side, as Miles continues:

> Momentum for outright separation is negligible: the economic benefits of remaining part of France (and the E.U.) are too great. . . . If the DOM-TOM passively accept their status as overseas projections of an erstwhile European colonizer, it is because they are conditioned to do so. The educational system, the media, and consumer values all reinforce the post-colonial message of departmentalization, stressing the benefit of the current arrangement. The elevated standard of living that DOMTOM peoples enjoy, however, comes at the cost of economic and psychic dependency. From this vantage point, the "democracy" that the DOM-TOM "enjoy" is a sham. The formal attributes of a democratic polity may be in place—even the pro-independence minority does not contest the transparency and competitiveness of elections held in overseas France—but this is an alien power's democracy, built on a history of colonial rule. (2005, 226–227)

This economic and psychic dependency imposed on the population is external in origin, and parallels the increasing domination by the departmental integrationist model of the local economy. The targeted erasure of a plantation economy that, for Antilleans, was synonymous with self-reliance, despite its origins in colonialism and slavery, was the most visible and, indeed, egregious element in this advancing diminution of local structures:

> The early years of departmentalization, characterized by a massive inflow of metropolitan funds and the emergence of a dependent development, also witnessed the vestigial fading of the plantation economy and the *rurabinization* of the Martinican peasantry. Calls for political autonomy, we have seen above, were largely coopted by the Socialist plan for *decentralization* which carried a unique resonance in the overseas departments throughout the 1980s. . . . At the same time, *bétonisation* of Martinique—the wholesale paving, construction, "concretization" of the island—has proceeded apace, thanks to both French and European fiscal incentives and developmental funds. (Miles 1995, 360–361; emphasis in the original)

As this quote from William F. S. Miles makes clear, the twin terrors of dependent development and *bétonisation* were intimately linked across the French Antillean landscape. In other words, growth on the urban side was paralleled by the steady reduction or elimination of local subsistence agriculture—leaving in place agricultural production geared toward export—and the concomitant triumphant spread of concrete and the category of development that came with it. The primary results of these phenomena were an increasing inability of these islands literally to feed themselves, along with submission to the centralized economic structures and practices that characterized the French metropole. Richard Burton effectively explains these interlinked phenomena:

> The agricultural base on which the traditional creole culture was founded has been eroded beyond all possibility of restoration, leaving that culture—where it survives at all—increasingly bereft of any anchorage in the actual lived experience of contemporary French West Indians and . . . succumbing by the day to what the increasing number

of Martinicans and Guadeloupeans who care scathingly call *bétonisa-*
tion: the remorseless spread of concrete in the form of hypermarkets
and housing developments, *résidences secondaires*, motorways and service roads, hotels and marinas across the countryside and beaches of
the two islands. (1993, 7–8)

The material results of such practices and priorities are undeniable, their
effect on the population at large clearly indicating a series of *étapes* presag-
ing the ultimate triumph of neoliberalism and the cost of living crisis that
overtook these territories in 2009. In "Mittérand in the Caribbean," Miles
points to a particular series of economic events that, taken together, transformed the social and economic landscape of Martinique—and, by extension, Guadeloupe—in very substantial ways by the early 1980s. For example,
he points to the precipitous drop in the number of rum distilleries—from
forty-two to eighteen—between 1963 and 1980; the drop in exports and the
parallel rise in imports between 1961 and 1982; the drop in the employment rate from 62 percent to 42 percent during the same period; and the
radical jump in the percentage of the Martinican-born population—from
4 percent in 1954 to 25 percent in 1979—living on the French mainland.[6]
Taken in sum and read diachronically, these phenomena announce a society and an economy collapsing on themselves, a prolonged wave of socioeconomic exploitation targeting the presumptively coequal subject of Antillean
neoliberalism.

This point was effectively driven home in a prescient article concerning
the production and consumption of food in Guadeloupe published around
the time of the 2009 uprising. Here, Pamela Obertan opens with the primary and paradoxical point that "after centuries as a French colony, this
French Caribbean *département* still imports around 80 per cent of its food."
The reasons for this, in her opinion, are grounded in both history and in
contemporary economics:

It is, however, very difficult for farmers to grow crops for the local market and to diversify their produce. The authorities have neglected subsistence agriculture and have favoured export crops, such as sugar cane

and bananas, which alone cover half of the island's cultivated land. This
paradoxical situation largely stems from certain unjust structures
imposed on the island in its history. Guadeloupe was a French colony
and was forced to send much of its agricultural production to France
and other markets. Little land was left for production for the local
market, and the island was therefore obliged to import most of its food
from France. (Obertan 2009, 14)

What Obertan's analysis shows clearly is that the colonial model of production and trade, well established since the days of mercantilism—whereby
the colonies on the periphery produced goods in their raw, unfinished
form and sent them to the metropole for refinement, whence they were
(re)imported into the periphery along with a wide range of consumer dura-
bles for colonial consumption—has changed little, if at all. The local market
remains of secondary importance, and the centralization of capital in the
metropole ensures that this pattern remains in place, shaping and re-
forming local patterns of taste and consumption. Obertan goes on to point
out that this practice "perpetuates a 400-year-old history of exporting primary produce with very little added value and importing much more
expensive refined and processed products. The result is a large trade deficit.
Moreover, the population's tastes are clearly westernised. Local people
often prefer to consume imported products, which are often cheaper than
local products" (2009, 14–15). In a word, then, this toxic brew of imports
over exports, westernized tastes, and declining local production, in conjunction with their chief corollary of an ever-rising cost of living, located
the Antilles ever further beyond the pale of a sovereignty that would
include the capacity for economic or political self-determination.

Looked at holistically, the facts and figures underlying this *décalage*
between production and consumption illustrate the point clearly. A few short
years before the uprising of 2009, even as the number of farms and the volume of agricultural production fell precipitously, "Guadeloupe imported
€2,274 million worth of goods and service during 2005. The majority of this
import expenditure went on manufactured goods including pharmaceuticals

and clothes; energy generating fuels, food, office equipment, construction materials, telecommunication and computer equipment."[7] Here, the scale and scope of Guadeloupe's imports make its submission to the hegemony of metropolitan capitalist production all but incontrovertible. At the same time, we learn that "in 2005, Guadeloupe exported €162.5 million worth of goods and services, an increase of 4.7 percent on the previous year's total. The majority of this was agriculture products (61 percent) and industrial products."[8] Similarly, in Martinique, we note that "exports grew in 2006 by 29.5 percent to reach €489.1 million, marking a return to the growth trend which had started in 1996 but was briefly interrupted in 2005. Imports also rose but by a smaller amount (8.9 percent) to reach €2.5 billion. The trade deficit reached the €2 billion mark."[9] These figures illuminate clearly the extent to which the entire Antillean economy is mired in the throes of a deficit trading model that advances the interests of metropolitan capital at the expense of the Antillean consumer.

The economic dependency outlined above impacts the black majority population to a disproportionate degree. By the same token, the historically privileged white elite, despite numbering fewer than three thousand, has been able to maintain and expand its dominance by allying their interests with those of metropolitan French capital, as together they seek to maximize their profits at the expense of the cohort of black labor that they continue to exploit. The end result of this racialized structure of profiteering is exemplified by Bernard Hayot, head of perhaps the most prominent béké family in Martinique and president of the Groupe Bernard Hayot; he is personally worth more than three hundred million euros and is reputedly the 119th-richest individual in France.[10] What we see, then, is a critical repositioning of this economically dominant béké minority within the new neoliberal framework, as Camee Maddox points out:

> The *béké* elites of Martinique have maintained economic control by transitioning from plantation owners to business executives in the consumption-driven import economy, tourism, and the service-oriented tertiary sector. Economic growth in Martinique has been the result of public

and social monetary transfers from France, rather than self-sustaining development models. . . . There are many factors contributing to the system of white *béké* privilege, including their economic and political alliances with the metropolitan French bourgeoisie and their control over the land. (2015, 93)

It is the sum total of this socioeconomic exclusion and dispossession that culminated in the grand paradox of citizenship as a deleterious catalyst undergirding the French Caribbean condition. Crucially, this dominance spanned both the economic and—through the hegemonic control of key media like television and radio—cultural domains, as Maddox goes on to point out: "French citizenship and the 'blind' consumption of goods produced externally have helped to establish this level of French cultural and economic hegemony" (2015, 94). In sum, neoliberalism had a broad impact on the economy as well as the culture of Guadeloupe and Martinique. Contesting the negative impacts of these changes was the primary goal of the LKP insurrections. Their name and rallying cry, the concept of "the costly life," their principal demand for a pay raise for the lowest-income earners, and their incisive portrayal of the exploitative relation between France and these two overseas departments spoke eloquently to the pressures that motivated this revolt. Those at the bottom of their neoliberalized dirigisme economies had been driven to a breaking point. The adverse trends in incomes, employment, and redistributive measures had to be forcefully stopped and reversed.

Given the scale of effects that the neoliberal era has wrought on the capitalist dimensions of the dirigisme economies of France, Martinique, and Guadeloupe, the question arises as to whether the insurrectionary powers and capabilities deployed by the LKP were well matched to contend with the increased powers of this latest phase of Western capitalism. We will conclude our essay with two responses to this issue. The first response, drawing on the Créolité movement, emphasizes the power and the contributions of the cultural upsurges produced by the LKP. The strong asserting of creole identities, the taking over of the L'Herminier Museum, the creating of an alternative television station, and the role of music in sustaining the insurrection would be cases in point. The second response, drawing on James's theory of collective action, will focus more on the collective persona behind the political and economic forces mobilized by LKP.

Créolité and the LKP Uprising

On the cultural side, the visible influence of the Créolité movement can be traced to the pronouncement of the *Eloge de la créolité* in May 1988 at the Festival caraïbe de la Saint-Denis and the publication of the *Eloge* a year later; however, the corresponding cultural impact of the *zouk* group Kassav', from its inception in 1979, also cannot be discounted. Certainly, these twin axes of cultural expression have been pivotal in mediating the articulation of Antillean identity both at home—in the islands—and abroad in the metropole as well as internationally. Indeed, one might argue that between the thirty-year span of the Créolité movement and the forty-year duration of Kassav's island, regional, and international renown, the depth and range of their dual roles in asserting the validity of French Caribbean cultural identity are beyond question, and their message links directly to the issues raised by LKP.

In terms of the discursive and thematic goal of the *Eloge*, the ultimate value of Créolité arguably lay in its instantiation of an enunciative framework for cultural identity. Its etymological origin may be located through the term *creole*, wherein complex contexts of ethnicity, cultural intersection, change, and exchange reveal it to be an inherently unstable category, shot through with the ambiguities, pluralities, and essentialisms of usage reflecting its origins in the colonial period. In the early 1970s, the late Barbadian poet and historian Kamau Brathwaite had moved these ideas forward as he examined the process of transculturation in the Caribbean, ascribing importance to an ethnic and cultural pluralism that produced new configurations and new methods for their articulation.

When the *Eloge* appeared, what it sought most to contest was a long-standing binary perspective that saw the Caribbean as part of an either-or, Africa-Europe continuum, with implicit singularities that originated in the concept of separation: "Neither Europeans, nor Africans, nor Asians, we proclaim ourselves Creoles." The aim of this coalescent vision was to use Créolité's primary instantiation in French Creole as a metaphor to help develop modalities for creative expression in the arts that would emphasize the region's creative intersectionality and prioritize local pluralities over metropolitan singularities, while performing the multiplicity and complexity of the creole mosaic through new perspectives and practices: "Our history is a braid of histories. . . . We are at once Europe, Africa, and enriched by Asian contributions, we are also Levantine, Indians, as well as pre-Columbian Americans in some respects. Creoleness is 'the world diffracted but recomposed,' . . . a Totality" (Bernabé et al. 1993, 75, 88; italics in the original). Clearly, then, while the *Eloge* emphasized that Créolité should be read as an ethnocultural intersectionality, its articulation was aimed primarily at enhancing multivalent modes of indigenous expression.

Créolité sought to broaden Caribbean identity by allowing multiple influences to coexist and to assert themselves by (re)valorizing neglected or forgotten aspects of encounters or expression germane to the local experience. Between Créolité and the work of Martinican philosopher Édouard Glissant, who had developed the principle of creolization and its corollary of Relation in his *Caribbean Discourse*, these discourses reveal a range of creolized popular cultural practices in a variety of locations, especially in food, music, syncretic religions, and Creole languages. Creolization should be understood as an open, fluid process that cannot be reduced to a single path or principle, and while it emphasizes the unpredictable results and transformative potential of cultural contact, its potential for conveying the cross-cultural elements shaping postcolonial societies should be evident. Between creolization and Créolité, then, new paths were opened up for the articulation of a range of local expressive forms, in literature and painting as well as theater, dance, and music. Authors from Maryse Condé to Suzanne Dracius, from Patrick Chamoiseau to Daniel Maximin, inscribed characters of Indian, Chinese, béké, *chabin*, Syro-Lebanese, and mixed-race origin into their texts in the 1980s, 1990s, and 2000s, some of whom expressed themselves in Creole—whether through a glossary or through (sometimes) translated passages of dialogue—in a literary strategy of cultural multivalence aimed at broadening the palette of authenticity in "French" representation even as it pluralized the putative ethnic makeup of the Antillean community.

Creolizing music as an identitarian practice brings us directly to Kassav' and indirectly to the key role of local music in the demonstrations. Indeed, *zouk* can be said to embody the concrete articulation of Antillean cultural identity through performance, and speaks directly to the concept of an evolving cultural identity as a framework for individual and communal representation. Read through the prism of a burgeoning recognition of non-Frenchness, this insistent articulation of a French Caribbean cultural identity brings to mind Stuart Hall's famous formulation of this discursive and cultural phenomenon. In "Cultural Identity and Diaspora," he speaks tellingly of "the ruptures and discontinuities which constitute, precisely, the Caribbean's 'uniqueness'. Cultural identity, in this second sense, is a matter of 'becoming' as well as of 'being'. It belongs to the future as much as to the past. It is not something which already exists, transcending place, time, history and culture. Cultural identities come from somewhere, have histories. But, like everything which is historical, they undergo constant transformation. Far from being eternally fixed in some essentialised past, they are subject to the continuous 'play' of history, culture and power" (Hall 1990, 225).

Here, Antillean cultural identity arguably recognizes and draws on its past to shape its social inscription in the present and for the future. In its core nonfixity we can see LKP appropriating the creolized praxis of transformation that responds to the patterns and practices of history and power to contest the hegemonies of metropolitan capital. In like manner, zouk can trace its origins and form to an insistence on valorizing the multiple musical heritages of the French Caribbean. In her book *Awakening Spaces*, Brenda F. Berrian charts the supergroup Kassav's route to success from its early beginnings as a Guadeloupe-based band, paying particular attention to the deliberate decision "to adopt a Creole term heard throughout the French Caribbean for its group and a Martinican Creole word for its music"

(2000, 40), as well as its fusion of numerous regional and African-American musical styles and its choice to sing in Creole. Ultimately, through this creolization of musical styles and influences, zouk as played by Kassav' is a fusion of musical genres heard across the Caribbean. Further, Kassav's songs are incontrovertibly political, as they voice the people's perspective on history, slavery, neocolonial domination, and cultural identity, and their repopularization of slave-based rhythms like the *gwo-ka* and use of the drum speaks directly to their incorporation of historical practices into contemporary Caribbean musical forms and current conditions; their 1984 international hit, "Zouk la sé sèl médikaman nou ni" (zouk is the only medicine we have), for example, is about economic hardship and unemployment in what is indisputably a departmental context.

If by valorizing language and history, Kassav' reinforces the notion of the Caribbean as a community of composite peoples and cultures, the group's vocal assertions of self-determination and continuity in the face of historical metropolitan depredations would provide direct inspiration for the traditional musical structure and slave-driven rhythm of the song that would undergird the 2009 uprising, "La Gwadloup sé tan nou." This became the LKP anthem, the chant that would echo through the streets of Guadeloupe during the massive, paralyzing demonstrations. In total, the song lyrics read, "La Gwadloup sé tan nou, la Gwadloup sé pa ta yo: yo péké fè sa yo vlé adan péyi an-nou." Translated from Creole, the lyrics are "Guadeloupe is ours, Guadeloupe isn't theirs, they won't do what they want, what they want with our land." Importantly, the anthem was sung in Guadeloupean Creole, an indigenous language dating back to the seventeenth century, and conveys its insurrectional intent through the sound of the conch shell—traditionally used to summon slaves to revolt—and the chant and *gwo ka* rhythm that also date back to slavery. The rhythm is played on the "ka" drum that slaves made from barrels destined for the transport of various goods, which was also used to announce clandestine meetings or revolts against sugarcane plantation owners. The *gwo ka* was inevitably banned by the colonizers and criticized by the church but remains a valiant staple of Antillean musical expression and cultural resistance, incorporated into the songs of contemporary artists from Kassav' to Njie. The rhythm undergirds songs that tell of the racialized division of Guadeloupe and Martinique and the resulting oppressive labor conditions, agricultural exploitation, and forced creation of a consumer society— persistent social questions voiced by the LKP and grounded in the realities of everyday life.

C.L.R. James and the LKP Uprising

Despite the power of the Créolité reading of the LKP uprising, in terms of the issues raised in the 2009 *Manifeste*—such as postcapitalism, ending economic dependence, and *lyannaj* or collective solidarity—"the text fails to offer any concrete, specific advice" (see Hardwick's article in chapter 2 of this volume). Particularly on the issues of collective solidarity and postcapitalism, James could be of help.

The starting point of James's Marxism is the inherent creativity of the human self, which is not a blank slate upon which society imprints its order and values. If, for James, society and its culture are creative projections of the self, creole identities would also be grounded in these self-formative powers of projection and introjection (Henry 2009, 178–205). These egogenic and sociogenic capabilities operate at both the individual and collective levels. At the collective level, James posited the existence of a We-self that is as creative as the I-self he posited at the individual level. Indeed, for James the I-self of everyday consciousness emerges out of the We-self of collective consciousness, which often remains more hidden. Via this We-self, we engage in a variety of collective behaviors—as members of our churches, universities, political parties, and trade unions—and act in concert. Here James saw forms of bonding that result from the socio-genic creativity of the We-self.

Indeed, James saw much of our culture, politics, and economics as outward creative projections of solutions to real social problems coming from the We-self. These creative projections could come from individuals, like the Créolité scholars, or they could come from the masses. However, when the masses project such creative solutions, these are "written," or better yet dramatized, in media of collective action such as sports, like cricket or football; theater; strikes; and insurrectionary activity, like that of the LKP. These activities are the texts of the masses, and they can sometimes reveal the creativity of the We-self better than the texts of individuals. James examined them as carefully as he examined the texts of Marx, Engels, Césaire, or Glissant, making intertextual connections between uprisings across cultures, decades and centuries.

For James, socialism, and hence ideas of postcapitalism, did not have their origins in the works of Marx or in the communist and socialist parties that followed. Rather, these ideas had their birth in the unwritten texts that were dramatized in the collective self-organizing of the Paris Commune and the Russian Soviets, and that continued in the workers' councils of the Hungarian Revolution, the insurrections that produced departmentalization, and the 2009 LKP uprising. Without these creative upsurges and projections from the We-self of the masses, the books written by individual socialists, including James himself, would have been without solid foundations. In short, socialism has been an insurrectionary response of working classes around the world to the negatives of capitalism, which helped to create the *lyannaj* or collective solidarity between the exploited masses who rose up in Martinique and Guadeloupe.

With regard to the Caribbean region, the We-self of the working class has been structured around strong attachments to island geographies; religious projections of Afro-Christian, Hindu, and Muslim faiths; ludic and carnivalesque projections of sports and merriment; black communist and black democratic socialist political projections; and economic projections of a cooperative and state-centered nature. These aspects of the Caribbean We-self are in dynamic tension, simultaneously advancing and receding. At bottom, James posited a domain of infinite creativity that usually remained hidden, elusive, and unknown. He often referred to the creative center of political and economic projections as the public self of a class or group. The self-formative growth and organizing capabilities of this public self allowed James to measure the socialist content dramatized in worker uprisings. As we seek to know the author of individual texts, so we must seek to know the We-self or author of the collective texts of worker uprisings.

Considering the LKP uprising from this Jamesian perspective, we would be best advised to look at it comparatively and intertextually. How do the solutions dramatized in the forty-four days of collective action compare with those of earlier uprisings, and what do they tell us about the increasing formation or de-formation of the collective self that authored those solutions? James would have been struck by its strategic actions taken, such as the blocking of ports and key arteries into the cities. These would have given LKP its distinct insurrectionary credentials. James would have been struck by the spontaneous creation of the alternative television station Télé Otonom in response to the established media's misreading of the carnivalesque modes through which workers dramatized their grievances. Reinterpreting the carnivalesque as a collective medium of expression would have led to the artists' takeover of the L'Herminier Museum as a site of LKP insurrection.

Compared with other uprisings, the LKP insurrection stands out as extremely significant but at the same time clearly circumscribed. Although the insurrection quite explicitly raised issues of racism, exploitation, and relations with France, these issues were addressed within the existing constitutional and departmentalized framework, excluding the LKP insurrection from the category of a "lutte de libération nationale" (struggle of national liberation). The increases in wages and changes in the tax structure, significant as they were, took place within the collapsing dirigisme economies of France, Guadeloupe, and Martinique. The temporary return to earlier practices of local food production was a powerful statement about food security but at the same time not a long-term practical solution. The setting up of more participatory media was another significant political statement by LKP, which echoed political demands from earlier Caribbean uprisings. But here too, the challenges of giving this idea a broader institutional expression were not met. Thus after the uprising ended, we saw a return to preinsurrectionary economic and political practices, which gave rise to the ambivalent feelings and outcomes that we noted at the beginning of this chapter.

From a Jamesian perspective, these outcomes can be understood with the aid of a number of supporting factors. The first was the isolated context of the uprising. In contrast to the uprisings of the 1930s or those of the 1960s, which were regional, Martinique and Guadeloupe were alone. Second, the unusually brutal suppression of the 1967 insurrectionary strike in Guadeloupe by the French military and CRS police—in which unknown numbers were killed, with estimates ranging up to one hundred or more—was both shocking and intimidating. The 2017 commemoration of the fiftieth anniversary of that event—and the reallocation of its official records as top secret—indicated its sobering impact even as it made clear the Algerian lengths to which France was prepared to go to keep Martinique and Guadeloupe. Third, the postcapitalist impulses of the uprising were certainly inhibited by the dramatic weakening of the international workers movement of James's time; the collapse of socialist experiments in Africa, Grenada, and Jamaica; and then the even more dramatic collapse of socialism in the Soviet Union and Eastern Europe. As a result, a context-driven pragmatism framed the actions of the LKP leaders.

But in spite of this strategic pragmatism, the uprising exposed and made clear for all to see the potentially revolutionary public self of workers in Guadeloupe and Martinique. It lifted the veils that kept this collective self hidden and revealed its specific creative responses to the increased pressures coming from a declining neoliberal order. Ultimately, this forty-four-day uprising set out a new framework for an unprecedented act of resistance, with the overarching neocolonial and neoliberal contexts codifying resistance as it takes shape within the particular ambiguities of the departmental relation. Homi Bhabha defines its particularity this way:

> Resistance is not necessarily an oppositional act of political intention, nor is it the simple negation or exclusion of the "content" of another culture, as a difference once perceived. It is the effect of an ambivalence produced within the rules of recognition of dominating discourses as they articulate the signs of cultural difference and reimplicate them within the deferential relations of colonial power—hierarchy, normalization, marginalization. . . . For colonial domination is achieved through a process of disavowal that denies the chaos of its intervention . . . in

order to preserve the authority of its identity in the teleological narratives of historical and political evolutionism. (Bhabha 1994, 110–111)

Read in this way, the imbrication of culture, economics, and politics is ineluctably and pellucidly clear, as hierarchy and marginalization become the unmistakable symbols of the accumulationist capitalist practices that demarcate the periphery from the center. In disavowing the character and intent of its actions even as it undertakes them, the imperial West's core principles of democracy and economic opportunity effectively become the masks behind which metropolitan capital continues its rapacious reign. In the cooperative and participatory solutions projected, then, and in the spontaneous takeovers of the movement, we have our most important recent update on the state of Caribbean socialism, and in particular its legacy in Guadeloupe and Martinique.

Circumscribed as it may be, let us read this update as carefully and objectively as James would, drawing the lessons from what the projected solutions achieved and did not achieve. Let us carry forward these insights as we continue the struggle for the more just, egalitarian, and post-capitalist society gestured toward by the LKP insurrection.

NOTES

1. See Alain Anselin, "West Indians in France," in *French and West Indian: Martinique, Guadeloupe and French Guiana Today*, edited by Richard D. E. Burton and Fred Reno, 112–118 (London: Macmillan Caribbean, 1995).

2. See Marc Tardieu, *Les Antillais à Paris d'hier à aujourd'hui* (Paris: Editions du Rocher, 2005), 175–176.

3. "The Caribbean Must Reduce Its Multimillion-Dollar Food Impost Bill, Stated the Head of the OECS," Inter-American Institute for Cooperation on Agriculture, July 20, 2018, http://www.iica.int/en/press/news/caribbean-must-reduce-its-multimillion-dollar -food-import-bill-stated-head-oecs.

4. Food and Agriculture Organization of the United Nations, *State of Food Insecurity in the CARICOM Caribbean-Meeting the 2015 Hunger Targets: Taking Stock of Uneven Progress* (Bridgetown, Barbados, 2015), 7.

5. Lurleen M. Walters and Keithly G. Jones, "Caribbean Food Import Demand: Influence of the Changing Dynamics of the Caribbean Economy," selected paper prepared for presentation at the Southern Agricultural Economics Association Annual Meetings, Birmingham, Alabama, February 4–7, 2012, 4.

6. See William F. S. Miles, "Mitterrand in the Caribbean: Socialism (?) Comes to Martinique," *Journal of Interamerican Studies and World Affairs* 27, no. 3 (Autumn 1985): 63–79, 64.

7. "Doing Business with Guadeloupe," Caribbean Export Development Agency, Saint Michael, Barbados, May 2007, 9.

8. "Doing Business with Guadeloupe," 10.

9. "Doing Business with Martinique," Caribbean Export Development Agency, Saint Michael, Barbados, May 2007, 7.

10. *Les derniers maîtres de la Martinique*, directed by Romain Bolzinger (Tac Presse, 2009).

REFERENCES

Balibar, Etienne. 2018. "'Gilets Jaunes': The Meaning of the Confrontation." *Open Democracy*, December 20.

Bernabé, Jean, Patrick Chamoiseau, and Raphaël Confiant. 1993. *Eloge de la créolité / In Praise of Creoleness*, bilingual ed., translated by M. B. Taleb-Khyar. Paris: Editions Gallimard.

Berrian, Brenda F. 2000. *Awakening Spaces: French Caribbean Popular Songs, Music, and Culture*. Chicago: University of Chicago Press.

Bhabha, Homi. 1994. *The Location of Culture*. New York: Routledge.

Burton, Richard D. E. 1993. "'Ki moun nou ye?' The Idea of Difference in Contemporary French West Indian Thought." *New West Indian Guide / Nieuwe West-Indische Gids* 67, no. 1/2: 5–32.

Césaire, Aimé. 2010. "Letter to Maurice Thorez," translated by Chike Jeffers. *Social Text* 28, no. 2 (103) (Summer): 145–152.

Childers, Kristin Stromberg. 2016. *Seeking Imperialism's Embrace: National Identity, Decolonization, and Assimilation in the French Caribbean*. New York: Oxford University Press.

Constant, Fred. 2001. "The French Antilles in the 1990s: Between European Unification and Political Territorialisation." In *Islands at the Crossroads: Politics in the Non-Independent Caribbean*, edited by Aaron Gamaliel Ramos and Angel Israel Rivera, 82–94. Kingston, Jamaica: Ian Randle Publishers.

Duménil, Gérard, and Dominique Lévy. 2004. *Capital Resurgent: Roots of the Neoliberal Revolution*, translated by Derek Jeffers. Cambridge: Harvard University Press.

Girvan, Norman. 2012. "Colonialism and Neo-colonialism in the Caribbean: An Overview." Paper prepared for IV International Seminar: Africa, the Caribbean and Latin America, St. Vincent and the Grenadines, November 24–26.

Guilluy, Christophe. 2018. "France Is Deeply Fractured. Gilets Jaunes Are Just a Symptom." *Guardian*, December 2.

Hall, Stuart. 1990. "Cultural Identity and Diaspora." In *Identity: Community, Culture, Difference*, edited by Jonathan Rutherford, 222–237. London: Lawrence and Wishart.

Henry, Paget. 2009. "C.L.R. James and the Creolizing of Rousseau and Marx." *C.L.R. James Journal* 15, no. 1: 178–205.

Maddox, Camee. 2015. "'Yes We Can! Down With Colonization!' Race, Gender, and the 2009 General Strike in Martinique." *Transforming Anthropology* 23, no. 2: 90–103.

Miles, William F. S. 1995. "Déjà Vu with a Difference: End of the Mitterrand Era and the McDonaldization of Martinique." *Caribbean Studies* 28, no. 2 (July–December): 339–368.

———. 2001. "Fifty Years of 'Assimilation': Assessing France's Experience of Caribbean Decolonisation through Administrative Reform." In *Islands at the Crossroads: Politics in the Non-independent Caribbean*, edited by Aaron Gamaliel Ramos and Angel Israel Rivera, 45–60. Kingston, Jamaica: Ian Randle Publishers.

———. 2003. "The Irrelevance of Independence: Martinique and the French Presidential Elections of 2002. In *New West Indian Guide/Nieuwe West-Indische Gids* 77, no. 3/4: 221–252.

———. 2005. "Democracy without Sovereignty: France's Postcolonial Paradox." *Brown Journal of World Affairs* xi, no. 2 (Winter/Spring): 223–234.

Obertan, Pamela. 2009. "The Food Crisis in Guadeloupe." *Seedling* (January): 14–15.

PART II

NEOLIBERALISM AND THE PARADOXES OF NON-SOVEREIGNTY IN THE WIDER CARIBBEAN

6

Criminalization, Punitive Neoliberalism, and the Puerto Rican Independence Movement

JACQUELINE LAZÚ

The exercise of competitive capitalism in Puerto Rico has meant control over political action and economic interests, and the control, criminalization, and punishment of oppositional thinking. The neoliberal project in Puerto Rico is both vintage and vanguard, as the island territory has been an incubator for that project's principles as well as an important landmark for challenging them. Since 1898 the question of U.S. citizenship has been inextricably tied to these issues. Even with infamously divided sentiments over the question of political status, culture and nationalism remain, arguably, the most powerful weapons against the U.S. political enterprise in Puerto Rico. For well over 120 years of U.S. rule, the Puerto Rican independence movement has been in the front of this resistance. Standing their ground on the function of cultural and political autonomy, the Puerto Rican independence movement has endured the network of legal, military, ideological and economic acts of repression and state crimes that harness the conditions uniting neoliberalism and empire.

For most observers, understanding the manifestations of complicity that they perceive among Puerto Ricans and other colonized people, with the systems that oppress them is challenging to say the least. Scholars have studied all of these systems in important and productive ways. In fact, Puerto Rico's intellectual history in response to U.S. imperialism and systems of power and domination is ubiquitous. I find the work of nineteenth-century philosopher Eugenio María de Hostos especially impactful for its

JACQUELINE LAZÚ

application of interdisciplinarity as decolonial practice before coloniality had been named (Berrios 1985, 81).

In more recent times, the discourses of coloniality and decoloniality have provided us with important tools to articulate the philosophical underpinnings of the colonial enterprise understood as the patterns of power that exceed the limits of colonial administrations to define culture, labor, intersubjective relations, and knowledge production (see Quijano 2001). While many other scholars have added layers to our understanding of coloniality, I want to highlight Puerto Rican philosopher Nelson Maldonado Torres's understanding of coloniality as a radicalization and naturalization of the non-ethics of war. In modernity, Maldonado-Torres explains, the idea of how a world is in conditions of war and the codes of behavior in that time is transformed through the idea of race. It becomes naturalized and the treatment of those defeated is legitimized long after the war is over (Maldonado-Torres 2016, 248).

While the independence movement has been marginalized in Puerto Rican politics, the potential for aggression or opposition that has been present from the very beginning in the colonial relationship with the United States was in fact repurposed into the racial profile of the docile, ungrateful, and unruly Puerto Rican in the imaginary of dominant culture. This trope was at the core of the canonical and influential essay written by Rene Marqués in 1960, "El puertorriqueño dócil." The text is both celebrated as a defense of Puerto Rican nationalism and challenged as a relentless example of the coloniality of literary discourse in Puerto Rico. One especially impactful critique came from Juan Gelpí; in *Literatura y paternalismo en Puerto Rico* (1993), he rigorously reveals the paternalism embedded in the Puerto Rican literary canon and the break from the tradition seen in later generations of writers. To Gelpí, Marqués's essay signals the final desperate plea of a nationalist and paternalistic discourse in crisis that has always supposed a relationship between those who have power and those subject to it. This would soon be replaced with a more diverse and heterogeneous view of identity and nationalism as represented, for example, in José Luis González's 1980 essay "El país de cuatro pisos" (Gelpí 1993, 2).

In effect, the trope of the docile Puerto Rican served to justify the domination, exploitation, and when necessary annihilation of Puerto Ricans to sustain the "new racial capitalism."[1] Maldonado-Torres's suggestion that we consider decolonial transdiciplinary methodologies to reach a wider and more complex understanding is key to confronting the complex nature of Puerto Rican nationalist discourse. To this end, Yolanda Martinez-San Miguel's work extending the discourse of coloniality is also an important point of reference. In *Coloniality of Diasporas* (2014) she offers three ideas that are especially important to this study. The first is her project of decentering the nation-state, which she argues obscures the ability to respond to coloniality in the Caribbean. Secondly, she posits the possibilities of the coloniality of cultural power to challenge the dominance of economic and political discourse in the narrative of identity formation and resistance in the Caribbean. Lastly, she exposes a critical bridge of decolonial possibilities by extending the narrative of Caribbean colonialism and resistance into the diasporic experience. In the case of Puerto Rico, all three of the ideas *are* the starting point. In applying a critical criminological lens to the study of historical narrative analysis I offer another level of transdiciplinarity and, as such, decolonial praxis that reveals similar interlocked pathways to the neoliberal, colonial politics of knowledge production in Puerto Rico.

These ideas became inherent in a historical trajectory that begins with the customization of a legal system that criminalized any opposition to U.S. colonialism. They were fomented by the formation of an insular political apparatus that secured the interest of the elite above the common good, and paramilitary actions that guaranteed the isolation of opposing interests as the United States implemented its formula for the neoliberal empire. Indeed to understand conditions of the neoliberal colonial state in Puerto Rico, most recently invested in a new stage of disaster capitalism, we must consider from multiple angles how systems *relied* on one another and were part of a continuum that effectively *guaranteed* mass complicity and compliance with its insidious progression.

Second-Class Citizenship and the Criminalization of Dissent

Since 1898, the most pervasive method of control in maintaining the colonial stronghold in Puerto Rico and any public opposition suppressed has been federal jurisdiction over the Puerto Rican judiciary system. The suppression of Puerto Rican self-determination has time and again taken precedence over the understanding and enforcement of justice relative to U.S. constitutional law. The primary target was the dissenting anti-capitalist advocating Puerto Rican independence. The secondary target was the Puerto Rican people, primarily the poor and working-class majority that would somehow need to be convinced that they deserved to be ill-treated and punished harshly for any attempt to undermine the colonial paradigm.

In the aftermath of Hurricane Maria in September of 2017, there was an unprecedented interest in the status of Puerto Rico and the conditions that led to the relationship between the United States and the island territory. Op-eds on the Foraker Act of 1900, the Jones-Shafroth Act of 1917, and the Merchant Marine Act of 1920 circulated widely on social media. A USA Today/Suffolk University poll conducted in March 2017 found that fewer than half of Americans (47 percent) believed that Puerto Ricans are U.S. citizens by birth (Gómez 2017). These federal laws were in fact precursors for the conditions that fomented the expansion of U.S. economic interests and the unidirectional trade benefits that characterize colonial neoliberal economies.

Provisions in all of these federal laws brought into question the status of Puerto Rican citizenship, particularly in the application of the U.S. Constitution and its statutes. There were a number of critical decisions that ensued relative to the Civil Code and the Codes of Civil and Criminal Procedure that marked the beginning of de jure suspension of constitutional rights to Puerto Ricans in criminal and civil cases that would be exercised at will against anti-colonial activists in particular. Under the Foraker Act, judicial power was vested in the courts and tribunals then existing in Puerto Rico, including its municipal and police courts. The act also created a federal judicial district for a court called the United States District Court for the District of Puerto Rico that succeeded the Provisional Court, which was established following the Treaty of Paris that ended the Spanish-American War and made Puerto Rico a possession of the United States under military rule. Unlike federal courts in state jurisdictions, federal court fees and expenses and salaries for the court's officers in Puerto Rico were payable out of the Puerto Rico treasury. Puerto Rico was literally made to pay for the imposition of federal oversight. Moreover, the Foraker Act also created a commission appointed by the president of the United States to compile and revise the laws of Puerto Rico and to frame and report recommendations for changes to Puerto Rico's laws moving forward (Rodriguez Vidal 2016, 3–4).

While there were immediate challenges to the Foraker Act, the U.S. Supreme Court picked and chose which it would consider. In 1901, it chose to hear five cases that it collectively referred to as the "Insular Cases." Christina Duffy Burnett and Burke Marshal provide a comprehensive analysis of the issues covered in the new territorial policy instituted by these acts in *Foreign in a Domestic Sense: Puerto Rico, American Expansion and the Constitution* (2001). Lanny Thompson extends the study of the Insular Cases by looking at the differential attitudes of the United States toward unincorporated territories, and the racialized discourses used to justify assimilation through colonial insularity. Among the most important of the cases that these studies point to is *Downes v. Bidwell*, which challenged the tariff as unconstitutional in violation of the uniformity clause, the no preference clause, and the no export duty clause of the U.S. Constitution. By a vote of 5–4, the Supreme Court ruled for the U.S. government to sustain the tariff, but it was clear that there was no shared rationale for the decision—in large part because the Court was unprepared to answer the greater question of Puerto Rico's relationship to the United States. The most interesting position relative to this study was Justice Byron White's middle-ground stance. He proposed that even though the Constitution did apply throughout the United States and its territories, the full set of protections applied only to those territories that the Congress had "incorporated" (Rodriguez Vidal 2016, 5). Since Puerto Rico remained unincorporated, Congress was free to impose the tariff. In effect, the United States maintained the right to colonize and it could also deny its possessions rights that apply to the states. In August 2019, the American Civil Liberties Union (ACLU), submitted a friend of the court brief seeking to overturn the racist precedents in the Insular Cases that have excluded Puerto Ricans from the same constitutional protections as other Americans. The brief came in connection with a case over the constitutionality of the financial oversight board, known colloquially as "La Junta" (a short form of "La Junta de Control Fiscal"), established for Puerto Rico by Congress in 2016 in the midst of the financial crisis on the island (Higgins 2019). The dispute was scheduled to be argued in October 2019, and a decision is expected by June 2020. The enduring effects of the Insular Cases on their own speak volumes to differential justice in Puerto Rico, but they hardly stand alone.

The Jones-Shafroth Act, also known as the Jones Act, signed on March 2, 1917, defined Puerto Rico expressly as "an organized but unincorporated territory" of the United States, an ambiguity that appeared aimed at justifying the racist legal precedents and those to follow. It also granted Puerto Ricans statutory, not constitutional, U.S. citizenship that made them eligible for the military draft. Only a few months after the enactment of the Jones Act, nearly twenty thousand Puerto Ricans were drafted to participate in World War I. Moving forward, Puerto Rico saw a deepening of U.S. presence on the island running into World War II, when the numbers of Puerto Ricans serving multiplied to proportions higher than those of any other ethnic or national group after Hawaiians (Falcón 1984, 47). The act also extended to Puerto Rico a bill of rights and instituted a republican form of government with three branches, maintaining the judicial powers already vested in the courts after the Foraker Act, as well as a few left over from when Puerto Rico was a Spanish colony—many of which *remain* in place *today*. Finally, the Jones Act also allowed for writs of error and appeals from final judgments of the Supreme Court of Puerto Rico to be taken to the United States Circuit Court of Appeals for the First Circuit (the federal appellate jurisdiction that Puerto Rico shares with Maine, Massachusetts,

New Hampshire, and Rhode Island) and subsequently to the U.S. Supreme Court (Rodriguez Vidal 2016, 5).

The Jones Act was also challenged, and Justice White's incorporation doctrine would resurface in the 1922 case of *Balzac v. Puerto Rico*. This criminal libel case was against Jesús M. Balzac, an editor for the newspaper *El Baluarte*, who wrote an article referring indirectly to the colonial governor at the time, Arthur Yager. The article was considered libelous. Pursuant to the Jones Act and its guaranteed citizenship, Balzac sought a jury trial under the Sixth Amendment (see Soltero 2006). The U.S. Supreme Court ultimately held that the Sixth Amendment did not require an extension of the right to jury trial to Puerto Rico as it was an unincorporated territory. While Puerto Rico eventually legislated to provide jury trials in criminal cases that resulted in prison sentences longer than six months, to this day there is no right to jury trial in civil cases brought before Puerto Rico courts. Balzac never even got to the most obvious argument for the exercise of his First Amendment rights. What the Balzac case finally revealed above all were the measures that the federal courts were willing to go through to silence opposition to colonial rule. In fact, pro-independence journalists have been targeted by the United States from the very beginning. In 1898, Izcoa Díaz, arrested and sentenced for publishing critiques of the occupying forces, became the first of many Puerto Rican political prisoners in the United States.

Coercion and open repression by legal means, continued to be distinctively present under U.S. rule. While it began with the incarceration of journalists and the closing of opposition newspapers by colonial authorities, it continued with the imprisonment of Nationalist Party leaders in the 1930s. Luis Nieves Falcón's bilingual legal summaries collected in *Violación de los Derechos Humanos en Puerto Rico por los Estados Unidos / Violation of Human Rights in Puerto Rico by the United States* (2002), Ché Paralitici's *Sentencia Impuesta: 100 Años de Encarcelamientos por la Independencia de Puerto Rico* (2004), and Ramón Bosque-Pérez and José Javier Colón Morera's *Puerto Rico Under Colonial Rule: Political Persecution and the Quest for Human Rights*

(2006), are just three of the book-length resources that offer distinct and wide perspectives on the actions of the courts against the legal and political rights of Puerto Ricans to speak and act against colonialism. As activists, many of these scholars offer firsthand experiences and testimonies to reinforce the otherwise hidden abuses against activists, and offering a much-needed transdisciplinary praxis to the scholarship (Nieves Falcón 2002, 19).

Among the many laws these scholars explore, Law 53 stands out as critical to reconstructing the victimology of state crimes against Puerto Ricans and their fight for self-determination through legal measures. The Gag Law, as it is popularly known, was enacted on May 1948 by the Puerto Rico legislature and made it a felony offense to "encourage, defend, counsel, or preach, voluntarily or knowingly, the need, desirability, or convenience of overturning, destroying, or paralyzing the Insular Government, or any of its political subdivisions, by way of force or violence; and to publish, edit, circulate, sell, distribute, or publicly exhibit with the intention to overturn . . . , as well as to organize or help organize any society, group, or assembly of persons who encourage, defend, or preach any such thing, or for other ends" (quoted in Acosta-Lespier 2006, 59). This law was a copy and direct translation of a section of the Alien Registration Act, a statute popularly known as the "Smith Act," the roots of which can be traced to the Alien and Sedition Acts of 1798 passed by the predominantly Federalist 5th United States Congress and approved by President John Adams. The Smith Act was aimed primarily at immigrants who supported the Democratic-Republicans and later the secessionists during the American Civil War. The Gag Law was defended by the president of the senate at the time, Luis Muñoz Marín, who would later become the first Puerto Rican elected governor, as a measure against the Nationalist Party that had gained some ground after the return of nationalist, independence movement leader Pedro Albizu Campos in 1947.

Ivonne Acosta-Lespier explains that even though Law 53 was passed in 1948, it is often said to be the result of the 1950 Nationalist revolt. She says, "It is thus deduced, incorrectly and in defiance of the truth, that the repression following the revolt was reasonable, as any government has the right to protect itself from attempts of being overturned by force or violence" (Acosta-Lespier 2006, 60). In fact, the law provoked more violence. The public immediately understood the interest that the law served for the United Sates, and there was strong civic opposition that was rigorously suppressed. Furthermore, explains Acosta-Lespier, the Gag Law was so severely enforced that it helped to decrease electoral support for independence, and began an "era of silence" at the University of Puerto Rico that lasted nearly two decades; hypervigilance and harassment provoked the Nationalists to resist with violence rather than be meekly led to jail (Acosta-Lespier 2006, 61).

The U.S. federal legal system would continue to find ways to dismantle the independence movement, which in turn adopted new modes of resistance. The first time that the U.S. government used the seditious conspiracy statute was in the 1930s against Puerto Rican Nationalists. 18 U.S.C.S. § 2384, Seditious Conspiracy, provides:

> If two or more persons in any State or Territory, or in any place subject to the jurisdiction of the United States, conspire to overthrow, put down, or to destroy by force the Government of the United States, or to levy war against them, or to oppose by force the authority thereof, or by force to prevent, hinder, or delay the execution of any law of the United States, or by force to seize, take, or possess any property of the United States contrary to the authority thereof, they shall each be fined under this title or imprisoned not more than twenty years, or both.

For more than sixty-five years since then, until 1986, the statute was used exclusively against Puerto Rican *independentistas* (Winter 1996, 185). In the 1930s, Pedro Albizu Campos, Juan Antonio Corretjer, Luis G. Velázquez, Clements Soto Vélez, Erasmo Velásquez, Julio H. Velazquez, Juan Gallardo Santiago, and Pablo Rosado Ortiz were accused of conspiracy to overthrow the U.S. government in Puerto Rico for their support of labor movements and other anti-colonial efforts. Seditious conspiracy charges were brought up again against Puerto Rican Nationalists in the 1950s including Lolita Lebrón, Rafael Cancel Miranda, Irivin Flores, and

Andrés Figueroa Cordero after they opened fire in the U.S. Congress to bring attention to the continued colonization of Puerto Rico. They, along with other Nationalists, were accused of a single continuous conspiracy operating from at least September 1950 to May 1954. Again, three different cases of seditious conspiracy in the 1980s were brought against Puerto Ricans in the pro-independence struggle. The immediate objective, as former political prisoner Elizam Escobar explains, was "to criminalize our struggle, labeling us terrorists and lunatics" (Torres and Velázquez 1998, 238). Seditious conspiracy is a powerful tool for the U.S. federal government as it allows for the imposition of lengthy and disproportionate sentences, justifies punitive and torturous conditions of imprisonment, and perpetuates the expansion of repressive legal authority over the Puerto Rican people. Seditious conspiracy feeds a patriotic, racist, and xenophobic mentality, and builds a face of neutral criminal prosecution by a "democratic" government (see Susler 2018).

In 1936, Secretary General Juan Antonio Corretjer of the Nationalist Party was asked to surrender party records to the grand jury. Corretjer's refusal on the grounds that U.S. courts had no legitimate jurisdiction over Puerto Rico incited a posture of noncollaboration with the antics of the federal legal system that has demonstrated the strength of the Puerto Rican people to withstand those antics for the cause of self-determination and independence (see Deutsch 1984). Activists in the 1970s and beyond have taken a similar stance against U.S. courts' finagling of politically and racially charged laws. In 1976, Lureida Torres Rodríguez, a schoolteacher in New York City, would be the first Puerto Rican subpoenaed by a federal grand jury. The FBI Counterintelligence Program (COINTELPRO), which had been infiltrating Black and Puerto Rican liberation movements in the United States since its inception in 1956, based Torres's case primarily on covert and illegal surveillance. Following the example of Corretjer, Lureida Torres stood up to a New York federal grand jury investigating the Puerto Rican independence movement and refused to cooperate. The price to pay for not collaborating with the grand jury is well known to those who support the independence movement. Torres spent three months in jail.

Between 1976 and 1979, eleven independence activists or simply supporters of the independence movement were jailed for civil or criminal contempt, or both, for refusing to take part in the investigation (López Rivera 2007, 172). Jan Susler, attorney at the People's Law Office in Chicago and member of the National Lawyers Guild, whose attorneys have represented several of the political prisoners, explains that like the other egregious legal precedents, the grand jury has been leveraged as "a tool for the political internment of independence activists"(Susler 2008, 7). The U.S. federal courts invidiously wield it against those seeking to end U.S. colonial rule over Puerto Rico.

Armed Resistance and the Emergence of Party Politics

Since the Foraker Act, the Jones Act, and the Gag Law, the exercise of state repression has been committed to depicting all colonial opponents as "terrorists" in an effort to criminalize their actions on behalf of liberation and deprive them of their human rights. Simultaneously, the persistence of a legacy of militant resistance continued to challenge the illegitimacy of the colonial establishment. Prior to the 1898 occupation, the movement against Spanish colonialism, under the leadership of Ramón Emeterio Betances and Segundo Ruiz Belvis, laid the strategic and symbolic foundations for the movement (see Paralitici 2004; Lidín 1981). El Grito de Lares on September 23, 1968, orchestrated by Bentances and Ruiz Belvis, continues to hold important symbolic meaning for the independence movement.

The powerful symbol of September 23 didn't escape notice of the U.S. government either. In the midst of the celebration on the 137th commemoration of El Grito in Puerto Rico, more than two hundred agents of the FBI, among them a score of snipers, surrounded the house of seventy-two-year-old pro-independence activist Filiberto Ojeda Ríos in the town of Hormigueros and gunned him down. The operation that killed Ojeda Ríos, which many believe to be part of the infamous extrajudicial execution "Kill List" under President Barak Obama (see Becker and Shane 2012), backfired terribly for the FBI. While Puerto Ricans, more often than not out of fear of the dire repercussions, have grown wary of independence movement leaders, these same Puerto Ricans did not take well to this killing by the U.S. government, particularly in a time of such dire economic and political repression. The Puerto Rican government had received no notice of the offensive. As journalist Félix Jiménez put it in a report on the event in the *Nation* (2005), it "turned the former fugitive from a Robin Hoodish patriot of reference into the consensual patriot of preference in Puerto Rico." Moreover, Jiménez rightfully reminded the public, "the timing of the execution could not have been more incendiary—it was staged during the commemoration of the 137th anniversary of El Grito de Lares . . . the most important date for independence advocates on the island, a holiday whose highlight for the past fifteen years had been a taped message by the man who was left dying."

The FBI shot down Ojeda Ríos one hour after his last political speech had been broadcast over radio and television, tapping an emotional nationalist nerve that for a brief but significant moment *united* pro-statehood, commonwealth, and independence advocates among the people denouncing the actions of the FBI. The island government responded quickly, understanding the symbolic capacity of the event, and to the chagrin of political opponents accorded all kinds of posthumous honors to Ojeda Ríos. Before his death was even announced officially to the public, the execution prompted massive protests on the island and in U.S. cities including New York, New Jersey, Boston, and Chicago. A riot at the University of Puerto Rico forced an administrative decree for an "academic recess" for students, staff, and faculty to attend Ojeda Ríos's funeral.

Ojeda Ríos had been the commander in chief of the Boricua Popular Army or *Los Macheteros*, one of a number of underground groups that emerged from the legal and covert criminalization tactics of the U.S. federal legal system in the 1970s. He was on the FBI's most wanted list for fifteen years after jumping bail on accusations of the infamous 1983 heist of a Wells Fargo Truck in Connecticut, netting $7.2 million. The spectacle of state terror staged in the execution of Ojeda Ríos was, again, neither unprecedented nor conclusive.

In "Puerto Rico: State Formation in a Colonial Context," Pedro Cabán identifies eight periods of political and economic change that in some way altered the conduct of U.S. colonial practice in Puerto Rico. The periods were characterized by shifts in local political coalitions that competed for the ability to administer the colony. Each period, he asserts, was also notably marked by insular economic restructuring precipitated by shifts in U.S. fiscal policies and changes in the economy, congressional efforts to address Puerto Rico's status, and changing perceptions of hemispheric challenges to U.S. national security. The periods that he identifies are (1) dismantling and replacing the Spanish colonial regime (1898–1900); (2) establishing the colonial state, (1900–1916); (3) consolidation and demise (1917–1931); (4) reworking the colonial formula (1932–1940); (5) relative autonomy (1941–1951); (6) Commonwealth and industrialization (1952–1968); (7) demise of Estado Libre Asociado (ELA) and annexation (1969–1988); and (8) reappraisal of the Commonwealth (1989–2000) (Cabán 2002, 172). While Cabán's study ends with the turn of the twentieth century, we could theoretically add another two periods: a ninth, from 2000 to 2017 marking a period of an unprecedented debt crisis, austerity measures, and the implementation of the fiscal control board; and a tenth, marked by the post–Hurricane Maria emergence of colonial disaster capitalism taking place since September 20, 2017, and the 2020 earthquakes.

I assert that each of the periods that Cabán identifies is also characterized by a surge of militant anti-colonial activity on the island and the metropolis. The establishment of a U.S. military occupation and the new era of U.S. colonialism after 1898 marked a new phase in the Puerto Rican independence movement. Most scholars tend to move directly into analyses of the 1930s nationalist movements led by Albizu Campos as the next most influential period for the movement. The 1920s, however, were critical to understanding the development of the political partnership and the nuances of Puerto Rican politics that reignited the political violence of the beginning of the century. The events of this era served as a precursor for the activities of the 1930s onward.

The emergence of the powerful political block that grew out of a labor base in the previous decades shifted the political landscape in the 1920s. The 1901 Hollander Act passed by the island's first civilian governor, Charles Herbert Allen, imposed taxes on farmers that aimed to ensure that Puerto Ricans lost their land in order to speed up the growing commercial demand for sugar and tobacco. The effects of Hurricane San Ciriaco in 1899, and the destruction of the coffee crops for which farmers received virtually no relief funds, further instigated the process. Out of desperation, farmers turned to predatory lenders that suddenly infiltrated the island, and by 1920 the majority of Puerto Rican farmers had lost their land to American Colonial Bank, Bankers Trust, or National City Bank. Charles Herbert Allen had become president of the American Sugar Refining Company, now known as Domino Sugar, which controlled 98 percent of the sugar-refining capacity in the United States. The brief economic boom during World War I, the crisis that followed, and the depression of the world sugar industry in the spring of 1920 yielded major losses at a time when the insular economy had invested its energies entirely in the cultivation of sugarcane. Cane sugar became a protected crop under the U.S. tariff system (Ayala and Bernabe 2007; Scarano 1993).

In response to these conditions, the Federación Libre de Trabajadores (FLT), led by Santiago Iglesias, organized tobacco factory and field workers, sugarcane cutters, millworkers, and dockworkers during the first decade of the century. By the end of World War I, membership in the FLT had tripled to twenty-eight thousand members, making the FLT a political and social threat to the hegemonic classes on the island. Moreover, Santiago Iglesias had won a seat in the Puerto Rican Senate in 1917, and members of the party began to call for the creation of an independent republic (Ayala and Bernabe 2007, 64). The Nationalist Party was founded in 1922 from a coalition of three pro-independence organizations that had formed on the island: the Asociación Nacionalista de Puerto Rico, which evolved from the Union Party; La Juventud Nacionalista; and La Asociación Independentista. The Nationalist Party that was evolving at this time took a somewhat timid approach to the struggle for independence and wavered in its allegiances to the Union Party. The leadership cadre of the party belonged to the Ateneo Puertorriqueño and would become a sort of intellectual branch of the independence movement (see Albizu-Campos Meneses and Rodríguez León 2007; Denis 2015). These conditions set the foundation for the various allegiances that emerged among the dominant classes and would start to give shape to the complex system of loyalties to U.S. rule.

The United States laid down the neocolonial gauntlet in Puerto Rico with the passage of Section 27 of the Merchant Marine Act of 1920 (also referred to as the Law of Cabotage). The Act required that all goods carried by water between U.S. ports be carried on U.S. flagged ships that are constructed in the United States, owned by U.S. citizens, and operated by U.S. citizens. The merchandise had to be loaded off the original carrier, loaded onto a U.S. ship, and only then delivered into Puerto Rico. The law covered the shipment of any product from anywhere (Denis 2015; Grabow, Manak, and Ikenson 2018). In effect, this maritime "protection" racket in the first two decades of the U.S. colonial government occupation of Puerto Rico began to truly shape the fundamental elements of disaster capitalism.

The people's demand for change was against a community economically and politically tied to the United States. Historian José Solá explains that the pressure of a growing militant labor movement and criticism by the United States led political leaders on the island to forge new alliances. Leaders representing the landowning interests (Union Party) and corporate sectors from the Puerto Rican Republican Party articulated a political discourse that was nationalist and reformist. Meanwhile, leaders among the remnants of the Puerto Rican Republican Party joined members of the Socialist Party to form the *Coalición* and called for the annexation of the island to secure Puerto Rican prosperity and American economic interests. What is clear is that the political realignments were based on fear of the working class taking over the political apparatus (Solá 2010, 5–6). While they observed the protocols of political competition on the surface, they orchestrated wide-scale coercion and violence against the poor and working-class electorate. The American colonial officials, expected to administer the island and look after the interests of American investors, conveniently tolerated the violence and left it to be dealt with by the local police.

The period of the 1930s stands as one of the most horrific demonstrations of state crime and spectacles of terror in the history of U.S. occupation in Puerto Rico. A number of things changed significantly enough to catch the attention of the U.S. government during this period, and initiated a period of particularly violent repression and resistance. In 1930, Dr. Pedro Albizu Campos took over the leadership of the Nationalist Party and steered it away from its methods of moderate opposition. He began to denounce and challenge colonial politics directly. This coincided with a series of workers' strikes supported by Albizu Campos and the Nationalist Party and a rise in the ideals of independence. The United States responded with the militarization of the Puerto Rican government. They appointed Blanton Winship as governor of the island, Elisha Francis Riggs as chief of police, and Robert A. Cooper as judge of the U.S. federal court in Puerto Rico. All of them had links to the U.S. armed forces.

Of the crimes committed by the state against Puerto Ricans, the bloodiest took place on March 21, 1937, in the Ponce Massacre. Members of the Nationalist Party had planned to hold a march. At the last minute, under direct orders from Governor Winship, the permits for the march were revoked, but the Nationalists did not comply. The police responded with an ambush that, according to the American Civil Liberties Union investigating the events of that day, no one could escape. The police fired on the crowd of unarmed people, which included uninvolved spectators, leaving nineteen people dead and more than two hundred wounded, with two police officers caught in their own cross fire. Between 1935 and 1940, at least forty-five members of the Puerto Rican Nationalist Party were sent to prison. Some were sentenced to life in prison and exonerated years later. The harshest sentence was given to Pedro Albizu Campos, who was indicted on charges by the federal grand jury in 1937 connected to the assassination of Riggs by two members of the Cadets of the Republic, the youth organization of the Nationalist Party. The U.S. government referred to the

Cadets as the "Liberation Army of Puerto Rico" and based some of the sedition charges against Albizu Campos, Corretjer, and the others indicted on their role in organizing the Cadets. The prosecutors claimed that the military tactics taught to the Cadets were for the purpose of overthrowing the U.S. government. A jury of seven Puerto Ricans and five non-Puerto Ricans acquitted the group by a vote of 7–5. Disapproving of the verdict, Judge Robert Cooper called a new trial with an intentionally selected and manipulated jury of ten non–Puerto Ricans and two Puerto Ricans, which found the defendants guilty and sent them to the federal penitentiary in Atlanta. Albizu Campos was not able to return to Puerto Rico until 1947 after nearly a decade of documented torture. Upon his release and return to the island, again he began to prepare for the armed struggle against the U.S. colonial enterprise (Paralitici 2006; Ayala and Bernabe 2007; López Rivera 2007; Denis 2015).

In the 1940s and 1950s, the next major surge in the resistance movement grew out of the release and return of Albizu Campos; the Gag Law; and Public Law 600, the Puerto Rican Commonwealth Act. The disintegration of the sugar monoculture economy became the target of Albizu Campos's fiery speeches condemning the United States for keeping Puerto Rico under economic bondage and its people in perpetual poverty. International pressures stemming from the Atlantic Charter and the shifting international view on colonialism led to the United States granting Puerto Ricans a semblance of self-government. This came in the form of the declaration of the commonwealth status and an amendment to Section 12 of the Jones Act granting qualified voters in Puerto Rico the right to elect their own governor (Otaño 2003, 1820).

On August 27, 1951, the people of Puerto Rico elected the members of the Constitutional Convention that would pass the resolutions necessary to make these happen under a new Constitution. The first was Resolution 22, which chose the word "Commonwealth" to name the political body of the insular state, which is "simultaneously connected to a larger political system and hence does not have an independent and separate status." Having no direct translation in Spanish, the convention chose the term "Estado

Libre Asociado," which translates literally to "Free Associated State." A second decision, Resolution 23, attempted to affirm some level of adjustment to the status of the island "within the terms of compact entered into with the United States" (Otaño 2003, 1840). Despite the obvious attempt to disguise the status quo, Puerto Ricans passed the Constitution in March of 1952, but not before approval and editing by the United States and with an additional amendment that required any change to the Commonwealth Constitution to be consistent with the U.S. Constitution, Public Law 600, and the Federal Relations Act.

Preempting the Constitutional Convention, from 1947 to 1951, the United States had submitted the requisite information to have Puerto Rico removed from the United Nations' list of non-self-governing territories, which under a new resolution (73e) required that countries inform the United Nations (UN) of any changes to the constitutional status of their territories. Exemption from that requirement amounted to a suspension of the need to send the UN information about the territory. Upon the creation of the Commonwealth, the United States informed the UN of the "change in government." In January 1953, the U.S. Department of State informed the UN that it would no longer transmit information as required by the UN resolution. The measure virtually ensured that cases involving Puerto Ricans brought before the international body would be approached with an entirely different type of diplomacy. The omission was all that the U.S. government needed to launch its most repressive campaign against the independence movement.

Movement leaders would not stand idle as the U.S. government took these illicit actions. By now movement leaders fully understood that electoral politics would not be a successful option against the anti-imperialist agenda. The only feasible solution they saw was a campaign of continued agitation that would make it too costly and difficult for the United States to maintain the colony. Albizu Campos explained: "Puerto Rico must create a grave crisis for the colonial administration in order that its demands be heard. What is needed is a rebel organization to make a clean break with the colonial regime and to request recognition of our independence from the free nations of the world" (quoted in Wagenheim et al. 1988, 168). In 1950, the movement launched some of its most aggressive responses yet in the form of notable armed insurrections. In October of 1950, under the leadership of Blanca Canales, the Nationalists burned down the police station in the town of Jayuya, overthrew the local authorities, and raised the banned Puerto Rican flag, declaring Puerto Rico an independent republic for two days. The plan, originally intended to take place in November of that year, was diverted when the Nationalists learned that government agents knew of their impending insurrection. Their long-term objective was to gain independence for Puerto Rico, but their short-term goal was to seize and retain military and political control of one or two large towns and pressure the UN to force the United States to allow Puerto Rico its right to exercise self-determination (Cabán 2005, 499). That week the Nationalist insurrection broke out in nine towns and cities, including Jayuya, the capital San Juan, Utuado, and Arecibo. For the first and only documented moment in history by many accounts, the United States bombed its own citizens as the U.S. National Guard launched a ground and air strike on the town of Jayuya that ended the insurrection (Denis 2015, 194; Cabán 2005, 499). The government responded with draconian measures.

Law 53 was used as the legal tool to arrest, convict, and jail hundreds of individuals affiliated or presumed to be affiliated with any pro-independence organization. Albizu Campos was convicted on twelve counts of violation of Law 53, and given prison terms ranging from twenty-seven to seventy-eight years of prison for attempted murder and conspiracy to overthrow the U.S. government. Twenty-one Nationalists were convicted of murdering a police officer and sentenced to life in prison. During his various prison sentences in the United States and Puerto Rico, Albizu Campos and his comrades were subjected to agonizing, inhumane methods of torture that would affect them for the rest of their lives. In 1958, a Civil Liberties Commission issued a report on Law No. 53 accusing the government of using the law "under a façade of legality . . . as a dragnet to punish members of minority groups, with the crime defined in a highly expansive manner to reduce or eliminate the problem of proof" (quoted in Cabán 2005, 499).

The second half of the twentieth century was marked by surges of repression and retaliation between the U.S. government and various pro-independence groups in Puerto Rico and in the Puerto Rican diaspora in the United States. The Nationalist Party, the Macheteros, and the Fuerzas Armadas de Liberación Nacional (FALN) followed the declarations of Albizu Campos, positing that the U.S. government would not respond to diplomacy—only armed resistance. The Nationalist uprisings were followed by an assassination attempt on U.S. President Harry Truman by Oscar Collazo and Grisello Torresola, residents of New York who attacked Blair House, where the president resided. Torresola was killed in the attack. Collazo survived and received a death sentence that was later commuted to life in prison by Truman. Once again, Collazo would explain that "it was not important if we did or did not reach President Truman. That was secondary. It was sufficient to create a scandal that focused world attention on the colonial case of Puerto Rico. And the assault was a success" (Fernández 1996, 182).

In another notable failed but symbolically important attack, led by Lolita Lebrón in 1954, four members of the Nationalist Party shot at members of the U.S. House of Representatives shouting "¡Viva Puerto Rico Libre!" Five congressmen were wounded. As Lebrón was being arrested, she proclaimed, "I did not come to kill anyone, I came to die for Puerto Rico!" Again, the Nationalists were sentenced to death—charges that were later commuted to life in prison. In fact, in time, the extreme sentences imposed on the Nationalists and the popular campaigns for their release would become too evident to ignore. In the late 1970s, after serving twenty-five years in prison, Lolita Lebrón, Irving Flores, and Rafael Cancel Miranda would have their sentences commuted by President Jimmy Carter, who cited humane considerations for their commutations, despite years of Puerto Rican urges for clemency. Many observers pointed to the coincidence of Fidel Castro's simultaneous release of several American CIA agents being held in Cuba on espionage charges.

To be clear, there were a number of movements that took varying positions on the approach to the independence of Puerto Rico with very different politics. The approach of the Nationalist Party and the Macheteros, and in the 1970s and 1980s the FALN, created a rift between those who saw electoral politics as an avenue, including the PIP (Partido Independentista Puertorriqueño), the MPI (Movimiento Pro Independencia), and the PSP (Paritido Socialista Puertorriqueño), among others. In the last half of the twentieth century, the independence movement saw the rise of the Fuerzas Armadas de Liberación Nacional (FALN) as the articulation of its positioning of armed resistance as the principal approach in the anti-colonial struggle. The clandestine movement was heavily influenced by Marxist ideologies and global approaches to anti-colonial efforts. On the other hand, there was consistent communication, collaboration, and negotiation as well. Despite the differences, a comprehensive chronology of armed struggle in Puerto Rico reveals many moments of solidarity between the public independence movement and the armed clandestine movement (see Committee in Solidarity 1979).

The FALN was unique in its attack of the U.S. colonial apparatus in that it positioned the armed clandestine struggle within the U.S. Puerto Rican diaspora, pushing the struggle to the margins of both the Puerto Rican independence movement and U.S. leftist movements (Power 2013, 152). In many ways informed by the actions of the Nationalist Party before them, the FALN challenged images of Puerto Rican passivity with "armed propaganda" combining armed resistance with rhetorical propaganda to inform the public about the political context within which the FALN acted, and highlighting the history of resistance of the Puerto Rican people. Between 1974 and 1982, more than one hundred attacks throughout New York, Newark, Hartford, Chicago, and Washington, D.C., were attributed to the FALN (see List of FALN Perpetrated Bombing and Incendiary Incidents). Between 1980 and 1985 alone, sixteen Puerto Ricans were arrested and accused of various crimes as members of the FALN. The transnational nature of FALN was consistent with a growing sense of anti-colonialism across the world in the early 1970s. In fact, on multiple occasions, the FALN acted on behalf of not only Puerto Rican liberation but also other anti-colonial struggles. During the 1982 bombing of Banker's Trust in Manhattan, the FALN dedicated their actions to the people of Palestine and indicted the United States for their participation in the global system of imperialist aggression (National Committee to Free Puerto Rican Political Prisoners of War 1983).

Of the numerous freedom fighters associated with the FALN, most were released in 1999 when the efforts of the popular campaign pressured President Bill Clinton to commute their sentences. People also pointed to political bargaining as Hillary Clinton was preparing to run for the Senate seat in New York and was vying for the influential New York Puerto Rican vote (see Dorfman 2017). Filiberto Ojeda Ríos and Oscar López Rivera carried the torch of radical resistance into the twenty-first century. For Ríos, that came about through the horrific spectacle of his assassination in 2005. For Oscar López Rivera, it came through a heroic act of resistance as a prisoner of war for a historic thirty-six years, twelve of which were spent in solitary confinement enduring various forms of torture and dehumanizing conditions meant to break him down physically and psychologically (Bannan 2017, 137). In the early 1980s, the FBI arrested López Rivera, Carlos Alberto Torres, Haydée Beltrán, and Ida Luz Rodríguez, whom they accused of seditious conspiracy and ties to the FALN. The FBI claimed that López and Torres were the reputed leaders of the FALN. López had been a target of the grand jury's "fishing expeditions" in the late 1970s and was forced to go underground from 1976 until his capture in 1981 to be able continue his political actions in secret. The ensuing trial of Oscar López Rivera was as revealing as others before him of the insidious and abusive nature of the legal system against Puerto Rican freedom fighters. Knowing this, Oscar López Rivera declared himself a prisoner of war: "Given my revolutionary principles, the legacy of our heroic freedom fighters, and my respect for international law—the only law which has the right to judge my actions—it is my obligation and my duty to declare myself a prisoner of war. I therefore do not recognize the jurisdiction of the United States government over Puerto Rico or of this court to try me or judge me" (López Rivera quoted in Nieves-Falcón 2013).

López Rivera was sentenced to fifty-five years in prison despite the lack of any evidence linking him with weapons or any human casualties. Later, another fifteen years were added to his sentence after he was accused of conspiring to escape from prison. In 1999, López Rivera refused to accept the Clinton commutation because the offer was not extended to all Puerto Rican political prisoners. His evident strength of character, sense of purpose, and commitment to solidarity led Puerto Ricans from nearly every political sector to join the massive media and propaganda campaign that led President Obama to commute his sentence in 2017.

Anchored in Chicago's Paseo Boricua Community and the work of the Juan Antonio Corretjer Puerto Rican Cultural Center, which López had helped found in 1973, the campaign gained strength between 2013 and 2014, commanding the attention of Puerto Rico's national press (Nieves-Pizarro 2016, 69). As the outgoing President Obama faced his final decisions about executive orders, he and the U.S. mainstream press could no longer ignore the pressure from the economically distressed and politically fed-up Puerto Rican transnational community. Oscar López Rivera was finally released on May 17, 2017.

Coloniality, Criminality, and the Neoliberal Empire

Oscar López Rivera's release from prison coincided with the worst economic depression in the recent history of Puerto Rico. The island faced more than $70 billion in debt, primarily as a result of high-risk bond schemes orchestrated by Wall Street financiers. After Hurricane Maria, President Donald Trump's Twitter declaration that the United States had done enough already for Puerto Rico and "will not bail out long outstanding & unpaid obligations with relief money" (October 23, 2018), pundits on either side took advantage and rallied behind the question of precisely why to continue to sustain this relationship. Despite more than 120 years of absolute negation, somehow the question that continues to surface is the question of full U.S. citizenship in the form of the debate for or against annexation of Puerto Rico as the fifty-first state in the United States. The incessant "plebiscite to nowhere," as a headline in the *Atlantic* put it just days after the June 2017 results of a referendum on the status on the island, repeats itself periodically. Flaunting the proverbial carrot of first-class citizenship in the faces of island residents, this question does little more than provide some media fodder for the pro-statehood Partido Nuevo Progresista (New Progressive Party) to continue to exist in some form differentiated from the Partido Popular Democrático (Popular Democratic Party), the party that advocates for the Commonwealth status quo. The turnout for the vote was historically abysmal for a normally enthusiastic electorate. Fewer than one-fourth of all voters voted after questions regarding Department of Justice certification of the ballot questions led to charges of corruption and a mass boycott among opposition parties. The fate of Puerto Rico could not have been more clearly stated: "the facts are that Congress is not bound by any aspect of the referendum vote on Sunday, and that Puerto Rico's right to self-determination—while an important theoretical international legal concept and germane to its own territorial constitution—simply does not exist in federal legislative terms" (Newkirk 2017).

The *Atlantic* article goes on to explain that although the thirty-seven states added to the original thirteen by the U.S. Congress understood from the beginning that they would become states and had clear pathways to doing so—including the use of referenda and self-determination—Puerto Rico was acquired with no such understanding. Under the Treaty of Paris, Puerto Rico was added as a colonial possession, an *unincorporated territory*. Even consideration for statehood would require incorporation, determined by Congress and three political criteria, explained as follows by Carlos Iván Gorrín Peralta, a professor at the InterAmerican University of Puerto Rico and a territorial-law scholar: "Those three criteria are the number of people in the territory who want statehood, the embrace of 'the fundamental values of American democracy' among the territory's population, and the territory's solvency" (Newkirk 2017). In effect, the most recent plebiscite actually further compromised the already very unlikely scenario that Congress would even consider taking on the matter at all.

For some time, many critics understood the U.S. fear of the "loss" of Puerto Rico as the protection of a strategic Caribbean outpost in military terms. This was especially impacted by Cold War fears of Cuba looming over the Americas as the Russian outpost. On the other hand, the colonial economic activities and intentions were always evident. These were the conditions that created the wealth of nations and positioned the United States at the forefront of the capitalist world economy. Perhaps less evident but not obscure was the role the island was to play in the safeguarding of capitalism in a United States–centered world empire. In fact, occupation of Puerto Rico has been a means, not the end, to a long list of ways to sustain U.S. economic power in what many began to declare a postcapitalist global economy.

Milton Friedman's *Capitalism and Freedom* (1962) laid out the principles that could extend the ailing *free private enterprise exchange economy* that helped to build the U.S. empire. Friedman, of course, as one of the founders of the Mont Pelerin Society in 1947, is among the members of that group credited for promoting the principles of a free market economic system. Of greatest interest in this study is his position on the role of government, which he insisted should be decentralized for the preservation of freedom. On the other hand he states that "government may enable us at times to accomplish jointly what we would find it more difficult or expensive to accomplish severally" (2002, 2). The idea was that government should abolish any regulation that interferes in the accumulation of wealth for "the free man." By trial and error, the U.S. government experimented with a number of different approaches to capitalize on the colonial subordination of Puerto Rico.

While the American public would have to wait until the passage of NAFTA (North American Free Trade Agreement) in 1994 to begin to hear and understand the phenomenon of neoliberalism that Friedman was articulating, by the end of the nineteenth century, a new hegemonic colonial structure was under way with the United States and the United Kingdom's maintenance of key colonial possessions. I assert that a unique strategy lies precisely in the "juridical-political framework" of the "colonial empire," an anomaly that has to be accounted for by the liberal standards of metropolitan thought. Recent studies that challenge the mutual exclusivity of neoliberalism and government or nation-state are especially helpful to this end (Lowe 2015; Slobodian 2018; Ince 2018). Following a much longer lineage dating back to the dependency theory, and even further back to the roots of capitalism and slavery, political theorist Onur Ulas Ince asserts that "a major corollary of the colonial perspective on capitalism is to underscore the constitutive role of extra-economic coercion in effecting capitalist social transformations. Within this picture, colonial land grabs, plantation slavery, and the forced deindustrialization of imperial dependencies configure as crucial moments in the global formation of capitalism" (Ince 2018, 4). The ideological nature of public opinion about the political and economic struggles of Puerto Rico, to be fully grasped, should be contextualized in the legal, political, and military investments that have shaped that opinion. Theories of coloniality, criminality, and punitive neoliberalism together offer additional insight to the extra-economic system of coercion that Ince describes. In fact, the criminalization of dissent was the backbone of punitive neoliberalism in Puerto Rico.[2]

In the case of Puerto Rico we have considered in this study the role of a monoculture economy, cabotage laws, and exorbitant land taxes drawing in predatory bankers and industrialization under Operation Bootstrap offering tax breaks to U.S. corporations, among other profit-driven decisions. To these we can add the free rein on distribution of low price government obligation bonds sold by the island between 2012 and 2014, leading to a debt of historic proportions, a massive default on rescue loans, and a hard-line austerity program led by yet another U.S. federal law, the Puerto Rico Oversight, Management and Economic Stability Act of 2016, with the very ironic acronym of PROMESA. As of January 2019 we could also add the approval of the COFINA debt plan aimed to restructure the bonds issued by the insolvent Government Development Bank, which is expected to yield massive profits for the hedge funds originally responsible for the crisis. The plan overwhelmingly approved by creditors is expected to be finalized with the approval of the federally appointed oversight board and U.S. Judge Laura Taylor Swain (Dennis and Connor 2019). The reduction of debt principal that the plan implies will likely be paid off by an increase in already extreme austerity measures.[3]

What the case of Puerto Rico offers us in a unique way is a blueprint for what we have seen reproduced on a global scale, not only by the United States, but also by all the enduring economic superpowers. As the concept of neoliberalism was revealed, many observers believed that we were in fact witnessing the demise of the modern empire. The case of Puerto Rico demonstrates how capitalism could be scaled in an increasingly globalized marketplace. To accomplish this, the United States had already learned that it would absolutely need to begin with some level of control over the likelihood of rebellion among those most adversely affected by the encounter between liberalism and colonial capitalism. Quinn Slobodian's important analysis in *Globalists: The End of Empire and the Birth of Neoliberalism* (2018) on the global public sphere of capitalism extends this argument into international civil society. In fact, Slobodian's story of neoliberalism begins in Stubenring in the 1920s, where the Vienna Chamber of Commerce first gathered and Ludwig Mises led a private seminar on classical liberalism that included Lionel Robbins, Frank Knight, John Van Sickle, and others who were also among the founders of the Mont Pelerin Society. This timeline not only exposes the context in which "future neoliberals formed their principles" but "also shows how their writing began with straightforward policy problems rather than abstract contemplation" (Slobodian 2018, 30). The abstract scenarios were not abstract at all. The scenarios played out throughout the colonial period in the Americas and ushered into the twenty-first century in the modern colonial state were predicated, not on the demise of the state, but on Mises's principles of "omnipotent government" and, in one of his most telling phrases, the state as "a producer of security" (Slobodian 2018, 33). By 1947, these principles were ready to be applied as adaptable policies on a global scale.

Lisa Lowe's genealogical method in *The Intimacies of Four Continents* (2015) further reinforces the historical ontology that I am proposing is critical to understanding Puerto Rico as an incubator of modern liberalism. Lowe articulates "the manners in which the liberal affirmations of individualism, civility, mobility, and free enterprise simultaneously innovate new means and forms of subjection, administration, and governance." She asserts that the social inequality of our time is part of a legacy that connects the colonial archive to the "archive of liberalism." This process reveals the mediation and resolution of liberalism's contradictions, and colonial governance as a strategic, permeable and improvisational process (Lowe 2015, 4). This genealogy necessarily takes us even further back than Stubenring to elucidate the foundations of the ideals that inform critical liberal ideologies. She links the emergence of liberties defined in terms of citizenship, rights, wage labor, free trade, and sovereignty with the systems of racial classifications and colonial divisions of humanity in the seizure of lands from native people and colonial slavery. Resistance was treated in the exact same way within these contexts, explains Lowe: "The native resistance to European intrusion was regularly cast as a threat to the security of settler sovereignty, which rationalized war and suppression" (Lowe 2015, 9).

Nelson Maldonado-Torres similarly grounds coloniality in the sociohistorical context of the conquest of the Americas and the colonial enterprise when capitalism was entangled with forms of domination and subordination. But it did not stay in the local context of the Americas. In fact, he says, it became a "model of power," the very basis of what was then going to become modern identity, inescapably framed by world capitalism and system of domination around the idea of race (Maldonado-Torres 2007, 244). In the *Coloniality of Being*, Maldonado-Torres extends Quijanos's discussion during the colonial period about the very humanity of native people to Enrique Dussel's application of the Cartesian *ego conquiro* ("I conquer, therefore I am"). This idea is understood as the unquestioned certainty of the self as a conqueror that informed modern European identity. It is sustained by a racist, imperial Manichean attitude of misanthropic skepticism (Maldonado-Torres 2007, 245). Maldonado-Torres goes on to explain that the lived experience of racialized people is deeply affected by the encounter with this misanthropic skepticism that marks them simultaneously as violent and "killable." This informs the non-ethics of war as a constitutive part of an allegedly normal world.

There is, however, another layer to non-ethics of war that should be understood as part of its doxa: financial repression. Readily accepted as the nature of capitalism itself, the term was coined by Stanford economists Edward Shaw and Ronald McKinnon to mean essentially that governments use the private sector to service debt. Financial repression, according to the first of a series of publications in *Forbes* that explored the concept, consists of "methods for governments to increase tax income and domestically-held debt" (Pham 2017). It is the term that should be used to describe the economic model suffocating the people of Puerto Rico for the past century, now liberally applied throughout the globe to funnel money toward government and its preferred economic sectors. For Puerto Rico, this has translated to crippling unemployment at nearly 11 percent, periods of mass migration of the working class, and widespread poverty at a rate of 45 percent *before* Hurricane Maria, according to Census Bureau information. This is twice the rate of poverty of the state of Mississippi, the highest in the continental United States at that time. To pay off its debt, the government turns to austerity measures that have to be explained and accepted.

To accomplish the necessary general acquiescence of people to what is now being called the "age of austerity," the narration of debt crisis presents these measures as a logical response to people living beyond their means. This has been critical to the public discourse of the Puerto Rican debt crisis since the early 2000s. If the responsibility lies exclusively on Puerto Ricans—their laziness and unwillingness to work, overspending, dependency on welfare, and so on—the government must justifiably bear down and punish them for their misdeeds. This logic rids colonial capitalism in Puerto Rico of any responsibility for the decades of corporate tax cuts, speculative irresponsibility, and excesses, instead blaming the poor. William Davies refers to a third stage of neoliberalism, characterized by the justification of austerity as punishment, as *punitive neoliberalism* (Davies 2016).

Since the 1990s, we began to see the function of austerity in the reinforcement of the dominant economic order; yet it remains coupled with isolation, creating both a repressive and an accepted measure. Puerto Rico with all of its colonial particularities has long ceased to be unique in some ways. Economic repression is among the contradictions of the dominant economic order. The debt crisis in Puerto Rico in 2006 was happening as the world was facing the worst economic disaster since the Great Depression in the form of the 2008 financial crisis. Yet Puerto Rico has been portrayed as if it were entirely different and isolated from that crisis. What does remain different is the root of the problem: colonialism, and the illegality of the debt to begin with. The United States enters and exits at will when it comes to "control" in Puerto Rican affairs, wholeheartedly exploiting the ambiguity of the political relationship. The unknown or misunderstood condition makes isolation even more accepted in the implementation of austerity policies in non-sovereign states.

The repeated implementation of extraordinary forms of punishment as we have seen in the case of Puerto Rican independence activists relied on a successful state campaign of criminalization, beyond legal measures, that mirrors the tactics of punitive liberalism to gain public approval. Rafael Bernabe offers some insight into why political repression has been important to sustaining an economic system of colonial neoliberalism. He explains that from its inception neoliberalism demands reduced democratic accountability, shifting policy decisions to unelected bodies. "This is often done and justified in the name of 'depoliticizing' decisions, of creating 'non-party,' 'non-partisan' or technocratic institutions or placing decisions in the hands of professionals or so-called 'experts'" (Bernabe 2017). Indeed, the members of the Fiscal Control Board were primarily bankers and corporate leaders, including some of the very people responsible for the schemes that created the crisis to begin with.

The sustained exercise of state repression on the independence movement, coupled with the efforts to label activists as criminals and terrorists, along with economic repression, makes Puerto Rican resistance costly and promotes political dynamics of accommodation even in progressive sectors (Dello Buono 1991, 125). Finally, and less often addressed when considering the general mood of acquiescence, is the sanctioning effect of fear, particularly when contextualized in the victimology of state crimes.

The challenges inherent in developing a theoretical and empirical criminology of the state have made research in this area scarce. In the 1980s and 1990s, there was a brief period of increased interest in understanding state malfeasance, but most of the work has focused on understanding and correcting harms caused by corporate and state agents. Many fewer studies have focused on a critical victimology of state-organized harms (Kauzlarich et al. 2001, 173). Developing a victimology of state crimes requires the enumeration of the victims and the offender, and an understanding of what constitutes a state crime. In the context of Puerto Rico, Kauzlarich, Matthews, and Miller's itemization is an important starting point. To begin with, they explain that it is important to understand state crime as "illegal, socially injurious, or unjust acts, which are committed for the benefit of a state or its agencies" (2001, 175). It is also important to see governmental and state crime as a form of organized crime. Finally, among the victims of state crimes identified by the literature, we must consider individuals suffering from racism (Hazlehurst 1991; Simon 2002), sexism (Calufield and Wonders 1993), and classism (Bohm 1993); countries and nations oppressed by powerful states (Barak 1993, 1991; Kauzlarich and Kramer 1998); workers (Aulette and Michalowski 1993); union organizers (Tunnel 1993); immigrants (Hamm 1995); prisoners (Kauzlarich and Kramer 1998); the natural environment (Kauzlarich and Kramer 1993); suspects in criminal cases (Hazlehurst 1991); and those subjected to cultural imperialism (Ross 1995). In defining the activities of a state as criminal, one may turn to international law, human rights standards, or domestic law (Kauzlarich et al. 2001). Throughout this study, not only have we been introduced to a fairly broad representation of the victimization of Puerto Rican activists by crimes of the U.S. state colonial apparatus, but we have also seen freedom fighters appeal to all these legal standards to no avail.

A recent study by Pickett, Roche, and Pogarsky (2018) on the theory of emotional deterrence examines fear as a strong predictor for criminal propensity and situational intentions to offend. This complex, in-depth study of fear versus apprehension, among many other things, has us think about offending-related victimization as an influential source of anxiety and cognitive judgments about the dangerousness of offending. The authors explain that "many factors, including characteristics of the local environment, prior victimization, and media consumption have indirect effects on fear of crime through perceived victimization risk" (Pickett et al. 2018, 30). The criminalization of resistance in Puerto Rico was in this way extremely effective for both vilifying those willing to *fight* and for instilling fear in those who even thought about expressing the most minimal desire for self-determination. In the summer of 1987, the public was finally made aware of more than 150,000 extensive files, *carpetas*, collected by the island's police for decades on so-called political subversives under police surveillance. The massive surveillance apparatus was aimed primarily, but not exclusively, against the independence movement.[4]

Conclusion: A New Era of Resistance

The U.S. government was invested in a larger struggle for the popular perception of the Puerto Rican independence movement, orchestrating legal maneuverings in the court *and* instilling fear about even associating with anyone remotely affiliated with the cause of independence. The independence movement, absent viable state structures, continues to silently feed an ailing but viable collective national consciousness for Puerto Rican self-determination. This consciousness is evident in the fact that despite the annoyance of politicians at the manipulation of circumstances following the assassination of Ojeda Ríos, the first response from multiple sides was indignation. Unfortunately, from the perspective of the United States, the first response was recognition. U.S. state agents had gone too far, but they had gone too far many times before, and a strategy to evade responsibility was not far behind.

And yet, once again, we are witnessing a broad spectrum of anti-liberal agitation. Some observers point out that many of the left-wing resistance movements that have emerged in Puerto Rico have moved away from the Marxist or nationalist dogmas that were ascribed to the politics of the independence movement before them. They aim to foster young leadership, articulate new solidarities, and revive the practice of community organizing (Tormos-Aponte 2018, 1). In fact, the austerity measures against the University of Puerto Rico (UPR) led to two massive university student strikes occurring in 2010 and 2017 after then governor Luis Fortuño announced cuts in resources and tuition hikes, and again after La Junta announced public-sector furloughs and more budget cuts to the university. The student strikes received enormous support from labor and social justice movements, leading to one of the largest general strikes in the island's history on May 1, 2017. Powerful coalitions have formed, like Todo Puerto Rico por Puerto Rico, aiming to ride the momentum of the UPR student strikes and direct action plans.

While Hurricane Maria and the resulting humanitarian crisis is once again testing the resistance movements, there has been a surge of creation of networks of mutual aid centers and solidarity brigades that are resisting the nonprofit-, corporate-, and government-led networks that do little more than collect money that never reaches the population. Moreover, through their efforts we have witnessed the self-sufficiency, creativity, and resiliency of even the most isolated communities on the island, and we are listening and learning from one another. In the summer of 2019, an unprecedented historical show of solidarity and anti-colonial resistance took place in Puerto Rico. Tens of thousands of Puerto Ricans took to the streets on the island and in the diaspora demanding the resignation of Governor Ricardo Roselló, not only for a barrage of offensive, obscene texts between him and his advisers, but for the long history of political, economic, and cultural repression now fully exposed to the people of Puerto Rico. On July 24, 2019, after weeks of arrogantly resisting public demands, Roselló announced his resignation. The Puerto Rican people won a major battle in the anti-imperialist war.

The resistance inherent to Puerto Rican cultural autonomy has always been a challenge to the U.S. colonial project. Puerto Rican nationalism (cultural and political) has made cultural assimilation difficult, if not impossible. Therefore, political assimilation is gridlocked and often volatile. Puerto Rican migration, another important strategy to maintaining the colonial state, has not improved conditions for Puerto Ricans, the U.S. economy, or the U.S. dominant cultural agenda. The assault of U.S. popular culture and consumerism has been disastrous, to say the very least. Puerto Ricanism retaliates, reinforcing its impacts on U.S. popular culture, particularly through grassroots arts, the entertainment industry, sports, and politics. While these impacts do not always translate to any type of social gain for the Puerto Rican *people*, there is no denying the role that these impacts play in reinforcing *identity* and provoking grassroots resistance. As much as the Spanish language has been deployed to attack the influence of, in particular, a deconstructed sense of nationalism that has proved to be painfully divisive, it also remains an unsubstantiated standard for relinquishing Puerto Rican cultural identity.

In "Designing Cultural Policy in a Postcolonial Colony: The Case of Puerto Rico," Javier Hernández-Acosta presents a critical historical timeline of Puerto Rico's attempts to implement cultural policies amid the influence of political status ideologies and within a "post-colonial colony scenario." Most of Hernández-Acosta's timeline is marked by obstacles to development, among them "the perception that preservation and dissemination of traditional expressions of culture are things from the past," which has excluded culture, including cultural expressions of traditional music and Black heritage, from economic plans and policies (Hernández-Acosta 2015, 296). At the end of his study, he does find a light at the end of the tunnel with the emergence of the role of cultural agents in Puerto Rico who go "beyond artwork" to consider intersections with anti-military movements, the environmental struggle, student activism, and community development—projects that nevertheless are marginalized in public institutions and funding opportunities because of their political and grassroots nature.

The leaders of the independence movement, as it was shaped in the past, can find elements of their approach to the struggle for self-determination within today's progressive struggles on the island and the metropolis. José López, brother of Oscar López Rivera, community activist and director of the Puerto Rican Cultural Center in Chicago, recognizes disunity as part of the contradictions and points of reconciliation for the independence movement.

Oscar's release is an important symbol of a new stage for the movement centered on solidarity and opening doors to other sectors of the Puerto Rican political system. "I see us as protagonists in that disunity," says López. "But on the other hand, I also see that we have grown and are able to be part of the national dialogue of Puerto Rico" (Power 2013, 60). An integral piece of that dialogue is the shared commitment to radical democracy and emancipation—self-determination.

NOTES

1. Here I am referring to ideas developed by Jodi Melamed in *Represent and Destroy: Rationalizing Violence in the New Racial Capitalism* (2011), where she explores the geopolitical conditions that cultivated today's massive amounts of information and certainty about race and oppression as part of the problem and solution for an anti-racist, liberal-capitalist modernity.

2. Marisol Lebrón's *Policing Life and Death: Race, Violence, and Resistance in Puerto Rico* (University of California Press, 2019) offers an insightful and meticulous case study of the rise of punitive governance in policing policies in Puerto Rico since the 1990s, as well as the response and collective efficacy of grassroots resistance and anti-violence activists.

3. The debt crisis combined, followed by the events surrounding Hurricane Maria in 2017 and the economic restructuring plan, may arguably be the most widely discussed and studied series of events in Puerto Rican economic history from the perspective of the United States in both public and intellectual spaces. For more in-depth discussions on the context for each of these phases of the debt crisis, I recommend the social media–circulated Puerto Rico Syllabus (https://puertoricosyllabus.com/additional-resources/extended-bibliography/) as a starting point for a live and interactive bibliography of related issues.

4. *Las carpetas: Persecución política y derechos civiles en Puerto Rico* (The Files: Political Persecution and Civil Rights in Puerto Rico), edited by Ramón Bosque-Pérez and José Javier Colón-Morera (New York: Centro para la Investigacion y Promocion de los Derechos Civiles, 1997), is a collection of articles and documents concerning political surveillance and repression in the island, based on evidence gathered after the 1987 scandal.

REFERENCES

Acosta-Lespier, I. 2006. "The Smith Act Goes to San Juan." In *Puerto Rico under Colonial Rule: Political Persecution and the Quest for Human Rights*, edited by R. Bosque-Pérez and J. Colon Morera. Albany: State University of New York Press.

Albizu-Campos Meneses, L., and M. Rodríguez León, eds. 2007. *Albizu Campos: Escritos*. Puerto Rico: Publicaciones Puertorriqueñas.

Aulette, J. R., and R. Michalowski. 1993. "Fire in Hamlet: A Case Study of State-Corporate Crime." In *Political Crime in Contemporary America*, edited by K. Tunnell, 171–206. New York: Garland.

Ayala, C., and R. Bernabe. 2007. *Puerto Rico in the American Century: A History since 1898*. Chapel Hill: University of North Carolina.

Bannan, N. 2017. "Oscar López Rivera: Hasta Su Regreso." *NACLA Report on the Americas; New York* 49, no. 2: 136–138.

Barak, G. 1991. *Crimes by the Capitalist State.* Albany: State University of New York Press.

Becker, J., and S. Shane. 2012. "Secret 'Kill List' Proves a Test of Obama's Principles and Will." *New York Times,* May 29, World.

Bernabe, R. 2017. "Punitive Neoliberalism and Financial Melancholia in Puerto Rico," CADTM, November 6. https://www.cadtm.org/Punitive-Neoliberalism-and,15427#nb2.

Berrios, M. 1985. "El filósofo latinoamericano, o la institución del polígrafo en la formación de la nacionalidad." In *Anuario de filosofía jurídica y social,* 79–92. Valparaíso: Sociedad Chilena de Filosofía Jurídica y Social.

Bohm, R. 1993. "Social Relationships That Arguably Should Be Criminal although They Are Not: On the Political Economy of Crime." In *Political Crime in Contemporary America,* edited by K. Tunnell, 3–30. New York: Garland.

Bosque-Pérez, R., and J. Colon Morera. 2006. *Puerto Rico under Colonial Rule: Political Persecution and the Quest for Human Rights.* Albany: State University of New York Press.

Cabán, P. 2005. "Puerto Rican Nationalist Uprising." *Latin American, Caribbean, and US Latino Studies Faculty Scholarship* 22. http://scholarsarchive.library.albany.edu/lacs_fac_scholar/22.

Caulfield, S., and N. Wonders. 1993. "Personal AND Political: Violence against Women and the Role of the State." In *Political Crime in Contemporary America,* edited by K. Tunnell, 79–100. New York: Garland.

Chen, M. 2017. "The Bankers behind Puerto Rico's Debt Crisis." *Nation,* June 8, 2017.

Committee in Solidarity with the Puerto Rican Movement. 1979. *Toward People's War for Independence and Socialism in Puerto Rico: In Defense of Armed Struggle.* https://www.marxists.org/history/erol/ncm-8/armed-struggle.pdf.

Davies, W. 2016. "The New Neoliberablism." *New Left Review* 101 (Sept.–Oct.): 121–134.

Dello Buono, R. 1991. "State Repression and Popular Resistance: The Criminalization of Puerto Rican Independentistas." *Humanity & Society* 15, no. 1: 111–131.

Denis, N. 2015. *War against All Puerto Ricans: Revolution and Terror in America's Colony.* New York: Nation Books.

Dennis, A., and K. Connor. 2019. "Hedge Funds Win, Puerto Ricans Lose in First Debt Restructuring Deal." American Prospect, February 8. https://prospect.org/article/hedge-funds-win-puerto-ricans-lose-first-debt-restructuring-deal.

Deutsch, M. 1984. "The Improper Use of the Federal Grand Jury: An Instrument for the Internment of Political Activists." *Journal of Criminal Law and Criminology* 75, no. 4: 1159–1196.

Dorfman, Z. 2017. "Why Did Obama Free This Terrorist?" *Politico,* January 24, 2017. https://www.politico.com/magazine/story/2017/01/oscar-lopez-commutation-barack-obama-214685.

Duffy Burnett, C., and B. Marshall, eds. 2001. *Puerto Rico, American Expansion, and the Constitution.* Durham, NC: Duke University Press.

Dussel, E. 1977. *Filosofía ética de la liberación,* 3rd ed., vol. III, *Niveles concretos de la ética latinoamericana.* Buenos Aires: Ediciones Megápolis.

———. 1995. *The Invention of the Americas: Eclipse of "the Other" and the Myth of Modernity,* translated by Michael D. Barber. New York: Continuum.

————. 2002. "World System and 'Trans'-modernity," translated by Alessandro Fornaz-zari. *Nepantla: Views from South* 3, no. 2: 221–244.

Falcón, A. 1984. "A History of Puerto Rican Politics in New York City." In *Puerto Rican Politics in Urban America*, edited by James Jennings and Monte Rivera. Westport, CT: Greenwood Publishing.

Fernández, R. 1996. *The Disenchanted Island: Puerto Rico and the United States in the Twentieth Century*. Westport, CT: Greenwood Publishing.

Friedman, M. 2002 (1962). *Capitalism and Freedom*. Fortieth anniversary edition. Chicago: University of Chicago Press.

Gelpí, J. 1993. *Literatura y paternalismo en Puerto Rico*. San Juan: Editorial del la Universidad de Puerto Rico.

Gomez, A. 2017. "Yes, Puerto Rico Is Part of the United States." *USA Today*, September 26. https://www.usatoday.com/story/news/world/2017/09/26/yes-puerto-rico-part-united -states/703273001/.

Grabow, C., I. Munak, and D. Ikenson. 2018. "The Jones Act: A Burden America Can No Longer Bear." *Policy Analysis*, Cato Institute, no. 845 (June 28).

Hamm, M. S. 1995. *The Abandoned Ones: The Imprisonment and Uprising of the Mariel Boat People*. Boston: Northeastern University Press.

Hazlehurst, K. 1991. "Passion and Policy: Aboriginal Deaths in Custody in Australia 1980–1989." In *Crimes by the Capitalist State*, edited by G. Barak, 21–47. Albany: State University of New York Press.

Hernández-Acosta, J. 2017. "Designing Cultural Policy in a Postcolonial Colony: The Case of Puerto Rico." *International Journal of Cultural Policy* 23, no. 3: 285–299.

Higgins, T. 2019. "ACLU Asks Supreme Court to Overrule Precedent That Established 'Second-Class' Status for Puerto Rico." *CNBC Politics*, August 30. https://www.cnbc .com/2019/08/30/aclu-supreme-court-must-erase-racist-precedent-in-puerto-rico-case .html.

Ince, O. 2018. *Colonial Capitalism and the Dilemmas of Liberalism*. New York: Oxford University Press.

Jiménez, F. 2005. "The Killing of Filiberto Ojeda Ríos." *Nation*, October 24, Regions and Countries.

Kauzlarich, D., and R. C. Kramer. 1993. "State-Corporate Crime in the U.S. Nuclear Weapons Production Complex." *Journal of Human Justice* 5, 4–28.

————. 1998. *Crimes of the Nuclear State: At Home and Abroad*. Boston: Northeastern University Press.

Kauzlarich, D., R. Matthews, and W. Miller. 2001. "Toward a Victimology of State Crime." *Critical Criminology* 10: 173–194.

Lidin, H. 1981. *History of the Puerto Rican Independence Movement*, vol. 1. Master Typesetting of Puerto Rico, Inc., Hato Rey.

List of FALN Perpetrated Bombing and Incendiary Incidents. 1997. Latin American Studies, December 15. http://www.latinamericanstudies.org/puertorico/FALN -incidents.pdf (accessed January 18, 2018).

López Rivera, O. 2007. "One Hundred Years of Puerto Rican Resistance," in *Warfare in the American Homeland: Policing and Prison in a Penal Democracy.*, edited by Joy James. Durham, NC: Duke University Press.

Lowe, L. 2015. *The Intimacies of Four Continents*. Durham: Duke University Press.

Maldonado-Torres, N. 2007. "On the Coloniality of Being," *Cultural Studies* 21, no. 2–3: 240–270.

———. 2016. "Transdisciplinariedad y decolonialidad." Quaderna, April 3. https://quaderna.org/transdisciplinariedad-y-decolonialidad/.

Martínez-San Miguel, Y. 2014. *Coloniality of Diasporas: Rethinking Intra-colonial Migrations in a Pan-Caribbean Context*. New York: Palgrave Macmillan.

Mignolo, W. 2000. *Local Histories/Global Designs: Coloniality, Subaltern Knowledges, and Border Thinking*. Princeton, NJ: Princeton University Press.

National Committee to Free Puerto Rican Political Prisoners of War. 1983. "FALN Communiqués." *Libertad*. In "A La Izquierda: The Puerto Rican Movement, 1923–2002," Archives of the Puerto Rican Diaspora Centro de Estudios Puertorriqueños, Hunter College, City University of New York, New York, microfilm reel 6.

Newkirk, V. 2017. "Puerto Rico's Plebiscite to Nowhere." *Atlantic*, June 13, Politics. https://www.theatlantic.com/politics/archive/2017/06/puerto-rico-statehood-plebiscite-congress/530136/.

Nieves Falcón, L. 2002. *Violation of Human Rights in Puerto Rico by the United States*. San Juan, PR: Ediciones Puerto.

———. 2013. *Oscar López Rivera: Between Torture and Resistance*, online ed. Oakland, CA: PM Press.

Nieves-Pizarro, Y. 2016. "Free Óscar López Rivera!: News Coverage of United States Domestic Human Rights Issues." *Centro Journal* 28, no. 2: 68–87.

Otaño, J. A. 2003. "Puerto Rico Pandemonium: The Commonwealth Constitution and the Compact-Colony Conundrum." *Fordham International Law Journal* 27, no. 5: 1806–1858.

Paralitici, Ché. 2004. *Sentencia Impuesta: 100 Años de Encarcelamientos por la Independencia de Puerto Rico*. San Juan, PR: Ediciones Puerto.

———. 2006. "Imprisonment and Colonial Domination, 1898–1958." In *Puerto Rico under Colonial Rule: Political Persecution and the Quest for Human Rights*, edited by R. Bosque-Pérez and J. Colon Morera. Albany: State University of New York Press.

Pham, P. 2017. "What Is Financial Repression?" *Forbes*, December 11. https://www.forbes.com/sites/peterpham/2017/12/11/what-is-financial-repression/#480c328817f5.

Pickett, J., S. Roche, and G. Pogarsky. 2018. "Toward a Bifurcated Theory of Emotional Deterrence." *Criminology* 56, no. 1: 27–58.

Power, M. 2013. "From Freedom Fighters to Patriots: The Successful Campaign to Release the FALN Political Prisoners, 1980–1999." *CENTRO: Journal of the Center for Puerto Rican Studies* 25, no. 1: 146–179.

Quijano, A. 2001. "Globalización, colonialidad y democracia." In *Tendencias básicas denuestra época: globalización y democracia*, edited by Instituto de Altos Estudios Diplomáticos "Pedro Gual," 25–61. Caracas: Instituto de Altos Estudios Diplomáticos "Pedro Gual."

Rodriguez-Vidal, C. 2016. "A Tale of Two 'Municipalities' (Detroit and Puerto Rico): Legal and Practical Issues Facing a Financially Distressed 'Municipality.'" Report submitted to the American Bar Association Section of State and Local Government. 2016 Spring Meeting, April 7–10, Intercontinental Hotel, San Juan, Puerto Rico.

Ross, J. I. 1995. *Controlling State Crime*. New York: Garland.

Scarano, F. 1993. *Puerto Rico. Cinco Siglos de Historia*. New York: McGill Press.

Simon, D. R. 2002. *Elite Deviance*, 7th ed. Boston: Allyn and Bacon.

Slobodian, Q. 2018. *Globalists: The End of Empire and the Birth of Neoliberalism*. Cambridge, MA: Harvard University Press.

Solá, J. 2010. "Partisanship, Power Contenders, and Colonial Politics in Puerto Rico, 1920s." *Caribbean Studies* 38, no. 1: 3–35.

Soltero, C. R. 2006. "Balzac v. Porto Rico (1922), the Insular Cases (1901), and Puerto Rico's Status in the American Legal System." In *Latinos and American Law: Landmark Supreme Court Cases*, edited by Carlos R. Soltero, 19–34. Austin: University of Texas Press.

Susler, J. 2008. "Puerto Rican Independence Movement under Attack in New York and San Juan." *Guild Notes* 34, no. 1: 6.

———. 2018. "Seditious Conspiracy: Puerto Rican Political Prisoners in the United States." Unpublished manuscript.

Thompson, L. 2010. *Imperial Archipelago: Representation and Rule in the Insular Territories under US Dominion after 1898*. Honolulu: University of Hawaii Press.

Tormos-Aponte, F. 2018. "The Politics of Survival." *Jacobin*, April 2.

Torres, A., and J. Velázquez, eds. 1996. *The Puerto Rican Movement: Voices from the Diaspora*. Philadelphia: Temple University Press.

Tunnell, K. D., ed. 1993. *Political Crime in Contemporary America*. New York: Garland.

Wagenheim, K., and O. Jiménez de Wagenheim, and L. Martínez Fernández, eds. 1988. *The Puerto Ricans: A Documentary History*. Maplewood, NJ: Waterfront Press.

Winter, B. 1996. "Invidious Prosecution: The History of Seditious Conspiracy—Foreshadowing the Recent Convictions of Sheik Omar Abdel-Rahman and his Immigrant Followers." *Georgetown Immigration Law Journal* 10, no. 185 (Winter).

7

Developing Disasters

INDUSTRIALIZATION, AUSTERITY,
AND VIOLENCE IN HAITI SINCE 1915

VINCENT JOOS

Eight years after an earthquake took the lives of more than three hundred thousand people and destroyed or damaged most of the built environment in the Port-au-Prince region, the downtown area of Haiti's capital is still in rubble. In Port-au-Prince, everything has changed. People wounded by the disaster, people who are still mourning their loved ones, live in a city that lost its main landmarks. Stalled construction sites and shattered buildings dot the urban landscape. The Parc Martissant, a forty-two-acre hillside where old and beautiful trees abound, has opened on the southern side of the city and offers a glimmer of hope in the form of a peaceful public park, a medicinal garden, and a library. Yet, not much has changed. In the summer of 2018, massive demonstrations against the rise of gas prices paralyzed the country. Following the recommendations of the International Monetary Fund (IMF), the government of Haiti's President Jovenel Moïse took a well-beaten path by suddenly imposing austerity measures that would increase state revenues on the back of middle- and low-income Haitians (Joos 2018; Regan 2018). Reforms that advantage Haiti's small agro-business and industrial sectors to the detriment of local farmers and low-income workers have plagued Haiti since the 1915 American invasion of the country.

Pushing a "business-friendly" climate by cutting public spending, downsizing the state workforce, and slashing import tariffs and corporate taxes—and by fostering political, administrative, military, and economic centralization in Port-au-Prince—the United States and the international financial institutions (IFIs) it supports have encouraged urban migration and led to the economic suffocation of the Haitian countryside, where a formerly powerful peasantry has lost, over the past hundred years, its capacity to sustain itself and to contribute to the food security of these regions. Since 1915, *all* Haitian state leaders have something in common: their economic and social policies are designed to attract foreign capital. The American strategy to "develop" the economy and to allow the flourishing of U.S. corporations during the occupation was simple: violently quashing rebellions, cracking down on unions or stifling their creation, and keeping wages, corporate taxes, and tariffs low (Pamphile 2015). This strategy remains today the political horizon of IFI-managed Haitian governments. In brief, the same old economic agenda—growing the export sector, creating free trade zones, concentrating public services and industries in the Port-au-Prince region, and so on—has greatly contributed to create the conditions that transformed a 7.0 magnitude earthquake into one of the greatest disasters of the Americas. These policies pauperized the nation and forced rural dwellers to settle in incredibly dense neighborhoods. The absence of the state when it comes to implementing construction codes or to managing urban planning led to the building of hazardous dwellings and to extreme urban density that, combined, led to massive destruction during the 2010 earthquake (Tobin 2013). After the catastrophe, international donors came up with a reconstruction plan based on this premise: the development of Haiti will be spurred by economic growth, which itself will be generated by the creation of a robust export sector. The same old colonial and neocolonial solutions are still in vogue. Indeed, not much has changed since the earthquake, and not much has changed since the violent American military and administrative occupation of Haiti (1915–1947).

In 1915, the U.S. marines invaded Haiti, declared martial law, and waged a five-year war against indigenous communities who resisted the military overtake of their administrations and lands. This war, which "must have resembled a massacre," left fifteen thousand dead and wounded on the Haitian side, and ninety-eight dead and wounded on the U.S. side (Gaillard 1982, 261). The military occupation of Haiti lasted until 1934. Through puppet governments and alliances with the small Haitian business elite, the

U.S. managed to impose policies that led to the economic withering of the provinces and to the centralization of political and administrative powers in Port-au-Prince (Danticat 2015). After the violent repression of their opponents, U.S. authorities cut the provinces' budgets and dismantled regional armies, while American corporations were taking over large swaths of land to grow cash crops or for mining (Anglade 1982a). The United States sponsored a rewriting of the Haitian Constitution that allowed aliens to own land and the creation of new Haitian security forces that safeguarded corporate interests, evicted people from their land, and coerced them to perform free labor on infrastructural projects that benefited a small Haitian and American private sector (Dupuy 1989; Trouillot 1990). Moreover, during the U.S. occupation of the Dominican Republic (1916–1924), U.S. corporations created large sugar plantations and used a Haitian workforce to work in the cane fields, putting in motion migratory flows from the western part of the island to the east and setting terrible work conditions for Haitians in the Dominican Republic that still endure today (Danticat 2015). The Haitian state—mainly composed of Haitian and American administrators who shared the benefits of weak industrial operations— functioned as an actuary of these corporations and imposed an austerity budget that reduced taxes for corporations, raised taxes on Haitian citizens, and created a mobile and cheap industrial workforce (McPherson 2016). In the 1920s, Haiti already functioned as a "corporate paradise," where almost nonexistent taxes, cheap labor, and low land prices were supposed to attract foreign investors (Dupuy 2014; Steckley and Shamsie 2015, 186). Unfortunately, Haiti kept being "open for business" even after the departure of the American army.

The U.S. army left Haiti in 1934, but a U.S. fiscal representative worked in the Haitian government until 1947. This representative had broad powers over customs collection, tariffs, taxes, and government spending. He also made sure the Haitian state repaid the loan it contracted with the United States in 1922 (Dubois 2012, 295). The loan was used to build infrastructures meant to foster an export economy Haitians had long refused and fought against. It is important to note that peasants were forced to build these bridges and roads because of the imposed *corvée*—a system of free labor that was widespread in the southeastern U.S. and that was introduced in Haiti by segregationist American administrators (Woolf 2015). This led to the creation of what Edwidge Danticat aptly named "a kind of national chain gang" (Danticat 2015).

American business ventures undertaken during the long American occupation (1915–1947) set up unbalanced state-corporation relations and catalyzed the erosion of national sovereignty, reinforced race-based social inequalities, ramped up deforestation, and imposed a regime of fiscal austerity that continues today to set Haiti up for political, economic, and "natural" disasters (Jean-Baptiste 2012, 98). Even though Haiti was extremely business-friendly, only a handful of short-term, devastating industrial and agricultural projects got off the ground in the past hundred years. They generated little state revenues, offered a small number of poorly paid jobs, and never contributed to the growth of other sectors of the economy. However, these projects had a disproportionate role in the shaping of Haitian economic policies and state-corporation relations over the past hundred years. They also had a disproportionate effect on the natural and social environment of Haiti.

I argue that private-public ventures—more precisely corporate takeovers of national resources facilitated through various assemblages of American and Haitian public institutions—have been the main engine of the extraction economy in Haiti since the beginning of the American occupation. I also argue that these short-lived industrial experiments forcefully contributed to shape both state institutions and the economic, legal, and fiscal landscape of Haiti. Under the guise of industrial development, a long string of one-off, poorly planned industrial projects have transformed a mostly decentralized agrarian region into a non-sovereign and hypercentralized country. With each industrial, fiscal, and legal intrusion in Haiti, the United States, along with IFIs, have pushed for the reduction of public spending on social services and the state workforce while lowering or ending import tariffs on goods (such as rice, beans, flour, and oil). As a small number of predatory Haitian elite members managed imports of subsidized—hence, artificially cheaper—American agribusinesses, local food production plummeted and state investments in agricultural infrastructure (such as irrigation systems, markets, roads) vanished (Anglade 1982b). In the meantime, each industrial and agro-industrial push reactivated revolutionary networks and new forms of counter-industrial and counter-colonial politics. Civil wars, mass strikes, and protests punctuate the devastating corporatization of the Haitian state during the past hundred years.

This chapter examines some of the major industrial intrusions in Haiti's rural provinces since the American occupation. Of course, the occupation and concomitant weakening of Haitian sovereignty did not happen in a vacuum. The occupation reactivated colonial practices of centralization and forced labor. In other words, many forms of French colonial legacies structure how the state and economy still function today. These legacies can be summarized as follows: utter environmental degradation, depletion of soils, and deforestation; the establishment of racial hierarchies and race-based inequality; the exclusion of rural dwellers from political and commercial life; the establishment of humanely and environmentally devastating cash crop economies; and the creation of global economic dependences. In order to analyze the effects of more than a hundred years of United States military and economic domination, I will first describe some of the legacies of the French colonial period, as they continue to infuse various development project on the island. In doing so, I want to understand how industrial and agro-industrial projects and neoliberal policies contributed to the economic and environmental degradation that pushed people toward Port-au-Prince for the past forty years and to the weakening of state capacities in basic social welfare and public infrastructure. This discussion will shed light on processes that transformed the earthquake into a mega-disaster, such as extreme urban density, absence of sound public infrastructure, and non-implementation of construction codes. Understanding how a hundred years of imposed austerity politics suffocated Haiti also helps to understand what led to the almost total subjugation of the national state by IFIs, international nongovernmental organizations (NGOs), and American state agencies after the devastating earthquake of January 12,

2010. I argue that each major industrial push furthered Haiti's global economic dependence, food insecurity, and vulnerability to disasters while weakening the Haitian state's capabilities in protecting the security and well-being of its citizens.

To use the words of Daniel Goldstein, the Haitian state is today a "manager, actuary, cop [that] controls dissent among citizens whose economic interests run counter to those of industry, and whose social rights impose unwanted and expensive restrictions on transnational commerce" (Goldstein 2012, 19). The waves of structural adjustment programs (SAPs) that accompany these industrial intrusions have rendered the state inoperative in the fields of health, education, sanitation, and so on, leaving a gap that was quickly filled, right after the quake, by the disaster industrial complex—a global system of extraction in which private and public interests conflate to promote "old, failed solutions packaged in 'new and improved' ways" (Svistova and Pyles 2018, 55). The 2010 "reconstruction" plans proposed by the Interim Haiti Recovery Commission—the official entity led by Bill Clinton—indeed favored old solutions: economic growth would be produced through the expansion of free trade zones, the construction of industrial parks, the renovation of port infrastructure, and so on (Katz 2015). Once again, the overused industrial scheme failed spectacularly and reinforced Haitian dependences, debts, and disaster vulnerability. Here, I am offering a brief overview of Haiti's industrial history by analyzing some key projects that were implemented before the earthquake and that led to increased structural violence in Haiti. The conditions that transformed a 7.0 magnitude earthquake into one of the greatest human disasters in the Americas are the result of long historical processes rooted in productivist and (neo)colonial ideologies that have generated violence against communities that refused wage-labor systems and large-scale environmental degradation.

Colonial Legacies

While American corporate imperialism largely contributed to transforming entire regions of the Caribbean into gigantic cash-crop operations during the long period of the Banana Wars (1898–1934), European colonialism had already engaged the same regions on the path of environmental degradation, centralization of political and economic powers, race-based and rural-urban social divisions and inequalities, and dependence on food imports, especially during the eighteenth-century sugar and coffee booms. The French slavery-based plantation system in Saint-Domingue, which would become Haiti in 1804, established a long-term pauperization process on the island while it allowed the formation of new business elites in France, especially in Bordeaux. In the 1772 revised version of his *Essai sur les Mœurs et l'Esprit des Nations*, Voltaire paints a scathing portrait of the French Saint-Domingue colony and reveals the core elements of the colonial enterprise:

> In 1757 there were about thirty thousand people in the French part of Saint-Domingue. Also, there were a hundred thousand Negro or Mulatto slaves who worked on sugar, indigo, and cocoa plantations, shortening their life expectancy for the sake of our new tastes and needs. We buy these Negroes on the Guinea Coast, the Gold Coast, and the Ivory Coast. Thirty years ago, one could buy one Negro for fifty pounds. This is about one fifth the price of a fat cow. Today in 1772, this human commodity costs about fifteen thousand. We tell them that they are humans like us and that they are being redeemed through the blood of a God who died for them. Then we make them work as mere beasts. We feed them poorly: if they run away, we cut their leg off, and once we give them a wooden leg, we make them use their arms to spin the sugar mill! And we dare speak about people's rights! The small islands of Martinique and Guadeloupe that the French started cultivating in 1735 supplied the same commodities as Saint-Domingue. These are dots on the map and events that peter out in the history of the universe; but these lands that we barely recognize on the globe are responsible in France for the annual circulation of sixty million commodities. (Voltaire 1963 [1809], 341–342; my translation)

The Atlantic trade enriched a powerful merchant bourgeoisie in French ports such as Nantes and Bordeaux and transformed these port cities into modern industrial and import-export poles. The French economy depended on the immense wealth created in its American colonies. Indeed, once the Saint-Domingue colony erupted in revolt in 1791, Bordeaux's economy dwindled and the whole region entered a recession (Duby 1972, 743). France's economy grew in proportion to the depletion of natural resources in the Caribbean colonies and human resources in West Africa (Rodney 1972). As Voltaire notes (and as analyzed in Trouillot 1995), French Caribbean colonies were "dots on the map and events that peter out in the history of the universe," places that official historiographies silence or misrepresent. However, they were economically crucial. In 1787, France exported 22 percent of the commodities it produced to its Caribbean colonies while receiving from them 37 percent of its total imports (Butel 2007, 151). This hyperproductivist system based on slavery and the regional dominance of port cities put in place the elements that would lead to the unraveling of the Haitian economy in the twentieth century.

As with subsequent colonial enterprises, French authorities imposed a system of political and economic suffocation of outposts they thought they couldn't fully control in order to tightly channel the routes of goods and capital through one strategic location. Though religious infrastructure was well distributed within Saint-Domingue, administrators made sure that provincial parishes could not grow on a commercial or military level. For instance, in Croix-des-Bouquets, a parish contiguous to Port-au-Prince, only "one surgeon, one locksmith, one saddler, one baker and one butcher" were allowed to ply their trades (Corvington 1992, 26). This growth limitation was accompanied by the allocation of the majority of the budget to the development of port-cities (de Vaissière 1909). The general suffocation of the provinces, and later the economic strangling of the peasantry, would become common tactics during the American occupation and the Duvalier dictatorship.

If recent analysis of urbanization in Haiti posits the American occupation as the prime vector of centralization (Etienne 2013; Lucien 2013), it is important to note that Port-au-Prince had already evolved as an urban area with concentrated wealth and power under French colonial rule. While the most visible form of centralization is the recent demographic regrouping of people in dense areas of the capital, military and administrative centralization began in 1749, when French royal powers sought to tighten their control of the fragmented island economy. The main consideration of colonial administrators was not the edification of a city but the development of a port. Until today, "commercial relations" still dictate the shape the city takes, regardless of its residents' desires. Since the devastating earthquakes of 1751 and 1770, authorities knew that the bay of Port-au-Prince was not suitable for urban living. However, given the strategic and central location of the port, social considerations vanished. Though Port-au-Prince has been destroyed several times by earthquakes, floods, fires, and sieges, its port activities have made it an urban phoenix that grew even larger during the multiple reconstruction periods that have punctuated its existence.

While French Saint-Domingue was the least urbanized of French Caribbean colonies on the eve of the 1789 French Revolution, with 94 percent of its population living in rural areas, the port cities of the island were commanding daily life on plantations (Butel 2007). The traders and merchants of Cap Français (today Cap Haitien), Saint-Marc, and Port-au-Prince gained political and economic power in the colony as they acquired property, coordinated hinterland trade with shipping activities, and more importantly functioned as bankers and managers of plantations whose owners lived abroad. In the meantime, an important group of affranchised people of mixed descent, "les gens de couleur libre" or *Mulâtres* (hereafter "mulattoes"),[1] gained economic and political importance. By the end of the eighteenth century, they became political competitors to white traders as they sought equal status in the administrative and legislative spheres (Trouillot 1986).

Once Haiti became independent in 1804, after thirteen years of revolution, the plantation system did not completely disappear. Haitian statesmen and elite members tried many times to reimpose coerced labor. However, because the country faced an economic embargo and contracted a huge debt with France in 1825 in order to compensate the planters who lost their properties, Haiti never had the chance to develop into a centralized nation with a modern industry in the nineteenth century. An export sector existed, but it generated too little revenue to have an impact on the island. Instead, a strong peasantry developed, and the country entered the long phase of what Haitian geographer Georges Anglade called the "period of regionalization." Based on small land ownership, subsistence agriculture, and the selling of produce surplus, the Haitian peasantry created a world away from the state and the plantation regimen (Barthélémy 2000; Gonzalez 2019). Culturally articulated around spiritual practices and with Kreyol as a common language, the nineteenth-century Haitian peasantry forged a system of self-governance that enabled people to create families and to control the land as they wished, for the privileging of food production (Mintz 2010). Nonetheless, peasant agriculture still produced goods for the export market, such as coffee, and was not completely based on subsistence agriculture. Even though forcefully autonomous, Haitians living in the provinces were integrated into the national and global economy (Alvarez and Murray 1981; Steckley and Shamsie 2015). However, the balance between food security based on the growing of food crops and participation in the agro-industrial export sector was fragile. The American occupation forced many peasants from their land and brought an abrupt end to the decentralized systems that enabled a majority of Haitians to live and work on their own terms. Cash crops were back, as were population displacements and rapid environmental devastation.

The Great Rubber Disaster

The American occupation was a forceful and violent attack on the Haitian peasantry and their economic systems, which were judged to be archaic by national and international business leaders who wished to revive the plantation system. During the occupation, agro-industrial ventures would plague the majority of Haitians and lead to guerilla warfare. The cultivation of export crops like sugar or bananas led to the eviction of hundreds of families from their land. For instance, in 1926, American businessmen backed by the American military government seized more than twelve thousand acres of fertile land from Haitian peasants in the Cap Haitien region to grow sisal, a fibrous plant used in weaving. To make room for this massive industrial operation, the U.S. Army evicted thousands of families from their land. According to Suzy Castor, the Americans displaced fifty thousand peasants to make room for sisal plantations, which she called a "classic colonial enclave" (Castor quoted by Naimou 2015, 244). Even though U.S. companies eventually left the region in the 1970s, state-owned companies continued to use the land in Caracol and Fort-Liberté to grow sugar and sisal until 1986. The intensive cultivation of just one crop over two decades so depleted the soil that food production across Cap Haitien was threatened. The evictions and the use of land to grow cash crops accrued food insecurity, deforestation, and soil depletion. The departure of the U.S. Army in 1934 didn't mark the end of this pattern.

The U.S. kept sponsoring agro-industrial and industrial projects in the years following the official end of the occupation. As mentioned above, an American fiscal agent who controlled the national budget, tariffs, and economic policy remained on the island until 1947 (Lundahl 2015, 372). This presence would enable some of the most devastating agro-industrial and mining operations in twentieth-century Haiti. I am taking here the example of rubber production to show how the Haitian state, American corporations, and international institutions have cooperated to implement projects that ultimately benefit a handful of individuals while ruining the livelihoods of thousands of Haitians. Rubber production in Haiti enabled the fusion of the Haitian political world with the American business sector. This alliance allowed a corporation to use state institutions in 1941 to evict people from their land and to reorient Haitian agricultural, commercial, and industrial programs (Gilbert 2016). As Myrtha Gilbert has powerfully demonstrated, this complete overtake of national institutions by a corporation would pave the way for similar destructive business ventures, even in the present moment. American agro-businesses along with experts from the U.S. Department of Agriculture and the Haitian Ministry of Agriculture pushed for the privatization of farmed lands through long-term rental agreements and put mechanisms in place to keep wages and corporate taxes low. Spurring "business confidence," by slashing public spending, state investments in industrial sectors, and taxes, is the hallmark of austerity politics (Blyth 2013, 41). In turn, the economic growth supposedly generated by this quasi-religious abstinence from intervention in the public sector and by a policy of extreme laissez-faire when it comes to financial and environmental regulations will foster "development." The example of the cultivation of rubber in Haiti contains, in a nutshell, all the elements that politically destabilize the island and increase its vulnerability to disasters and global economic downturns.

Until 1947, the United States implemented projects that were in line with F. D. Roosevelt's Good Neighbor Policy in the Caribbean. The Haitian government had very little say in the country's development and spent state revenues on the repayment of international debts and on large agro-industrial projects that broke entire self-sustaining communities in the countryside. The Good Neighbor Policy translated into the replacement of military intervention by violent economic subjugation. The rubber experiment in Haiti is a case in point. In *Les Arbres Musiciens*, a novel published in 1957, Jacques Stéphen Alexis described how the U.S.-imposed cultivation of rubber led to the destruction of Haitian livelihoods, thriving ecosystems, and religious worlds during the World War II period. Through the eyes of Gonaïbo, an adolescent man who lives in communion with the verdant hills of the Jérémie region, Alexis depicted the mass evictions and bulldozing of their land by a "cavalry of white men, in khaki, [riding] strange iron horses at a crazy speed, like an unrush of destructive angels pouncing on the land still wet with dew" (Alexis translated by Dash 1981, 199). In the meantime, he described how Haitian president Elie Lescot's anti-superstition campaign, which targeted Vodou practitioners, helped to nullify the resistance to the imposition of an export economy relying on cash crops. As historian George Eddy Lucien notes, both the regimes of Sténio Vincent (1930–1941) and of Elie Lescot (1941–1946) "constitute a period during which the bases of neocolonialism were laid. Their financial and commercial policies reflect this pattern. They obeyed American commands to the letter. Their politics is to render the country attractive to foreign capital. Their development politics rely on loans" (Lucien 2013, 47; Joseph 2017, 126). As this chapter suggests, internationally sponsored industrial projects in Haiti follow a pattern: they lead to the tearing apart of both the social fabric of communities that have lived autonomously in Haiti since 1804 and the fertile soils sustaining them, while they corrode the sovereignty of the Haitian state and accentuate the country's economic vulnerability.

The planting of 4,800 hevea rubber plants bought from the Goodyear Rubber Company's plantation in Mindanao, Philippines, started on April 9, 1941, in the Grand Anse region. It led to the wiping out of nearly fifty thousand acres of residential areas, fields, and forests in one of Haiti's most fertile regions and to the destruction of solidarity networks established through Vodou practices (Dubois 2012, 314). As Alexis's novel suggests, Haitian peasants lived the sudden arrival of rubber corporations in Haiti as a tragic repetition, as if they were "the guards of the Great Anacoana" witnessing the apocalyptic coming of the conquistadors. However, as Alexis also noted, the 1940s brutal assault on the life and land of peasant farmers relied on new governmental assemblages. Through the creation of the Society for Haitian and American Agricultural Development (SHADA), a private-public venture financed by a loan of $5 million from the Export–Import Bank of the United States, American agronomists and businessmen paired up with Haitian governmental officials to organize a lucrative corporate venture. In 1941, SHADA was granted a fifty-year monopoly of the sale and export of rubber and "acquired land in various regions of the country for a total of 133,400 hectares, or 21.5% of the total cultivated area of Haiti" (Dupuy 1989, 45). The Haitian state and American corporate interests fully conflated without the need of military intervention to create an industry that only responded to the United States' immediate needs in rubber (Gilbert 2016). In 1944, after an unusual drought and the fall of rubber prices, the already fledging rubber industry mostly vanished from southern Haiti, leaving behind deforested lands, depleted soils, and landless farmers.

The rubber experiment in Haiti reveals the forces that have been at play in the establishment of isolated, poorly coordinated, and short-term industrial projects that considerably increased the country's vulnerability to "natural" disasters and global economic fluctuations. These repeated attempts at growing an export economy and at forcing people into a wage-labor system reinforced the dominant position of "the 1 percent to 2 percent of the population that constituted the Haitian bourgeoisie (both 'mulatto' and black)" (Dupuy 1989, 146). By favoring "mulattoes" in positions of power, the American occupants reactivate what Leslie Péan named "l'engrenage coloriste mulâtriste" (the colorist and mulatrist cycle) and exacerbated the divides between people of mixed descent who inherited most of the plantation system's remnants after 1804 and a large majority of "black" Haitians who remained, for the most part, excluded from the high spheres of commerce and government (Péan 2003, 58). Even though some members of the "black bourgeoisie" and urban middle classes regained power under the presidency of Dumarsais Estimé (1946–1950) and the dictatorship of François Duvalier (1957–1971), the same extractive economic system based on the exploitation of peasant labor and heavy taxation of basic goods remained in place (Trouillot 1990). In other words, the American occupation transformed a weak Haitian state plagued by international debts into a predatory apparatus controlled by fraudulently elected leaders who, as Michel-Rolph Trouillot stated, "made their personal fortune the very raison d'être of state revenues" (Trouillot 1994).

The Bauxite Scheme and the Illusion of Sovereignty

From 1934 to 1957, the Haitian economic structure did not change much; nor did the political elites that controlled both the state and private sector. President Sténio Vincent, who led the country from 1930 to 1941, gave Haiti its "second independence" by negotiating the departure of the U.S. Army. However, Haiti's economy and budget were still controlled by the U.S. while Vincent reinforced racial divisions. Vincent's "mulatrism" was in line with American segregationist practices (Kaussen 2000, 20). The independence was illusory, and the same old developmental recipes—economic growth through industrialization will magically "develop" the country—were reinforced over the years. The Estimé presidency (1946–1950) temporarily shifted political power to the "black" middle-class and bourgeoisie but did not reduce the economic dominance of the Port-au-Prince merchant elites that were constituted of "mulattoes" and of families that immigrated to Haiti toward the end of the nineteenth century—mainly from Syria but also from Germany, Denmark and England (Jackson 2011, 231). The doors were also kept open for American corporations, which took advantage of low-wage labor and optimal fiscal conditions. The example of bauxite mining shows once again how Haiti is conceived of as an extractive colony and how surplus value made from the island's raw materials benefits U.S. businesses. The bauxite push, in the Caribbean, coincided with the forceful entry of IFIs in the region (Girvan 1971). Negotiations pertaining to mining were a way to weaken environmental regulations and corporate tax burdens in the Caribbean basin. The bauxite industry in Haiti benefited the U.S.-based Reynolds Mining Corporation but left almost nothing behind in Haiti, economically speaking, except environmental degradation and social instability.

Until the ascent of François Duvalier to power in 1957, the same shady "industrialization" deals with the United States went on. But they did not follow a sustained politics of industrialization. Rather, they were again isolated operations that benefited the very small and bilateral import-export elite. After the rubber fiasco, American corporations focused on cash crop production (the Standard Fruit and Steamship Company kept the monopoly on banana exports from 1935 to 1946) and on mining operations. While U.S. authorities officially left the country in 1947, the important mission conducted by the United Nations in 1948—the first of a long string of "peacekeeping" missions—put Haiti back on the path of development through internationally led (mainly U.S.-led) industrialization. U.N. observers argued that a "strong" state would be best for Haiti's development, and the mission opened up new industrial possibilities, which in turn translated into the providing of loans by USAID and other IFIs (Schuller 2007, 150). I will take here the example of bauxite mining to briefly show how bilateral industrial schemes kept Haiti under American and IFIs economic purview and how they reinforced social and financial vulnerability at all level during the Duvalier era. The flamboyant nationalism of François Duvalier could not mask the utter lack of economic sovereignty and of long-term planning. As Michel-Rolph Trouillot aptly noted, "François Duvalier's government had always given the United States the most tangible sign of its submission: unconditional support of U.S. capital" (1990, 202). Following a well-known pattern, American corporations "worked" with the government to acquire land and fiscal advantages in order to implement their projects. The mining industry is a case in point, as negotiations on bauxite extraction coincided with the forceful entry of the IMF into the Caribbean.

In Haiti, the U.S. based Reynolds Mining Corporation monopolized the extraction and export of bauxite starting in 1953 (Johnson 1953, 48; Fellom 1953, 30). As sugar was refined in France from the raw materials imported from Saint-Domingue during the colonial period, aluminum was produced in U.S. factory from bauxite mined in the Caribbean. In other words, the surplus value was created abroad and benefited foreign corporations, and, adjacently, foreign states. The same year, Haiti was accepted as a member of the International Monetary Fund and of the World Bank (IMF 1953, 86; Buss 2009, 58). Both institutions supported the corporate mining of bauxite in the Caribbean, and helped to reinstate the "typical features of plantation economy which are reproduced - better still, ratooned - in the features of the company-country relationship in the bauxite industry" (Girvan 1971, 378). With the administrative (and often military) support of the United States, aluminum companies negotiated low fiscal obligations and advantageous lease terms where they enrolled the Haitian government as an eviction and repression agent. As Jamaican economist Norman Girvan has shown, aluminum companies sealed provisions that turned "governments and other public institutions [into] appendages of the corporate system, i.e., they are incorporated into the system of control and exploitation relationships through which the companies operate in the countries" (1971, 417). Bauxite mining was the Trojan horse of the IMF and of the World Bank in the Caribbean. Since 1953, IFIs have mushroomed and have consolidated global dependencies in the Caribbean. Haiti fell under the tutelage of many international lending institutions that are still dictating economic policies in the country today. These IFIs, and their local political allies, prevented the decentralization of power and the equitable distribution of state revenues while they transformed the Haitian state into a fierce defender of international private interests.

The big bauxite push, and the concomitant memberships with IFIs, happened under François Duvalier's rule. In 1959, the Haitian government gave Reynolds access to 150,000 acres of land, which led to the displacement of hundreds of families (Doura 2001; Sansavior 2015, 196). As Haitian economist Fred Doura has demonstrated, the impact of the bauxite industry on the Haitian economy and on Haitians' well-being was null. The small amount of mining-related taxes collected during the Duvalier era were siphoned off by the dictator's family and inner circle. Between 1957 and 1961, Reynolds paid only 7% of its total revenues in taxes to the Haitian state and employed only 0.5% of the industrial workforce of the country (Trouillot 1990, 202; Coupeau 2008, 146). The main impact of the mining economy was, *once again*, the massive displacements of peasant farmers and the aggravation of food insecurity. While Duvalier widely opened his country for mining, he also reinforced Haiti's dependency to IFIs by adhering, in 1959, to the Inter-American Development Bank (thereafter IDB).

Through the expansion of the bauxite industry in Haiti, U.S. dominated international lending agencies established the *modus operandi* for doing international business in Haiti. Corporations and their institutional allies have worked together to weaken state capabilities when it comes to social or environmental regulations while they contributed to reinforce its repressive and autocratic structures. Adhering to the IMF, for instance, meant to frame Haiti's 'underdevelopment' as the result of a lack of industrialization—a process itself hindered by the supposed 'backwardness' of Haitian rural citizens. Hence, every effort meant to 'open Haiti for business' was already inscribed in the teleological narrative of "development," which is here synonymous with an ideological, technocratic import and a tool of cultural and economic imperialism (Escobar 1995). As Nevers Constant, who was Duvalier's Minister of Agriculture and Natural Resources, declared in a private meeting where the Haitian government asked for a major IMF funding increase in 1966: "Everyone here around this table, Haitian or American, knows that Haiti's key problem is a problem of production. Our national salvation can only come from the development of our production. [IMF] funding is a primary condition for the growth of our production" (Guichard 2010, 18). Already in 1966, clearing the path for industrial production and attracting foreign investments by downsizing state economic, social, and environmental oversight was the central strategy to "develop" Haiti.

The Great Neoliberal Plunge

In May 1980, Radio Haiti reporters Marvel Dandin and Harold Isaac described how the Reynolds Mining Co. managed to circumvent the minimal taxation and regulations they had negotiated with the Haitian government since 1944 (Radio Haiti Archive 2018). Leaving almost no trace in the national economy and resource-depleted lands behind them (Garrity 1974), bauxite mines started to close in the countryside. As Dandin and Isaac report, Haitians employed by Reynolds in the Miragoane mines, worked in "hell-like conditions" and saw no improvements in their communities. Foreign-born and local upper-class administrators, by contrast, lived in comfortable buildings in the fenced-off American City, while local public schools didn't see any improvements from the opening of the mine in 1957 to its closing in 1987 (Radio Haiti Archive 2018). As Monique Garrity noted in 1974, the trickle-down benefits for local citizens were almost nonexistent: locals were allowed to use the 12-bed hospital opened for Reynolds employees if they paid for their meals and prescriptions and got access to drinking water. The disadvantages, in the meantime, were many. The Plateau de Rochelois, where mining operations took place, was, until the early 1960s, a place where farmers thrived. "There is no region with such a combination of productions," wrote Paul Moral in 1961. "Bananas, coffee, red beans, sugar cane, fruits" used to dot the hilly landscape of the Plateau (Moral 1961, 157). But mining operations left behind landless peasants and intensified the environmental problems of the region by accruing erosion

and soil depletion. Even though the initial and renegotiated contracts stip-
ulated that Reynolds should rehabilitate mined-out land, "the company's
record in this area is rather dismal" (Garrity 1974, 202).

Haitian economist Fred Doura, in his analysis of extractive economies
in Haiti, shows that mining and mono-crop enclave industries have modeled state-corporation relations in a way that prevents any industrial or
economic development in Haiti (Doura 2012). Export-based industries
function as extractive enclaves that do not have linkages to other sectors of
the economy, and leave nothing behind for a majority of Haitians, except
accrued environmental degradation. As was the case with sugar during the
colonial period, the raw products are processed and refined outside of
Haiti. For instance, the bauxite that is transformed into final products
abroad generates 95% of added value. The impact of bauxite mining was
minimal for the Haitian economy, but it proved critical to the well-being of
Reynolds industries in the U.S. (Garrity 1974). Even though the tourism and
garment industry picked up in the 1970s, creating an annual 5% of economic growth during this period, living conditions for Haitians were
quickly degrading (IMF 2006). At the beginning of the 1980s, renewed
political violence was accompanied by widespread economic and agricultural crisis in the countryside. In other words, economic growth didn't
trickle down: provincial irrigation systems, markets, and roads were not
maintained, and the lower tariffs on food imports meant that Haitian farmers had a hard time competing with foreign agrobusinesses. The situation
quickly unraveled. Chronic episodes of famine, political violence, along
with widespread and visible state corruption led to two processes: massive
immigration movements and rebellions (Nicholls 1986, 1244; Farnsworth
1984). Being open for business never lifted living standards for Haitians.
Instead, neoliberal policies fueled the proletarization of Haitian farmers
and led to the disappearance of basic state welfare functions.

The closing of mines coincided with a crackdown on the free press, a
return of the state militias (Tontons Macoutes), and large increases in foreign
aid. In 1983–1984, the United States aid to Haiti came to represent $44.7 mil-
lion, while an IMF agreement allowed the disbursement of $63 million in loans

covering the period 1983–85 (Southerland 1984). Haiti had remained fiercely open for business since the 1915 occupation, but foreign capitals did not follow suit. And when they did, the impact on state revenues was small. Successive Haitian governments kept tariffs and taxes low, regulations were quasi nonexistent, and nationalist leaders made sure a "docile" pool of poorly-paid laborers would be available at all times. Nonetheless, these optimal conditions never led to any form of industrial development. Even during the short periods when the economy grew, Haitians didn't see any improvements in infrastructures or basic services. The Haitian state, since 1957, heavily relied on U.S. controlled IFIs loans, especially IMF loans, to keep state expenditures afloat. These loans came with strings attached: transforming Haiti into a free-trade zone and keeping labor cheap were, and are still, considered as the path to economic growth. According to the credo of productivist religions, economic growth is the key engine of the always vaguely defined 'development'. While IMF lending is supposedly temporary and lasts on average five years, Haiti spent 21 years under consecutive arrangements up until 1990, imposing various destructive structural adjustment programs (Ottersen 2013, 36).

As economist Stanley Fisher explains, IMF loans come with a package of conditions such as "trade liberalization, price liberalization, privatization, the introduction of indirect means of monetary control, foreign-exchange market liberalization, banking-system restructuring, tax reform, subsidy cuts, and changes in the structure of government spending" (Fischer 1997, 25). By the early 1980s, the IMF and other lenders forcefully downsized the size of the state and slashed the number of state employees while they helped open the market to food imports, which was supposed to help Haitians as they transited from a food security-centered economy to a free market economy. Of course, having fewer state employees means having less state supervision when it comes to environmental and social regulations. Allied with U.S. institutions like the United States Agency for International Development (USAID), IFIs have steadily pushed neoliberal initiatives like Ronald Reagan's Caribbean Basin Initiative, an economic plan that led, in 1984, to the redirecting of 30 percent of Haiti's domestic food production toward export crops (Mullin 2018). The conditions imposed by IFIs have led, for instance, to the destruction of rice production and to accrued food insecurity. Not able to compete with American subsidized rice, Haitian farmers were the direct victims of a "free" market economy that heavily favored the U.S. (Holt-Gimenez and Patel 2012, 38–39). Neoliberal measures transformed Haiti into one of the most open economies in the world and contributed to shrinking an already small horizon of stable livelihoods for most Haitians.

Eventually, these old recipes had an effect in the 1970s. From 1970 to 1980, assembly industries became a key sector of Haiti's economy, employing 80 percent of the industrial workforce of the country (Péan 1987). However, they functioned on the same enclave model: international corporations manufacturing baseballs or electronic goods in Haiti benefited from tax and tariffs exemptions and paid no taxes on materials and machineries imported for goods production. In brief, these corporations' operations contributed little to the national treasury and did not generate trickle-down effects for other sectors of the economy (Opitz 2004, 110). The low salaries of sweatshops' employees were cut off in a vile fashion. For instance, employees had to pay for toilet paper and drinking water and were confronted with seasonal layoffs. Meanwhile the 9 percent taxes taken off their salaries was readily siphoned off by Duvalier and his inner circle (Schuller 2007). The enclave industrialization schemes contributed to three forms of "development" in Haiti: development of wealth for a small circle; development of environmental disasters and food insecurity in the countryside; development of dense urban centers in regions where factories allowed for the illusory dream of finding employment. By 1980, Jean-Claude Duvalier couldn't hide the utter failure of his own "economic revolution" anymore. Bolstered by the election of Ronald Reagan, who turned a blind eye to human rights issues while offering financial aid to Haiti, the Haitian state resorted to violence to contain the growing anger of citizens who had been repeatedly harmed by allied local and international elites.

The history of the first half of the 1980s in Haiti seemed to be coming straight out of a science fiction book, given the absurdity of the policies backed by international partners and their implementation by docile Haitian administrators. In 1980, Jean-Claude Duvalier and his inner-circle siphoned $20 million of aid disbursed by the IMF (Southerland 1984). In return, the IMF scolded Haitian leaders for their misuse of public funds. However, things were back to normal after the state implemented superficial fiscal reforms advocated by the IMF. The loans quickly resumed, even though embezzlements of public funds never ceased.

The five-month tenure of Marc Bazin, a World Bank economist, as a minister of finance and economy in 1982 helped to shed light on these embezzlement mechanics. However, he was quickly ousted and replaced with Frantz Merceron, a French-trained economist who covered the Duvaliers' shady business deals while forcefully implementing the IMF-backed reforms required to receive IFI loans (Abbott 2011). Meanwhile, most of the Haitian elites who benefited from investing in the industrial and agro-industrial sector didn't pay the taxes that would have helped build robust public education or health sectors. As journalist Keith Richburg noted, "Haitian investors accounted for more than $250 million deposited in American and offshore Caribbean banks [in 1985], and Duvalier and his family members are widely assumed to be among those depositors" (1986). For instance, Ernest Bennett, a coffee exporter who was almost bankrupt by the end of the 1970s, became one of the wealthiest Haitian businessmen after his daughter Michèle married Jean-Claude Duvalier in 1980. By 1985, he ran lucrative businesses in all kinds of sectors and became the first importer of luxury cars in the country. Many members of the Haitian business elite lined up, and still line up, with IFI recommendations as doing so enables them to pay little to no taxes and to have access to a wider, and less supervised, import-export market (Gros 2012). While, logically, state revenues should be used to build roads, schools, and markets and to hire doctors and teachers, in Haiti the meager state revenues were directly siphoned off by small political and economic circles while the task of taking care of the country was left to external institutions. A wide array of international financial lending institutions and, since the beginning of the 1970s, a growing apparatus of international NGOs, took on the task of "developing" the country while the state made supplemental efforts to attract foreign capital.

During the waning days of Duvalierism (1980–1986), the IMF insisted that the Haitian government impose a politics of fiscal austerity: cutting government spending, slashing welfare programs, dwindling the number of state employees while increasing taxes for the majority of Haitians contributed, along with brutal political repression, to create the climate of revolt that started to shatter the country in 1985. The IMF agreement with Haiti was a two-year program of reforms that led to $63 million in loans for the 1983–1985. As Daniel Southerland reported in 1984, "Merceron claims to have been implementing most of the provisions of this program. According to Merceron, these moves have included cuts in government spending over the past two years of more than 25 percent and revenue increases of more than 40 percent" (1984). Once again, putting in order the "balance of payment and foreign exchange position"—the key criteria for an IMF loan— meant to *peze souse* (squeeze and suck) the Haitian peasantry with heavy tax burdens while keeping the country attractive for business by cutting corporate taxes and slashing tariffs.

In the meantime, the Reagan administration's Caribbean Basin Initiative (CBI), initiated in 1983, further damaged the Haitian economy and considerably undermined its food security. Under the CBI, duty-free "privileges" accorded to twelve nations of the Caribbean led, in Haiti, to the flooding of the Haitian market by U.S. subsidized food. The CBI simply led to a large increase in U.S. exports toward the Caribbean while U.S. imports remained weak (Katz 2013, 292). Not able to compete with the artificially low prices of U.S. imported food, the Haitian agricultural sector declined abruptly (Trouillot 1990). While these policies transformed Haiti into a small-scale "supplier of garments, dolls, magnetic tapes, and electronic equipment" (Trouillot 1990, 202), the swift and violent slaughter of Haitian pigs broke the economic spinal cord of the Haitian peasantry. As Mark Schuller writes, "responding to an outbreak of swine fever, the U.S. government killed off Haitian pigs, de-facto bank accounts, replacing them with high-maintenance pink U.S. pigs, amounting to Haiti's 'great stock market crash'" (Schuller 2007, 150). This series of man-made economic disasters, along with accrued political repression, triggered massive migration movements and led to the ousting of Jean-Claude Duvalier in February 1986. After almost thirty years of violent dictatorship and constant economic sabotaging, Haitians lived in a country devoid of public services and basic infrastructure.

The failed rubber experiment, the Reynolds takeover of Haitian bauxite, the almost nonexistent economic impact of the 1970s apparel and assemblage industry, and the devastating creole pig slaughtering campaign seem to shed light on the profound lack of state agency in Haiti. However, Haitian business elites and a small political cohort belonging to the middle classes and bourgeoisie fully cooperated with American corporations and institutions. For instance, the initial contract between Reynolds and the Haitian state that was signed in 1944 was so advantageous to the American corporation that they named the bauxite found in Haiti the "Lescotite" (Jamaica Bauxite Institute 1980, 191) in homage to then president Elie Lescot, a staunch proponent of "mulatrism," who gave a blank check to American investors willing to do business in Haiti. In the rubber case, Lescot and his Haitian associates were on the board of the Haitian-American corporation that devastated the Jérémie region to cultivate hevea plants. And once again, in the pig slaughter case, the Haitian government fully cooperated with USAID to eliminate creole pigs. It appears that the Haitian state is not so weak after all. Through various institutional assemblages where the lines between the private and public sectors are blurred, it uses its small margins of sovereignty to fully engage in collaborations that are nefarious to the majority of Haitians. The state acts as a cop and actuary of foreign corporations and institutions to impose pro-business policies that constantly shifted the tax burden to low-income Haitians. However, when it comes to social welfare, environmental regulations, and public infrastructures, the state is almost nonexistent. More than a hundred years after the American invasion, austerity politics, defined by Mark Blyth as the constant adjustment of the economy by reduction of tariffs, corporate taxes, public spending, and wages to restore "competitiveness," are still plaguing Haiti today.

Liquidating the Haitian State: Aristide, Clinton, and the Structural Devastation of Haiti

In previous sections, I took the example of extractive economies to show how state-corporation relations modeled economic policies in Haiti. By the end of the Duvalier dictatorship, it was clear that extractive industries fostered ecological vulnerability, centralization and urban density, and economic dependency. The 1985 popular revolt indicates that Haitian people were not the passive recipients of physical and fiscal repression. Even though the state security apparatus suffocated popular resistance for twenty-nine years, a renewed democratic movement was taking shape in the 1980s. The ousting of Duvalier was followed by a period of political instability where Duvalierists controlled the state (Barthélémy 1990). However, the landslide election of Jean-Bertrand Aristide in December 1990 was an extraordinary affirmation of popular political desires and practices that had been forged in the *longue durée*. With the election of Aristide, Haiti had the chance to reorient and decentralize its economy and to establish a system of wealth redistribution. During its eight-month tenure, "the Aristide regime increased enforcement of tax collection, including import fees and arrears. As a result, the Direction Générale des Impôts registered a historic increase in total revenues. It also put into place price controls on products such as rice and wheat" (Naidu et al. 2017). Not surprisingly, Aristide was ousted by a coup on September 29, 1991, with the support of local business elites and of various foreign actors.

The military junta that came to power brutally repressed the democratic movement, killing peasant leaders and human rights activists while using terror as a mode of government (Caple-James 2010). The return of necropolitics—defined by Achille Mbembe as the use of political power to determine who can live or die—and of business as usual plunged once again the island in complete disarray and propelled massive movements of migration (Mbembe 2019). Given space constraints, I cannot detail the complexity and nuances of the post-Duvalier era. Excellent studies of the 1986–2010 period show that popular resistance, even if weakened, did not disappear, and that the push to implement IFIs structural adjustment programs was a catalyzer for foreign-backed right-wing repression (Fatton 2002; Dupuy 2007). In this section, I briefly describe how history repeats itself as a macabre farce: the return of austerity politics in 1994 along with the U.S. invasion of the country mark once again a period of great economic decline for a majority of Haitians.

Following years of economic embargo and of paramilitary violence, Aristide signed the Governor's Island Accord in 1994 that allowed him to resume his presidency. The accord provided amnesty to the coup terrorists and even gave them seats in Aristide's government. Moreover, Aristide had no choice but to implement drastic structural adjustment programs (Dupuy 2007). Once again, opening Haiti for business was a violent endeavor. A U.S.-backed U.N. force comprising thirty thousand soldiers occupied the country and suppressed popular resistance to the newly imposed austerity measures in the name of stabilization and peacekeeping. Aristide himself became a tame advocate of capitalism and development through economic growth. Under the tutelage of Bill Clinton, the second Aristide government, and the many successive governments that followed it, implemented the same neoliberal pattern of measures that further pauperized Haiti.

U.S.-backed IFIs' grand plans to develop Haiti through the fostering of economic growth led to the same old results: the crippling of small-scale farming, the spectacular rise of food insecurity and concomitant dependence on American food imports, and the establishment of extractive sweatshop ventures that provided a small number of poorly paid jobs. As Doug Hellinger writes, "though mindful of the misery caused by a long history of elite rule in Haiti, the Clinton team, along with the international financial institutions, have insisted on control over the Haitian economy through a structural adjustment program that gives priority to the interests of foreign investors over those of the Haitian poor" (McGowan 1997, 2). The usual suspects—the IMF, the World Bank, USAID, and the IDB—promised to

provide two billion dollars of aid upon implementation of pro-business policies. To take a few brief examples, international donors asked the government to lay off half of its civil servants, to decrease minimum wages, to
privatize nine state enterprises, to limit state regulation and intervention
in the economic field, to create free-trade zones, and to provide tax incentives to foreign businesses (McGowan 1997).

The IMF had the most powerful role as it provided short-term and mid-
term loans and it acted as the gatekeeper for other IFIs' loans. The IMF
worked with the government and imposed macroeconomic measures that
led to the elimination of tariffs and regulations that protected local food
crops, cuts in government spending, and so on. As many scholars have
shown, these measures led to the abrupt decline of small-scale agriculture,
to an almost total reliance on food imports, and to a deep political instability (Richardson 1997; Farmer 2012; Steckley and Shamsie 2015). The radical
decreases of tariffs in the 1990s and 2000s allowed subsidized American rice
to flood the country and sapped the vibrant Haitian rice agriculture—a
process of decline for which Bill Clinton apologized in 2010 (O'Connor
2013). Slashing import tariffs meant slashing state revenues. However, the
economic growth that is supposed to be generated by free trade never came
and never filled state coffers. Budget deficits may be alleviated through
IFIs' temporary loans and cuts in public spending, but these "solutions" are
not sustainable in the long term. Each structural adjustment program
undermines state capacity and augments global economic dependency. As
Jean-Germain Gros suggests, structural adjustment programs are not a
"cure" but the very element that provokes "the contagion of the disease" as
they foster state fragility, international debt, and the massive dwindling of
state revenues (Gros 2010, 983). Slashing tariffs in Haiti indeed spurred economic activity, but only for the rice farmers of the Mississippi Valley. The
return of austerity politics and military occupation clearly went against the
needs and desires of the Haitian population. From the reelection of Aristide in 2000 to the 2010 earthquake, the country suffered from political violence and instability while food prices skyrocketed. While attractive
conditions for the business sector were forcefully put into place, foreign

investors didn't flock to Haiti. Once again, pro-business policies spectacularly failed.

On the eve of the 2010 earthquake, Haitians had access to a small pool of low-wage industrial jobs and relied on food imports to make ends meet. Since 2004, after a coup d'état that sent Aristide into exile for a second time, the country has been occupied by U.N. forces. Successive governments were in constant negotiations with the IMF, which continued to act as a loan gatekeeper. At this point, it seems that the Haitian government was doing nothing but negotiate terms with IFIs. Food insecurity was on the rise while waves of political violence plagued the entire country. The 2008 financial crisis along with devastating hurricanes and tropical storms led to sharp food price increases, which in turn engendered large protests against "lavi che"—the high cost of living—in Haiti. While, in 2009, Guadeloupe and Martinique's massive protests against the neocolonial system that kept non-*béké* populations captive to global price fluctuations were unfolding, a weakened but clairvoyant popular movement asked to end the neoliberal agenda promoted by IFIs and put in place—even though often reluctantly—by Président René Préval's government. In response to the ongoing food crisis and political instability, then U.N. secretary Ban Ki-Moon sent Bill Clinton as a special envoy to Haiti in June 2009. As Jonathan Katz has astutely described, Clinton, who was dubbed "le Gouverneur" by the Haitian press, came with a premade "vision and a plan" outlined in a nineteen-page report (Katz 2013, 138).

"Clinton's Gospel" had been authored by economist Paul Collier, a former World Bank administrator who had traced a "new" path for Haiti. In his report "Haiti: From Natural Catastrophe to Economic Security," Collier advocated for the creation of export zones that would attract the global garment industry to Haiti, in turn solving the unemployment problem. In brief, Collier offered newly packaged old "solutions" that had utterly failed during the Jean-Claude Duvalier era. The embargo at the beginning of the 1990s had wiped away the few remaining garment factories of the Duvalier era, but rebuilding the sector, argued Collier, would put Haiti on the path to economic security. Of course, the Haitian government would have to make an effort for the economic miracle to happen: keeping wages low, deregulating labor laws, and loosening customs enforcement were part of the package (Katz 2013, 140). The Haitian government adopted the key measures advocated by Clinton and Collier, and plans to transform Haiti into a little Taiwan were *once again* on the table.

Post-earthquake Industrial Politics and the Development of Disasters

On January 12, 2010, more than three hundred thousand people died in a 7.0 magnitude earthquake that rocked the Port-au-Prince region. An estimated three hundred thousand houses collapsed or were permanently damaged, and more than 1.9 million people instantly became homeless (Bell 2012). Decades of economic suffocation of the countryside and human-provoked ecological devastation pushed rural dwellers to migrate to the capital, where services and industries are centralized. If Port-au-Prince comprised fifty thousand inhabitants in the 1950s, by 2010, more than two million people lived there, mostly in substandard housing units located in neighborhoods devoid of basic infrastructure (Tobin 2013). If the structures of economic, administrative, and political centralization were put in place during the colonial and occupation periods, the extreme demographic concentration that contributed to transforming the earthquake into a catastrophe happened during the Duvalier regimes and subsequent years of neoliberalism that pushed people away from the provinces to the cities. Once again, the slashing of rice tariffs in 1995, for instance, ruined thousands of people relying on rice cultivation in the Artibonite valley. Going to Port-au-Prince is often not a choice but a necessity for people who cannot generate any income through agriculture. The extreme density of Port-au-Prince, reinforced by the centralization of NGO services after the earthquake, is one of the key elements that transformed an earthquake into a mega-disaster (Marcelin et al. 2016). In the meantime, the Haitian state was severely affected by the earthquake: an estimated 25 percent of public servants died, and the National Palace collapsed, along with ministry buildings, schools, hospitals, and so on. In other words, major parts of a state that already had little say in the national economic agenda disappeared. All of a sudden it became easier for IFIs, Western states, and NGOs to simply bypass the Haitian state and to transfer the missions of public institutions to large NGOs.

This takeover happened quickly. Immediately after the quake, the U.S. Army coordinated relief efforts in a disorganized fashion while the United States and the IFIs and NGOs it supports took over the reconstruction plans for the country. The massive donations to NGOs that were already active in Haiti, along with state and IFI donations, would be coordinated by U.N. special envoy Bill Clinton and Haitian prime minister Jean-Max Bellerive. Both led the Interim Haiti Recovery Commission (IHRC), an entity created by presidential decree on April 21, 2010. As Paul Collier noted in 2011, the Haitian government, supposedly, could not be trusted with the management of the recovery, and an entity independent of the government should coordinate large donations. The IHRC was this entity. If it looked like a new international and Haitian partnership on paper, the IHRC actually functioned without the input of Haitian state actors. As Jonathan Katz astutely demonstrated, the IHRC simply recycled old economic solutions that, by then, should have put Haiti on the path to economic security at least fifty years earlier (Katz 2013).

The IHRC did not take into account the input of Haitian actors—they were a cosmetic presence in the commission that implemented an agenda created well before the earthquake. In December 2011, the twelve Haitian members of the IHRC wrote a letter describing their marginalization. As they stated, "the twelve Haitian members present here feel completely disconnected from the activities of the IHRC. . . . In spite of our role in the governance structure of the institution, we have so far received no follow-up on the IHRC activities" (Johnston 2011). Bill Clinton had the power to orient the reconstruction upon his own neoliberal vision. The 2009 Collier report was refurbished into a disaster recovery plan—the Action Plan for the Recovery and Development of Haiti. Under the motto of "Building Back Better" (who would want to build back worse?), the Action Plan replayed the same old song: free-trade zones and industrial parks meant to house the garment industry would kick start economic growth, and that would in turn generate long-term recovery. *Once again.*

The IHRC set budget priorities and privileged the creation of "growth poles" where the clothing industry would play a pivotal role. While this institution didn't have large financial powers, Clinton was nonetheless able to orient the economic policy of Haiti, especially after the fraudulent election of pro-business president Michel Martelly. In 2011, such a "growth pole" emerged in Caracol, in the northern part of the country. The Caracol Industrial Park, Bill and Hillary Clinton's pet project, is a six hundred-acre industrial facility meant to house garment factories. U.S. taxpayer money via USAID and the IDB financed the construction of the park. As the previously mentioned letter of the Haitian IHRC board members stated, "in reality, Haitians members of the board have one role: to endorse the decisions made by the Director and Executive Committee."

As Haitian administrators were mostly bypassed, the construction of the park was swift. In order to make room for the project, "366 families were displaced from their land. . . . Also negatively impacted by the Caracol Industrial Project were 720 agricultural workers and thousands of resellers, food processors and pastoralists, as well as rural community members who relied on the agricultural production of the land for food and livelihood or used it to access water" (Chérestal 2015, 3). Actually, 442 families were displaced by the construction (Accountability Counsel 2018). The park was supposed to create sixty thousand jobs in five years, but as of 2018, only about thirty-five thousand people work in the Haitian apparel industry, with approximatively nine thousand people working in the Caracol Industrial Park (Haiti Libre 2018).

Tè Chabé, the site where the industrial park was built, was a concentration camp during the American occupation. In 1918, Haitian leader Charlemagne Péralte led a rebellion against the American occupants who had maintained a forced-labor system called the *corvée* in the north (Dubois 2012). Moreover, as mentioned earlier, peasant farmers were also protesting the massive displacements caused by the U.S. sisal plantations (Castor 1978). Péralte led an army of more than five thousand peasant farmers—les

Cacos—in warfare against the American occupants. "After years of resisting the U.S. occupying forces, Péralte was captured and killed on October 31, 1919, by two U.S. marines, Herman Henry Hanneken and William
Robert Button, who infiltrated his camp disguised in blackface" (Philogène
2015, 109). Many Caco rebels and displaced farmers were then imprisoned
and sent to the Cap Haitien prison or to the Tè Chabè concentration camp.
According to Dantès Bellegarde, 5,475 prisoners died in the Tè Chabè camp.
The American authorities dismissed this massacre, stating dryly that
repressing Haitian brigandage evidently entailed the loss of Haitian lives
(Bellegarde 1937, 56–57). Péralte's body was buried in a concrete cast to prevent his followers from exhuming the body or to resurrect it (Michel 1996,
42; Philogène 2015, 112). Before then, however, the U.S. Army put his body
on display in Grand Rivière, so Haitian local officials and people who knew
Péralte could see him dead. An anonymous U.S. Marine photograph took
the picture of Péralte's body, tied to a door, partly covered in white cloth.
The U.S. army then disseminated the image by airplane in the countryside
as a warning to the Caco rebels. However, this image, which unintention-
ally evokes a crucifixion, became a symbol of resistance for the Haitian
peasantry. The Cacos did not back down and led a second war against the
U.S. Army that ended in 1920. Péralte became a symbol of resistance to the
occupant, a symbol for Haitian peasants who fight to preserve their autonomy and livelihoods.

Building the Caracol Industrial Park on a site deemed sacred by many
of the people who live in Caracol and who worked the fertile lands of Tè
Chabè may not be an intentional erasure of history on the part of IDB, the
Haitian government, or the Clinton Foundation–USAID assemblage. However, the bulldozing of one of the last strongholds of today's Haitian peasantry and the building of factories in a place where people who fought
against the brutal return of the plantation system in their region is an
affront to many Caracol peasants. Bulldozing Tè Chabè is an uprooting of
the peasants' cosmology, value systems, and social cohesion. It is an indirect form of history silencing that has long been a practice of the Haitian
creole state, defined by Barthélémy as the wealthy political elites allied

with international partners who aim to "develop" the nation through top-down industrialization (Barthélémy 1990, 58). Development in the Caracol region has meant displacement, dispossession, and pauperization for peasant farmers and their families. These displacements echo the violent "anti-superstition campaigns" of the U.S. Marines or the Haitian government that lasted from the 1920s to the early 1940s. These led to the killing of Vodou practitioners, the destruction of their temples, and the confiscation of their ritual objects.

Moreover, the Caracol Bay, which "includes a breathtaking barrier reef and the largest remaining mangroves in Haiti," will (or has already) greatly suffer from the pollution engendered by the factories, a rapidly growing population, and the deep sea port slated for construction in the near future (Chéry 2015). This area was home to hundreds of farmers and fishermen who ensured the food security of an entire region. But since small-scale agriculture has never been considered viable, the IHRC put forth a model that has repeatedly failed: the creation of a pool of low-wage workers relying on food imports. Once again, eight years after the implementation of Collier and Clinton's neoliberal recipes, the results are clear: evictions, accrued food insecurity, environmental devastation, and meager economic benefits for Haitians.

Meanwhile, Haiti continued to be occupied by U.N. military forces and saw a massive influx of U.S. soldiers right after the earthquake. U.S. soldiers guarded humanitarian convoys, which simply slowed down relief operations in the days after the earthquake, greatly augmenting the death toll of the disaster. The MINUSTAH (United Nations Stabilization Mission in Haiti), after many years of actively being engaged in or supporting the repression of political activists who oppose the neoliberal agenda of U.S.-backed puppet governments, was responsible for the cholera epidemic that killed an estimated 8,767 people between 2011 and 2014 (UNCT 2014). While the U.N. was trying to sweep its responsibility under the rug, international NGOs, such as the American Red Cross or Oxfam, along with Christian missionaries achieved their takeover of the social welfare functions of the Haitian state by expanding their operations in the fields of infrastructure and housing (re)building, health care, education, and so on. While I only briefly touch on this subject here, an overwhelming number of scholars have detailed the nefarious long-term effects of NGOs on state capacity, disaster preparedness and recovery, and the economic well-being of local populations in Haiti (Schuller 2012a; Wagner 2014; Farmer 2012; Trouillot 2012).

The first NGO "explosion" happened in the early 1980s, as structural adjustment programs eroded state capacity by downsizing already meager social welfare budgets. After the earthquake, an estimated ten thousand international NGOs operated in Haiti without state supervision. If NGOs like Partners in Health or Fokal collaborated with the Haitian state in order to rebuild state capacity, they were exceptions. For example, NGO management of temporary shelter camps and of housing construction was a spectacular failure. Laura Sullivan affirmed that the American Red Cross, which received half a billion dollars in donation, built six houses between 2010 and 2015 in Haiti (Sullivan 2015). Even though this account needs to be nuanced (large NGOs redistribute some of their funds to smaller local NGOs, and so on), Sullivan pointed to a key problem: incompetent international actors who are non-Creole speakers received large salaries for doing work that ultimately could be summed up as what Haitian film director Raoul Peck dubbed as "assistance mortelle"—lethal assistance (Peck 2012).

As anthropologist Mark Schuller has brilliantly demonstrated, NGOs act as "gap fillers" in states eroded by neoliberalism and propose alternatives of state social welfare that are temporary and unsustainable; they reproduce and perpetuate social inequalities by creating new semi-elites who receive comfortable salaries in the global South; they "present institutional barriers against local participation and priority setting" (Schuller 2009, 85). Moreover, they keep alive the "corruption" discourse that frame global South governments as entities that are unable to address the issues citizens confront in pauperized regions (Svistova and Pyles 2018). In other words, NGOs help to reproduce the racist trope of Haitians being inept at governing themselves, which propelled the 1915 American invasion in the first place, and impede the development of a local qualified workforce by diverting what should be the jobs of Haitian public servants to a new class of privileged NGO workers who are often completely disconnected from the people they are supposed to help.

Eight years after the 2010 catastrophe, the IHRC industrialization projects did not generate sufficient economic growth to foster the always loosely defined "development" of Haiti and did not create stable living environments where Haitian people would thrive. On the contrary, the concentration of NGO services in the capital reactivated the processes of urban centralization and density, making the people living in Port-au-Prince once again vulnerable to earthquakes. Many NGOs in Haiti work in the murky waters that stand between temporary crisis intervention and long-term development projects, such as urban planning, housing construction, and so on. NGOs that improvise themselves as infrastructure builders led projects that, overall, made a bad situation worse. Some NGOs, like Médecins Sans Frontières (MSF; Doctors without Borders), are involved not only in emergency care but also in the building of clinics throughout the Port-au-Prince region. The failures of MSF are an example that sheds light on the larger foreign NGO developmental catastrophe that is still unfolding in Haiti. Simply put, the fact that NGOs are meant to temporarily help countries in situations of crisis entails the reality that sustainable, long-term projects are not on the table.

In 2011, MSF, an NGO with many international chapters that has been in Haiti since 1991, was able to quickly build a hospital in the Léogâne and Port-au-Prince region. Reaching far beyond its emergency help role, this medical organization stepped into infrastructure building and did so efficiently. For instance, the Chatuley hospital in Léogâne opened in 2010 and offered between four thousand and six thousand free consultations a month. Because MSF offers only temporary services, the hospital closed down in 2015. Over a short period of time, the free services proposed by all medical NGOs in the region dried up an already frail local health economy (Lemay-Hébert 2018, 4). The temporary MSF hospital may have offered services that were inaccessible to people before the earthquake, but once the structure closed down, it left behind a medical desert. NGOs are indeed meant to offer temporary solutions, and people living in Léogâne can now feel the brunt of such one-off practices, having today less access to medical services than before the quake. MSF plans to close two more hospitals located in Port-au-Prince in 2018 and 2019. This will lead to the layoff of more than a thousand of Haitian doctors, nurses, and technicians. As Evelyn Trouillot astutely noted, medical NGOs opening these temporary hospitals destroyed local health systems by offering free services past the post-earthquake emergency period, which led to the closing of many Haitian doctors' offices that could not compete with the free clinics, and by taking away doctors and a skilled workforce from local institutions (Trouillot 2012, 106). Once again, the model of one-off, poorly planned projects providing non-Haitian "experts" with comfortable salaries and offering ephemeral job opportunities is what weakened the Haitian public and private health system.

Not all NGO work has the dire consequences noted here. Haitian-led NGOs that have been operating in the country for a long time, that work with truly participatory methods, and that employ a majority of Haitians at all hierarchical levels have achieved major results. For instance, Zanmi Lasante—Partners in Health, an NGO founded by anthropologist Paul Farmer that has been operating in Haiti for more than thirty years, is working with the Ministry of Health to provide health care to more than four million Haitians and employs more than five thousand doctors throughout the country. This NGO, in full partnership with the state, also administers a state-of-the-art university hospital in Mirebalais that caters to more than eight hundred patients a day. While there are tensions arising with the Haitian state, Zanmi Lasante nonetheless established a solid partnership with key Haitian institutional actors and contributes to build state capacity in the health sector. Likewise, FOKAL—Fondasyon Konesans ak Libète, an NGO led by former Haitian prime minister Michèle Pierre-Louis, is a force of good in Haiti. The recent preservation of the Martissant Park and the large urban renovation of the neighborhoods southeast of Port-au-Prince are models for efficient cooperation between the state and local NGOs (Couet and Grandidier 2013). FOKAL helps rebuilding state capacity in many domains and is engaged in participatory urban planning, the production of major cultural events, and the promotion and formation of young Haitians in fields as varied as environmental justice, journalism, and education. These two models have in common their work with the state and their aim to create institutions and to establish processes (such as peaceful relocation and fair compensation of residents who are being relocated during urban planning phases for FOKAL) that are culturally sound and that help to rebuild state sovereignty. Unfortunately, if these nongovernmental actors have the ability to establish long-term projects that reinforce the state welfare's capacity, this is not the case for a majority of foreign NGOs who have, ultimately, worsened the 2010 disaster on many fronts in the past eight years (Schuller 2012a).

Conclusion: *Désoccupation et Désenveloppement*

More than a hundred years after Haiti's brutal occupation by the U.S. Army, and after decades of "Good Neighbor Policy" marked by repeated military interventions, the Haitian state functions as an entity that violently protects international business interests and as an eviction agent. Each major industrial push—from the rubber fiasco to the garment factory invasions of the 1970s and their spectacular return in 2011—contributed to solidifying the political domination of predatory elites and to eroding state capacity when it comes to social welfare, the state workforce, and public infrastructure. However, considering that Haiti's fate is conditioned only by neoliberal forces or a predatory state means silencing this country's main actor: Haiti's people. While this chapter aimed to show how enclave industries paved the way for the great neoliberal plunge that started in the 1980s by forging state-corporation relations that ultimately eroded state-people relations, I would like here to briefly bring back Gonaïbo, Jacques Stephen Aléxis's protagonist in *Les Arbres Musiciens*.

In Marxist-influenced literature, Gonaïbo stands out as a unique character. As he witnesses the devastation brought about by rubber cultivation in the Jérémie region, and as he painfully experiences the loss of his land and the destruction of the forests and fields he cherishes, Gonaïbo realizes that social and economic equity is indissociable from environmental justice. Rather than subscribing to the "modernization through industrialization" and anti-peasant Marxist doxa of his time, Aléxis forges a new kind of socialism based on the anti-colonial practices generated during the 1791–1804 revolution and the pantheist reading of nature of Vodouyzan peasants for whom, even if "musician trees may fall from time to time, the voice of the forest keeps being powerful." Even if often accused of being the main engine of deforestation, a majority of Haitian people who have long been opposing export economies and extractive systems know that their well-being and their chance to sustain disasters resides in the ecological healing of their country. The anti-IMF protests of the 2000s, along with the 2018 protests against the rise of gas prices advocated by the IMF, are not spontaneous "mob" movements but actions rooted in a deep understanding of the economic, social, and political corrosion brought by IFIs and their local collaborators (Joos 2018).

In 1983, Georges Anglade published a brilliant essay entitled "Ochan pou Malere." In this short text, Anglade analyzes how a "civilization of poverty" has optimized the human, environmental, and material conditions surrounding it to create viable lives and economic systems. Instead of considering poverty as a problem and assimilating it to misery—defined as a complete absence of survival means—Anglade proposes to study and sustain the collective modes of work, such as "compagnonage," the risk-averse diversified agriculture, and the egalitarian systems of resource redistribution that the Haitian peasantry has forged over the long term. Doing so means privileging polycultures over export-centered mono-crops: privileging local food security and land tenure over wage-labor systems that foster dependence on food imports; and privileging Haitian people's values, desires, and practices over grand projects designed by foreign technocrats. The 2009 mass strikes in Guadeloupe and Martinique, and the many big and small protests that have rocked Haiti's political landscape since the 2008 financial crisis, have put forth what Gonaïbo has long been dreaming of, and what Georges Anglade had long argued before passing away in the 2010 earthquake: the popular resistance to neocolonial empires is not a mere response to oppression but a holistic practice that ties together ecology, collective memory, *vivre-ensemble* (living together), and economic well-being.

Modern development through mass tourism, industrialization, and neoliberal trickle-down illusions has repeatedly failed. *Désenveloppement* (de-development)—defined by Anglade as the "processus d'accès de chacun à la pauvreté du nécessaire pour construire la richesse nationale collective" (process that allows everyone to access basic necessities to build the collective national wealth)—would mean building or repairing the infrastructures that help local economies to thrive; creating policies that foster food security and rural decentralization; and mainly respecting and protecting the cultural, religious, social, and economic values of a people who managed to create, in the nineteenth century, systems that "provided a better quality of life than that of African descendants anywhere else in the Americas" (Dubois and Jenson 2012). Repairing the roads that lead to regional markets and (re)building the produce markets that dot this side of the island, along with trade policies that would protect rural economies, for instance, would go a long way. The Haitian peasantry is not an eternal entity that exists separate from the vicissitudes of capitalism. On the contrary, Haitian peasants have repeatedly been "proletarized" through evictions and displacements. Nonetheless, decentralization and the return of food crops in the hills and valleys of Haiti must be considered as an ecologically and socially sound path to recovery.

As Edwidge Danticat argues, Haiti must also experience a "désoccupation" and a return to sovereignty. In other words, the U.S. and its allies must stop intervening in Haitian elections and IFIs must stop pushing austerity in a nation that is in dire need of investment in its institutions, infrastructure, and people. The Caribbean community (Caricom) established a ten-point reparation plan that could open a path to autonomy and self-governance for regions that are still enduring the economic, psychological, and cultural legacies of European colonization and American imperialism. In 2015, French president Francois Hollande promised that France would pay its "moral debt" to Haiti. However, this promise is not enough. For more than a hundred years, Haiti bore the brunt of a debt contracted with France in 1825 to compensate slave owners who had lost properties in Saint-Domingue, which crippled the development of the country. As the Caricom plan proposes, canceling debts and directly funding state projects in the domains of health, culture, and education would be a first step toward reparations. Instead, in Haiti, a new class of foreign NGO workers and international experts reap the benefits of a lucrative disaster industrial complex. A people-driven reconstruction that pays attention to the needs and desires of a majority of Haitians by investing in local food, health, educational, and cultural economies may not be a silver bullet that will fix all of Haiti's problems, but it would be a good first step toward independence. Financial reparations along with a full formal apology from the nations that engaged in the Atlantic slave trade and in post-slavery coerced labor systems, and not charity, are crucial for the process of international reconciliation and justice.

NOTE

1. The terms *mulâtre* and *mulattoe* are fraught categories that have often been used in a racist fashion. However, in current Haitian scholarship, and among Haitian Creole speakers, the terms *mulattoe* or *milat* refer mainly to the light-skin color commercial and political elites who ascended to power during the American occupation. For instance, former Haitian president Elie Lescot is described as a fierce proponent of "mulatrism" as he placed only *mulattoes* in positions of power in his government and in the military. For thoughtful analysis of these terms, see Daut (2015) and Pierrot (2019).

REFERENCES

Abbott, Elizabeth. 1991 (1988). *Haiti: The Duvaliers and Their Legacy*. New York: Simon and Schuster.

———. 2011. *Haiti: A Shattered Nation*. New York: Overlook Duckworth.

Accountability Counsel. 2018. "Haiti: Caracol Industrial Park." https://www.account abilitycounsel.org/client-case/haiti-caracol-industrial-park/#case-story (accessed March 21, 2020).

Allen, Theodore William. 2001. "Be Fair: Reverse Discrimination." *Z Magazine*, January 24.

Alvarez, M. D., and G. F. Murray. 1981. *Socialization for Scarcity: Child Feeding Beliefs and Practices in a Haitian Village*. United States Agency for International Development.

Anglade, Georges. 1982a. *Atlas critique d'Haïti*. Montréal, Québec: Groupe d'études et de recherches critiques d'espace, Département de géographie, Université du Québec à Montréal; Centre de recherches caraïbes de l'Université de Montréal.

———. 1982b. *Espace et liberté en Haïti*. Montréal, Québec: ERCE & CRC.

————. 1990. *Cartes sur table*. Port-au-Prince, Haïti: Editions Henri Deschamps; Etudes et recherches critiques d'espace.

"Ayiti Kale Je." 2013. http://haitigrassrootswatch.squarespace.com/.

Barthélémy, Gérard. 1990. *L'univers rural haïtien: le pays en dehors*. Paris: L'Harmattan.

————. 1992. *Les Duvaliéristes après Duvalier*. Paris: L'Harmattan.

————. 2000. *Créoles–Bossales: Conflit en Haïti*. Petit-Bourg, Guadeloupe: Ibis Rouge Éditions.

Beaubrun, Yvens, et al. 1999. "Asosyasyon Plantè avèk Distilatè Leyogàn, pwodiksyon nasyonal, fo kleren (etanòl) (2)." *Face à l'opinion*, Radio Haiti, Port-au-Prince, January.

Bellegarde, Dantés. 1937. *L'Occupation américaine d'Haïti*. Montréal: Editions Beauchemin.

Blumenthal, Max. 2004. "The Other Regime Change: Did the Bush Administration Allow a Network of Right-Wing Republicans to Foment a Violent Coup in Haiti?" Global Policy Forum, July 16.

Blyth, Mark. 2013. "The Austerity Delusion: Why a Bad Idea Won Over the West." *Foreign Affairs* 92, no. 3: 41–56

Butel, Paul. *Histoire Des Antilles Francaises*. Paris: Perrin, 2007.

Caple-James, Erica. 2010. *Democratic Insecurities: Violence, Trauma, and Intervention in Haiti*. Berkeley: University of California Press.

"Caracol Industrial Park." 2018. USAID. Revised August 16. https://www.usaid.gov/haiti/caracol-industrial-park.

Castor, Suzy. 1978. *La Ocupación Norteamericana de Haití y sus Consecuencias, 1915–1934*. La Habana: Casa de las Américas.

Charles, Jacqueline. 2018. "Haiti Has Put a Fuel Hike on Hold. But Is It Enough to Save the Prime Minister's Job?" *Miami Herald*, July 7. https://www.miamiherald.com/news/nation-world/world/americas/haiti/article214497129.html.

Chen, Michelle. 2014. "How Humanitarian Aid Weakened Post-Earthquake Haiti." *Nation*, September 2. https://www.thenation.com/article/how-humanitarian-aid-weakened-post-earthquake-haiti/.

Chérestal, Kysseline Jean-Mary. 2015. "Building Back Better? The Caracol Industrial Park and Post-earthquake Aid to Haiti." Washington, DC: ActionAid. https://www.actionaidusa.org/wp-content/uploads/2016/09/building_back_better_the_caracol_industrial_park_and_post-earthquake_aid_to_haiti.pdf.

Chéry, Dady. 2015. "Haiti's Open Vein at Caracol Industrial Park." http://newsjunkiepost.com/2015/05/07/haitis-open-vein-at-caracol-industrial-park/.

Corvington, Georges. 1970. *Port-au-Prince au cours des ans*. Port-au-Prince: Impr. Henri Deschamps.

————. 1992. *Port-au-Prince au cours des ans: La ville coloniale 1743–1789*. Port-au-Prince: Deschamps.

————. 2003. *Port-au-Prince au cours des ans*. Montréal: Les Éditions du Cidihca.

Couet, Lucie, and Estelle Grandidier. 2013. "L'espace public au cœur de la reconstruction: l'exemple de Martissant à Port-au-Prince, Haïti." *Field Actions Science Reports*, special issue 9. http://journals.openedition.org/factsreports/2828.

Danticat, Edwidge. 2015. "The Long Legacy of Occupation in Haiti." *New Yorker*, July 28.

Dash, J. Michael. 1981. *Literature and Ideology in Haiti, 1915–1961*. London: Palgrave Macmillan.

Daut, Marlene. 2015. *Tropics of Haiti: Race and the Literary History of the Haitian Revolution in the Atlantic World, 1789–1865*. Liverpool, UK: Liverpool University Press.

"Deux hôpitaux ferment, un millier d'emplois supprimés: Il faut éviter que ces professionnels de la santé ne partent." 2018. *Le Nouvelliste*, March 5.

de Vaissière, Pierre. 1909. *Saint-Domingue; La société et la vie créoles sous l'ancien régime (1629–1789)*. Paris: Perrin et cie.

"Doctors Without Borders Closing 2 Hospitals in Haiti Capital." 2018. *U.S. News and World Report*. July 20. https://www.usnews.com/news/world/articles/2018-07-20/doctors -without-borders-closing-haiti-hospital-for-women.

Dubois, Laurent. 2005. *Avengers of the New World*. Cambridge, MA: Harvard University Press.

———. 2012. *Haiti: The Aftershocks of History*. New York: Macmillan.

Dubois, Laurent, and Jean Casimir. 2010. "Reckoning in Haiti." http://www.ssrc.org /features/pages/haiti-now-and-next/1338/1395/.

Dubois, Laurent, and Deborah Jenson. 2012. "Haiti Can Be Rich Again." *New York Times*, January 8.

Duby, Georges. 1972. *Histoire de la France*. Paris: Bibliothèque historique Larousse.

Dupuy, Alex. 1989. *Haiti in the World Economy: Class, Race, and Underdevelopment since 1700*. Boulder, CO: Westview Press, 1989.

———. 1997. *Haiti in the New World Order: The Limits of the Democratic Revolution*. Boulder, CO: Westview Press.

———. 2007. *The Prophet and Power: Jean-Bertrand Aristide, the International Community, and Haiti*. Lanham: Rowman & Littlefield, 2007.

———. 2010. "Beyond the Earthquake: A Wake-Up Call for Haiti." *Latin American Perspectives* 37, no. 3 (May).

———. 2014. *Haiti, from Revolutionary Slaves to Powerless Citizens: Essays on the Politics and Economics of Underdevelopment, 1804–2013*. New York: Routledge.

Etienne, Harley F. 2013. "Urban Planning and the Rebuilding of Port-au-Prince." In *The Idea of Haiti: Rethinking Crisis and Development*, edited by Polyné Milerry, 165–180. Minneapolis: University of Minnesota Press.

Farmer, Paul. 2012. *Haiti after the Earthquake*. New York: PublicAffairs.

Farnsworth, Clyde H. 1984. "In Explosive Haiti, Much Hunger and Little Hope." *New York Times*, June 8. https://www.nytimes.com/1984/06/08/world/in-explosive-haiti-much -hunger-and-little-hope.html.

Farwell, Scott. 2010. "Haiti's Private Medical Sector Collapsing as Charities Rush to Provide Free Health Care." *Dallas Morning News*, June.

Fass, Simon. 1980. *The Economics of Survival: A Study of Poverty and Planning in Haiti*. Washington, D.C.: Office of Urban Development, Bureau for Development Support, Agency for International Development–International Development Cooperation Agency, 1980.

———. 1988. *Political Economy in Haiti: The Drama of Survival*. New Brunswick, NJ: Transaction Books.

Fatton, Robert. 2002. *Haiti's Predatory Republic: The Unending Transition to Democracy*. Boulder, CO: Lynne Rienner Publishers.

———. 2007. *The Roots of Haitian Despotism*. Boulder, CO: Lynne Rienner Publishers.

————. 2014. *Haiti: Trapped in the Outer Periphery.* Boulder, CO: Lynne Rienner Publishers.

Fischer, Stanley. 1997. "Applied Economics in Action: IMF Programs." *American Economic Review* 87, no. 2: 23–27.

Gaillard, Roger. 1973. *Les cent-jours de Rosalvo Bobo; Ou, une mise à mort politique.* Port-au-Prince: Presses nationales.

————. 1982. *Charlemagne Péralte Le Caco.* Port-au-Prince: R. Gaillard.

Gilbert, Myrtha. 2016. *SHADA: Chronique d'une Extravagante Escroquerie.* Port-au-Prince: Bibliothèque Nationale d'Haïti.

Giraud, Alexandre. 2018. "Haïti: Démission du premier ministre Jack Guy Lafontant." *RCI.FM.* July 15. https://www.rci.fm/infos/politique/haiti-demission-du-premier-ministre-jack-guy-lafontant.

Girvan, Norman. 1971. "Bauxite: The Need to Nationalize, Part I." *Review of Black Political Economy* 2, no. 1: 72–94.

Godard, Henry. 1988. "Port-Au-Prince: Les mutations récentes de l'organisation spatiale." *Mappemonde* 3: 6–9.

Goldstein, Daniel M. 2012. *Outlawed: Between Security and Rights in a Bolivian City.* Durham, NC: Duke University Press.

Goldstein Sepinwall, Alyssa, ed. 2013. *Haitian History: New Perspectives.* New York: Routledge.

Gonzalez, Johnhenry. 2019. *Maroon Nation.* New Haven, CT: Yale University Press.

Gros, Jean-Germain. 2010. "Indigestible Recipe: Rice, Chicken Wings, and International Financial Institutions: Or Hunger Politics in Haiti." *Journal of Black Studies* 40, no. 5: 974–986.

————. 2012. *State Failure, Underdevelopment, and Foreign Intervention in Haiti.* New York: Routledge.

"Haiti Bucks Privatization." 1995. *Multinational Monitor* 16, no. 11. https://multinationalmonitor.org/hyper/mm1195.03.html.

"Haiti: Cholera Outbreak—2010–2017." 2018. Reliefweb. Accessed September 30. https://reliefweb.int/disaster/ep-2010-000210-hti.

"Haiti—Economy: SONAPI Wants to Attract New Investments in the Industrial Sector." 2018. *HaitiLibre*, August 21.

"Haïti: La Mort Liquide (Partie 3)." 2012. *AlterPresse*, April 23. http://www.alterpresse.org/spip.php?article12745#.W7FKjWhKiM_.

"Haïti: MSF met un terme à ses activités d'urgence à Léogâne." 2015. Médecins Sans Frontières. July 31. https://www.msf.ch/nos-actualites/communiques-presse/haiti-msf-met-terme-ses-activites-durgence-leogane

"Haiti Tense after Unpopular Fuel-Price Hike." 2018. *Jamaica Observer,* July 8. http://www.jamaicaobserver.com/latestnews/Haiti_tense_after_unpopular_fuel-price_hike.

"Haïti-Zones franches: Extraversion économique et sous-développement." 2012. *AlterPresse*, March 24.

Holt-Gimenez, Eric, and Raj Patel, eds. 2012. *Food Rebellions: Crisis and the Hunger for Justice.* Oakland, CA: Food First Books.

"IHRC Board Meets amidst Mounting Criticism." 2011. Center for Economic and Policy Research, April 8. http://cepr.net/blogs/haiti-relief-and-reconstruction-watch/ihrc-board-meets-amidst-mounting-criticism (accessed September 30, 2018).

International Monetary Fund. 2014. "Haiti: History of Lending Arrangements as of November 30, 2014." https://www.imf.org/external/np/fin/tad/extarr2.aspx?member Key1=400&date1key=2014-11-30.

Ives, Kim. 2018. "Haiti's Popular Uprising Calls for President Jovenel Moïse's Removal." *Counterpunch*, July 13. https://www.counterpunch.org/2018/07/13/haitis-popular -uprising-calls-for-president-jovenel-moises-removal/.

Jackson, Regina O. 2011. *Geographies of the Haitian Diaspora.* London: Routledge.

Jamaica Bauxite Institute. 1980. *JBI Journal*, vols. 1–3. Jamaica: Bauxite Institute.

Jean-Baptiste, Chenet. 2012. "Haiti's Earthquake: A Further Insult to Peasants' Lives." In *Tectonic Shifts*, edited by Mark Schuller and Pablo Morales, 97–100. Boulder, CO: Kumarian Press.

Jeanty, Gérard, Jr. 2018. "Le gouvernement augmente le prix des produits pétroliers à la pompe." *Le Nouvelliste*, July 10. http://www.lenouvelliste.com/m/public/index.php /article/189854/le-gouvernement-augmente-le-prix-des-produits-petroliers-a-la-pompe.

Johnston, Jake. n.d. "Analysis: Workings Behind Haiti Gas Increase Revolt." *Haitian Times.* https://haitiantimes.com/2018/07/15/analysis-workings-behind-haiti-gas-increase -revolt/ (accessed September 30, 2018).

———. 2011. "IHRC Board Meets amid Mounting Criticism." Center for Economic and Policy Research, April 8. https://www.cepr.net/ihrc-board-meets-amidst-mounting -criticism/.

Joos, Vincent. 2018. "Haiti's Deadly Riots Fueled by Anger over Decades of Austerity and Foreign Interference." *The Conversation*, July 26. https://theconversation.com /haitis-deadly-riots-fueled-by-anger-over-decades-of-austerity-and-foreign -interference-100209.

Joseph, Celucien L. 2017. *Thinking in Public: Faith, Secular Humanism, and Development in Jacques Roumain.* Eugene, OR: Wipf and Stock Publishers.

Katz, Jonathan. 2013. *The Big Truck That Went By: How the World Came to Save Haiti and Left Behind a Disaster.* New York: Palgrave Macmillan.

———. 2015. "The Clintons' Haiti Screw-Up, As Told By Hillary's Emails." *Politico*, September 2. https://www.politico.com/magazine/story/2015/09/hillary-clinton-email -213110.

———. 2016. "The Clintons Didn't Screw Up Haiti Alone. You Helped." *Slate*, September 22. https://slate.com/news-and-politics/2016/09/the-truth-about-the-clintons -and-haiti.html.

Kaussen, Valerie Mae. 2000. *Romancing the Peasant: History and Revolution in the Modern Haitian Novel.* Santa Cruz: University of California Press.

Klarreich, Kathie. 2008. "Food Crisis Renews Haiti's Agony." *Time Magazine*, April 9.

Lemay-Hébert, Nicolas, et al. 2018. "Haïti: Tensions entre aide humanitaire et développement dans le secteur de la santé." *Alternatives humanitaires*, July.

Lucien, Georges Eddy. 2013. *Une modernisation manquée: Port-Au-Prince (1915–1956).* Port-au-Prince: Éditions de l'Université d'État d'Haïti.

Lundahl, Mats. 2013. *The Political Economy of Disaster: Destitution, Plunder and Earthquake in Haiti.* New York: Routledge.

———. 2015. *The Haitian Economy: Man, Land and Markets.* New York: Routledge.

Marcelin, L. H., T. Cela, and J. M. Shultz. 2016. "Haiti and the Politics of Governance and Community Responses to Hurricane Matthew." *Disaster Health* 3, no. 4: 151–161. http://doi.org/10.1080/21665044.2016.1263539.

Marcello, Elizabeth M. 2005. "Structural Adjustment in Haiti: The Impact on Agriculture and Implications for Sustainability." Bachelor's thesis, University of California, Santa Cruz.

Mbembe, Achille. 2019. *Necropolitics*. Durham, NC: Duke University Press.

McGowan, Lisa. 1997. "Economic Justice Denied: Structural Adjustment and the Aid Juggernaut in Haiti." Development Group for Alternative Policies.

McPherson, A. 2016. *A Short History of U.S. Intervention in Latin America and the Caribbean*. Chichester, UK: Wiley Blackwell.

Michel, Georges. 1996. *Charlemagne Péralte and the First American Occupation of Haiti*. Dubuque, IA: Kendall/Hunt.

Mintz, Sidney Wilfred. 1984. *From Plantations to Peasantries in the Caribbean*. Washington, DC: Latin American Program, Woodrow Wilson International Center for Scholars.

————. 2010. *Three Ancient Colonies: Caribbean Themes and Variations*. Cambridge, MA: Harvard University Press.

Moral, Paul. 1978. *Le paysan haïtien: Étude sur la vie rurale en Haïti*. Paris: G. P. Maisonneuve et Larose.

"MSF ferment leur hôpital à Delmas 33." 2018. *Le Nouvelliste*, July 17. https://lenouvelliste .com/article/190234/msf-ferment-leur-hopital-a-delmas-33.

Mullin, Leslie. n.d. "How the United States Crippled Haiti's Rice Industry." Haiti Action Committee. https://haitisolidarity.net/in-the-news/how-the-united-states -crippled-haitis-domestic-rice-industry/ (accessed October 2, 2018).

Naidu, Suresh, James A. Robinson, and Lauren E. Young. 2017. "Social Origins of Dictatorships: Elite Networks and Political Transitions in Haiti." CDEP-CGEG Working Paper Series 31: 1–47.

Naimou, Angela. 2015. *Salvage Work: U.S. and Caribbean Literatures amid the Debris of Legal Personhood*. New York: Fordham University Press.

Nicholls, David. 1974. *Economic Dependence and Political Autonomy: The Haitian Experience*, 9 vols. Montreal: Centre for Developing-Area Studies, McGill University.

————. 1986. "Ideology and Political Movements in Haiti, 1915–1946." *Annales-economies societes civilisations*.

————. 1996. *From Dessalines to Duvalier: Race, Colour, and National Independence in Haiti*. New Brunswick, NJ: Rutgers University Press.

O'Connor, Maura R. 2013. "Subsidizing Starvation." *Foreign Policy*, January 11. https:// foreignpolicy.com/2013/01/11/subsidizing-starvation/.

Opitz, Gotz-Dietrich. 2004. *Haitian Refugees Forced to Return: Transnationalism and State Politics 1991–1994*. Piscataway, NJ: Transaction Publishers.

Ottersen, Idun Berge. 2013. "The Effects of IMF Lending Arrangements: A Study of the Intentions of the International Monetary Fund, and the Macroeconomic Effects of their Lending Arrangements." Master's thesis, University of Agder, Norway.

Pamphile, Leon D. 2015. *Contrary Destinies: A Century of America's Occupation, Deoccupation, and Reoccupation of Haiti*. Gainesville: University Press of Florida.

Péan, Leslie. 1987. "Trade in Manufactures: Haiti 1970–79." IESCARIBE Study for Interamerican Development Bank.

————. 2003. *Haïti, économie politique de la corruption: De Saint-Domingue à Haïti (1791–1870)*. Paris: Maisonneuve & Larose.

Peck, Raoul. 2012. *Fatal Assistance*. Paris: Velvet Film.

Philogène, Jerry. 2015. "'Dead Citizen' and the Abject Nation: Social Death, Haiti, and the Strategic Power of the Image." *Journal of Haitian Studies* 21, no. 1: 100–126.

Pierre-Louis, Francois. 2011. "Earthquakes, Nongovernmental Organizations, and Governance in Haiti." *Journal of Black Studies* 42, no. 2. https://www.jstor.org/stable/41151335.

Pierrot, Gregory. 2019. *The Black Avenger in Atlantic Culture*. Athens: University of Georgia Press.

Pyles, Loretta. 2015. *Disaster Recovery in Post-Earthquake Rural Haiti: Research Findings and Recommendations for Participatory, Sustainable Recovery*. Albany, NY: School of Social Welfare. https://www.albany.edu/ssw/assets/HaitirecoveryreportNSF_final.pdf.

Richardson, Laurie. 1997. *Feeding Dependency, Starving Democracy. USAID Policies in Haiti*. Boston, MA: Grassroots International. http://grassrootsonline.org/sites/default/files /Feeding-Dependency-Starving-Democracy.pdf.

Richburg, Keith. 1986. "Duvalier's Wealth Put in Millions." *Washington Post*, February 18.

Rodney, Walter. 1972. *How Europe Underdeveloped Africa*. London: Bogle-L'Ouverture Publications.

Saint-Pré, Patrick. 2018. "Un record de 375 millions USD d'investissements directs étrangers pour Haïti en 2017." *Le Nouvelliste*, July 12. http://www.lenouvelliste.com /article/190052/un-record-de-375-millions-usd-dinvestissements-directs-etrangers -pour-haiti-en-2017.

Sanders, Richard. 2007. "The G184's Powerbrokers—Apaid and Boulos: Owners of the Fourth Estate; Leaders of the Fifth Column." *Press for Conversion!*, September. http:// coat.ncf.ca/our_magazine/links/61/42-43.htm.

Schöneberg, Julia Maria. 2017. "NGO Partnerships in Haiti: Clashes of Discourse and Reality." *Third World Quarterly* 38, no. 3: 604–620.

Schuller, Mark. 2007. "Haiti's 200-Year Ménage-à-Trois: Globalization, the State, and Civil Society." *Caribbean Studies* 35, no. 1.

———. 2009. "Gluing Globalization: NGOs as Intermediaries in Haiti." *PoLAR: Political and Legal Anthropology Review* 32: 84–104.

———. 2012a. *Killing with Kindness: Haiti, International Aid, and NGOs*. New Brunswick, NJ: Rutgers University Press.

———. 2012b. "Homeward Bound? Assessing Progress of Relocation from Haiti's IDP Camps." *Bureau des Avocats Internationaux*, November 16.

Shamsie, Yasmine. 2014. "La construction d'un parc industriel dans l'arrière-pays rural d'Haïti. Quelques observations sur le partenariat état-société et les capacités de l'état." *Cahiers des Amériques latines* 75: 79.

Southerland, Daniel. 1984. "Haitian Finance Officials Try to Plug Nation's Leaky Ledgers." *Christian Science Monitor*, October 2. https://www.csmonitor.com/1984/1002/100219.html.

Steckley, Marylynn, and Yasmine Shamsie. 2015. "Manufacturing Corporate Landscapes: The Case of Agrarian Displacement and Food (In)Security in Haiti." *Third World Quarterly* 36, no. 1: 179–197.

Sullivan, Laura. 2015. "In Search of the Red Cross' $500 Million in Haiti Relief." *NPR*, June 3. http://www.npr.org/2015/06/03/411524156/in-search-of-the-red-cross-500-million -in-haiti-relief.

Svistova, Juliana, and Loretta Pyles. 2018. *Production of Disaster and Recovery in Post-earthquake Haiti Disaster Industrial Complex*. Abington, UK: Taylor and Francis.

"Thousands March in Haiti Demanding Return of Aristide." 2009. HaitiAction, March 2. https://www.haitiaction.net/News/HA/3_1_9/3_1_9.html.

Tobin, Kathleen. 2013. "Population Density and Housing in Port-Au-Prince: Historical Construction of Vulnerability." *Journal of Urban History* 39, no. 6 (June 6). https://doi.org/10.1177/0096144213491224.

Trouillot, Evelyne. 2012. "Abse sou Klou: Reconstructing Exclusion." In *Tectonic Shifts: Haiti since the Earthquake*, edited by Mark Schuller and Pablo Morales, 103–107. Sterling, VA: Kumarian Press.

Trouillot, Michel-Rolph. 1986. *Les racines historiques de l'état Duvaliérien*. Port-au-Prince, Haiti: Deschamps.

———. 1990. *Haiti, State against Nation: The Origins and Legacy of Duvalierism*. New York: Monthly Review Press.

———. 1995. *Silencing the Past: Power and the Production of History*. Boston, MA: Beacon Press.

UNCT. 2014. "Haiti Cholera Response." ReliefWeb, December 31. https://reliefweb.int/report/haiti/haiti-cholera-response-december-2014.

United Nations. 2010. *Report of the United Nations in Haiti 2010: Situation, Challenges and Outlook*.

Voltaire. 1963 (1809). *Essai sur les mœurs et l'esprit des nations et sur les principaux faits de l'histoire depuis Charlemagne jusqu'à Louis XIII*, edited by René Pomeau.

Wagner, Laura Rose. 2014. "Haiti Is a Sliding Land: Displacement, Community, and Humanitarianism in Post-earthquake Port-Au-Prince." PhD diss., University of North Carolina at Chapel Hill.

Woolf, Christopher. 2015. "When America Occupied Haiti." *WLRN*, August 7. https://www.wlrn.org/post/when-america-occupied-haiti#stream/0.

8

A "New" Antillean DOM Arts Scene, or the Pragmatic Aesthetics of Patience

ARTINCIDENCE, ANNABEL
GUÉRÉDRAT, DANIEL GOUDROUFFE,
HENRI TAULIAUT, AND
JEANNETTE EHLERS

ALESSANDRA BENEDICTY-KOKKEN

It's not a French thing.

—Santigold, interviewed about her
second single, "L.E.S. Artistes" (2008)

Pa ni plézi an méchansté
Sav, ki an lespri ékilibré
pou richèché sensérité

. . . .

Elas!
Elas péyi mélé
Elas Matinik, nou piti, nou piti, nou piti
Nou ké gran

—Kolo Barst, "Péyi nou," from the
album Lot bô so *(2004)*

This chapter looks at how the artistic production of Annabel Guérédrat (dancer and performance artist) and Henri Tauliaut (environmental, digital, and installation visual artist, as well as performance artist), who along with others form the art collective Artincidence, and Daniel Goudrouffe (photographer)[1] engage with what I term a *pragmatic aesthetics of patience*. I use the terms *aesthetics, pragmatism,* and *patience* as critical lenses with which to view the artists' oeuvre, but I also employ them as a prism to better understand a possible turn in the French Caribbean intellectual sphere that complements other currents in contemporary Africana thought, as well as more broadly scholarship that is not necessarily, or at least explicitly "Africana": that is, as scholars who observe gross discrepancies worldwide, we are increasingly understanding most world spaces to be de facto postcolonial. As such, we are turning to Africana thought to think through the vexed and more often than not violent relationships that we have to one another, based on histories and aftermaths of colonial encounters. Emine Fişek, a scholar of contemporary theater among immigrant communities in Paris, argues that "theater" "function[s] as both a representation of a certain identity and the space where that identity is openly understood to be the outcome of social rehearsal" (Fişek 2017, 4). As such, although Goudrouffe's medium is photography, I argue that the performative aspect of theater, as deliberated on by Fişek, undergirds his photography in ways comparable to how Guérédrat and Goudrouffe embody their veritable performances on stage, in nature, and in urban space. More specifically, I suggest that Guérédrat, Goudrouffe, and Tauliaut's nurturing of a *pragmatic aesthetics of patience* offers a possibility for reconciliation: reconciliation with one's own relationship to a geopolitical *home*; reconciliation as regards the varied polemics that have surrounded Guadeloupe's and Martinique's 1946 departmentalization; and reconciliation among beings, both living (that is, humans, animals, plants) and materially man-made (for example, clothing, trucks). I argue that Guérédrat, Tauliaut, and Goudrouffe nurture an artistic practice that, in its largest sense, provokes "interventionist practices" (Danbolt 2016, 3), whose ethos cultivates the patience needed to deal with, confront, and even reoperate the historical and present-day violence that continues to create oppressive conditions, even among the supposedly most tolerant-minded contingents of our societies.

I am particularly mindful of Kobena Mercer's supplication that as critics we not forget the aesthetic when discussing the artist. Mercer has problematized the critical reception of artists said to be "Caribbean," whereby their importance as "from the Caribbean" figures more largely than the actual transformative effects that the Caribbean arts scene has had on the notion of moral personhood writ large. Running the risk of overly emphasizing the artists' "biographical identity" at the expense of detracting "attention from the aesthetic intelligence embodied in actual works of art as objects of experience in their own right" (Mercer 2016, 1–2), I suggest that for varying reasons, the notions of "Guadeloupe" and "Martinique" constitute local and translocal forces that nurture their artistic practice.

While the two islands are often referred to collectively as the "French Caribbean," or the Caribbean DOM (*départements d'outre-mer*), the way they are each signified separately (and compared with each other) is not irrelevant: the relationship between the two and the stereotypes around each island affect the philosophical-aesthetic imaginary in which Guérédrat, Tauliaut, and Goudrouffe work. More specifically, in the popular imaginary, Guadeloupe is understood as more rebellious, less "European," and far more feminist, while Martinique (or at least its elite) is associated with a certain ease (or assimilationism) in regard to its relationship to France. These categorizations are buttressed by how quite iconic intellectual figures and movements are associated with one or the other island and, as such, undoubtedly hover in the background of this "new" Antillean DOM arts scene. For Martinique, Aimé Césaire, Edouard Glissant, Raphaël Confiant, and Patrick Chamoiseau are male intellectuals whose theoretical and literary output has been essential, if not groundbreaking, for the establishment of Africana thought. While Frantz Fanon was also born in Martinique and put Martinique at the center of much of his writing, his deeply psychoanalytical diagnosis of blackness in *Peau noire, masques blancs* (*Black Skin, White Masks*) (1952) followed by an unequivocal anticolonialist stance in *Les damnés de la terre* (*The Wretched of the Earth*) (1961) renders him a rather controversial figure for many Martinicans (and scholars throughout the North American and European academe), who are more comfortable with the poetic discourses of notably Césaire, Chamoiseau, and Glissant. Confiant's positionality as regards discourses of eventual Martinican independence from France is quite complex: that is, while these discourses provoke, they are also fraught with identity politics and in recent years have caused a more mainstream international audience to dismiss his anger as anti-intellectual.[2] For Guadeloupe, Maryse Condé, Simone Schwarz-Bart, and Gisèle Pineau, as well as the well-known unionized protests of the 1970s and more recently 2009, position it as a more defiant island, which is often compared to Haiti, a sovereign nation-state since 1804. Although, in this article, I do not directly address all of these intellectuals or movements, the realpolitik magnanimity of notably Glissant's notion of "opacity" as well as the confrontationally autonomous sensuality[3] of Condé's prose linger in the background as veritable variables of the zeitgeist that I argue informs Guérédrat's, Goudrouffe's, and Tauliaut's work, as well as that of Ehlers, who is based in Denmark. More concretely, I perceive Guérédrat, Goudrouffe, and Tauliaut as artists who are "at ease" operating from—and between—both Guadeloupe and Martinique, imbricating the iconic afore-mentioned intellectual and politically engaged spaces one within the other, yet at the same time juxtaposing them provocatively with global Northern and global Southern art scenes. Of course, the very notion of what it means to be "at ease" undergirds the interrogation of this article and notably ques-tions what is at stake in working and thinking *from* a certain geographic location (and its public sphere) as opposed to another.[4]

Guadeloupe and Martinique are certainly geographic entities, but drawing on Millery Polyné's designation of Haiti as both place and "idea," I propose that Guadeloupe and Martinique also constitute *ideas*, evoking affective loci that are Caribbean and French; geographically located in the Americas but politically incorporated into the French nation-state and hence the European Union; "very small" (Barst, see epigraph) in terms of their surface area, but loomingly grandiose as regards their intellectual, political, and literary histories. Such ease does not mean that Guérédrat, Goudrouffe, and Tauliaut are complacent in the economics of the art mar-ket; rather, they actively operate an artistic practice that grounds their work in the specificity of what it means to practice citizenship, in all of its complexities, in a DOM space.[5] In particular, I suggest that their work engages, both explicitly, but also more delicately, a particular encounter between concepts understood by global Northern art market and art historian sensibilities to constitute two separate and even oppositional aesthetic traditions: one French, and more generally understood as European; and the other Haitian, and more generally apprehended as African or black. As such, in my analyses of the artists' practices, and especially in the third part of my article, I assert *place* as a critical category that is inextricably entangled in questions of geopolitical positionality, cultural identity, sovereignty, independence, freedom, gender, sexuality, and race.

I argue that if Guérédrat, Tauliaut, and Goudrouffe are at the avantgarde of the arts scene of the late 2010s and early 2020s, it is because they deploy—at times overtly and more often implicitly—a Haitianist and also a Vodouyizan perspective as part of their professional praxis. I look particularly at how their artistic production dialogues with *Haiti*, as both a geopolitical neighbor and as an aesthetic concept, one in line with Lewis R. Gordon's notion of "Black aesthetics" versus "black aesthetics," a distinction that designates what it means to have value from a certain epistemic location. What does it mean to create art from a space that is less constantly under the direct epistemic oppression of a white order (i.e., a Vodouyizan lived experience)? Of course, the oppression of white supremacist discourses and geopolitical realities does not mean that a Vodouyizan episteme is not affected by white supremacy. Instead, what this article interrogates is how to create in a space that actively theorizes what it means to have value in ways that are not prescribed by a white supremacist Enlightenment aesthetic philosophical regime (Gordon 2017, 26). Gordon articulates the challenge: "A problem with constructing black aesthetics is, then, as proposed at the outset, whether aesthetics has been so colonized that its production would be a form of colonizing instead of decolonial practice" (24). In the end, Gordon, drawing on Paul C. Taylor's *Black Is Beautiful: A Philosophy of Black Aesthetics* (2016), asserts what it means to create value for oneself despite a white supremacist order that constantly denies such value: "Though aware, and critical, of the derisive lowercase b of black, where the humanity of racially designated black subjects is brought into question,

Taylor is interested in the lived reality of such people as subjects of value"
(26). Gordon argues that since "aesthetic reality . . . emerges as how human
beings live *as deserving value* in its full range" (24), "the questions of Black
aesthetics and Black humanity are, then, symbiotic" (26). The implications
of what it means to live more or less in the constant onslaught and presence
of whiteness has to do in part with place and notably how a given place's
public sphere is informed by white supremacy, inhibiting, allowing, or
encouraging black lives to matter. Does place affect how black aesthetics
take place? That living in the DOM is somehow free of white supremacy is
absolutely not what I suggest, but to think through what it means to produce art in a place that is more aware of the violence of colonialism and
slavery and that in certain prominent parts of the public sphere actively
honors rather than exploits "the facts of the lived experience of most black
and especially Black people" (Gordon 2017, 29) may affect how an artist's
work is interpreted and received. In keeping Gordon's, Zakiyyah Iman
Jackson's, and Taylor's invitation to think through the critical categories of
the *human* and *aesthetics* through the lens of *b/B/lackness*, this article's gesture is to interrogate how Guérédrat, Tauliaut, and Goudrouffe dialogue
with Haiti, working from a space that is circumscribed politically within
the European Union, but is geographically close to *Haiti*—as place, idea,
and intellectual and aesthetic practice—functions representationally in a
specific relationship to *Europe*, and in particular to the "unfinished histories
of colonial-aesthetic injustice" (Danbolt 2016, 3). In so doing, the artistic
production of these three artists, as well as Ehlers, working also within the
European Union, but from a completely different public sphere, eloquently
and incisively contributes to global discourses on cosmopolitanism concerned with what it means to be a being in a world uncertain about its
political and environmental futures.

The article then is divided into three parts. First, I provide an overview
of intellectual and social contexts that I argue inform Tauliaut's, and Goudrouffe's artistic production, even if not explicitly Guérédrat's—notably
how Haiti has figured into the general public discourse of Guadeloupe and
Martinique since the 1980s and the role of internationally renowned Gua-

deloupean and Martinican intellectuals in nurturing a particular set of interrogations as regards colonial memory and political agency. Second, I engage an analysis of each artist's work. Third, in drawing on analyses of Jeannette Ehlers's performance and video art, I suggest that Guérédrat, Tauliaut, and Goudrouffe craft an aesthetics that is mindful of how Martinique and Guadeloupe allow them a certain agility in their artistic practice, an agility that they might not have were they to practice elsewhere. I suggest that Guadeloupe's and Martinique's intellectual history affords these artists the possibility to actively resist the essentializing idea of *being from* a specific place. Instead, they craft these spaces into a specific trans-geo-aesthetic intellectualism that allows them to nurture, in Adlai Murdoch's words, an "evolving mosaic of difference, emphasizing pluralism of being as the core of a postcolonial subjective position [which] demonstrated the anathema of fixity and singularity" (Murdoch 2017, 185). In other words, Guadeloupe and Martinique are absolutely present, then and now, as geopolitical experiences that shape the artists' aesthetic practices, not as rigid entities, but as places that engage transnationally in ever-changing ways.

In between Haiti and Europe: Politico-intellectual Contexts

What does an article dedicated to the contemporary arts scene of the Antillean DOMs have to do with a volume concerned with "neocolonial empire and resistance to it" (Murdoch, p. 4, this volume)? How does the contemporary arts scene have anything to do with an analysis of the forty-four-day mass general strike that brought the French overseas territories of Guadeloupe and Martinique to a standstill? The short answer is, "everything," for the 2009 events are inextricably linked to a series of other important sociopolitical contexts, which in the late 2010s have created an intellectual public sphere that distinguishes itself quite radically from previous discussions around identity, marginalization, exclusion, belonging, and even suffering. In addition to the 2009 general strike, this chapter keeps present the suite of initiatives that the French government undertook around the recognition of its role in the trade of enslaved persons and slavery. These events are largely the result of mass demonstrations. Madeleine

Dobie writes, "Notably, on May 23, 1998, some forty thousand Antilleans marched in the streets of Paris, presenting what was an unprecedented display of community identity" (Dobie 2010, 293). These events include the commemoration of the 150th anniversary of the second abolition of slavery in 1998; "the impulsion of the socialist law of 21 May 2001 qualifying slavery and the trade of enslaved persons as crimes against humanity"; the governmental decree of January 5, 2004, which "founded the Comité pour la mémoire de l'esclavage [Committee for the Memory of Slavery], originally headed by the Guadeloupean Maryse Condé"; the designation of May 10 as a national date for commemorating the abolition of slavery; and, President François Hollande's inauguration on May 10, 2015, of Mémorial ACTe, also known as the Centre caribéen d'expressions et de mémoire de la traite et de l'esclavage, an institution based in Point-à-Pitre on the site of the former Darboussier sugar factory.

At some level, each of the aforementioned post-1998 events quintessentially engages the "idea of Haiti" (Polyné 2013, 1). As anthropologist Paul Brodwin points out, the role of Haitian workers ambivalently informs the difficult conversation around workers' rights, notably in Guadeloupe. Brodwin writes: "Haitians originally came as cane cutters in the midst of a bitter struggle over unionization in the declining Guadeloupean sugar industry. Without their knowledge, Haitian men were used as strikebreakers by the owners of sugar plantations, and in 1975 they became the target of violent opposition (including lynch mobs) led by pro-union Guadeloupeans" (Brodwin 2010, 18). For his part, historian Philippe Zacaïr explains that the controversial employment of Haitian cane workers did not just apply to the sugar industry in Guadeloupe, but also to the banana industry in both Guadeloupe and Martinique (Zacaïr 2010, 45). Zacaïr examines how labor conflicts of the late 1970s matured into a full-blown societal scapegoating of Haitians culminating in the heavily mediatized anti-Haitianism of "Ibo Simon, a former singer turned politician and popular television host," who in September 2001 was "charged with repeatedly calling for racist hatred and violence against Haitian immigrants and other Afro-Caribbeans residing in Guadeloupe" (Zacaïr 2010, 43).

In contrast to such flagrant anti-Haitianism, which took place in the DOM from the late 1970s to the early 2000s, DOM intellectuals such as Edouard Glissant in *Caribbean Discourse* (1989) and Patrick Chamoiseau and Raphaël Confiant in *Lettres créoles* (Creole Letters) (1999) explicitly extol Haiti as perhaps the only place in the Caribbean that has successfully nurtured an "authentic" aesthetic that has developed itself largely independently of a European influence (Glissant 1989, 460; Benedicty-Kokken 2012, 297–298). As Michal Obszyński's work on Guadeloupean, Guyanese, Haitian, and Martinican literary manifestos and programmatic texts illustrates, over the course of the twentieth century, Caribbean writers have put forth the notion that Haiti represents a "real" Caribbean beingness, which must be celebrated rather than denounced (Obszyński 2016, 96). And, as the respective writings on Haitians living in Guadeloupe of Brodwin, sociologist Laënnec Hurbon, and Zacaïr show, Haitians themselves are invested in a narrative of Haiti as the most genuine identity of the Caribbean for, through such a narrative, "Haitians claim cultural intimacy with Guadeloupeans" (Brodwin 2010, 31). Drawing on Hurbon, Zacaïr explains that the notion of "authenticity" for Guadeloupeans is a vexed one: one they fear, for it distances them from assimilation to a French republican order of things; but also one they desire, for at least in the past, "authenticity" has presented itself as an inevitable prerequisite to national self-determination. More simply put, Haiti represents an aspiration for sovereignty and also all the trepidation about what such independence might entail (Zacaïr 2010, 43).

Presently, however, Haiti-as-idea represents a less divisive space, one that corresponds to a public discourse on DOM-ness, which has found more comfortable ways to articulate the paradoxical asymmetries of what it means to be at once part of, but also separate from France.[6] In her study of "how contemporary labor activists in Guadeloupe wrestle with the conceptual arsenal of political modernity—including the seductive but constraining categories of freedom, sovereignty, nation, and revolution," anthropologist Yarimar Bonilla (2015, 3) shows that Guadeloupeans have deliberated on a "pragmatic vision" (xiii) that "evokes a new model of community and collective possibility outside of the traditional categories of citizenship and nation" (177). In the later decades of the twentieth century, "Haiti" represented the debate around whether or not the DOM should pursue political separation from France; in contrast, since the 2000s, as Bonilla's and Zacaïr's work suggests, Haiti no longer needs to be used as the example to (or not to) follow.

That said, it is not possible to claim that "Haiti" is no longer of importance when discussing Guérédrat, Tauliaut, and Goudrouffe's artistic practice. Guérédrat, Tauliaut, and Goudrouffe are at some level part of a generation that has been part of a DOM society that has conscientiously engaged discursively with Haiti as a means to better understanding itself. The same generation that has born witness to such ambivalent uses of Haiti-as-an-idea has also been present in what Bonilla argues are some of the most subtle articulations of contemporary global political practice and thought to date, especially as regards what it means to determine oneself in our present-day neoliberal order. Moreover, Guérédrat, Tauliaut, and Goudrouffe are also part of a generation that has seen, for better or worse, real change as regards official French recognition of its colonial past. It is significant that Guadeloupe now houses Mémorial ACTe, "the first major institution in the Caribbean" to commemorate the legacy of slavery not just in the French Antilles, but in the entire Caribbean. Mémorial ACTe's edifice is "composed of two buildings that form a gigantic serpent covered in black granite," which are at once connected and covered by "a monumental arc" made of an anodized aluminum lattice (Flandrin 2015). Moreover, if we consider that Goudrouffe was invited to be the guest of honor and chief curator for Mémorial ACTe's first Festival of the Caribbean Image, it becomes clear that the art scene is both an agent and a recipient of the changing landscape of the DOMs relationship to the French "métropole" (Arts des Caraïbes-Amériques 2020).

More specifically, I suggest that one of the reasons that Guérédrat, Tauliaut, and Goudrouffe are able to agilely hold on to such varied and conflicting meanings of what it means to be *rich, successful, poor, victimized,* or *marginalized* is that it is possible to situate their work within a geo-intellectual relational landscape: they are at once from Guadeloupe and Martinique, but they are also from a conceptual space that is *between Haiti and . . .* , wherein the *and*s are prolifically multiple. Guérédrat's, Tauliaut's, and Goudrouffe's work as artists based at least part-time in Guadeloupe and Martinique takes place quite literally between Haiti and Guadeloupe; Haiti and Martinique; Guadeloupe and Haiti; Haiti and France; Haiti and the United States; Haiti and Guyana; Haiti and Chad; Haiti and Réunion, or Haiti and Madagascar. In other words, the artists' work puts into play the historical injustices of the quadruple legacies of the Middle Passage, slavery, indigenous genocide, and a centuries-old neoliberal order. The work interrogates but does not outright reject the vexed relationship of the DOMs to France and the European Union, a relationship that has afforded the DOMs a certain level of infrastructural security (that is, hospitals, schools, urban planning); and the reality that such infrastructural stability does not translate into individual wealth, so that the large majority of DOMians continue to live under the poverty line. In regard to their aesthetic engagements, Guérédrat, Tauliaut, and Goudrouffe proudly feature the artistic proficiencies that they have garnered from their citizenship in Guadeloupe and Martinique. Yet, they also actively seek that their work be put into relation with communities to which they feel affinities. For example, Guérédrat's performance work is informed by her proficiency in spiritual communities that privilege embodied knowledge, such as Butoh, Halprinian postmodern dance and healing, Regla de Ocha, shamanism, and Vodou. This multiplicity, what Murdoch describes with all the potential of the *negative*—that is, the negative in its photo-filmic sense, as the "anathema of fixity" (Murdoch 2017, 185)—puts Guérédrat, Tauliaut, and Goudrouffe at the forefront of our contemporary global arts scene.

Artincidence, At the Stardust Café and Titans, Performance and Video Art

In July 2015, two figures enter the Stardust Café in Le Moule, on the eastern coastline of Grande Terre, Guadeloupe. The bar is located close to the city-center's nineteenth-century church, built sturdily to withstand the hurricanes and tornadoes to which Le Moule is particularly privy. Once named by the

British "Portland," Le Moule is a significant harbor, the historical home to the island's most lucrative sugar factory, where the population once comprised a seven-to-one ratio of enslaved persons to non-enslaved persons (Karukera). Both figures enter the Stardust Café, quietly, with a slow hesitation. They sit down at a wooden table and say nothing. Each is dressed in an integral full body suit: one suit is grayish white, the other beigeish white. They remain completely silent. The integrality of their bodysuits is such that they have no openings, not even for their mouths or eyes. Beautiful peacock-like LGBTQ+-rainbow-flag-hued headdresses crown the figures' heads. Quietly, proudly, and cautiously, the two sit, possibly unaware that they are being watched.

They are nonetheless being filmed multiple times over, by the camera that is meant to follow them on their Le Moule journey but also by the cell phone of someone at the bar. A client who knows the café well immediately and superbly caringly comes over to them to take their order. They say nothing. Someone steps out of the bar to ask a woman on the street to come in, maybe to watch, maybe to help out. She enters. A couple of women stand at the doorway, cautiously, leaning toward the street, not sure whether they are ready to enter. Unable to serve the two, since they do not speak, drink, or eat, the client asks the owner of the bar to bring a couple of glasses, straws, and a bottle of water. Meanwhile the bar's owner, from behind the bar, explains to a man—whom we later learn is Guérédrat and Tauliaut's photographer, Robert Charlotte—that the owner had seen the two earlier in the day outside the church. He proposes that they are-and/or-represent saints whom the priest had asked to leave the church. He explains that during the mass, his daughter had not yet arrived at the café. It is now that she is present that they come, as if it were her presence that allows the angels to seek safety at the Stardust. The café owner says: "Et là, le Bon dieu me les envoie" (And now, the Good God sends them to me). The understanding is that the two are not quite the type of saints who belong in a church.

The reaction that they solicit resonates with so much of the scholarship generated around the very European and Euro-American designation of embodied thought systems as *marvelous* or *magical realism*, an ontological relationship to the world that does not function according to distinct schisms between dream and reality; life and death; then and now; human and animal; male and female.[7] Of course, as recent publications of Vanessa Agard-Jones, Christian Flaugh, and Charlotte Hammond argue, questions of sexuality and gender in Guadeloupe, Haiti, and Martinique falter between the categories that as academics we are obliged to implement in our commitment to the clarity that is academia's exigency. Whereas in other work, Guérédrat and Tauliaut very conscientiously play with and subvert categories such as cisgender, transgender, transvestite, same-sex-desiring, queer, dominatrix, in *At the Stardust Café*, especially when the two are seated, they are beings in the full sense of the word as conceived by posthumanist scholarship. In other words, these two *Stardust Café* beings nurture the "non-human experience as site of knowledge" (Ferrando 2012, 10), with the natural world and the highly mechanical and digitized worlds merging into a being that is profoundly equipped with a way-of-being-in-the-world that cultivates an ethics of belonging that is anything but exclusionary, what Jackson refers to as "texts that critique and depose prevailing conceptions of 'the human' found in Western science and philosophy" (2020, 1).

For its part, the performance piece filmed at night, *Titans* (2015), offers a stunning example of the organic rapport that is possible between the natural and the mechanical. In *Titans*, Guérédrat and Tauliaut stage the entry of two trucks that belong to two drivers who transport sugarcane. Tauliaut recounts that the two men live in the neighborhood in which they grew up and that he had often noticed the decorativeness of the trucks. He invited them to the video performance taking place at and after sunset. The trucks enter an empty parking lot. In the horizon, the spectator sees the lights of cars on the highway, as well as the light of the sun that is setting. The trucks enter side by side, extremely slowly. Their deliberateness; the brightness of their headlights but also the decorative lights that surround their front grilles and fenders; the elegance of the swanlike side exhausts; and the pride of the truck's cab, which stands alone, all exude the regality of true confidence.

As the sun descends, the camera again offers the spectator a wide-angle panoramic shot, but this time from the other side of the parking lot; only now, in the dark, as spectators, we are no longer aware that the terrain is that of a parking lot. The line of action becomes clear: we are privy to a meeting among the trucks and the two smaller figures, who as in *At the Stardust Café* don iguana-like headdresses. The lights of the trucks illuminate the smaller human iguana-like figures.[8] Slowly, they begin a dialogue-dance; the larger mammoth protagonists (played by the trucks) move in response to the smaller two-legged beings (played by Guérédrat and Tauliaut), and vice versa. The parking lot of Le Moule Gardel Sugar Factory, the last surviving small sugar factory in Guadeloupe according to Tauliaut, transforms into a terrain that is anything but industrial, yet also not quite uniquely of the "natural" order, for the trucks' lights—one's more reddish, the other's more greenish—appear as at once electronic and biological, creating what the artists describe as a sort of "totem-contemporary art."

Such melding, then, of art, science, the present, and the past, intersects with Afrofuturists' mixing of "science fiction and fantasy . . . to decode and represent such concepts as blackness, Caribbeanness, and freedom" (Josephs 2013, 127). As such, *Titans* resonates with literary scholar Kelly Baker Josephs's description of the Afrofuturist aesthetic project, which crafts "a fertile space from which to conceive positive visions of a single black past and a cooperative diasporic future" (Josephs 2013, 127). *Titans* also reminds us that black diasporic humanism has always been posthumanist, for as philosopher Francesca Ferrando admits, posthumanism is profoundly Eurocentric (Ferrando 2012, 13–14), failing to take account of Afrofuturism (and I would add here embodied spiritual and intellectual practices such as Vodou), which articulate beingness as far more than the human, a space that is linked profoundly to the most peaceful and also violent realities of nature, to constantly evolving human modernity, and to the pretentiousness of "humancentrism" (Ferrando 2012, 10). *Titans*, then, exemplifies the aspirational anthropocenic equilibrium that seeks to balance two forces often posited as oppositional. In this way, *Titans* serves as an embodied pedagogy, which models what it teaches: that nature and the man-made can coexist, but only if all the actors recognize the integral life power of the other: that is, each possesses a personhood (or animalhood, or machinehood), which must recognize the other's beingness.

Henri Tauliaut, Biological Visual and Installation Art

Tauliaut's installation art absolutely beckons a *mise-en-relation* with Firelei Báez's visual oeuvre, for both artists draw on the conception that the vegetal, the natural, the technical, and the digital are capable of merging into what Tauliaut characterizes as "ecosystems." It goes without saying that narratives that posit the natural against the mechanical invade our present-day worries about the future. For example, present-day scientific discourse unequivocally shows that the environmental degradation of the earth will end in the destruction of life as we know it. Another more aesthetically deliberated example illustrative of the destructive oppositional relationship between nature and machine is that of early twentieth-century Italian and German art scenes, which staged the end of the natural world and thus humanity through the dominance of industrialization, in the films of Fritz Lang, for example; or the urban built environment's imposition of solitude, even if elegant, on the human subject, in the paintings of Giorgo de Chirico.

In contrast, Tauliaut's and Báez's visual work emphasizes the notion of the community of beings, asserting the natural and the man-made as life forms in their own right, neither dominating the other. Most important, their oeuvre decenters the human, putting the human on par with the other beings of our contemporary ecosystems. Much in the same way as Báez paints the human body into nature or nature into the human body, Tauliaut immerses the human into the biospheric. For example, for the Havana Biennial in 2014, Tauliaut developed *Jungle Sphère*, an installation piece that produced a man-made jungle (see figure 8.1). *Jungle Sphère* was composed of two spheres, one almost four meters in diameter and the smaller one three meters, one embedded in the other. Tauliaut was able to create a space in which rare plants grew thanks to the warmth provided by the exhibit's visitors, whose hands on the outer biosphere prompted sounds and lights that generated the plant growth. Tauliaut's work then makes us

Figure 8.1 *Jungle Sphere 3.0*, Bienal de la Havana, May 2015.
Copyright © 2015. Henri Tauliaut—photographer: Henri Tauliaut.

aware that the mechanical, the natural, and the human exist in a code-
pendent relationship that can work well together. His practice then phi-
losophizes the very "question du Vivant, sa complexité, sa beauté, son
extraordinaire foisonnement et sa banalité" (Cultures Outre Mer n.d.; question of the Living, its complexity, its beauty, its extraordinary abundance, and
its banality).

Annabel Guérédrat, Dance and Performance Art

For her part, Guérédrat, unlike perhaps any artist I know except Yasujirō
Ozu, the master of cinematic slowness, has cultivated the aesthetic of
embodied deliberateness, through dance, movement, and performance.
Her absolute comfort—and the spectator might say, bliss—in enacting
slowness is undoubtedly related to her advanced training and collaborative
experiences, which merge the spiritual, the philosophical, and the embodied: U.S.-American Anna Halprin's postmodern dance and healing; Chadian
modern dancer Hyacinthe Abdoulaye Tobio's elaboration of disequilibrium

Figure 8.2 *Shadows of Frida #3*, directed, filmed, and montage by Henri Tau-
liaut. Performed by Annabel Guérédrat and Gwladys Gambie. Mediathèque,
Trois-Ilets. June 2016.
Copyright © 2017. CieArtincidence—photographer: Jean Baptiste Barret.

as slowness; Regla de Ocha; shamanism; and Vodou. Even when she sings,
she inhabits a soprano voice, as in for example, the video performance
piece *Shadows of Frida I* (2016) (figure 8.2). Guérédrat's *slow work* unsettles
because it holds on to a measured unctuous softness that calms at the
same time that it draws the spectator into realities that are far from
peaceful.

Certified in geography, French language and literature, and history,
having taught in a *lycée* in Gagny, France for two years, Guérédrat's work
also includes a repertoire that is far more explicitly aggressive, harnessing
into her own work her admiration for feminist-activist artists such as
Audre Lorde and Ana Mendieta. In works such as *A Freak Show for S* (2015),
Guérédrat pays homage to Sarah Baartman and more expansively to women,

and in particular those whose bodies have been brutally exposed to exploitation by a global white capitalist exchange: exchange as slavery, trafficking, labor, culture, or art. *A Freak Show for S* was performed at the Grace Exhibition Space in New York for "The Sphinx Returns," a four-months performance series that took place in 2015. Even in these more overtly disconcerting performances, Guérédrat imposes slowness as a mode of keeping her audience present. She harnesses gradualness as it is often understood, as peacefulness. Most important, however, like Ozu, she lets us linger in it long enough that we take note of how the worst violence is often that which in Rob Nixon's term constitutes "slow violence," whose destruction takes centuries to lay bare, whether it is violence against the environment or that against female bodies, whereby the source of their violence is one and the same.

The merger then of Guérédrat and Tauliaut's practices is one that nurtures an ethics of belonging that is acutely aware of how black bodies are continuously excluded, abused, and compromised. In other words, the artists' work asserts belonging as a right, one that is complexly layered in Guadeloupe and Martinique by a double belonging, to both the global North and the global South—one that renders them, in the eyes of so many, privileged and, in the eyes of others, victimized. The artists' patient work resists slipping into representations that inspire pity, and they carefully choreograph anger, and even rage, to assure its most effective (and affective) import. In emphasizing the slowness of being and notably the slowness of how violence works itself into and onto the bodies of humans—but also of plants, rocks, waterways, churches, artificial biospheres, and sugarcane-carrying trucks—the two engage in a pedagogy of how to belong. Their individual and collective work thus nurtures an ethics of "being a part of" that harnesses the power inherent to marginality, theorizes it, cultivates it, and redefines practices of what it means to carry within one's being the traumas of the past and the present, the precariousnesses of tomorrow, and the beauty—often painful and violent and false beauty—of what it means to engage in an "interrogation of power in its most intimate dimension" (Sexton 2011, 29).

Guérédrat and Tauliaut's formal brilliance is to superimpose Weltanschauung upon Weltanschauung. Their whitish integral suits topped by the colorful headdress at once play the advertising game. Like the clichéd photo advertisement of a woman's hand clenching a beer bottle, in which the receiver of the image can either see a cold beer or alternatively a sweating phallus, so Guérédrat and Tauliaut offer their spectators what they are predisposed to see: an LGBTQ couple; angels; Maman-Dlô (a river or water spirit and goddess) and her lover; peacocks; iguanas; aliens. *At the Stardust Café, Titans, Jungle Sphère,* and *Shadows of Frida I* illustrate what Maja Horn explains is the indispensable contribution of the late José Esteban Muñoz to performance studies. Horn writes of Muñoz's *Disidentifications: Queers of Color and the Performance of Politics* (1999): "Ultimately, *Disidentifications* was for me both a call to cultural specificity, to understand what specific given (national) cultural protocols constrain or enable performances, and an example for productive forms of theoretical traffic, namely, how Muñoz's Caribbean-inflected use of hybridity offered a critical approach for apprehending subjects who did not fit comfortably into (singular) US minoritarian identity molds" (Horn 2015, 82). As artists who intentionally weave together spaces that engage the translocal politics of being minority in major national spaces, but also as artists who craft a practice that brings together artists working throughout the globe, Guérédrat and Tauliaut's *At the Stardust Café* is exemplary of how Muñoz's theoretical corpus quietly but insistently spins a web that entangles its reader in "a reparative project that retains a kernel of the negative" (Alvarado 2015, 107). In other words, their work processes what it means to be forced into minority citizenship to the world, always and incessantly dealing with the unspeakable intergenerational traumas inflicted by more or less recent histories of oppression. Ultimately, then, Guérédrat and Tauliaut's work takes account of both how global politics render certain subjects "subjectless," and also how these violent "discourses bring the subject into being" (Alvarado 2015, 110). That is, the two figures *At the Stardust Café* are born into personhood thanks to the bar owner and his clients' articulation of what the figures might need and who they might be. In fact, *At the Stardust Café* is accompanied entirely by an instrumental score. It is through subtitles that the spectator views the words of the bar's human subjects.

It is this ethico-aesthetic landscape of compassionate slowness, a space generative of posthuman angels, which leads me to comprehend Guérédrat and Tauliaut's work as a pragmatic aesthetics of patience. I use the words *comprehend* and *apprehend* with both Emmanuel Levinas and Edouard Glissant in my theoretical rearview mirror: with Levinas reminding me that one can only become aware of the other through the mode of the unexpected, in which my "initial approach of the other person" takes place "in terms of astonishment or surprise" (Beavers 1995, 5); and with Glissant insisting on the etymological presence of ap*prehension* and com*prehension*, both of which teach us that any knowledge-based activity around understanding otherness, in a neoliberal, post-slavery, postcolonial, and neocolonial economy, can be undergirded only by the desire to own, possess, and exploit (Moatamri 2007). In other words, to encounter the other in an Enlightenment-informed episteme is to subject the other to some level of exploitation. It is in this gesture of holding the manipulative close to the compassionate that one feels the vital vulnerability of Guérédrat and Tauliat's art, and the potentiality for what is offered by thinking otherness to "relationality," which "signals that life is interrelationship and interdependence, always and at every level" (Escobar 2020, 92).

Daniel Goudrouffe, Photojournalist and Photographer

I begin my discussion of Daniel Goudrouffe's mostly documentary blackand-white photography with my own personal critical analysis—and yes, unabashed judgment—of Goudrouffe's work. That is, to date, I have yet to see the work of a non-Haitian documentary photographer who is capable of framing Haiti in such a way that the photos inspire the comforting poetic realism of the ordinary, an ordinary, which resists the violent exceptionalism that Cécile Accilien and Kaiama L. Glover criticize in so much of their commitment to how Haiti is represented in media and scholarship: work; love; family; moments of laughter, disappointment, reflection, sadness, and stoicism. Goudrouffe describes his three photographic projects to date as "cycles." *Beyond Paradise* chronicles a period of fourteen years of travel and extended stays throughout the black hemispheric Atlantic (1998–2016), notably to Haiti, Cuba, Guyana and Suriname, Dominica, Trinidad, and Puerto Rico. *Caribbean Diaspora in New York*, an ongoing project, reflects on his relationship as a Caribbean artist living and working between Guadeloupe, Massachusetts, and New York. And *Memories*, his most recent endeavor, experiments with nondocumentary techniques, such as superimposition of images and light painting, to comment on what it means to keep the past and future present in the now-time of the photographic medium.

Having first trained under Magnum photographer Guy Le Querrec, whom Goudrouffe met in October 1995 in Guadeloupe, Goudrouffe adheres to a Magnum philosophy that restrains one from interpreting one's own photos, a viewpoint perhaps best articulated by another Magnum photojournalist, Elliot Erwitt: "Little is more irritating to me than photographers pontificating about photography or talking about their pictures in public" (2017). Similarly, Goudrouffe refuses to comment on the meaning of his work or even on how it might intervene with theoretical considerations of photography as a medium to access information, promote activism, or reshape contemporary aesthetics of the visual. Instead, in his interviews and talks, he constrains himself to providing technical information about a given photograph: when and how it was shot; how it was developed; and in which photography or art exhibits he has exposed it. In hearing him speak, Haiti comes up explicitly as a major point of return, even a home base, for his oeuvre, as the place where he truly began his practice as a photographer—the literal place and the intellectual and visual mindscape to which he has returned most frequently.

In the picture that the editor and photographer have generously allowed me to feature here, I purposefully restrain from extended commentary. In part, I take my cue from both Erwitt and Goudrouffe, and instead of analyzing the specific photos, I have chosen to share his professional trajectory and praxis. Unlike the visual and performance art of Guérédrat and Tauliaut, the very medium of Goudrouffe's photography does not invite an actively interactive engagement with it. And in fact, were I to further describe the photos, I would indeed commit the injustices that pertain so painfully to what Glover describes as "outwardly benign discourses," which are nonetheless "conditioned by the uncomfortably linked issues of race, space, poverty, and fear" (Glover 2017, 236).

In a May 2017 interview, with anthropologically informed worries about the relationship between the camera and the subject being photographed, I asked Goudrouffe if he sought permission from those human subjects whom he photographed. Goudrouffe responded that the Magnum pedagogy is to nurture truth through the "instantané" (instantaneous), which means "voler les images" (stealing the images). Goudrouffe explained that Magnum's practice is to expose truth. Goudrouffe succinctly and movingly stated how he has adapted Magnum's praxis: "J'essaie d'être juste, mais dans quoi? Je suis juste dans ma subjectivité peut-être." (I try to be fair, but in what? Maybe I am fair in my own subjectivity.) The confident hesitation, expressed as a question and not an answer, corresponds to how I read Guérédrat, Tauliaut, and Goudrouffe in the same theoretical space, which proposes that their work is characterized by a *pragmatic aesthetics of patience* that in Goudrouffe's instance means trusting his own instinct that the poetry he and his camera produce outweigh any possible exploitation of the persons photographed.

A similar conversation to which I was privy a couple of months later only underscored the notion of patience and pragmatism. In July 2017, while in attendance at the Sixth Afroeuropeans Conference in Tampere, Finland, an audience member asked one of the keynote speakers, Johny Pitts, a writer and photographer, and also the founder Afropean.com, the same question I had asked Goudrouffe. Pitts's response was that if Henri-Cartier Bresson (one of the founders of Magnum) did not ask permission, neither would he. Pitts also went on to elaborate that the very method by which he works, like that of Goudrouffe, requires spending time in a place among its citizens, nature, and built environments, early in the morning, late at night, and throughout the busiest moments of a day. The very method is one that asks continual permission, a permission that does not "steal." In fact, the key to the *photographic practice of justice* that Goudrouffe and Pitts engage in has to do with what Goudrouffe brilliantly and humbly asserts as ownership of his subjectivity: "Maybe I am fair in *my* subjectivity" (my emphasis).

Here Goudrouffe reminds us of Michel-Rolph Trouillot's assertion that "the Western gaze remains the stumbling block that makes it impossible for the native to become a full interlocutor" (Trouillot 2003, 133). But, what happens when the gaze is not "Western"? What happens when the person taking the photograph is informed by sensibilities that at once strike a balance between what Jared Sexton deliberates on as always at once both Afro-Pessimism and Black Optimism. In contemplating the relationship among the work of Frantz Fanon, Lewis Gordon, Orlando Patterson, Sylvia Wynter, and Saidiya Hartman, Sexton writes:

> Though it may appear as counterintuitive, or rather because it is counterintuitive, this acceptance or affirmation is active; it is willing or willingness, in other words, to pay whatever social costs accrue to being black, to inhabiting blackness, to living a black social life under the shadow of social death. This is not an accommodation to the dictates of the antiblack world. The affirmation of blackness, which is to say an affirmation of pathological being, is a refusal to distance oneself from blackness in a valorization of minor differences that bring one closer to health, to life, or to sociality. (Sexton 2011, 27)

Goudrouffe's photos reflect visually the Poetic of Relation that Glissant made a lifelong project of deliberating in words. Goudrouffe's very being-in-the-world—that is, his heightened sensibility to beingness in its multiple connections to the world, compounded by his complex gaze—serves as a "repository for . . . memory" (Agard-Jones 2012, 339) where both his own being, and those he renders "still" on the various mediums that are considered photographic must be read as "a palimpsest and as a thing in a state of permanent becoming," which bear "the traces of multiple forms of power"

(Agard-Jones 2013, 187). In other words, it is precisely Goudrouffe's subjectivity, and at once his self-effacing confidence, which reflects, yes, the complexity, but also the pragmatism of "relation."

Thus far, the aspects of Goudrouffe's subjectivity that I have delineated are limited to facts largely beyond Goudrouffe's control, notably the biographical facts that inform his social being. I turn now to a discussion of Goudrouffe's aesthetic practice that "unsettle[s] long-standing habits and traditions in the humanities [and] opens our understanding of art to a broader range of interpretive pathways" (Mercer 2016, 3). To date, all three of Goudrouffe's projects put forth images of what it means to be mindful of how one's personal dignity is largely dependent on how one maintains balance between oneself and one's environment, and if one's environment even allows the conditions for such balance to be achieved. Goudrouffe's images are *not* about "the generation and quest for 'salvation goods' in the form of . . . especially *worthiness*" (Rey and Stepick 2013, 5), which Terry Rey and Alex Stepick argue is the unavoidable reality of being Haitian in a U.S. space, in which both art and religion provide "a sense of dignity and respect that transforms boat people into people, beasts into gods" (201). *Neither* are Goudrouffe's images about showcasing what Glover claims are Haiti's exceptional narratives, whereby "Haitian exceptionalism . . . ultimately conflates the *super-* and the *sub*human" (Glover 2012, 201).[9] And Goudrouffes's photos are also *not* about showcasing Haitians' supposedly outstanding human capacity for "resilience" (Clitandre 2011, 151). Rather, Goudrouffe's are images that reveal Caribbean people as de facto dignified: the question of whether or not they are majestic, super or sub, or resilient doesn't even cross the visualizer's mind. Goudrouffe's images strike neither pity nor jealousy.

For example, in *Haïti Léogane 3* (2010), Goudrouffe sits close to the older gentleman (see figure 8.3). Goudrouffe is seated low enough, perhaps on the ground, in such a way that his camera offers us a perspective in which the man's carefully crossed feet and hands take up as much of the photographic surface as his face. *Haïti Léogane 3* is distantly reminiscent of Italian late Renaissance painter Andrea Mantegna's *Lamentation of Christ* (c. 1480), nota-

Figure 8.3 *Haïti Léogane 3* (2010).
Photographer: Daniel Goudrouffe. Reprinted with permission.

bly in the fact that the perspective privileged by both the photographer and
the painter foreshortens the human body in such a way that the feet, hands,
and head take up equal amounts of space on the physical artistic surface that
they occupy—only, in Mantegna's painting, Christ's figure lies on its back,
invoking the insecurity, fear, and sadness of those who mourn him; whereas,
in Goudrouffe's photograph, the older man's figure sits upright, suggesting
that the vitality of life is dependent as much on the body as it is on the history that the body carries within it. In Mantegna's painting, the feet stare at
us aggressively, reminding us of Christ's painful passion: we are obliged to
work to move past Christ's wounded feet, across his nude torso, to make it
to his face. Goudrouffe instead puts a similar foreshortening perspective
into play, but in a much less extreme way, to emphasize the equilibrium
between the man's feet, hands, and face. The balance between the feet, that
is, those bodily instruments that support us and allow us to feel the earth
beneath us; the hands, which allow us to enter into contact with the world
around us, assuring our efficiency (and perhaps even our potential for

generosity, sensuality, or violence); and the face, which communicates our personality, reminds us that wisdom-of-being comes only when we manage a relationship among all parts of our body. The photo, taken after the 2010 earthquake in Haiti, insists that the knowledge that defines a life worth living has everything to do with balance: balance between the mind and the body; balance between oneself and one's environment.

And it almost goes without saying that to sit below, just slightly below, one's subject is to assume a position of reverence, but a reverence that refuses to over-romanticize the photographer's visual interlocutor. It is by taking on such a confidently humble stance that Goudrouffe's photos offer images that successfully steer away from pathologizing the body, while holding close the racial and gendered tensions that continue to produce global injustices. Most important, Goudrouffe's images fight for a space in which we learn to trace a calmer relationship to other beings. In this way, I suggest that Goudrouffe's poetics avoid creating extreme affective states, such as the Kantian *sublime*, for *to sublimate* is to engage at some level in a process in which the recipient of the aesthetic process gets lost in the experience of contemplating the given object of art. The subject loses reason, as it were, and enters the confused but cathartically healing spaces of passion, melancholia, or revelation. Most important, the onlooker *uses* the experience of the sublime for self-gain: the inebriating quality of the sublime depends on *taking from* the object of art. Crudely put, when the image represented is that of a real person, the result can be the unsettling but seductively addictive experiences of eros, melancholia, or pathos. Onlookers, especially those who look through a gaze of whiteness, may not necessarily sublimate their desires, but at least they contemplate their own desiring mechanisms quite literally *using*, in the case of Mantegna, the image of Christ's body or the images of Haitian bodies.

Goudrouffe's work then, like Guérédrat and Tauliaut's, quietly but aggressively and rigorously fights back. More precisely, Goudrouffe nurtures a visual process in which onlookers feel themselves absolutely unable to enter into such a selfish relationship with the persons depicted in the photos. His oeuvre sustains a sense of dialogue with the human image(s) replicated on the photographic paper, the printed page, or the online screen. He assures a dynamic of relationality, in which the photographer and the person photographed enter into contact and the receiver of the object of art *becomes aware* of the person printed onto the photographic paper. In so doing, Goudrouffe nurtures an aesthetic practice that in many senses does not correspond to what many deem aesthetic: he does not overly emphasize a self-reflexive formalism; he does not encourage a sublime fascination with the liminality between desire and death. Instead, his poetic practice creates a healthier space in which onlookers *take notice of* and maybe conduct an *inner dialogue with* the persons depicted but find themselves *unable to use* the persons and the environments framed by the contours of the photographic image to gratify an impulse toward "the abjection and ontologizing plasticization of 'the African'" (Jackson 2020, 29).

From "Where" We Do Our Art Criticism Matters: Jeannette Ehlers in Conversation with the DOM Art Scene

In the most general and theoretical of terms, this essay has sought to ask the question, Can aesthetic practice nurture an ethos of patience while at the same time channeling the solemn, tragic, infuriating, and ever more apparent consequences of colonial and neocolonial violence? To give a better sense to my question, and to return to the question of place to which Mercer holds critics accountable, I enter into dialogue with Jeannette Ehlers's performance and artwork. I select Ehlers's work because she engages in comparable mediatic practices to those of Guérédrat, Tauliaut, and Goudrouffe, but mostly in a public sphere that is quite different from theirs. Indeed, Ehlers is Caribbean and European, but the public-sphere circumstances of her Caribbean-Europeanness are far from similar to those of Guérédrat, Tauliaut, and Goudrouffe. The intention of this attention to Ehlers's work is to honor her work by putting her into dialogue with Artincidence and Goudrouffe, and to question how the context of where artists exercise their art affects how their practice is critically received.

Ehlers's *Whip It Good* (2013) is a performance that also has been exhibited as an audiovisual piece (2014). In the piece, a woman is dressed in white with coats of white paint covering her flesh, layers drawn to suggest the combination of the scars and fresh wounds of a human body that has been whipped incessantly by a master who is terrified of what the subjugated human being might do. Art historian and critic Mathias Danbolt writes that the female body (performed by Ehlers) "carefully smears a large black leather whip with charred coal from a bowl on the floor." Danbolt explains that in the video montage the woman whips a series of "white plaster casts of antique reliefs and statues" (Danbolt 2016, 2). Danbolt continues: "But the camera is not the only spectator to the scene. The jump cuts between the white plaster-cast statues and the woman whipping, position the statues participants of sorts in the act, participants that are not only witnesses, as they also figure as the imaginary targets of the retribution" (Danbolt 2016, 3). Danbolt's extended analysis of *Whip It Good* argues that Ehlers's piece draws attention to the perilous "white innocence" (Wekker 2016, 1) that generates new acts of violence while continuing to eschew difficult conversations about European colonial histories. In Danbolt's words, Ehlers's performance whips white surfaces black—whether they are statues or canvases—reminding her spectator-participants of the omnipresence of "white supremacy," which is "driven by the desire for clean slates central to the rhetoric of beyonding that informs our so-called post-historical, post-race, post-identity, and post-feminist times" (Danbolt 2016, 5).

While I absolutely agree with Danbolt's analysis, it is also important to point out that the woman self-reflexively smothered in white paint textured to look like the scars and wounds of a whip's lashes is not so much taking revenge as she is re-enacting the violent and tragic ridiculousness of the white master possessed by the brutal sadomasochistic pleasure needed to whip another human body. In other words, she is not smothered in brown or black paint, nor are the portions of the paint meant to look like open wounds depicted in red. Ehlers's body is a representation of the very absurdity of the inextricability of race and violence. The white paint also recalls how "white clay body paint" is used to "construct" and invoke "spirit identities" in West and Central Africa (Gundaker 1998, 116–117). One need only think to the cover image of Aisha M. Beliso-De Jesús's *Electric*

Santería: Racial and Sexual Assemblages of Transnational Religion (2015), titled
Jura by photographer Marta María Pérez Bravo, or to those who in July pil-
grim to Sodo, or Saint d'Eau, in Haiti, who enter the water often having
covered themselves in "a combination of various medicinal plants (particularly basil), possibly accompanied by soap or another lathering agent" with
the "psychological and physiological impact . . . as one experiences an ultimate release of a former 'unhealthy' or imbalanced, unwhole self" (Daniels
2016). Interpreted through the lens of whipping, Ehlers's body *enacts* the
lack of control of a white establishment that is incapable of taking note of
its own irrationality. Interpreted through the perspective of Africana diasporic spiritual thought, the performance is a means of reestablishing equilibrium and balance in a Danish public sphere that has drastically eschewed
the memory of slavery from its national narrative. In other words, as art
historian Joaquín Barriendos argues, in performing the violence of the
white master, in taking on the persona of whiteness, Ehlers's female brown
body comes to its audience as phantom, a specter that is in complete control of itself (Barriendos 2015). Ehlers is not an angry, uncontainable body
that seeks revenge. She is a body performing a lesson, one that teaches,
much as Hannah Arendt so controversially did in 1963, of the "banality of
evil," how easy it is for violence to become repeatable and exponential. And
at the same time, her practice is one that seeks balance and healing. Ehlers's
pedagogy is one that patiently endures the emotional labor of explaining to
the ignorant majority how Enlightenment ideals that purport a more
democratic human order in fact inculcate a rigid and irrevocable violent
racial order.

The importance of place as regards notably the production of a performance piece becomes apparent when thinking of Ehlers's *Whip It Good*
alongside Guérédrat and Tauliaut's *At the Stardust Café*. Ehlers performs her
piece, in which she whips the canvas, before and alongside an audience that
is predominantly Danish; and she stages the whipping of the statues in a
historical Danish building, built explicitly with profits from a Danish colonial history in the Caribbean. The context then is a northern European
nation-state, in which the citizens are even less aware of Denmark's role

in a contemporary racial order than are, say, French or U.S.-American citizens.[10] In contrast, Guérédrat and Tauliaut's *At the Stardust Café* presents a performance whose intertexuality to slavery is less explicit than Ehlers's. In fact, it is the café-goers who read the two figures as not-quite-Catholic angels but closer to those ancestors-turned-angels who since the Middle Passage inhabit the depths of the Atlantic. Similarly, when Guérédrat and Tauliaut don the same integral bodysuits in Flatbush (Brooklyn, New York City), the reaction is completely different, but their performance solicits an equally gentle reaction, one that slows the passersby into the lull of the two figures' quiet patience for each other and for their surroundings.

Glissant's notion of opacity is perhaps the most appropriate articulation of how as conscious beings we are obligated to relate to one another and to our surroundings, and that this relation, is necessarily in the mode of "the Tragic." Alexandre Leupin, writing in 2016, comments on Glissant's notion of opacity in Glissant's *Poétique II*, published in 1997: "l'opacité, la résistance de l'autre, est fondamentale de sa connaissance; que seulement dans l'opacité (le particulier) l'autre se trouve connaissable. Enfin, que le dévoilement est le principe même du Tragique" (Leupin 2016, 232; opacity, to resist the other, is fundamental to its process of knowledge; only in opacity [the particular] the other finds recognition for itself. In the end, that the unveiling is the principle of the Tragic). The tragedy need not be understood as violent. We must not expect that to live together, we need to understand one another. In many cases, we cannot and should not understand one another, nor is it pragmatically possible to empathize with one another's experiences. Rather, living together means that we accept one another's differences as different: that is, we accede to the fact that "the other," whoever that *other* is to *us*, however we position ourselves at any given moment, can be utterly opaque to us. That is, to be in Glissantian Relation, we must admit that at times, or even quite frequently, we can but be completely opaque to ourselves, to one another. Such opacity, such resistance to being normative can come across as soft, benign, outgoing—but it may also come off as angry, enraged, morose, pessimist—and how it comes off depends on our respective subjectivities. If it is of the latter register, such affects are not to be read as violence (especially to a "white" public-sphere sensibility), but rather as opacity. They are limits set for self-preservation and self-care; they are not aggressions. And the wisdom to understand them as such is the *pragmatics of patience* that allows Tauliaut to contemplate and produce models for solutions to ecological disaster; Guérédrat and Ehlers to control with extreme agility the affects that they elicit in those who interact with their performances; and Goudrouffe the confidence to photograph an image without "stealing" it.

Articulated yet differently, Ehlers's practice is just as patient as that of the Martinican artists, yet the analytic possibilities at the disposal of those scholars and audiences who choose to be in the presence of her work are much less informed by the ethics of a DOM intellectual history. Emily Sahakian, an expert of French Antillean DOM theater, explains that throughout the 1990s and early 2000s much analysis around Glissant's notion of opacity has wondered "to what extent can creolization be generalized beyond the Caribbean?" (Sahakian 2017, 21). With the sustained reflections on Glissant's work of the late J. Michael Dash, Celia Britton, Adlai Murdoch, and Alexander Leupin, but also with the word *opacity* as an ethical stance entering the lexicons of writers who are not Caribbean,[11] it becomes clear that opacity is increasingly understood as a means of thinking through the inevitability of differences, and it makes sense that its most avant-garde and agile practitioners are those who have grown up multigenerationally in its presence.

Performance arts scholar Soyica Diggs Colbert writes about "how artists imagine, use, and call forth performance practices to constitute racial identity and interrupt the dehumanization of black people," emphasizing the "possibilities and dangers that representations of black suffering provide" (Colbert 2017, 5). For Colbert, performance is constantly about "possibilities and dangers"; for Sahakian, performance constitutes the fact that "embodied knowledge is necessary to any effort to grasp the ethics of creolization" (Sahakian 2017, 205).

A *pragmatic aesthetics of patience* is one in which the geopolitical and socio-intellectual contexts are such that an artist may choose to engage in an agility of ethical and aesthetic practices that abrasively contest a stubborn, myopic white order; allow the seemingly common person to be a magnanimous philosopher; underscore black social death for a mostly ignorant and unrepentant white order; or delve into what it means to valorize the potentialities of black social death (Sexton 2011, 27). I do *not* argue that Guérédrat, Tauliaut, and Goudrouffe engage in an artistic practice that is more Black Optimist than Ehlers. Instead, I make the claim that the pragmatic circumstances are such that when practicing in the global North, audiences and critics, despite best intentions, employ, or are obligated to employ, rather limited discourses, discourses restricted by the public spheres in which they operate, ones regimented by the violent phenomenon of the "smug ignorance" of mostly white intellectuals (Essed and Hoving 2013, 1). Guadeloupe and Martinique are also oppressed by a white order, not always in the same way, but they offer intellectualisms, which allow the artist to come into contact with a more capacious set of circumstances with which to practice one's art.

What I am trying to suggest is that Guadeloupe and Martinique are spaces that have nurtured a black intellectual scene for centuries. What is most important, as U.S.-American based writer Ta-Nehisi Coates wrote in a letter to his son, is "we could—and must—fashion the way of our walk" (Coates 2015, 69). The performance staged, whether as bodily performance, as installation art, or as photographic image, must make it clear that opacity's "Tragedy" be palpable: again in Coates's words to his son, "I am sorry that I cannot make it okay. I am sorry that I cannot save you—but not that sorry. Part of me thinks that your very vulnerability brings you closer to the meaning of life, just as for others, the quest to believe oneself white divides them from it" (107). The "new" Antillean DOM arts scene, but also Ehlers's work, inscribes itself into a larger world space that understands that to be ethical means to hold "the Tragic" of Glissantian opacity close, neither to fetishize it, nor to lament it, but to honor its presence and the work it does to make us more compassionately aware one of the other—not necessarily with the goal of understanding one another but rather with the understanding that to live alongside one another we must become ever more comfortable with what it means to be different from one another. As such, Guérédrat, Tauliaut, and Goudrouffe create an art—and operate from an intellectual sphere—that allow an artist to practice, engage with, and gain attention for work that refuses the "conscripts" (Scott 2004, 1) of a global Northern space that corners "black diaspora artists" (Mercer 2016, 3) into being understood in certain ways. These artists' *pragmatism* is then to be constantly at once *local, translocal, national,* and *transnational,* incorporating but also reoperating notions of what and to whom aesthetic practice belongs, in such a way that they constantly hold themselves accountable to their own practice.

NOTES

1. The artists' respective websites are http://artincidence.fr/, http://henritauliaut .com/, and https://danielgoudrouffe.com/. For Jeannette Ehlers's work: http://jeannet teehlers.dk/.

2. See Benedicty-Kokken, "Raphaël Confiant and Jewishness, or the Fraught Landscapes of French, Martinican and Franco-Martinican Intellectualisms," in Sarah Phillips Casteel and Heidi Kaufman, eds., *Caribbean Jewish Crossings: Atlantic Literature and Theory* (publication expected in 2020–21).

3. See the forthcoming book by Kaiama L. Glover, *Disorderly Women: On Caribbean Community and the Ethics of Self-Regard* (Durham, NC: Duke University Press).

4. The notion of "thinking from" and "with," I owe to Wayne Modest, head of the Research Center for Material Culture at the Nationaal Museum van Wereldculturen in the Netherlands and professor of material culture and critical heritage studies in the faculty of humanities at the Vrije Universiteit, Amsterdam (VU). https://www.material culture.nl/en/research/labs/thinking.

5. I make these assertions based on conversations that I had with the artists and conversations to which I was privy on several occasions. The students whom I have had the privilege of learning from at the Division of Interdisciplinary Studies at the Center of Worker Education at the City College of New York have guided the conversations around the work of Guérédrat, Tauliaut, and Goudrouffe in ways that have led me to the terminology *pragmatic aesthetics of patience.* Former students whom I especially want to thank are Deborah Browne, Gabrielle Gallo, Jess Narvaez, Jessie Salfen, Wilfredo Taveras, and LaVoya Woods-Hofer. All of the facts included in this article have been confirmed with the artists in e-mail exchanges between May and August 2017. The conversations took place on three occasions: first, in March 2016, upon Guérédrat and Tauliaut's visit to my class at the City College of New York's Center for Worker Education (City University of New York); second, in September 2016, when Goudrouffe and Sophie Saint-Just visited New York from Williams College, where Saint-Just is assistant professor of Caribbean film and literature; and finally, in May 2017, when Goudrouffe and Saint-Just generously agreed to travel back to New York to participate and attend another event organized with Guérédrat and Tauliaut at the City College of New York. In May 2017, I interviewed Goudrouffe formally.

6. I draw on the Canadian model of "assymetrical federalism," negotiated principally by Quebec but also notably benefiting other provinces such as Alberta.

7. See, for example, Jacques Stephen Alexis's groundbreaking and by now canonical essay, "Haitian Marvelous Realism," based on a text he published in *Présence africaine* in 1956 titled "Du réalisme merveilleux des Haïtiens," as well as the speech of the same title that he delivered at the First International Conference of Black Writers and Artists at the Sorbonne in the same year.

8. Tauliaut explains that the iguana is a representational figure that encapsulates one of the "states" of their artist practices.

9. See Sibylle Fischer's discussion of Bruce Gilden's "book of photographs titled *Haiti*," published in 1996 based on photography captured in Haiti between 1984 and 1995: Fischer, "Haiti: Fantasies of Bare Life," originally published in *Small Axe* in 2007 and updated in Millery Polyné's *The Idea of Haiti: Rethinking Crisis and Development* (2011). For more general work on exceptionalizing narratives of Haitian bodies, see Kaiama L. Glover's "Flesh Like One's Own: Benign Denials of Legitimate Complaint" (2017) in *Public Culture*.

10. For work on the Danish participation in the slave trade, see Erik Göbel, *The Danish Slave Trade and Its Abolition* (Leiden: Brill, 2016). See also commemorations of "Transfer Day," when the U.S. Virgin Islands were "transferred" from Denmark to the United States on March 31, 1917: Vanessa K. Valdes, "Commemorating Transfer Day," *SX Salon*, October 2017, http://smallaxe.net/sxsalon/discussions/commemorating-1917 (accessed July 6, 2020).

11. Writers such as Leupin, whose academic specializations are medieval studies and later Lacanian psychoanalysis; Camerounian political philosopher Achille Mbembe, whose *Critique de la raison nègre* (2013), recently translated into English as *Critique of Black Reason*, significantly references and incorporates Glissantian theory; Eritrean-French writer Abdourahman Waberi's novels and essays; and Italo-Somali novelist Igiaba Scego, whose recent novel *Adua* (2015), translated into English in 2017, pay significant attention to Glissant's work and the notion of "opacity."

REFERENCES

Accilien, Cécile. 2007. *Just below South: Intercultural Performance in the Caribbean and the U.S. South*. Charlottesville: University of Virginia Press.

A Freak Show for S. By Annabel Guérédrat. Directed by Whitney V. Hunter. Performed by Annabel Guérédrat. Grace Exhibition Space, New York, Fall 2015 (created in 2010). https://vimeo.com/154473274.

Agard-Jones, Vanessa. 2012. "What the Sands Remember." *GLQ: A Journal of Lesbian and Gay Studies* 18, no. 2–3 (2012): 325–46.

———. 2013. "Bodies in the System." *Small Axe* 42: 182–92.

Alvarado, Leticia. 2015. "'What Comes after Loss?': Ana Mendieta after José." *Small Axe* 47: 104–110.

Arendt, Hannah. 1963. *Eichmann in Jerusalem: A Report on the Banality of Evil*. New York: Viking Press (1961, *New Yorker*).

Arts des Caraïbes-Amériques. 2020. "Daniel Goudrouffe." https://www.reseau-canope.fr/art-des-caraibes-ameriques/artistes/daniel-goudrouffe.html (accessed July 20, 2020).

Association internationale des critiques d'art. 2015. "Henri Tauliaut à la Biennale de La Havane." *Aica Caraïbe du Sud*, March 23. https://aica-sc.net/2015/03/23/henri-tauliaut-a-la-biennale-de-la-havane/.

At the Stardust Café (Au Stardust Café). Performed by Annabel Guérédrat and Henri Tau-liaut. Stardust Café, Le Moule, Guadeloupe. July 2015.

Barriendos, Joaquin. 2015. "Spectres of L'Ouverture. A Ghost Is Haunting Your Museum: The Ghost of the Black Copenhagen." *Emisférica* 12.1, Special issue titled *Rasanblaj*, guest edited by Gina Athena Ulysse. http://hemisphericinstitute.org/multimedio /ehler-eng/ (accessed July 26, 2017).

Barst, Kolo. 2010 (2004). "Péyi nou." *Lot bò so*. By Kolo Barst. Produced by Debs Music. Fort-de-France.

Beavers, Anthony F. 1995. "Introducing Levinas to Undergraduate Philosophers." http:// faculty.evansville.edu/tb2/PDFs/UndergradPhil.pdf (accessed July 16, 2017).

Beliso-De Jesús, Aisha M. 2015. *Electric Santería: Racial and Sexual Assemblages of Trans-national Religion*. New York: Columbia University Press.

Benedicty-Kokken, Alessandra. 2012. "'Towards an Intellectual History of Possession: Reading 'la crise' as a Textual Space in Vodou and André Breton's Haitian Lectures and *Nadja*." *Studies in Religion/Sciences Religieuses* 41, no. 2: 280–305.

———. 2016. "On 'Being Jewish', on 'Studying Haiti' . . . Herskovits, Métraux, Race, and Human Rights." *The Haiti Exception: Anthropology and the Predicament of Narrative*, edited by Alessandra Benedicty-Kokken et al., vol. 7, 52–73. Liverpool: Liverpool Uni-versity Press.

Bentley, Nancy. 2012. "Warped Conjunctions: Jacques Rancière and African American Twoness." In *American Literature's Aesthetic Dimensions*, edited by Christopher Looby and Cindy Weinstein. New York: Columbia University Press.

Bonilla, Yarimar. 2015. *Non-sovereign Futures*. Chicago: University of Chicago Press.

———. 2017. "Freedom, Sovereignty, and Other Entanglements." *Small Axe* 53: 201–208.

Brodwin, Paul. 2010. "Marginality and Subjectivity in the Haitian Diaspora." In *Haiti and the Haitian Diaspora in the Wider Caribbean*, edited by Philippe Zacaïr, 13–41. Tallahas-see: University Press of Florida.

Chamoiseau, Patrick, and Raphaël Confiant. 1999. *Lettres créoles*. Paris: Editions Gallimard.

Clitandre, Nadège. 2011. "Haitian Exceptionalism in the Caribbean and the Project of Rebuilding Haiti." *Journal of Haitian Studies* 17, no. 2: 146–153.

Coates, Ta-Nehisi. 2015. *Between the World and Me*. New York: Spiegel & Grau.

Colbert, Soyica Diggs. 2017. *Black Movements: Performance and Cultural Politics*. New Brunswick, NJ: Rutgers University Press.

Csikszentmihalyi, Mihaly. 2014. *Flow and the Foundations of Positive Psychology: The Col-lected Works of Mihaly Csikszentmihalyi*. Dordrecht: Springer.

Cultures Outre Mer. n.d. "Henri Tauliaut: Artiste du bio-art et des arts numériques." Cultures Outre Mer. http://www.cultures-outre-mer.com/fr/artistes/henri-tauliaut (accessed July 18, 2017).

Danbolt, Mathias. 2016. "Striking Reverberations. Beating Back the Unfinished History of the Colonial Aesthetic in Jeannette Ehlers' 'Whip It Good.'" In *Say It Loud! Jean-nette Ehlers*, edited by Lotte Løvholm, 2–9. Copenhagen: Forlaget Nemo.

Daniels, Kyrah Malika. 2016. "The Coolness of Cleansing: Sacred Waters, Medicinal Plants and Ritual Baths of Haiti and Peru." *ReVista: Harvard Review of Latin America*. https://revista.drclas.harvard.edu/book/coolness-cleansing-sacred-waters-medicinal -plants-and-ritual-baths-haiti-and-peru-0.

Dobie, Madeleine. 2010. *Trading Places: Colonization and Slavery in Eighteenth-Century French Culture*. Ithaca: Cornell University Press.

Erwitt, Elliott. 2017. *Family Photographs, Curators' Comments*. In *Magnum Manifesto*, curated by Clément Chéroux, Clara Bouveresse, and Pauline Vermare. International Center of Photography, New York, May 26–September 3.

Escobar, Arturo. 2020. *Pluriversal Politics: The Real and the Possible*. Durham, NC: Duke University Press.

Essed, Philomena, and Isabel Hoving. 2013. "Innocence, Smug Ignorance, Resentment: An Introduction to Dutch Racism." *Thamyris/Intersecting* 9–30.

Fanon, Frantz. 1952. *Peau noire, masques blancs*. Paris: Editions du Seuil, 1952.

———.1961. *Les damnés de la terre*. Paris: Éditions François Maspero, avec préface de Jean-Paul Sartre en 1968, et puis chez Éditions Gallimard à partir de 1991.

Ferrando, Francesca. 2012. "Towards a Posthumanist Methodology. A Statement." *FRAME: Tijdschrift voor litteratuurwetenschap* 25, no. 1: 9–18.

Fischer, Sibylle. 2007. "Haiti: Fantasies of Bare Life." *Small Axe: A Caribbean Journal of Criticism* 23: 1–15.

Fisek, Emine. 2017. *Aesthetic Citizenship: Immigration and Theater in Twenty-First-Century Paris*. Evanston IL: Northwestern University Press.

Flandrin, Antoine. 2015. *Cinq choses à savoir sur le Mémorial ACTe, en Guadeloupe*, May 10. http://www.lemonde.fr/afrique/article/2015/05/10/cinq-choses-a-savoir-sur-le-memorial-acte-en-guadeloupe_4630682_3212.html.

Flaugh, Christian. 2013. "Crossings and Complexities of Gender in Guadeloupe and Martinique: Reflections on French Caribbean Expressions." *L'Esprit Créateur* 53, no. 1 (Spring): 45–59.

Glissant, Edouard. 1989. *Caribbean Discourse: Selected Essays*, edited by J. Michael Dash. Charlottesville: University of Virginia Press.

———. 1997 (1981). *Le discours antillais*. Paris: Editions Gallimard.

Glover, Kaiama L. 2012. "New Narratives of Haiti; or, How to Empathize with a Zombie." *Small Axe: A Caribbean Journal of Criticism* 16: 199–207.

———. 2017. "Flesh Like One's Own: Benign Denials of Legitimate Complaint." *Public Culture* 29, no. 2.82: 235–260.

———. In press. *Disorderly Women: On Caribbean Community and the Ethics of Self-Regard*. Durham, NC: Duke University Press.

Gøbel, Erik. 2016. *The Danish Slave Trade and Its Abolition*. Boston: Brill.

Gordon, Lewis R. 2017. "Black Aesthetics, Black Value." *Public Culture* 30, no. 1: 19–34.

Guadeloupe Karukera Visit. n.d. "LE MOULE la grande ville de l'Est de la Grande Terre." http://www.guadeloupe-karukeravisit.fr/la-grande-terre/la-cote-est/le-moule/ (accessed July 16, 2017).

Gundaker, Grey. 1998. *Signs of Diaspora. Diaspora of Signs*. Oxford: Oxford University Press.

Hammond, Charlotte. 2018. *Entangled Otherness: Cross-gender Fabrications in the Francophone Caribbean*. Liverpool: Liverpool University Press.

Horn, Maja. 2015. "José E. Munoz's Critical Caribbean Crossroads." *Small Axe* 47: 78–84.

Hurbon, Laënnec. 1983. "Racisme et sous-produit du racisme: Immigré Haïtiens et Dominicain en Guadeloupe." *Les Temps Modernes* 39: 441–442.

Iguanesque Wedding Parade #3 [Parade Nuptiale Ignanesque #3]. 2016. By Henri Tauliaut and Annabel Guérédrat. Performed by Henri Tauliaut and Annabel Guérédrat. Flatbush, Brooklyn, New York, March.

Jackson, Zakiyyah Iman. 2020. *Becoming Human: Matter and Meaning in an Antiblack World*. New York: New York University Press.

Josephs, Kelly Baker. 2013. "Beyond Geography, Past Time: Afrofuturism, The Rainmaker's Mistake, and Caribbean Studies." *Small Axe* 41: 135.

Lemarchand, René. 2009. *The Dynamics of Violence in Central Africa*. Philadelphia: University of Pennsylvania Press.

Leupin, Alexandre. 2016. *Édouard Glissant, philosophe: Héraclite et Hegel dans le Tout-Monde*. Paris: Hermann Éditeurs.

Lockward, Alanna. 2016. "Striving for Self-Education, Consciousness and Knowledge. A Dialogue with Jeannette Ehlers." In *Say It Loud! Jeannette Ehlers*, edited by Lotte Løvholm, 10–13. Copenhagen: Forlaget Nemo.

Mbembe, Achille. 2001. *On the Postcolony*. Berkeley: University of California Press.

Mercer, Kobena. 2016. *Travel & See: Black Diaspora Art Practices since the 1980s*. Durham, NC: Duke University Press.

Moatamri, Ines. 2007. "Poétique de la Relation: Amina Saïd et Edouard Glissant." *Trans-Revue de littérature générale et comparée* 3 (February 4). https://trans.revues.org /180#bodyftn23.

Munoz, José Esteban. 1999. *Disidentifications: Queers of Color and the Performance of Politics*. Minneapolis: University of Minnesota Press.

Murdoch, H. Adlai. 2017. "Créolité, Creolization, and Contemporary Caribbean Culture." *Small Axe* 52: 180–198.

Murdoch, H. Adlai, and Anne Donadey. 2005. *Postcolonial Theory and Francophone Literary Studies*. Gainesville: University of Florida Press.

Nixon, Rob. 2011. *Slow Violence and the Environmentalism of the Poor*. Cambridge, MA: Harvard University Press.

Obszyński, Michal. 2016. *Manifestes et programmes littéraires aux Caraïbes francophones: En/jeux idéologiques et poétiques*. Boston: Brill.

Polyné, Millery. 2013. *The Idea of Haiti: Rethinking Crisis and Development*. Minneapolis: University of Minnesota Press.

Rey, Terry, and Alex Stepick. 2013. *Crossing the Water and Keeping the Faith: Haitian Religion in Miami*. New York: NYU Press.

Sahakian, Emily. 2017. *Staging Creolization: Women's Theater and Performance from the French Caribbean*. Charlottesville: University of Virginia Press.

Santigold. 2008. "L.E.S. Artistes." By Santogold. Released by Downtown Records/ Atlantic Records.

Scott, David. 2004. *Conscripts of Modernity: The Tragedy of Colonial Enlightenment*. Durham, NC: Duke University Press.

Sexton, Jared. 2011. "The Social Life of Social Death: On Afro-Pessimism and Black Optimism." *InTensions* 5: 1–47.

Shadows of Frida I. 2016. By Annabel Guérédrat. Directed and filmed by Henri Tauliaut; montage by Henri Tauliaut. Performed by Annabel Guérédrat and Gladys Gambie. Mediathèque, Trois-Ilets, Martinique, June.

Taylor, Paul C. 2016. *Black Is Beautiful: A Philosophy of Black Aesthetics*. Chichester, UK: John Wiley & Sons.

Tinsley, Omise'eke Natasha. 2010. *Thiefing Sugar: Eroticism between Women in Caribbean Literature*. Durham, NC: Duke University Press.

Titans. 2015. By Annabel Guérédrat and Henri Tauliaut. Performed by Annabel Guérédrat and Henri Tauliaut. The Gardel Sugar Factory, Le Moule, Guadeloupe, September 3. https://www.youtube.com/watch?v=E7n36L4-9xk.

Trouillot, Michel-Rolph. 2003. *Global Transformations: Anthropology and the Modern World*. New York: Palgrave Macmillan.

Vázquez, Rolando. 2016. "Against Oblivion." In *Say It Loud! Jeannette Ehlers*, edited by Lotte Løvholm. Copenhagen: Forlaget Nemo.

Wekker, Gloria. 2016. *White Innocence: Paradoxes of Colonialism and Race*. Durham, NC: Duke University Press.

Whip It Good. 2013. By Jeannette Ehlers. Performed by Jeannette Ehlers. Ballhaus Naunynstrasse, Berlin. With 2014 video piece at Vestindisk Pakhus ("The West Indian Warehouse") in Copenhagen.

Zacaïr, Philippe. 2010. "The Trial of Ibo Simon: Popular Media and Anti-Haitian Violence in Guadeloupe." In *Haiti and the Haitian Diaspora in the Wider Diaspora*, edited by Philippe Zacaïr, 42–57. Tallahassee: University Press of Florida.

9

Buskando nos mes

GIVING MEANING TO NATIONAL
IDENTITY IN CURAÇAO, PAST
AND PRESENT

ROSE MARY ALLEN

Curaçao is a nonindependent Caribbean nation, an autonomous part of the Kingdom of the Netherlands, with a population that is ethnically fairly diverse. Like most Caribbean nations, race relations generally appear more relaxed, and the socioeconomic and political position of people of African descent seems on average better than in countries like the United States and Brazil. However, that does not mean that all is well, or clear. In the early twenty-first century, race, color, ethnicity, class, gender, and religion are relevant factors of social stratification in Curaçao. They are also controversial subjects of debate, and they intersect with concerns about cultural and national identity and identity construction. Identity still represents a challenge for Curaçao as it does for other Caribbean societies, albeit perhaps in different forms.

Like the rest of the region, Curaçao has been shaped historically by colonialism and slavery. Not so long ago, based on the stratification factors just mentioned, a large segment of the population was excluded from a broad range of civil and political rights and social benefits. Industrialization and modernization, induced by the arrival of an oil refinery in 1915, were later accompanied by a significant influx of immigrants who diversified the ethnic and cultural fabric of the Curaçaoan society. The cultural dynamics that have evolved from the relationships between the various social groups, drawn from some 150 national origins, are complex and have influenced the ways in which Curaçaoans define and experience citizenship, belonging and identity (Allen 2017).

Curaçao tends to brand itself as an autonomous (internally self-governing) "country" that asserts a certain "indigeneity" or "Curaçaoanness" by distinguishing its culture from that of the Netherlands, but it also often parades its membership in the Kingdom of the Netherlands. The relationship with the Netherlands is ambivalent: sometimes it is seen as colonial, at other times it is seen as a safeguard against local corruption, crime, and poverty, and as a stepping-stone toward global citizenship (Allen 2010). This may reflect the duality of "the colonial other and the self" as expressed by Edouard Glissant, the late philosopher and poet from Martinique. He (1989) states that in a colonial situation, the colonial mother operates as both the other and the self. Recent constitutional reform in Curaçao has again fed the sometimes hidden but always present concerns of Curaçaoans about cultural and national identity, as the reform raised controversial issues such as Dutch budgetary supervision and Dutch-derived legislation on "ethical" matters (same-sex marriage, euthanasia).

Identities in Curaçao seem flexible and situational rather than fixed, as people may hold on to several identity categories at the same time, and move in and out of them in complex and dynamic ways, as they attempt to balance idealism and pragmatism. In addition to claiming to be both Curaçaoan and Dutch-European, Curaçaoans may under varying circumstances also claim to be Antillean, Caribbean, or Latin American. Globalization, which is often seen as a threat to national identities and cultures, makes Curaçao's search for greater self-determination and self-governance seem more paradoxical. But globalization has also introduced new dimensions to the concept of identity, and these are fervently debated (nowadays also on social media), continually negotiated, and at times convincingly claimed (Allen 2017).

The complex, multilayered, and multidimensional situation surrounding identity in Curaçao may seem to involve contradictory thoughts and behaviors, and has even led some local scholars to speak of an identity crisis. The issues at play and the ways in which Curaçaoans construct identities may not always be clear to outsiders or even to insiders. The complexity of the matter seems to invite further scholarly investigation, including comparison with the wider Caribbean.

The objective of this chapter is to discuss how concerns over identity and national belonging have been addressed in Curaçao in the twentieth and early twenty-first century, and how Curaçao compares to the rest of the region in addressing these concerns. The main questions are, How do certain identity concerns that are latent in a society become foregrounded from time to time as part of the public discourse? What type of historical events may enable the debate on these contested issues to flare up? I will highlight two milestones in Curaçao's recent history through which identity issues clearly (re)entered the national discourse. These are the labor uprising and social movement of May 30, 1969, and the change in Curaçao's constitutional status on October 10, 2010. I also place the search for identity in Curaçao within a wider Caribbean context. The purpose of this chapter is neither to conduct a comprehensive analysis nor to provide conclusive answers, but to raise issues and contribute to discussion on a topic that has great potential for further study.

"Nibbling" on Coloniality in Curaçao in the Twentieth Century

Cases of violent internal conflict sometimes confront societies with identity issues that have not reached some measure of closure. Hernandez (2014) sees "closure" as effectively establishing structural arrangements of social interaction that empower parties to cope with their differences.[1] There are moments in Curaçao's history when its people have contested, sometimes violently, sometimes less so, the unequal power relationships in the society that are a part of its colonial legacy. One of these contestations in the twentieth century was the social uprising of May 30, 1969, popularly known simply by its date as "Trinta di Mei." At first glance it seemed to be a labor strike that got out of hand. The strike was directly caused by the fact that on that day a few workers of CPIM oil refinery[2] were laid off and sent to work for one of the refinery's contractors at a lower wage. This action caused an outburst among the workers; the strike grew in size and soon involved other protestors. What began as struggle for higher wages turned into a demand for recognition and respect. It was more than an ordinary labor conflict as it also became a social movement in which structural imbalances based on racial, ethnic, and class hierarchies in the society were questioned.

Since its establishment in the second decade of the twentieth century, the CPIM oil refinery had gradually transformed the Curaçaoan society, as the arrival of large numbers of labor immigrants of different ethnic and cultural backgrounds led to rapid and significant population growth. The labor immigrants came from South Asia, China, the Middle East, Portugal, Suriname, and the English-speaking Caribbean, as well as the Netherlands. Each of these immigrant groups added new degrees of diversity and complexity to the already multicultural fabric of the Curaçaoan society. Curaçao, which did not have a mono-crop, plantation-based, agricultural production economy like the rest of Caribbean but rather a trade-oriented economy, became one of the first industrialized economies in the region. It became a society in which the working class was no longer solely dependent upon the old elites (estate-owners and merchants) for employment, but could find work at the oil refinery in large numbers. Important to state is that some of these immigrants, such as the British West Indians and the Surinamese, had labor movement experience. Based on their connection to labor activism in their country of birth or elsewhere, they became quite influential in the labor movement in Curaçao. Some who never returned to their home country eventually came to occupy important leadership positions in Curaçao's labor unions.

These economic, demographic, and sociocultural transformations eventually also led to political changes. Already in the 1940s there was increased political consciousness, characterized by nationalism expressed particularly in popular literature and songs. Evidence of the growing self-awareness and resistance on the island starting in the 1940s is provided by historian Margo Groenewoud in her recent dissertation (2017). Activism contributed to the attainment of universal adult suffrage in 1949, which in turn was an essential step toward translating political consciousness into a struggle for more political autonomy for the island vis-à-vis the Netherlands. However, the acquired right to exercise citizenship through the general franchise could not erase social inequality. Ethnicity, color, and race continued to determine many aspects of life in Curaçao, even after the island, as part of the Netherlands Antilles federation, obtained autonomy or internal self-governance in 1954 (Roe 2016).[3]

The 1960s and 1970s were again relatively turbulent years as people in Curaçao no longer wanted to abide by the persisting social divisions and contradictions of the old society and began to more openly claim their rightful place. One approach was to raise awareness about the slave revolt of August 17, 1795, when the enslaved on the western part of the island, under the leadership of Tula and others, had started a revolt against their owners and demanded freedom. It was the biggest slave revolt in the island's history in terms of the number of enslaved involved, the number of days that the revolt took to be quelled, and its transnational links with the independence struggles of Haiti and Venezuela.

Commemorating the slave revolt was viewed at the time (the 1960s) as an act against the establishment, and it can be seen as an act of anticolonialism or as countering what Gloria Wekker (2016), following Edward Said, has called the "cultural archive" of colonialism. Already in the 1950s, an author, Pierre Lauffer, wanted to have the revolt and its leaders recognized.[4] In the 1960s the demands became more intense and more widespread, as shown by the following case study, based on a newspaper article from 1967, supplemented by an interview of mine with one of the activists in 1995 (Allen 1996).

Case Study

On July 26, 1967, a few young people went to the monument at the place called Rif, where the remains of Tula and the other leaders of the largest slave revolt in Curaçao in 1795 were thrown into the sea after their execution in 1795.[5] At this site, the young people held a commemorative meeting. Even though they meant well, the fact that they chose July 26[6] and not August 17 indicates some lack of historical knowledge. During an interview in 1995 with Andechi Albert, who was one of the persons giving a speech on that day, he acknowledged this fact. He attributed his ignorance to the deficiency of the educational system, which at the time did not pay attention to that aspect of history. He also blamed this ignorance of historical knowledge on colonialism.[7] In his 1967 speech, Albert emphasized the effects of colonialism on the mind of the people when he posed the following question to the crowd: "Why are our schools still called 'Peter Stuyvesant' or 'William the Silent'?"[8] The crowd shouted in unison: "Because we still live under colonialism and have a colonized mind."[9] Along with the reproach of colonialism came an emphasis on identity, as parallels were drawn between the new society that young people wanted to construct and the one that Tula had already envisioned in 1795, based on the ideas of liberty, equality, and fraternity.[10]

In a radio interview in 1983, Richard Hooi (1950–2017), who had been a member of the nongovernmental organization (NGO) called Komishon 17 di ougùstùs (17th of August Commission), recalled that a small group of people used to commemorate the 1795 slave revolt in the 1960s and early 1970s and that each year a large police contingent would be present at the place of commemoration.[11] Someone else who remembers those meetings is Stanley Brown, who in the late 1960s published a magazine named *Vitó* dedicated to exposing injustices in the society. He became one of the main players of Trinta di Mei, the labor strike and social movement of May 30, 1969 (Oostindie, 1999).

As mentioned earlier, Trinta di Mei was the principal expression of protest against the unequal power structure of the Curaçao society in the second half of the twentieth century. The sociologist René A. Römer signals the racial undertones of this event by pointing to certain aggressive behavior that was directed at white Curaçaoans and non-Curaçaoans (Römer 1979, 116). A poem titled "Tata makamba" (Father is a Dutchman) by Heske Levissin, published in 1974, five years after Trinta di Mei, shows how white Curaçaoans experienced the uprising. He wrote: "You left holes in Punda [town], and you planted hatred instead of respect. How dare you tell me that you alone are *Yu di Kòrsou* [Curaçaoan]. Because I was born white, does that mean that I cannot be *Yu di Korsou?*"[12] It is known from oral history that during Trinta di Mei, white creole Curaçaoans would try to differentiate themselves from non-Curaçaoan whites from the Dutch metropole and identify themselves as Curaçaoan by stressing the fact that they spoke the local Creole language, Papiamentu.

The existence of color- and race-based tensions in 1960s Curaçao was also corroborated by the American sociologists William Anderson and Russell Dynes, who conducted research locally in the aftermath of the uprising. In their report of findings, *The Organizational and Political Transformation of a Social Movement: A Study of the 30th of May Movement in Curaçao* (1973), they stated that the islands of the Netherlands Antilles at the time were still marked by cultural, racial, and economic strains. They emphasized that a large part of the population of African descent was still underrepresented in skilled labor and professional occupations. In terms of identity, many people continued to measure themselves by Dutch norms and were more likely to perceive themselves as failures than to develop and embrace an Antillean culture and identity that would lead to self-respect and to overcoming the legacies of colonialism and slavery (Anderson and Dynes 1973, 48). Their findings confirm the analysis of internalized standards of self-denial, rootlessness, and a conflicted sense of identity among Afro-Curaçaoans in Alejandro Paula's seminal publication *From Objective to Subjective Social Barriers* (Paula 1967, 31–32). Paula (1937–2018) has been one of the leading black intellectuals on the island, focusing on the subservient consciousness of the Afro-Curaçaoans.

Trinta di Mei is generally recognized as an important turning point in Curaçaoan history. The younger generations in particular played an important role. They were the ones who challenged the traditional beliefs still upheld by older generations and tried to forge a new consciousness. Ironically, most of the protagonists were intellectuals who had come back from the Netherlands with ideas that seemed radical for the Curaçaoan society of the time. They had been shaped by an experience of more overt racism in the Netherlands. The following excerpt from an interview I conducted in 1989 with the late Amos Nita testifies to the role of the younger generations in Trinta di Mei. Amos Nita and his brother Amador Nita (1921–1970), who died in the armor as minister of social affairs and public health, were among the principal leaders of Frente Obrero i Liberashon Trinta di Mei, a worker-based political party established immediately after Trinta di Mei.

Amos Nita argues in retrospect: "In the 1960s there was a lot of tension in the society. Our eyes slowly opened. When you turned your television on, you would never see someone of your own color. People carried a lot of hatred within themselves. Young people in those days were very critical and would open their mouth and protest against social injustice. They had character. Nowadays [1989] they have given them 'base' [crack] to shut their mouth. They have made them stupid, and they are now fighting where they shouldn't be fighting."[13] The late 1960s and the 1970s saw the rise of several organizations in Curaçao that drew attention to Afro-Curaçaoan history and culture. These organizations advocated for the recognition and equitable inclusion of black Curaçaoans in all sectors of the society. Culture and its expression through the arts (literature, theater, painting) were very important in their discourse. Examples of such organizations are the Fundashon Identidat Antiano (Foundation for Antillean Identity) led by Alejandro Paula and the Movementu 17-8-1795 (August 17, 1795, Movement), both established in 1968,[14] and the Fundashon Tula (Tula Foundation), established in 1974 by Guillermo Rosario. They aimed at forging a decolonized self-image, shaped by a shared historical struggle against slavery and racism by Afro-Curaçaoans in particular. Slogans such as "Ta di nos e ta" (It's our thing) and "Awor ta nos ta manda" (Now it's our turn to rule) showed the longing for recognition, self-pride, and self-confidence. It was through the struggles of these civil society organizations that after 1969 national symbols such as Curaçao's anthem and flag were officially instituted. As mentioned, in 1984 the government finally recognized the slave revolt of August 17, 1795, by proclaiming August 17 as the Day of the Struggle for Freedom.[15] And much later again, in 2010, exactly 215 years after the slave revolt, Tula, the leader of the slave revolt, was declared a national hero and received absolution posthumously.

These events show that Trinta di Mei brought about a more positive disposition toward the explicit recognition, inclusion, and advancement of the Afro-Curaçaoan as part of the island nation of Curaçao. However, attitudes about Trinta di Mei tend to be ambivalent. On one hand, as an openly race-based conflict, it is seen as a momentum of the reinforcement of Afro-Curaçaoan identity that produced societal changes for this particular group that were long overdue. On the other hand, it is also viewed more negatively as an event that involved an eruption of societal discontent, that halted economic development, as well as something that should never happen again (Oostindie 1999). This ambiguity, which might appear to be a characteristic of Curaçao, influenced the end results of the struggles of the 1960s and 1970s.

In the 1980s and 1990s, the topic of identity was less prominently present in the public discourse, but it resurfaced in the first decade of the new millennium.

Giving Meaning to National Identity in Curaçao in the Twenty-First Century

At the start of the twenty-first century, when most Caribbean countries had long left their colonial past behind and some were already preparing to celebrate fifty years of independence, Curaçao and the other four islands comprising the Netherlands Antilles were preparing for constitutional change. Through a series of referendums held during the 2000s, four of these five islands voted to change the constitutional status that had defined the federation of the Netherlands Antilles since 1954.[16] The issue was not so much independence from the Netherlands but whether the five islands should remain together or should split up, each obtaining a more direct link with the mother country. It is within this context of constitutional reform that identity issues flared up again in Curaçao. This development underlines the idea that cultural and national identities are not predetermined and fixed but are influenced by sociohistorical events, as several studies by Stuart Hall have shown.

The change in constitutional status eventually came into effect on October 10, 2010. On that day, the Netherlands Antilles federation ceased to exist, and Curaçao became an internally self-governing entity or "country" within the Kingdom of the Netherlands, with direct ties to the Netherlands. The change, popularly known by its date as "10-10-10," was preceded by much conflict and division, as illustrated by multiple public discussions and demonstrations. Much of these focused on the 2006 *Slotverklaring* (Final Declaration), the framework document that outlined the future constitutional and administrative relationship of Curaçao with the Netherlands and with the other Dutch Caribbean islands. The signing of the Slotverklaring in late 2006 caused intense debate in Curaçao, which involved anxieties about not only autonomy and governance but also matters such as citizenship, belonging, identity, and culture. Several demonstrations were held during 2007–2008, making these anxieties visible and showing that constitutional reform and citizenship are not just about legal issues but encompass less tangible matters as well. The so-called *Si ku Nò* (Yes or No) referendum held in May 2009 gave expression to the internal divisions on the island, as 52 percent of the voters agreed to Curaçao's impending constitutional change while 48 percent rejected it.

Some of the protest questioned the role of the Netherlands as a colonial entity. The anthropologist Francio Guadeloupe (2009), commenting on the situation at the time, said that it seemed as if *Hulanda* (the Papiamentu word for the Netherlands) was constantly present in the discourse of Dutch Caribbean people. He used the term *zombie* to denominate this haunting presence of *Hulanda* (Guadeloupe 2009, 52–53). In Caribbean folklore a zombie is a ghost-like figure, which is invisible but can still be present in people's life and disturb them. Hidden behind the main discourse on reform were sub-discourses on the less tangible and often more emotionally laden issues of national belonging, cultural diversity, and difference, intermixed with race and ethnicity, as well as feelings of rootedness, togetherness, loyalty, and trust.

It could also be noticed that around 2010, the Curaçaoan search for identity and belonging and the struggle for inclusion and membership, rights and benefits, became increasingly politicized. Identity became a significant matter in political debate and conflict. The government saw 10-10-10 as a momentous juncture in the history of the island. Two examples may illustrate how the spirit of this new beginning became expressed in a more assertive politics of identity, again by focusing on the Afro-Curacaoan identity.

In September 2010, one month before the dissolution of the Netherlands Antilles, at the opening of the official cultural and tourism program *Kulturismo*, the then commissioner of culture of the island territory of Curaçao—who soon afterward became the first minister of culture of the new country of Curaçao—expressed that Curaçao's national identity is essentially rooted in Afro-Curaçaoan culture. In doing so, a government representative officially legitimized Curaçao's African heritage and openly introduced black ethnicity into the discourse on national identity. His statement was immediately met with sharply dissenting and often quite emotional responses that laid bare the racial divisions in the society. Here is one such response:

> Mister Rene Rosalia, the current commissioner and possibly the future minister of culture for the new country of Curaçao, has recently brought turmoil to the island with his statement about the cultural position of the Afro-*Yu di Kòrsou* [Afro-Curaçaoan]. [The statement involved] some perhaps not very well formulated thoughts of a rookie member of government, who must now defend his emphatic viewpoints. Rosalia, however, should revise his vision of the Afro-Curaçaoan as the dominant population group of the island, as soon as possible. Not because of incompleteness, discrimination, an urge to dominate, or lack of financial cultural capacity or the fact that, for example, Curaçao's traditional, popular form of musical expression, as can be heard for instance on the radio, has practically been decapitated by other, foreign expressions.[17]

The second example is a decision in December 2010, by the same person, now in his capacity as minister of culture, to replace the name of a public secondary school from Peter Stuyvesant College to Kolegio Alejandro Paula. The Dutchman Peter Stuyvesant (1610–1672) was seen as a symbol of

Curaçao's colonial heritage, while the earlier-mentioned Alejandro Paula was a well-recognized local Afro-Curaçaoan scholar. The name change included a switch from a school name in the Dutch language to one in Papiamentu. And Peter Stuyvesant's statue, which had always stood quite visibly near the entrance of the school, was removed from the school's premises. The whole affair provoked fierce reactions from people with an opposing opinion. Their discontent was expressed in several ways, primarily through opinion pieces on social media and in newspapers, which platforms sometimes reflected a certain racial, class, or political alignment. However, a large segment of the population also did not voice a clear opinion, and the affair did not become a step toward dismantling other monuments with a colonial connection or a debate on what should be government's policy on contested cultural heritage items.

The two examples just given, from the period just before and after 10-10-10, show how identity can become politicized. It looks like a dialectic response to a complex, contradiction-laden situation in which power interests dating back to colonialism intermix with new issues related to globalization. While certain administrations and population segments may at times more forcefully assert a sense of identity or a form of cultural nationalism, this has not led to a significant political nationalism that seeks a definite break away from the island's "coloniality of being." This may be an illustration of the effects of what Walter Mignolo (2007) calls the "coloniality of power, whereby culture, labor and intersubjective relations and knowledge production are defined well beyond the strict limits of colonial administrations."[18] On the other hand, it could be a case of pragmatism motivated by the idea of being a small society in a large globalizing world. There certainly seems to be a persistent ambivalence in Curaçao that complicates the understanding of national belonging.

Curaçao from a Wider Caribbean Perspective

In the rest of the Caribbean too, there is an ongoing dialogue and search to reconcile the competing and conflicting demands of difference and unity in the (re)construction of desired homogenous societies (Sheller 2007). Rex

Nettleford (2003) states that "cultural and national identity continued to be a persistent quest by the Jamaican and Caribbean people for place and purpose in a globalized world of continuous change." From Sheller and Nettleford it follows that former colonies like Jamaica, even after some fifty years of independence, continue to search for a comfortable balance between the processes of modernization and globalization on one hand and the affirmation of traditional culture and local production on the other.

For most Caribbean nations, to greater or lesser extent, the construction of national identity has been tied to the search for political independence or autonomy and economic self-sufficiency, development, or survival (Hall 1995; Nettleford 2003). This may appear not to be the case for Curaçao, but as mentioned, there has been a search for self-realization and a process of self-affirmation within the colonial context. The French Antilles have received some attention in Curaçao from both those in favor and those against a stronger grip of the Netherlands on Curaçao. Some point to the social benefits, facilities, and (perceived) economic success of the French Antilles relative to independent Caribbean countries. Others feel that the inhabitants of the French Antilles are second-class French citizens and point to capital repatriation, limited indigenous business ownership, and high unemployment. H. Adlai Murdoch (2008, 258) states that the people of the French Caribbean have become the "inheritors of a double perspective, marking a transatlantic duality of location that increasingly separated them both from their politically independent Anglophone Caribbean counterparts and from the social and cultural materialities of the metropole, to whom they remain inexplicably linked in a complex symbiosis of contentious subordination." Murdoch's statement would seem to apply to the relative disappointment experienced by Bonaire, Saint Eustatius, and Saba after October 10, 2010, when they became overseas municipalities of the Netherlands and came to be referred to as "the Caribbean Netherlands."[19]

Maintaining a relationship with the European metropole is not as clearcut for Curaçao as it may seem for the French Antilles. According to Ellen M. Schnepel (2004), the political assimilation of the French Antilles with France in 1946 was not an abrupt or unexpected modification of their constitutional status, but rather a logical culmination of a centuries-long process of progressive incorporation into the political and legal framework of the French state—a process that had begun with the abolition of slavery in 1848. In contrast, scholars have observed that there is a wide cultural divide between the Netherlands and its Caribbean colonies.

As one illustration of this cultural divide, Oostindie (1996) points to the fact that Papiamentu is the lingua franca in Curaçao, even among the local, creole Dutch who have been present on the island for many generations. Indeed, Curaçaoans take pride in the fact that Papiamentu, unlike the creole languages of most other colonized nations, is not derived primarily from the language of the mother country but from Portuguese, Spanish, African, and Amerindian languages and some English, in addition to Dutch. Papiamentu has always been considered a key symbol of Curaçaoan nationhood, with its long history of being spoken by all social classes and ethnic groups, which also sets it apart from most other creole languages in the Caribbean (Römer 1974). Documents from the eighteenth and nineteenth centuries show that Papiamentu was already spoken by the local, creole Dutch in their communication with the local Sephardic Jews and with the enslaved and free African descendants. Linda Rupert (2012) studied the role of both the African and the Sephardic Jewish groups in the historical development of Papiamentu. Rupert and Alan Benjamin (2002) underscore that Papiamentu has become a key marker of a creolized Curaçaoan identity of which people are very proud. In the government's 2001 cultural policy, drafted by René Rosalia, titled "Rumbo pa independensia mental: 'Konosé bo historia i kultura pa bo konosé bo mes': Plan di maneho i akshon di kultura pa Kòrsou," Papiamentu appears as an important criterion for differentiating the in-group from the out-group, a role the language has always had. Papiamentu's stature was further legitimized in 2007 when it became one of the three official languages of Curaçao (together with Dutch and English).

However, the importance given to Papiamentu as a cultural signifier coexists oddly with a preference often extended to Dutch as the language of choice for upward social mobility. Many Curaçaoans still view the Dutch language as important cultural capital, beside English as today's global language of communication. A decades-long, ongoing discussion in Curaçao on whether and how to use Papiamentu as a language of instruction in the education system reflects some of the persistent paradoxes and challenges of national identity in Curaçao.

The selective preference for Dutch as social capital cannot be separated from the preference to remain within a Dutch constitutional framework. Even though there has always been some desire in Curaçao for independence, the outcome of the April 2005 referendum suggests that the percentage of people who want the island to remain a part of the Dutch Kingdom is quite high: 95 percent. The outcome confirms the results of opinion polls carried out in 1997–1998 and reported on by Oostindie and Verton (1998). More recent research by Wouter Veenendaal (2016) also illustrates the willingness of a majority of Curaçaoans to remain within the Kingdom of the Netherlands: only 14.4 percent of the population want to become completely independent.[20] Local nationalist groups explain that attitude as stemming from colonialism, ignorance, and a lack of agency. Others, such as Curaçao's Minister of Culture in 2011, point to the Dutch cultural influence in Curaçao, which he termed a "two-headed monster" as it is believed to be embodied by both Dutch expatriates and locals who have returned to the island after a period of residence in the Netherlands.[21]

That is not to say that there is no nationalism or no nation-building in Curaçao. There is; however, it is often not framed in anti-colonial discourse. For example, it may come packaged in government policies to unify "the people" under the banner of an assumed shared history and culture. Whereas in most nations, national symbols such as anthems and flags are (re)designed to meet the moment of decolonization and to stand as marks of independence, in Curaçao the institutionalization of national symbols went somewhat differently (Allen, 2017). For instance, an island's anthem was officially established on July 26, 1979, replacing the unofficial and outdated anthem that had been composed by a Dutch friar in celebration of the 1898 coronation of Queen Wilhelmina of the Netherlands.

The text of the new anthem includes words that are very common in anthems of independent states, expressing liberty, struggle, grandeur, pride, and patriotism. In 1984, the date of July 2 was institutionalized as the "Dia di Himno i Bandera di Kòrsou" (Hymn and Flag Day of Curaçao). July 2 was chosen to commemorate the day in 1951 on which the Island Legislative Council came together for the first time. Every year on July 2 citizens who have done extraordinary work for the community are conferred a national medal of merit. Since 2010 the government's nation-building agenda appears to promote solidarity, unity, cohesion, and patriotism based on an idealized and homogenized Curaçaoan cultural identity that seeks to embrace all inhabitants, both those with long historical roots on the island and those who are relative newcomers, as Natasha van der Dijs (2011) argues.

One term that attempts to describe societies in which the majority of the population wants to maintain constitutional ties with a Metropole is *extended statehood* (De Jong and Kruijt 2005). The essence of extended statehood is that people have chosen to remain under the dominion of a mother country. Consequently, one cannot speak of colonies or colonization because that presumes forced dominion. The concept of decolonization is also no longer seen as a process that should necessarily and ultimately lead to full independence, as was the general assumption following World War II. Extended statehood is portrayed as a very pragmatic way of dealing with long-term relationships of a colonial origin, which during the course of time may have taken on a variety of forms. Its proponents appear to use it to find ways in which former colonizer and formed colonized can come together to pursue mutual benefits.

However, the concept of extended statehood fails to consider the unequal power relationship that has endured since colonial times and that tends to be reinforced by the present global order. The term suggests equality within a system that from the outset has been unequal. That is why those who are opposed to it describe the situation instead as recolonization (Ansano 2012). Those who overlook the unequal power relationship are repeatedly surprised by certain actions of the metropole.[22] The concept of extended statehood also ignores the way in which the culture of the colonized nation is viewed within the multicultural constitutional arrangement and within the globalized setting. Generally, the Western powers will claim that certain values and norms to which they adhere are universal in the sense that all human beings should adhere to them. However, the way in which these values and norms are presented to their overseas territories continues to reflect the power differential between the constitutional partners.

Conclusion

In this chapter, I have looked at the ways in which Curaçao has addressed challenging issues related to cultural identity and national belonging in the twentieth and early twenty-first century. I have done so by examining in particular two milestones through which these latent issues prominently (re)entered the island's public discourse. The events that took place surrounding Trinta di Mei (the labor uprising and social movement of May 30, 1969) and 10-10-10 (the constitutional change of October 10, 2010) show that difficult, controversial, and often emotional issues of collective significance are bound to resurface from time to time if they are not addressed effectively and if some degree of closure is not achieved. The situation in Curaçao appears to reflect a certain ambivalence that ranges from asserting cultural nationalism to maintaining modern forms of political colonialism.

In closing I would like to give some suggestions for further research. First, ambivalence is a concept that needs to be understood better. Valuable theoretical tools to help us understand ambivalence in relation to identity may be provided by Stuart Hall's approach toward identity as something that is not fixed but constantly in a process of both "being" and "becoming," as well as by his critical analysis of how power and dominance and the resistance against them manifest themselves through the production of political consciousness.

Second, it would seem fruitful to compare the Curaçaoan search for identity with the cases of other nonindependent territories in the region, especially those where constitutional reform has also remained on the political agenda and may affect prevailing notions of identity and citizenship. Possibilities would include the former Dutch colony of Suriname, which became independent in 1975; the Dutch overseas municipality of Saint Eustatius, which since February 2018 is being administered by the central government of the Netherlands[23]; the Turks and Caicos Islands, where the United Kingdom suspended self-government between 2009 and 2012; the three French overseas departments where referendums on constitutional reform were held in 2003 and 2010; and Puerto Rico, where a consultative plebiscite was held in November 2012 and whose colonial relationship with the United States has strongly reentered the public debate in the aftermath of Hurricane Maria (September 2017).

Acknowledgment

I would like to thank Adlai Murdoch and Peter B. Jordens for their review and helpful comments.

NOTES

Buskando nos mes is Papiamentu (the lingua franca of Curaçao) for "searching for ourselves."

1. Ariel Hernandez, *Nation-Building and Identity Conflicts* (Wiesbaden: Springer Fachmedien Wiesbaden, 2014), https://doi.org/10.1007/978-3-658-05215-7_1.

2. The original name of the refinery, CPM (NV Curaçaoasche Petroleum Maatschappij), was changed to CPIM (Curaçaosche Petroleum Industrie Maatschappij) in 1925. Popularly it was always known simply as "Shell."

3. The various Dutch possessions in the Caribbean had always been grouped together in one way or another for the Netherlands' overseas governance purposes. "Netherlands Antilles" was the name of a Dutch-Caribbean federation of islands that existed between 1954 and 2010. With the entry into force of the *Statuut* [Charter] of the Kingdom of the Netherlands in 1954, the Netherlands Antilles became an autonomous partner within the Kingdom. At the time, the Netherlands Antilles federation consisted of Curaçao and five other Dutch Caribbean islands: Aruba, Bonaire, Saint Martin, Saint Eustatius, and Saba. The Kingdom further consisted of Suriname and of course the Netherlands.

4. Manuscript of the priest M. D. Latour called *Geschiedenis van R.K. Missie op de Nederlandse Antillen vanaf 1870* no. IV, 1950. See also "Ban Rapa Historia," *Nobo*, July 1, 1995.

5. August 17, 1795, marks a very important date in the history of Curaçao. Although the slave revolt that started on that day was ultimately not successful (slavery in the Dutch Caribbean was not abolished until 1863), the revolt had its impact on the society. The revolt led to laws regulating the quantity of food, clothing, and free time that the enslaved should receive from their masters. Lack of food and better treatment had been

among the driving forces behind the revolt, which today is known as one of the largest slave revolts in the history of the Dutch-governed islands of the Caribbean.

6. On July 26, 1499, the Spaniard Alonso de Ojeda first set foot on the island of Curaçao.

7. Interview by R. M. Allen with Andechi Albert, March 1995. See also interview in *Vito*, jaargang III, no. 5 (1967).

8. Peter Stuyvesant was a major Dutch figure in the early history of New York City. William I, Dutch Prince of Orange (1533–1584), was also known as William the Silent or Taciturn.

9. *Amigoe*, July 27, 1967.

10. *Amigoe*, July 27, 1967.

11. Interview by the Z-86 radio station, August 17, 1983. Richard Hooi could say this in 1983, one year before the Curaçaoan government recognized the slave revolt and proclaimed August 17, 1795, to be the Day of the Struggle for Freedom.

12. *Amigoe*, 1974.

13. Interview by R. M. Allen with Amos Nita, May 1989.

14. *Amigoe*, May 17, 1968.

15. It is called "Dia di Lucha pa Libertat." "Eilandsbesluit of August 7, 1984," in *Afkondigingsblad Curaçao*, no. 33 (1984).

16. The constellation of the Kingdom of the Netherlands has undergone several changes in the course of time. In 1975 Suriname became independent and left the Kingdom. In 1986 Aruba seceded from the Netherlands Antilles federation to become an autonomous country, still within the Kingdom. The five remaining islands of the Netherlands Antillean reached agreement with the Netherlands and one another on constitutional reform in 2006, leading to the restructuring of 2010 when Curaçao and Saint Martin each became an autonomous country within the Kingdom, while Bonaire, Saint Eustatius, and Saba each became overseas municipalities of the Netherlands. Hence, since 2010 the Kingdom consists of four partners: one independent country (the Netherlands), which includes three overseas Caribbean municipalities (Bonaire, Saint Eustatius, Saba), and three autonomous countries in the Caribbean (Aruba, Curaçao, Saint Martin).

17. Hitzig Bazur, "Kuantu Afro Kurasaleño tin anto? / Hoeveel Afro-Curaçaoënaars zijn er toch?," in *Caraïbisch Uitzicht*, October 1, 2010, https://werkgroepcaraibischeletteren .nl/kuantu-afro-kurasaleno-tin-antohoeveel-afro-curacaoenaars-zijn-er-toch.

18. Quoted in Nelson Maldonado-Torres, "On the Coloniality of Being: Contributions to the Development of a Concept," *Cultural Studies* 21, nos. 2 and 3 (2007), 243.

19. See articles in *Bonaire Nu*: "Drie jaar na staatkundige vernieuwing: Bonaire is verdeeld" (Three years after constitutional changes: Bonaire is divided); "10-10-10 bracht Bonaire niet de veranderingen waar men op hoopte" (10-10-10 did not bring Bonaire the changes it had hoped for).

20. W. Veenendaal, *Eindrapport CCC-Opinieonderzoek* (Leiden: KITLV, 2016). This is a report on an opinion survey carried out on the islands of Curaçao and Aruba between September 4 and December 1, 2015, by the KITLV/Royal Netherlands Institute of Southeast Asian and Caribbean Studies.

21. Freek van Beetz, *Het einde van de Antillen: Kroniek van een adviseur op Curaçao* (Delft: Eburon, 2013), 307.

22. For example, one source of much discussion and indignation in Curaçao is the recurring attempts by certain political parties in the Netherlands to get a bill of law approved in Dutch Parliament that would enable the Dutch government to deport Curaçaoans who have committed a felony or crime in the Netherlands. It is seen as evidence that there are different classes of Dutch nationality within the Kingdom, with Curaçaoans apparently counting as second-class Kingdom citizens.

23. See for example these two news articles: http://www.caribbean360.com/news/corruption-abuse-allegations-prompt-dutch-take-government-st-eustatius; "Dutch Government to Run 'Lawless' St Eustasius," *Jamaica Observer*, February 9, 2018, http://www.jamaicaobserver.com/business-report/dutch-government_to_run_%26%238216;law less%26%238217;_St_Eustatius_124679?profile=1056.

REFERENCES

Allen, Rose Mary. 1996. "In Search for Identity: An Analysis of the Commemoration of the Slave-Revolt of 17th of August 1795 in Curaçao." Paper presented at the Conference on Caribbean Culture Jamaica, March 3–6, Institute of Caribbean Studies in association with the faculty of social sciences, University of West Indies, Mona, Jamaica.

———. 2010. "The Complexity of National Identity Construction in Curaçao, Dutch Caribbean." *European Review of Latin American and Caribbean Studies / Revista Europea de Estudios Latinoamericanos y del Caribe* 89: 117–125.

———. 2017. *Reflecting in the Spirit of Stuart Hall on Cultural Identities within a Localized Form of Cultural Studies in Curaçao.* Paper presented at international conference on Stuart Hall, "Whither the Caribbean? Stuart Hall's Intellectual Legacy," June 1–3.

Anderson, William, and Russell Dynes. 1973. *The Organizational and Political Transformation of a Social Movement: A Study of the 30th of May Movement in Curaçao.* Working paper 39, Disaster Research Center. Columbus: The Ohio State University.

Ansano, R. 2012. "To Question Identity: Public Discourse and Transpersonal Ethics in Curacao." In *Multiplex Cultures and Citizenships: Multiple Perspectives on Language, Literature, Education and Society in the ABC-Islands and Beyond*, edited by Nicholas Faraclas, Ronald Severing, Christa Weijer, and Elisabeth Echteld, 55–67. Curaçao: Fundashon pa Planifikashon di Idioma (FPI), University of the Netherlands Antilles.

Benjamin, A. 2002. *Jews of the Dutch Caribbean. Exploring Ethnic Identity on Curaçao.* New York: Routledge.

Branche, J. 2008. *Race, Colonialism, and Social Transformation in Latin America and the Caribbean.* Gainesville: University Press of Florida.

Clarke, Richard. 2001. (Re)conceptualizing Caribbean Cultural Identity: Epistemic Shifts. *Caricom Perspective: Projections for the Future* 70.

De Jong, Lammert, and Dirk Kruijt, eds. 2005. *Extended Statehood in the Caribbean: Paradoxes of Quasi Colonialism, Local Autonomy, and Extended Statehood in the USA, French, Dutch, and British Caribbean.* Amsterdam: Rozenberg Publishers.

Eikrem, O. 1999. *Contested Identities. A Study of Ethnicity in Curaçao, the Netherlands Antilles.* PhD thesis, Norwegian University of Natural Science and Technology (NTNU).

Glissant, Edouard. 1989. *Caribbean Discourse: Selected Essays*, translated and with an introduction by J. Michael Dash. Charlottesville: University Press of Virginia.

Groenewoud, Margo. 2017. "'Nou koest, nou kalm': de ontwikkeling van de Curaçaose samenleving, 1915–1973: van koloniaal en kerkelijk gezag naar zelfbestuur en burgerschap." PhD diss., University of Leiden.

Guadeloupe, Francio. 2009. "De verdrijving van *Hulanda*. De Sabanen en hun toekomst als BES-eilanders." *Justitiële verkenningen* 35, no. 5: 48–62.

Hall, S. 1995. "Negotiating Caribbean Identities." *New Left Review* 209: 3–14.

Haviser, J. 1995. "Ethnic Diversity on Curaçao and the 'Yu di Korsow.'" Paper presented at the 23rd International Society for Intercultural Education Training and Research (SIETAR) Conference, June 5, Curaçao.

Hernandez, Ariel. 2014. *Nation-Building and Identity Conflicts: Facilitating the Mediation Process in Southern Philippines*. Wiesbaden: Springer VS.

Hoetink, H. 1958. *Het patroon van de oude Curaçaose samenleving. Een sociologische studie*. Assen: Van Gorcum (reprinted in 1987; Amsterdam: Emmering).

Mignolo, Walter D. 2007. "Introduction: Coloniality of Power and De-colonial Thinking." *Cultural Studies* 21, no. 2: 155–167.

Murdoch, H. Adlai. 2008. "Creole Counter Discourses and French Departmental Hegemony." In *Race, Colonialism, and Social Transformation in Latin America and the Caribbean*, edited by Jerome Branche, 257–277. Gainesville: University Press of Florida.

Nettleford, R. 2003. *Caribbean Cultural Identity: The Case of Jamaica; an Essay in Cultural Dynamics*. Kingston, Jamaica: Randle.

Oostindie, G. 1996. "Ethnicity, Nationalism and the Exodus: The Dutch Caribbean Predicament." In *Ethnicity in the Caribbean. Essays in Honor of Harry Hoetink*, edited by G. Oostindie, 206–231. London: Macmillan Caribbean.

———, ed. 1999. *Dromen en littekens: Dertig jaar na de Curaçaose revolte, 30 mei 1969*. Amsterdam: Amsterdam University Press.

Oostindie, G., and Peter Verton. 1998. *Ki sorto di Reino? / What Kind of Kingdom? Visies en verwachtingen van Antillianen en Arubanen omtrent het Koninkrijk*. The Hague: Sdu Uitgevers.

Paula, P. 1967. *From Objective to Subjective Social Barriers: A Historico-Philosophical Analysis of Certain Negative Attitudes among the Negroid Population of Curaçao*. Curaçao: De Curaçaosche Courant.

Reindersma, Tjioske. 2007. *Yu di Korsou of Makamba pretu? Thuisgevoel en identiteit van Curacaose terugkeerders*. Master's thesis, University of Utrecht.

Roe, Angela E. 2016. "The Sound of Silence: Ideology of National Identity and Racial Inequality in Contemporary Curaçao." *FIU Electronic Theses and Dissertations* 2590. http://digitalcommons.fiu.edu/etd/2590.

Römer, R. 1974. "Het 'wij' van de Curaçoënaar." *Kristòf* 1, no. 2: 49–60.

———. 1979. *Un pueblo na kaminda. Een sociologisch historische studie van de Curaçaose samenleving*. Zutphen, the Netherlands: De Walburg Pers.

Rosalia, R. 2001. *Rumbo pa independensia mental: "Konosé bo historia i kultura pa bo konosé bo mes": plan di maneho i akshon di kultura pa Kòrsou*. Willemstad, Curaçao.

Rupert, L. M. 2012. *Creolization and Contraband: Curaçao in the Early Modern Atlantic World*. Athens: University of Georgia Press.

Schnepel, Ellen M. 2004. *In Search of a National Identity: Creole and Politics in Guadeloupe*. Hamburg: Helmut Buske Verlag.

Sheller, Mimi. 2007. "Virtual Islands: Mobilities, Connectivity, and the New Caribbean Spatialities." *Small Axe: A Journal of Criticism*, no. 24: 16–33.

Van der Dijs, N. 2011. *The Nature of Ethnic Identity among the People of Curaçao*. Curaçao: Curaçaosche Courant, 2011.

Veenendaal, W. 2016. *Eindrapport CCC-Opinieonderzoek*. Leiden: KITLV.

Wekker, Gloria. 2016. *White Innocence: Paradoxes of Colonialism and Race*. Durham, NC: Duke University Press.

10

The Parallels and Paradoxes of Postcolonial Sovereignty Games in the Dutch and French Caribbean

THE END OF THE NETHERLANDS ANTILLES AND CONSTRUCTION OF NEW DUTCH CARIBBEAN POLITICAL ENTITIES AND RELATIONS

MICHAEL SHARPE

The 2009 protests in the French Caribbean overseas territories reflect a broader trend of negotiation of autonomy and integration in the non-sovereign world. This chapter attempts to understand twenty-first century neocolonial domination and the strategic use of "post-colonial sovereignty games" (Adler-Nissen and Gammeltoft-Hansen 2008; Adler-Nissen and Gad 2013) by using the case of the Netherlands and its dependent territories. The chapter focuses on developments around the dissolution of the Netherlands Antilles on October 10, 2010 ("10-10-10"), and its relative impacts, including both resistance and accommodation. The contemporary Kingdom of the Netherlands consists of the Netherlands and the Dutch Caribbean islands of Aruba, Curaçao, and Sint Maarten, while the Dutch Caribbean islands of Bonaire, Sint Eustatius, and Saba (BES) have been fully integrated as "public bodies" (*Openbare Lichamen*; similar to Dutch municipalities) of the Netherlands. Up until 10-10-10, the Dutch Kingdom was made up of the Netherlands in Europe and the Netherlands Antilles and Aruba in the Caribbean. The Netherlands Antilles was a federation of the islands of Curaçao, Bonaire, Saba, Sint Eustatius, and Sint Maarten, with Aruba having its own separate autonomous status. As was formerly the case with the Netherlands Antilles and Aruba, today Curaçao and Sint Maarten are Dutch "autonomous countries" with defense, foreign affairs, and nationality remaining the responsibility of the Dutch Kingdom. All Dutch Caribbean islanders hold Dutch and European Union (EU) citizenship with the permanent "right of abode" in the Netherlands. As in the case of the French Caribbean overseas territories and France, both scenarios of Dutch Caribbean integration and autonomy come with their own sets of opportunities and challenges but each reflects a "democratic deficit" vis-à-vis the Netherlands. This chapter discusses "post-colonial sovereignty games" in the way that autonomy and integration have been instrumentalized by the Dutch islands and the Netherlands with varying effects.

The Post-10-10-10 Kingdom of the Netherlands

Since 10-10-10, the transatlantic Kingdom of the Netherlands has transformed into a set of postcolonial non-sovereign autonomous and integrative island relationships with the Netherlands. The contemporary Dutch Kingdom consists of the Netherlands and Aruba, Curaçao, and Sint Maarten. Before October 10, 2010, the Dutch Kingdom comprised the Netherlands, the Netherlands Antilles, and Aruba. The Netherlands Antilles was a federation of the six small Caribbean islands of Curaçao (administrative capital), Bonaire, Saba, Sint Eustatius, Sint Maarten, and Aruba.[1] Aruba left the Netherlands Antilles in 1986 and officially gained "status aparte" as an autonomous country within the Dutch Kingdom. As a result of island referendums, the Netherlands Antilles was dissolved on October 10, 2010. The Netherlands took on much of the large Antillean debt in exchange for more financial supervision of Curaçao and Sint Maarten. Curaçao and Sint Maarten respectively gained autonomous statuses similar to Aruba with defense, foreign affairs, and nationality under the authority of the Dutch Kingdom. Similar to postwar French departmentalization of Martinique, Guadaloupe, French Guyana, and Réunion, Bonaire, Sint Eustatius, and Saba (BES) have been integrated into the metropole as Openbare Lichamen or "special municipalities" of the Netherlands and are now known as the Caribbean Netherlands. As inhabitants in the French Caribbean have French citizenship, French/ EU passports, and free mobility within the French republic and

EU, so also Dutch Caribbean islanders have Dutch citizenship and Dutch/ EU passports, and can, for the most part, freely travel, live, and work in the Netherlands and the EU. However, unlike the French Caribbean, which are integral parts of the EU as Outermost Regions, the Dutch islands are components of the EU's Overseas Countries and Territories (OCT). The distinction is that OCTs have exceptional status in EU law (*acquis*). Freedom of movement applies for EU citizens from OCTs to member states but not the other way around. Restrictions on freedom of movement between member states are prohibited, but within a member state, such as the Dutch Kingdom, movement can be regulated. Hence, migrants from the Dutch OTC must take an integration test (*inburgering*) in the Netherlands required of most non-Western foreigners (Kochenov 2011a, 50; 2011b, 213).

Rounding the Circle: The Costs and Benefits of Postcolonial Sovereignty Games

The concept of a "sovereignty game" is defined by Adler-Nissen and Gad as "two or more players who, in their interaction, make strategic claims about authority and responsibility with reference to a traditional 'either/or' concept of sovereignty" (2013, 10).[2] Postcolonial sovereignty is considered within a first round of twentieth century decolonization and independent states and a second round of decolonized but "still dependent new states" (Adler-Nissen and Gad 2013, 11). Putnam (1988) introduced the notion of two-level games to understand bargaining between states as well as negotiators and domestic constituencies. "Postcolonial sovereignty games" are said to be practiced in a triangular relationship between the EU, dependent territories as parts of the EU's Overseas Countries and Territories, and the former colonial metropole (Adler-Nissen and Gad 2013, 3, 11). The concept of "postcolonial sovereignty games" (Adler-Nissen and Gad 2013) is useful in attempting to understand the players, negotiations, and leverage politics of postcolonial Dutch Kingdom relations.

The advantages and disadvantages of non-sovereign status are often debated in terms of economic, political, ideological, and psychosocial arguments. Non-sovereignty has been characterized as "the best of all possible worlds" (Baldacchino 2006, 860) as well as "last" or "modern colonies"

(Aldrich and Connell 1998, 3; Grosfoguel 2003, 178, 180). Some point to peri-odic contestation (Ramos and Rivera 2001; Oostindie and Klinkers 2003; Clegg and Pantojas-Garcia 2009), and still others call for a revaluation of postcolonial non-sovereign arrangements as alternatives to independence (Hintjens 1995). This could incorporate non-sovereignty as a form of "extended statehood" (De Jong 2005a) or "partially independent territories" (Rezvani 2014, 20). Some arguments for non-sovereignty include general economic outperformance of their independent counterparts, higher stan-dards of living, better governance, security, territorial integrity and disas-ter relief, access to economic aid and preferential trade agreements, and metropolitan passports (Oostindie 2006, 611; Veenendaal 2015, 17; Rezvani 2014, 20). Other arguments against non-sovereignty involve external political interference, uncompetitive consumer economies, nearly exclu-sive metropolitan orientation, democratic deficits, brain drain, and ideo-logical and psychological identity issues (Oostindie 2006, 612; Veenendael 2015, 18; Aldrich and Connell 1998, 3). Some contend that non-sovereign territories satisfy geopolitical interests of metropolitan states (Miles 2001, 48; Ramos and Rivera 2001, 1–2). Rezvani surmises that "partially indepen-dent territories" can offer advantages to metropoles including cooperation, resources, geopolitical interests but even without these formal and unwrit-ten rules and "constitutional morality" defend the constitutional union (2014, 20, 119, 277). The advantages and disadvantages of postcolonial non-sovereignty in the Dutch and French Caribbean as well as the consisten-cies and departures inform this chapter on the ways in which the former Netherlands Antilles, Aruba, and the Netherlands negotiate power, author-ity, and legitimacy.

Argument

This chapter argues that there are several under-addressed similarities and differences between the Dutch and French non-sovereign Caribbean that reveal some of the parallels and paradoxes of non-sovereignty and add to the discussion of postcolonial sovereignty games. The post-1954 Kingdom of the Netherlands constitutes ongoing post-colonial sovereignty games

(Adler-Nissen and Gad, 2013) and a multilevel game among the Dutch Caribbean island governments and the Netherlands, island negotiators and domestic constituencies, as well as the EU and the international community.[3] The chapter begins with a discussion of the 1954 Charter for the Kingdom of the Netherlands, or *Statuut*, and the establishment of the Netherlands Antilles. This is followed by an analysis of the Curaçao 1969 uprising and Dutch military intervention and how these events influenced Suriname's 1975 independence. The preceding provides background for Aruba's 1986 secession as a prelude to an analysis of the 2010 dissolution of the Netherlands Antilles. In conclusion, there is an assessment of acts of resistance to rising costs of living, increased supervision and oversight, democratic deficits, and second-class citizenship, that are in some ways coextending the 2009 French Caribbean uprisings, in these latest iterations of Dutch Caribbean postcolonial sovereignty games.

Opening Dutch Postcolonial Sovereignty Games and the Contradictions of De Jure and De Facto Equality: 1954 Charter for the Kingdom of the Netherlands (*Statuut*)

The Dutch Empire initiated its exploits in the seventeenth century under the patronage of the Dutch East Indies Company and the Dutch West India Company; its reach included New Amsterdam (New York), Cape Coast (South Africa), Brazil, Caribbean islands, Suriname, and the Dutch East Indies (Indonesia) (Sharpe, 2008). By the mid-twentieth century, all that remained of the Netherlands' colonial possessions were the Dutch Caribbean islands, Suriname, and Indonesia. The Netherlands began its colonization of the Dutch Caribbean in the seventeenth century, but consolidation of sovereignty there did not occur until the nineteenth century. The islands have been Dutch since the 1630s (Oostindie 2009, 171), and Suriname since later in that period. With the end of the Napoleonic wars, the previous Republic of the Unified Netherlands was succeeded by a Dutch Kingdom in 1815, with its Caribbean colonial possessions as Suriname and the Dutch Caribbean islands. Colonial rule came under the direct control of the first king, King Willem I, who attempted reforms of the West India Company.

King Willem initiated the organization of Dutch Caribbean colonial authority into the three divisions of Suriname, Curaçao, and its dependencies, but this proved unsatisfactory, and the Dutch colonies were reestablished in 1828 as a single administrative unit with a Suriname-based governor. As this also was deemed unsatisfactory because of the geographic distance between Suriname and the Dutch islands, in 1848, the islands were separated from Suriname and became Curaçao and Dependencies (Sharpe 2008). The Netherlands' prioritization of its most profitable colony of the Dutch East Indies (Indonesia) until the 1940s and comparatively lackluster concern with its Dutch Caribbean colonies have been characterized as "careless colonialism" (Oostindie and Klinkers 2003, 57). The French "old colonies" in the Caribbean were colonized as early as 1635 (Guadeloupe and Martinique) and 1642 (French Guiana) and thus have been French or French territories longer than some parts of metropolitan France such as Nice and Alsace-Lorraine (Murdoch 2008, 15). Unlike France, with its close link to the French "old colonies," the Netherlands was rather sequestered from the Dutch Caribbean well into the twentieth century.

The postcolonial sovereignty games of the Netherlands and its colonial territories start with negotiations between the Netherlands and the colonies and at the international level with the 1954 Charter for the Kingdom of the Netherlands, or Statuut. The Charter (Statuut) had at least two objectives from the perspective of the Netherlands. These include the retention of Indonesia (the Dutch East Indies) and concerns about the maintenance of a positive international image. After a tumultuous colonial war, the Netherlands lost its highly valued Indonesian colony in 1949. Nevertheless, the Netherlands attempted to keep Indonesia within the Kingdom and in doing so, the embarrassed Dutch government granted Curaçao and its Dependencies (which included the aforementioned Dutch islands) and Suriname more autonomy and participation in government. This was sold as a "model decolonization" (Oostindie and Klinkers 2003, 73) process and resulted in the 1954 Charter for the Kingdom of the Netherlands. The Charter (Statuut) represents the official end of Dutch colonial relations (De Jong 2009, 25; Sharpe 2014a, 61).

In 1946, almost a decade before the 1954 Charter (Statuut), the French National Assembly passed the law of assimilation, which ended French "colonial" relations with the "Old Colonies" and transformed them into administrative districts of the French state, or *départements d'outre-mer* (DOM; French overseas departments) with French citizenship, representation in the French parliament, and rights to vote for the French president. In a departure from French integration, the Dutch Charter established the autonomous Dutch Kingdom "country" of the Netherlands Antilles and Suriname with the status of equal partners with the Netherlands within the Dutch Kingdom and representation in The Hague, the seat of the Dutch government. Defense, foreign affairs, and nationality were the only governmental functions left under the mandate of the Dutch Kingdom, which effectually meant the Netherlands. The French departmentalization was in part motivated by an attempt to apply republican ideals of "liberty, equality, and fraternity" through postwar era integration into the metropolitan French state with the application of metropolitan French laws and social benefits in the "old colonies" (Bishop 2009, 123). In contrast, the Dutch government viewed the "equal status" of its Dutch Caribbean partners as a temporary and instrumental measure toward holding on to highly valued Indonesia, improvement of its international reputation, and the eventual independence of the Dutch Caribbean.

Accordingly, fearing negative stigma attached to its actions in the Indonesian colonial war and bearing witness to international decolonization, the Netherlands wanted to update its stature before the United Nations and the world. Oostindie and Klinkers write: "The American press was generally positive; and on the grounds of the Charter, the United Nations relieved the Netherlands in 1955 from its obligation to report on the progress of the decolonisation process in its former Caribbean colonies" (2003, 85). Hillebrink argues that the Charter's notions of equivalence and voluntariness were more than likely designed to persuade the world that "the era of colonial domination had ended" (2008, 147). Nevertheless, some local democratic empowerment was made possible by the Charter. It is notable that by the time of the introduction Charter Suriname and the Netherlands Antilles had a Dutch-style system of parliamentary democracy, universal suffrage, and public administration (Oostindie and Klinkers 2003, 65). With the exceptions of Suriname's 1975 independence and Aruba's 1986 "status aparte," the preceding constitutional and political arrangements remained mostly uninterrupted until the dissolution of the Netherlands Antilles in 2010.

Oil, Uprising, Dutch Military Intervention, and Independence

Dutch Caribbean postcolonial sovereignty games ensued in the early and middle twentieth century between island negotiators, domestic constituencies, and those from the Netherlands. Several important events that shaped this include the beginnings of oil refinement in Aruba and Curaçao in the 1920s, Curaçao's 1969 "Trinta di Mei" uprising and Dutch military intervention under the Charter, and Suriname's 1975 independence. The sighting of oil in Lake Maracaibo, Venezuela, and Aruba's and Curaçao's close proximity, deep harbors, and the legal and military security offered by the Netherlands were the precursors for the 1920s opening of Lago Oil Company (Esso/Exxon) in Aruba and Isla Oil Company (Royal Dutch Shell) in Curaçao. Lago and Isla refined Venezuelan oil and shipped it to international markets. The two companies produced economic success and rapidly became the most important employers and influential players on the islands (Sharpe 2005, 2014a). During World War II, Lago became a leading fuel source for fuel and ultimately the world's largest oil refinery (Baker 1992, 24). Aruba and Curaçao possessed the world's two largest oil refineries by the middle of the twentieth century.[4] The 1954 Charter was promulgated during a period of some decline of oil sector expansion and increasing unemployment on the two islands.

Curaçao's racial and class hierarchies and inequalities were revealed in the 1969 Trinta di Mei, the May 30 uprising as designated in the native Papiamento language (Anderson and Dynes 1975; Römer 1998, 166). Curaçao's black majority experienced a somewhat racially segregated society and the dominance of the white, Protestant led Democratic Party as a situation bordering dictatorship (Sharpe 2005, 2009). These factors resulted in the Trinta di Mei revolt of May 30, 1969, with Dutch military intervention in Curaçao under the Charter. Wilson "Papa" Goddett, Amador Nita, popular unionists, and other critical figures of the original Frente Obrero Liberashon (FOL) were involved in the May Movement of 1969. The most immediate cause was a deadlock in negotiations in over a collective labor agreement between the Curaçao Federation of Workers (CFW) and Werkspoor Caribbean (WESCAR), the main contracting company within Royal Dutch Shell (Römer 1998, 166). However, "the real causes . . . were more deeply rooted and were intimately related to the racial social structure" (Römer 1998, 166).

The CFW wanted a wage agreement similar to one previously negotiated for Shell employees by another union, the Petroleum Workers Federation of Curaçao. Earlier in May 1969 the CFW escorted workers on a strike against WESCAR and were joined by a sympathy strike against Shell by the Petroleum Workers Federation of Curaçao and others. Wilson "Papa" Godett and other leaders made speeches to crowd of thousands and eventually led them on a march from Shell headquarters to Fort Amsterdam, Curaçao, the seat of the government, calling for its overthrow as an affront to the workers' demands. As the march proceeded, the police intervened, and Godett was eventually shot and wounded. The crowd then broke into smaller groups and spread through the downtown area setting buildings on fire, overturning cars, breaking windows, and looting stores. On May 30, a curfew was imposed for the weekend, and on June 1 the Dutch military arrived in Curaçao from the Netherlands to assist the police (Anderson and Dynes 1975, 5–6; Sharpe 2009). While some perceive this as a labor uprising, others view it as a revolt against racism and oppression, with end results of Curaçao's first black governor, Ben Leito, and first black prime minister, Ernesto Petronia, and an entry point for black working-class Curaçaoans and other Antilleans (van Hulst 2000, 98; Sharpe 2009). The events sparking the Trinta di Mei in the Curaçao capital of Willemstad were the result of a labor dispute between workers and management embedded in a race and class hierarchy. This event is generally accepted as a turning point in a shift away from a predominantly white minority ruling elite to a majority black-dominated society marked by intermittent anti-*makamba* (antiwhite European Dutch) politics (*makamba* is a local Papiamento pejorative word for Dutch) (Oostindie 2005, 126–127).

The 1965 Trinta di Mei postcolonial uprising and Dutch military intervention was perceived by some as Dutch "neocolonialism," and this perception impacted Dutch negotiations with Suriname. The Netherlands' desire to eliminate the specter of "neocolonialism" and to curb increased immigration from Suriname made the Netherlands more receptive to Suriname's nationalists. As such, the Netherlands advocated for independence rather than "autonomy." Suriname became an independent country in 1975 with nearly half of its population emigrating to the Netherlands. There are interesting parallels around the status of the Dutch Caribbean at this stage of its political development and the post-1946 departmental dismantling of the French Caribbean economy (Murdoch 2008, 18). Although the 1954 Charter advanced a fictional "equality" between the Dutch Caribbean and the Netherlands, increasing unemployment, worker displacement, and racial hierarchy resulted in the 1969 Trinta di Mei and Dutch military deployment in Curaçao. Similarly, while post-1945 departmentalization promoted a rhetorical equality between center and periphery, social uprisings with violent conflict between metropolitan police and workers took place in Martinique in 1959 and Guadeloupe in 1967 around racist attacks, salary increases, and parity in terms of social rights (Jalabert 2010).[5] The contradictions are apparent in these Dutch and French Caribbean postcolonial sovereignty games.

Aruba's 1985 Secession *Status Aparte*: Template for the Dissolution of the Netherlands Antilles

Aruba's 1986 "status aparte," or secession from the Netherlands Antilles and benefits associated with the autonomy in leaving the Netherlands Antilles but remaining within the Dutch Kingdom, would soon be something desired by each of the Dutch Caribbean islands. This demonstration had a central effect on the 2010 dissolution of the Netherlands Antilles. Antillean Prime Minister Juancho Evertsz cautioned that "the Netherlands Antilles minus Aruba equals 6 minus 1 = zero" (De Jong 2005b, 98). Aruba and the other Dutch islands of Netherlands Antilles had long begrudged the administrative dominance of Curaçao. Alofs and Merkies (2001) and Oostindie (2000, 2005) note Aruba's self-projection of a majority Euro-mestizo island, in opposition to the majority black Curaçao, and how this was employed to justify Aruba's "status aparte" in its negotiations with the Netherlands.

De Jong (2005b) contends that Aruba wanted separation from Curaçao and the Netherlands Antilles since the 1930s. This desire for separation from the Netherlands Antilles began with Henny Eman Sr. in the 1930s and was inherited by his son Shon Eman, and then his son Henny Eman Jr., the leader of the Arubaanse Volkspartij (AVP), Aruba's often pro-Dutch rightleaning party during the 1970s. Although the AVP advocated for separation, it the Movemiento Electoral di Pueblo (MEP) led by Betico Croes that broke away from AVP and dominated Aruban politics during the 1970s and 1980s. Aruban political elites viewed the Trinta di Mei Curaçao revolt of 1969 through the lens of the "black power" movements of the 1960s (Sharpe 2009). Aruba's separation from Curaçao and the Netherlands Antilles was partly based on the idea that Aruba was not black and should not be subjugated by black Curaçao (De Jong 2009, 39). The Trinta di Mei gave the Arubaanse Volkspartij (AVP) the momentum to expedite its demands for secession from the Netherlands Antilles.

After a referendum in 1977, some unrest erupted in Aruba, and the Dutch were forced to consider Aruba's "status aparte" from the Netherlands Antilles, especially Curaçao (Oostindie and Klinkers 2003, 123). Aruba's "status aparte" was pursued under the guidance of Betico Croes, who surprisingly died suddenly before it was realized. As the MEP party sustained a loss at the polls, the initial Aruban cabinet was presided over by AVP's Henny Eman (Oostindie and Klinkers 2003, 130). It was negotiated that Aruba would become independent in 1996 but this was eventually phased out. Aruba has fought against full independence, and its more recent prime minister Mike Eman argued autonomy is better because of the island's small size and vulnerability as well as access to EU networks (Kochenov 2011a, 14; Eman 2011, 434, 435).

The string of crises in then recently independent Suriname impacted events in Aruba. In addition to the race discourse mentioned earlier, Aruba's 1986 "status aparte" was bargained with Curaçao in mind as well Dutch apprehensions around the invocation of "neocolonialism." Despite the Netherlands' wish for Aruba's full independence, island leaders have negotiated the current political arrangement without leaving the Dutch Kingdom.

Dissolving the Precarious Semi-federation of the Netherlands Antilles

The Netherlands Antilles never came together as an autonomous entity or "nation" with a shared identity. The three Papiamento-speaking Leeward Islands (Aruba, Curaçao, and Bonaire) and the three English-speaking Windward Islands (Sint Maarten, Sint Eustatius, and Saba) are very different and a good distance from one another. In theory, the Netherlands Antilles was designed to make it easier for the Netherlands to deal with the islands through a single administrative structure. However, the significant cultural and geographic differences prevented the emergence of a common Antillean identity (Veenendaal 2015, 20). It was not until 2000 that an Antillean national anthem was even adopted. After Aruba's secession, the remaining islands felt even more subjugated by Curaçao. Individual island self-interest was pursued with relation to Curaçao, but Curaçao also began express that it bore too much of the financial burden of the smaller islands (Veenendaal 2015, 20).

Antillean officials had warned that if one island left, the federation would soon liquefy (De Jong 2009, 29). Antilleans governments found difficulties in the complex structure of the Netherlands Antilles, noted more by island divisions than a shared Antillean identity (Oostindie 2006, 618). The five remaining islands of the Netherlands Antilles tried to decide whether or not to continue as the Netherlands Antilles and entered a phase of "restructuring" in the early 1990s (De Jong 2005, 98). Despite the Dutch wish for the Dutch islands' independence, by the 1990s the political rhetoric had changed to an emphasis on good governance and the development of durable institutional structures (De Jong 2005, 87). There were concerns about the islands' vulnerability to drug trafficking and money laundering, and about the Netherlands' international responsibility. The Netherlands surmised that it would be "practically impossible as well as immoral and reproachable by international standards" to enforce independence on the Dutch islands (Oostindie 2006, 618). By the 2000s, the Netherlands became increasingly troubled by the difficulties of the Netherlands Antilles in controlling socioeconomic, crime, administrative, and financial problems, and increasingly negotiated bilaterally with each island (Veenendaal 2015, 20).

Referendums as Prelude to Dissolution

Despite the Antillean government and political parties campaigning for the end of the Netherlands Antilles, referendums held on the five islands in 1993–1994 showed a strong preference for continuation (Oostindie 2006, 620; De Jong 2009, 30). The year 2000 was an important one because the political winds had changed, and referendums held in Sint Maarten favored "status aparte" similar to Aruba. This initiated a series of referendums on the other four islands that beckoned toward termination of the federation.

Although there was a general notion that Antilleans voted in the 1990s to continue their relationship with the Dutch Antilles to show their dissatisfaction with their local leaders, by the 2000s the general consensus was that each island should deal with the Netherlands on a one-to-one basis (Oostindie 2006, 620). These referendums indicated a wish for a dissolution of the Netherlands Antilles and little want for independence. A majority in Sint Maarten as well Curaçao opted for a status similar to Aruba's "status aparte" and majorities in Saba and Bonaire voted for a one to one link with the Netherlands. Only Sint Eustatius voted for the maintenance of the Netherlands Antilles but later received the same integrated status as Bonaire and Saba. De Jong notes that the actions of the Netherlands actually encouraged the dissolution of the Dutch Antilles by bypassing the Antillean national government and negotiating one-on-one with island governments (2005b, 99). Following these referendums, a Round Table conference of the governments of the Netherlands Antilles and the Netherlands was organized in 2005, and it was agreed that Curaçao and Sint

Maarten should obtain "status aparte" and that the three other islands, undeterred by Sint Eustatius's vote for continuation of the Netherlands Antilles, should be integrated into the Netherlands. As mentioned earlier, it was agreed that the Netherlands would assume and write off €1.7 billion of the €2 billion public debt of the Netherlands Antilles. In exchange, Curaçao and Sint Maarten would have to submit to increased Dutch supervision of their finances and public budgets (Veenendaal 2015, 21). In later closing agreements over the next two years, a date of December 15, 2008, was set for the Netherlands Antilles to be dissolved but this proved untenable; a later date was set and finally implemented on October 10, 2010.

The Paradoxes of Postcolonialism: Democratic Dilemmas and Deficiencies

A central paradox of postcolonial non-sovereignty in the Dutch Caribbean is that although the 1954 Charter or Statuut undoubtedly somewhat democratically empowered Dutch islanders on the local level, like their non-sovereign counterparts in the French Caribbean, there are conspicuous democratic dilemmas and deficiencies. The 1954 Charter (Statuut) does not permit the Netherlands to impose independence or secede from the Kingdom. There must be agreement among all Dutch Kingdom partners, and so theoretically unilateral dissolution or secession is not possible (Oostindie 2013, 205, 206). In this way, each island has achieved its main goal of unilateral relations with the Netherlands (Oostindie 2013, 209, 210, 214). This rejection of independence has been referred to as "upside down decolonization" (Baldacchino 2013, vi) as well as "internal devolution" (Adler-Nissen and Gad 2013, 2). It is noted that the Netherlands is now a Caribbean country because its border extends to the "Caribbean Netherlands" (BES islands). On the one hand, the refusal of independence and negotiation of autonomy is an affirmation of Antilleans' democratic agency, but on the other, there are several issues of democratic accountability that give voice to the classification of neocolonialism.

It is democratically problematic that there was never a popular vote to approve the Charter or Statuut (Veenendaal and Oostindie 2018, 33; Duijf

and Soons 2011). Dutch legislative structures generally lack island representation. Following the arrangements of the former Netherlands Antilles, the
governors of Curaçao, Sint Maarten, and Aruba are appointed by and represent the Dutch monarch, and these Caribbean Dutch Kingdom partner
governments choose ministers plenipotentiary (resident ministers) who
represent the partner governments in the locality of the Dutch government in The Hague. The ministers are allowed to engage in discussions of
the Kingdom Cabinet but are not accountable to parliament (Koulen and
Oostindie 1987, 15–16). Kingdom-level issues are decided by the Kingdom
government, which is composed of Dutch cabinet ministers and the ministers plenipotentiary. There is no Dutch Kingdom parliament where Dutch
Caribbean residents or autonomous countries are represented (De Jong
2009, 38), and only a Dutch parliament, so the Netherlands is the final judge
(Oostindie 2013, 207, 208). Article 43 of the 1954 Charter or Statuut states
that the Dutch Kingdom is accountable for the protection of human rights,
the rule of law, and good governance. Despite the Charter's notions of
equality and mutual assistance among Dutch Kingdom partners, this is
impractical because of the dominance, size, and resource capacity of the
Netherlands. It is rather unclear when the Netherlands or the Dutch Kingdom is acting (Oostindie 2006; Veenendaal 2015, 16). This lack of clarity has
given rise to discussion of the Dutch Kingdom as the "Kingdom from the
Netherlands" rather than the Kingdom of the Netherlands. It is notable that
Sint Eustatius never voted for BES integration, which is likely an infringe-
ment of the UN right to self-determination (Duijf and Soons 2011, 60–61;
Veenendaal 2015, 21). Again a paradox of this postcolonial non-sovereignty
is that it can be regarded as both a violation of the right of self-determination
(Grosfoguel 2003) as well as evidence (Veenendaal 2015) of the people's
democratic will to remain constitutionally connected to the metropole.

Many European Dutch do not view themselves as sharing the Dutch
nationality with Dutch Caribbean people or have a privileged European
view of inclusion in the Kingdom of the Netherlands (Sharpe 2014a). It is
remarkable that it was not until the 2000s that the Antilles became a focal
point of debate in the Dutch parliament (Oostindie 2011, 38), in contrast to

the experience of the French Caribbean. French Antilleans are just about 1 percent of the total French population (Murdoch 2008, 43). In a similar vein, Dutch Antilleans and Arubans number just 153,469, or less than 1 percent (0.9 percent), of the total population of the Netherlands of 17,081,507 in 2017.[6] However, there is focused Dutch media attention on a small number of Antillean youth involved in criminal activity. Dutch historian Piet Emmer spoke to this issue in his 2007 article in the Dutch daily *NRC-Handelsblad,* in which he suggested that unlimited Antillean immigration has caused a "national trauma" and extensive damage to the Dutch society (Emmer, 2007). Laws drafted to attempt to challenge Antillean and Aruban freedom of movement to the Netherlands include the 2010 *Rijkswet Personenverkeer* (Maas 2014, 263) as well as the 2014 Bosman Law to limit migration from Aruba, Curaçao, and Sint Maarten with restrictions such as residence permit, proof of employment, and so on (Oostindie 2009, 169, 172, 173).[7] One public opinion poll in the Netherlands in 2008 indicated that more than half of the European Dutch favored the Netherlands severing all connections with the Netherlands Antilles.[8] A 2016 poll suggested that most European Dutch wanted the islands to leave the Dutch Kingdom.[9] Hero Brinkman, a member of Gert Wilders Dutch far right Partij voor de Vrijheid (PVV), even proposed that the Dutch islands be sold on eBay (*Expatica* 2009). Some island elites have argued that the Dutch Caribbean islands can provide a hub for Dutch and European interests in the Caribbean and Latin America, but many European Dutch attach little value to the islands.

Non-sovereignty and Déclassé Citizenship

The 1954 Charter (Statuut) establishes equal legal citizenship in the metropole as well as the non-sovereign periphery. Hintjens argues that only in the non-sovereign territories have individuals' socioeconomic and political rights been given priority in the decolonization process (1995, 46). Oostindie notes a "postcolonial bonus" in terms of the advantages of postcolonial ties, legal citizenship, and permanent right of abode for first-generation postcolonial immigrants in the Netherlands (2011, 22). There are some interesting parallels and dissimilarities in the Dutch and French Caribbean with regard to de jure citizenship and equality as well as institutional, social, racial practices, and implications. Under the doctrine of French republicanism, all French citizens born and raised within the French republic are only French with no official recognition of contingent identities, such as French Caribbean and so on (Milia-Marie-Luce 2009, 207). Beriss (2004) writes about French Caribbean (Antilleans) in France and the apparent contradictions between their legal status and their treatment.

Despite their legal status and their socialization into French culture, the categorization of Antilleans in France with immigrants makes it impossible for them to claim that they are simply French. They are linked by origin and skin color to the kinds of people who, in the French view, are unable to adopt French culture. They become immigrants, part of the "immigrant problem" in French society (Beriss 2004, 20–21).

Although they possess French legal citizenship French Caribbean people in France have long been subject to racial discrimination and "otherness." Whereas France does not formally admit the existence of minorities, the Netherlands both recognizes and categorizes them (Milia-Marie-Luce 2009, 207; Sharpe 2014a). Nonetheless, similar to the assumptions of nonbelonging in France, despite being born and raised as Dutch citizens, former Dutch Antilleans and Arubans in the Netherlands are classified as "Niet Westers allochtoon" or "non-Western, non-native" Dutch. These categories refer to the main ethnic minorities of Antilleans and Arubans, Turks, Moroccans, Surinamese, as well as those from Africa, Latin America, or Asia and others born outside of the Netherlands or in the Netherlands to one or two foreign-born parents (van Hulst 2000, 20).[10] De Jong writes, "Generations of New Dutch nationals are stigmatized with the label allochtoon as opposed to autochthon, The True Dutch with both parents born in the Netherlands. You may be born in Holland and you may be a Dutch citizen but neither automatically confers being Dutch" (2009, 35).

Dutch Caribbeans experience racism and discrimination in the Netherlands on a regular basis (Essed 1991; Essed and Hoving 2014; Sharpe 2014b). There is a commonsense notion of Antilleans and Arubans in the Netherlands

as "foreigners with a Dutch passport" (van Niekerk 2000, 2002). Even naturalized immigrants remain *allochtoon* thus reinforcing their nonbelonging
and otherness and reifying a particular type of white European "Dutchness" (de Hart 2004, 161). An example of this is 100 percent control policy
around suspicions of Antilleans at Amsterdam's Schiphol airport and feeling Antilleans to be "second class citizens" (De Jong 2009, 32; Allen 2010,
121). Likewise, Antilleans don't perceive themselves as Dutch but rather as
Curaçaoans, Sint Maarteners, Bonairians, and so on (De Jong 2009, 36).
Regardless of different contexts of de facto or de jure minority status, similar results and parallels are produced.

Although both the French and Dutch Caribbean are prosperous relative to much of the region, there remains a situation of high unemployment and cost of living. The unemployment rate in mainland France is
some 8 percent and in the French Antilles is 22 percent (Murdoch 2007, 43).
Departmentalization in the French Caribbean resulted in some 90 percent
of all goods being imported from France, with high prices reflecting trans-
Atlantic transportation costs (Murdoch 2007, 43). From 2011 to 2017, the
unemployment rate in Curaçao was 12–14.1 percent, Aruba 6–7.7 percent,
Sint Maarten 9–11 percent (reduced to 6.2 percent in 2017), Bonaire
5.8–6.7 percent, Sint Eustatius 4.9–7.1 percent, and Saba 4.4–3.3 percent,
compared with the rate in the Netherlands of 5–4.9 percent. Dutch Caribbean islanders in the Netherlands have consistently some of the highest
rates of unemployment of all *Niet Westers allochtoon* or "non-Western, non-
native" ethnic minorities, with a rate of some 15.1 percent in 2016 compared
with rates among the native Dutch at 6.0 percent in 2016 and 4.9 percent in
2017.[11] In ways similar to *la vie chére* (the expensive life) of the departmentalized French Caribbean (Bonilla 2010, 129), the cost of basic goods and services can be relatively high in the Dutch Caribbean as most items are
imported. This is particularly salient as a consequence of the 2010 BES integration into the Netherlands and the very small size and scale of these
economies. Pommer and Bijl (2015) write: "Price rises have had a major
impact on the purchasing power of island residents. . . . What is clear is that
local businesses raised their prices in response to higher taxes, higher costs

and the introduction of the US dollar." These inequities around democracy, citizenship, unemployment, and cost of living threaten the legitimacy of the post-1954 postcolonial Dutch Kingdom political enterprise.

Postcolonial Non-sovereignty and Resistance

The 2009 French Caribbean uprisings around unbearable price and cost-of-living increases have resonated in acts of resistance in the Dutch Caribbean, particularly with regard to 10-10-10. As a consequence of the 10-10-10 integration, the BES has the U.S. dollar as its the standard currency; most metropolitan Dutch laws apply to these islands; and education, health care, social services, and infrastructure are targeted to be raised to levels near the rest of the Netherlands. The BES has its own tax system, general health care insurance, and environmental laws. Veneendaal notes significant gains in terms of health, education, and infrastructure[12] and generally positive attitudes about expected improvements in these areas, immigration services, and the police (2015, 23). However, as previously stated, there is dissatisfaction with the status quo in the Dutch Caribbean that has produced resistance in various forms.

In an effort toward implementation that could present as a neocolonial action, hundreds of civil servants were flown from the Netherlands to the islands multiple times at great expense to set up Dutch government offices and services. For this reason, the visage of 10-10-10 integration is that of the white European Dutch civil servant.[13] Some people in Bonaire have the "feeling the Dutch are taking over," and demonstrations proliferate when there is a European Dutch political presence on the island, such as the royal family or Dutch parliamentary representatives.[14] Island residents have shown their dissatisfaction with taxation, purchasing power, and wages related to the cost of living (Veneendaal 2015, 23), poverty, and unemployment. A perception study finds that 67 percent of Caribbean Netherlands residents "experienced a decline in purchasing power since 10-10-10" and a majority believe the situation on their island has deteriorated when compared to 10-10-10 (Curconsult 2013, 4, 5). There is a view of immediate negative costs of BES integration, in terms of increased taxes; inflation; unemployment;

crime; the promulgation of Dutch metropolitan laws on same-sex marriage, abortion, and euthanasia that some locals have found "immoral"
(Allen 2010, 122; Oostindie 2013, 20); and more Dutch control, as well as the
persistence of historic racial hierarchies and perceptions of second-class
citizenship. Some Antilleans fear that the post-10-10-10 Netherlands presence in the BES will marginalize local culture; threaten autonomy; and
extend Dutch influence, norms, and "immoral laws" to all of the Dutch
islands (Allen 2010, 122, 9)

There have been long-standing sentiments of anti-colonial resentment
toward the Netherlands that predate the 1969 Trinta di Mei uprising. Cola
Debrot, a white Bonairean and the first native-born governor of the Netherlands Antilles, had the white Curaçaoan main character of his 1935 short
story My Black Sister, on his return from the Netherlands, say: "I hated
those pale faces in Europe with their fishlike frigidness, their want of
brotherly love and sisterly feeling" (Rojer and Aimone 2008, 17; van Hulst
2000, 97). Van der Pijl and Guadeloupe characterize the atmosphere since
10-10-10 as a negative attitude "towards all things Dutch" (2015, 90), and
Veenendaal and Oostindie warn that the "anger and bitterness towards the
Dutch metropole have unquestionably increased, creating a potentially
explosive situation" (2018, 43). The Dutch Caribbean island governments,
politicians, negotiators, and their populations have played a multilevel
game of defiance to increasing Dutch intervention that some have attributed to neocolonial structures. These political actors have invoked island
autonomy, the Netherlands, EU law and institutions, and international
norms in these postcolonial sovereignty games.

As previously mentioned, many Dutch Caribbean islanders feel the
encroachment of a metropolitan liberal model of "Dutchness"[15] and a
diminishment of local values, traditions, and autonomy. The "Asosashon di
Pastornan Kristian" (APK), Curaçao's association of Christian ministers,
protested against this "tsunami of immoral laws."[16] A silent demonstration
was held for first time in the history of Saba to protest the new tax structure and what some deem nefarious laws.[17] Sint Eustatius warned it would
appeal to the United Nations to protest the promotion of these laws.[18] By

2018, there was another silent protest in Sint Eustatius against a Dutch government emergency measure, with no local discussion, to dissolve its local government as the result of allegations of financial mismanagement, lawlessness, and corruption as well as the placement of many European Dutch police officers.[19] The "Concerned Bonairians" group cautioned then governor Lydia Emerencia in 2012 that there could be riots in Bonaire on par with that of Curaçao 1969 uprising over increasing prices and taxes since 10-10-10.[20] Radio Netherlands Worldwide quoted a protester as saying, "You can take it as a threat, but after today we're done talking. We'll go to jail if we have to, in the name of justice and of the people."[21] The same report discussed Dutch Queen Beatrix, on another official visit to Bonaire escorted by her son, then–Dutch Prince Willem Alexander, and her acceptance of a petition from the group in 2011 to address the island's poverty and an additional referendum on the island's status. Following his mother's abdication in 2013, King Willem Alexander spoke to protesters during his official visit to Bonaire and accepted a new petition from them with similar concerns and demands.[22]

The now autonomous Dutch Kingdom "countries" of Curaçao, Sint Maarten, and Aruba have respectively rejected degrees of Dutch interference and intermittently dabble in the discourse of local autonomy and even independence. The Netherlands Antilles prime minister, de Jong-Elhage, denounced "racist violence" against European Dutch in July 2008 after "race" riots over the island council conceding to more Dutch control over finances in exchange for debt forgiveness. A rather new development in Antillean history is the emergence of the pro-independence Curaçaoan political party Pueblo Soberano, founded in 2005. Pueblo Soberano (PS) has on occasion called politicians in the Netherlands "terrorists" and labeled some Curaçaoan politicians as puppets of the Netherlands.[23] The Sint Maarten politician Theo Heyliger of the United People's Party was accused of buying votes in the 2014 election. In a move Heyliger and others called a neocolonial measure, the Dutch government, out of a voiced concern about corruption, proposed a "pre-screening process for public officials."[24] Aruba's Prime Minister Mike Eman, of the then ruling Arubaanse Volkspartij

(AVP), went on a weeklong hunger strike in July 2014 to protest unnecessary Dutch government involvement in Aruba's 2014–2015 budget. The Dutch government requested Aruba's governor not to sign the budget into law because it wanted a review to correct the island's underperforming economy.[25] The Dutch government wanted the Aruban government to enact International Monetary Fund–style austerity measures. Eman argued that his hunger strike was a "last resort" against an attack on Aruba's autonomy.[26] By 2016, the Dutch government broke with protocol and defied Mike Eman's choice, instead appointing Juan Alonso Boekhoudt as the governor, prompting anger and debate about independence from all actors in both the islands and in the Netherlands.[27] In a way similar to Martinique's ascension as an associated member of the Organization of Eastern Caribbean States in 2016, during Aruba's budget debacle, Aruba's government began an initiative to connect with English-speaking neighbors to exchange ideas and opportunities within the region and benefit from Aruba's infrastructure and ecotourism.

Dutch and EU law and institutions have been invoked on several occasions in these postcolonial sovereignty games. The French territories are simultaneously Caribbean, French, and European (Bishop 2009, 119), and, for the most part, the same can be said of the Dutch territories.[28] There was a Dutch electoral law that limited Aruban and Antillean participation in European parliamentary elections only to those islanders who had lived at least ten years in the Netherlands. Paradoxically, most Dutch citizens living in the Netherlands Antilles and Aruba could not vote for the European Parliament, but Dutch citizens living abroad were allowed to vote. The case of *Eman and Sevinger* challenged this as a breach of the fundamental rights protected by the European Union (Kochenov 2011b, 202). The European Court of Justice (ECJ) concluded on September 12, 2006, that the principle of equal treatment prohibited the different treatment of Dutch citizens living abroad and those in the Netherlands Antilles and Aruba in the electoral process. The Dutch parliament subsequently changed the election law and, since June 2009, Dutch Antilleans and Arubans have been allowed to vote in European parliamentary elections.

As previously noted, a media and policy narrative has emerged around the "criminality" of Antillean/Aruban youth in the Netherlands, and steps have been taken to limit their citizenship rights around freedom of movement. A draft bill was proposed in 2005 by the Dutch political party D66 (social liberal) along with the hardline former minister for immigration and integration Rita Verdonk, of the Volkspartij voor Vrijheid en Democratie (VVD; conservative liberal), to deport Antillean youth who committed a crime or remained unemployed for several months. This bill was found to be in violation of the European Convention on Human Rights and unworkable because of the islanders' Dutch citizenship. Additionally, there were bills calling for the establishment of a database to monitor "troubled" Antillean youth. These bills were also criticized by the Antillean and Aruban governments, as well as Stichting Overlegorgaan Caribische Nederlanders (OCAN) (Consultative Body of the Caribbean Dutch), and were removed from consideration by 2008. Other attempts to limit Antillean movement, such as the 2014 Bosman Law mentioned earlier, were not backed by the Dutch government coalition partner Partij van de Arbeid (PvDA; social democratic) and were strongly opposed by the governments of Aruba, Curaçao, and Sint Maarten. The Bosman Law was deemed to be discriminatory on the basis of race and ethnicity by OCAN as well as the European Commission against Racism and Intolerance (ECRI) of the European Council.[29] Mass protests, a curfew, and more than two hundred arrests in The Hague occurred in 2015 over the death in police custody of Mitch Hernandez, a forty-two-year-old Aruban man, which some call a result of racial profiling in the Netherlands.[30] There has been a groundswell in civil society against the racist Dutch Christmas tradition of Sinterklaas, with Saint Nicholas accompanied by a helper, Zwarte Piet (Black Peter), who appears unintelligent and servile in minstrel-like fashion and is played mostly by whites in black face with exaggerated red lips, large gold earrings, and frizzy hair. This tradition prompted much protest and a national debate, with many arrests; in 2015 the United Nations Committee for the Elimination of Racial Discrimination (CERD) called on the Netherlands to eliminate or alter the practice to protect the dignity of people of

African descent.[31] As in the case of the 2009 French Caribbean uprisings, these acts of refusal draw attention to the broader contradictions and inequities of the Dutch Kingdom.

Conclusion

This chapter has attempted to comparatively highlight the parallels and paradoxes of Dutch Caribbean and French Caribbean postcolonial non-sovereignty within the context of postcolonial sovereignty games. The French Caribbean has been associated with France longer than some parts of mainland France, and the Dutch Caribbean has had a distant relationship with the Netherlands well into the twentieth century. The French and Dutch Caribbean "postcolonial sovereignty games" began in the postwar period, with the 1947 departmentalization of the "old colonies" into overseas departments and the 1954 Charter (Statuut) ending colonial relations, establishing the Netherlands Antilles as a political entity, and conferring the status of equal Dutch Kingdom partners on the Antilles and Suriname. While the French extension of full integration was in a part a fulfillment of the universal ideals of French republicanism, the Dutch inclusion of the Netherland Antilles and Suriname into the Dutch Kingdom was designed to retain Indonesia and a temporary measure toward complete independence that has been consistently rejected. The French and Dutch postcolonial projects reflect respective tendencies of idealism, instrumentalism, integration, and autonomy within these postcolonial sovereignty games.

By the 1960s and 1970s there were calls for more autonomy in the French Caribbean as a manifestation of the gap between republican ideals and French Caribbean realities. This tension between integration and autonomy is reflected in the 2003 constitutional revision allowing some French overseas territories more autonomy as *collectivities d'outre mer* (COMs). Similarly, the May 1969 Trinta di Mei uprising, Aruba's 1986 departure from the Netherlands Antilles, and the 2010 dissolution of the Netherlands Antilles all called for more local control within the Dutch Kingdom. The dissolution of Netherlands Antilles in 2010 resulted in negotiated autonomy as well as a quasi-French style departmentalization of the BES (albeit with the

U.S. dollar as its standard currency), its own tax system, and environmental laws. Notwithstanding Suriname's 1975 declaration of independence, the Dutch islands demand more autonomy while at the same time defy the Dutch wish for their independence.

French departmentalization and Dutch integration, and the 2009 French Caribbean uprising and Dutch Caribbean acts of resistance, have much resonance with each other around high prices and cost-of-living increases that have brought light to larger issues of democratic accountability and second-class citizenship. French Caribbeans are French citizens with full voting rights and representation in the French National Assembly and European parliament but their limited numbers, at some 1 percent of the French population, means they have little political weight. The Dutch Caribbean has limited if not perfunctory representation in Dutch legislative bodies. Although those resident in the autonomous countries generally cannot vote in Dutch national elections if they have not lived in the Netherlands for at least ten years, those on the BES can, and now all Dutch islanders have the franchise for the European Parliament. Similar to French Caribbeans, at just 1 percent of the population Dutch Caribbeans both in the Netherlands and the islands have very small numbers and constrained electoral power. Although there are different political contexts of legality, similar realities of political marginalization are produced and reproduced.

All of this is particularly relevant in this age of populist nationalism, in opposition to immigrants and citizens of color, threatening the liberal democratic order. One can assess the quality of a democratic and inclusive society by the way it treats its most vulnerable citizens—in this case those with a "postcolonial bonus." In this way, both French and Dutch Caribbeans, as advantaged postcolonial citizens, can be the miner's canary for the French Republic and the Dutch Kingdom. While France refuses to recognize its de facto minorities, opting for an overriding French identity, the Netherlands actively classifies its minorities, obscuring one's ability to become truly Dutch. There are competing realities of high unemployment and high cost of living of the Dutch and French Caribbean when compared to the metropoles. These realities, along with the realities of racism and discrimination, compound the perceptions and realities of second-class citizen status. There have long been calls for independence in Martinique and Guadeloupe, but this has only recently been invoked in the Dutch Caribbean. The place of Dutch Caribbeans and French Caribbeans both in their territories as well as in the Netherlands and in France can be a litmus test of societal, civic, and democratic inclusion. The failure to address inequities and democratic deficiencies ultimately weakens the ideals and legitimacy of the French republic and the Dutch Kingdom as some of the oldest examples of postwar liberal democracy in these latest iterations of postcolonial sovereignty games.

NOTES

This chapter expands with comparison to the French Caribbean the originally published Michael O. Sharpe, "Extending Postcolonial Sovereignty Games: The Multilevel Negotiation of Autonomy and Integration in the 2010 Dissolution of the Netherlands Antilles and Dutch Kingdom Relations," *Ethnopolitics* (April 2020): https://doi.org/10.1080/17449057.2020.1726031.

1. The Leeward Islands of Aruba, population 110,615 (2016) (Aruba Central Bureau of Statistics), http://cbs.aw/wp/wp-content/uploads/2017/09/QDB122017.jpg (accessed May 9, 2018); Curaçao, population 160,337 (2017) (Curaçao Central Bureau of Statistics); and Bonaire, population 19,408 (2016) (Statistical Bureau of the Netherlands), are located just off the coast of Venezuela. The Windward Islands of Sint Eustatius, population 3,193 (2016); Saba, population 1,947 (2016) (Statistical Bureau of the Netherlands), https://opendata.cbs.nl/statline/#/CBS/en/dataset/83774ENG/table?dl=B699 (accessed May 9, 2018); and Sint Maarten (Dutch side), population 40,535 (2017) (Department of Statistics St. Maarten) http://stat.gov.sx/ (accessed May 9, 2018) are located just east of Puerto Rico. Dutch is an official language, with Papiamento, a Portuguese Creole, the vernacular of Aruba, Curaçao, and Bonaire, and English as the common language of Sint Eustatius, Sint Maarten, and Saba.

2. Adler-Nissen and Gammeltoft-Hansen (2008) maintain that states engage in new practices and modify understandings of their own sovereignty in horizontal and vertical "sovereignty games" to reassure legitimacy, power, and control with the result of sometimes "strengthening their position vis-à-vis other actors" (3, 15–16).

3. Based on research and more than thirty interviews with politicians, bureaucrats, scholars, and local leaders in the Netherlands, Aruba, Curaçao, and Bonaire, 2011–2014.

4. "Curaçao, Aruba Seek Pan-American Aid to Attain Independence," *Chicago Daily Tribune (1923–1963)*, February 4, 1948, 14.

5. Susannah Savage, "50 Years On: Guadeloupeans Remember French Brutality," *Al Jazeera*, June 2, 2017, https://www.aljazeera.com/indepth/features/2017/05/50-years-guadeloupeans-remember-french-brutality-170525130554921.html.

6. CBS.nl, "Population; Key Figures," http://statline.cbs.nl/Statweb/publication/?DM=SLNL&PA=37296ned&D1=32,40,48&D2=0,10,20,30,35,40,45,50,55,60,65-67&VW=T

(accessed May 9, 2018); CBS.nl, "Bevolking; kerncijfers," https://opendata.cbs.nl/statline /#/CBS/nl/dataset/37296ned/table?ts=1524756215396 (accessed May 9, 2018).

7. "The Bosman Law Explained," *Curaçao Chronicle*, March 10, 2014, http://curaçao chronicle.com/politics/the-bosman-law-explained/.

8. "Helft Nederlanders wil af van Antillen," *De Telegraaf* (Binnenland), January 10, 2008, http://www.telegraaf.nl/binnenland/2961008/_Helft_Nederlanders_wil_af_van _Antillen_ . . . ; *de Volkskrant*, https://www.volkskrant.nl/nieuws-achtergrond/helft -nederlanders-wil-af-van-antillen~b6750283/ (accessed May 9, 2018).

9. "Meerderheid Nederlanders wil af van Antillen," *AD.nl*, October 7, 2015, https:// www.ad.nl/buitenland/meerderheid-nederlanders-wil-af-van-antillen~ad7077a4/.

10. "Westerse Allochtoon" includes most Western European countries, North America, and Oceania, as well as Japan and Indonesia, and hence is a socioeconomic and cultural characterization rather than a geographic one. The term *autotochtonen* refers to the "native Dutch" or those people whose parents were both born in the Netherlands, regardless of where they themselves were born. Central Bureau of Statistics of the Netherlands (Voorburg/Heerlen, 2006).

11. "Werkloosheid naar herkomst," *CBS.nl*, February 2, 2017, https://www.cbs.nl/nl -nl/achtergrond/2017/07/werkloosheid-naar-herkomst; https://opendata.cbs.nl/statline/# /CBS/en/dataset/82309ENG/table?dl=ACCD (accessed May 9, 2018).

12. "Bonaire Protests during Dutch Officials Short Visit," *Overseas Territories Review*, November 1, 2011, http://overseasreview.blogspot.com/2011/11/bonaire-protests-during -dutch-officials.html.

13. Interview with official of the University of Aruba, August 11, 2011.

14. Interview with director of communication, Rijkdienst Caribisch Nederland, July 10, 2014.

15. "Bonaire Protests during Dutch Officials Short Visit," *Overseas Territories Review*, November 1, 2011, http://overseasreview.blogspot.com/2011/11/bonaire-protests-during -dutch-officials.html.

16. "Protest against Immoral Laws," *Daily Herald*, March 23, 2010, https://thedailyherald .com/index.php?option=com_content&view=article&id=1817:protest-against-immoral -laws&catid=1:islands-news&Itemid=54.

17. "Saba Protests Conditions of New Political Status," *Overseas Territories Review*, October 21, 2011, http://overseasreview.blogspot.com/2011/10/daily-herald-sint-maarten -silent.html.

18. "Resistance against Same Sex Marriage on St. Eustatius," *Radio Netherlands Worldwide*, April 22, 2010, http://www.rnw.org/archive/resistance-against-same-sex-marriages -st-eustatius (accessed May 11, 2018).

19. Esther Henry, "Silent Protest against Dutch Intervention St. Eustatius," *Caribbean Network*, February 8, 2018, https://caribbeannetwork.ntr.nl/2018/02/08/silent-protest -against-dutch-intervention-st-eustatius/.

20. "Threat of Rioting on Dutch Caribbean Island," *Radio Netherlands Worldwide*, June 4, 2012. http://www.rnw.org/archive/threat-rioting-dutch-caribbean-island (accessed May 11, 2018)

21. "Threat of Rioting on Dutch Caribbean Island."

22. Audrey Graagnoost, "King Talks with Protestors," *NL Times*, November 17, 2013, http://www.nltimes.nl/2013/11/17/king-talks-protesters/.

23. "Curaçao MP: 'Politicians in The Hague Are Terrorists,'" *Curaçao Chronicle*, October 8, 2014, http://Curaçaochronicle.com/politics/Curaçao-mp-politicians-in-the-hague-are-terrorists/.

24. "Theo: Dutch Want to Prevent Me from Being Prime Minister," *Daily Herald*, October 20, 2014, http://beta.sxmelections.com/news/2890/default.aspx; Arxen A. Alders, "Obstacles to 'Good Governance' in the Dutch Caribbean: Colonial- and Postcolonial Development in Aruba and Sint Maarten," master's thesis, Utrecht University, 2015, http://deugdelijkbestuuraruba.org/wp-content/uploads/2016/04/AldersUUmaster thesis-aug-2015.pdf.

25. Maria Gabriela Díaz, "Aruba Prime Minister 'Prepared to Die' for Island's Autonomy," *Panam Post*, July 20, 2014, http://panampost.com/marcela-estrada/2014/07/16/aruba-prime-minister-prepared-to-die-for-islands-autonomy/ (accessed May 11, 2018)

26. "Starving Out the Dutch," *Timaru Herald*, July 5, 2014.

27. "Aruba Politics: Quick View—Independence Agenda Rekindled," *EIU Viewwire*, New York, November 17, 2016.

28. The twenty-six OCTs comprise eleven U.K. OCTs—Anguilla, British Virgin Islands, Cayman Islands, Montserrat, Turks and Caicos Islands, Saint Helena and the Dependencies, Falkland Islands, South Georgia and South Sandwich Islands, British Antarctic Territories, British Indian Ocean Territories, and Pitcairn; seven French—French Polynesia, New Caledonia and the Dependencies, Wallis and Futuna Islands, Mayotte, Saint Pierre and Miquelon, the French Southern and Antarctic Territories, and Saint Barthélemy; six Dutch—Aruba, Bonaire, Curaçao, Saba, Sint Eustatius, and Sint Maarten: and one Danish—Greenland. Bermuda by its own request has never had an association agreement with the EU. The Netherlands Antilles was counted as a single OCT until it fragmented into five separate entities on October 10, 2010 (Curaçao, Sint Maarten, Bonaire, Saba, and Sint Eustatius). Saint Barthélemy changed its status from an "outermost region" to an OCT on January 1, 2012, and Mayotte is expected to change its status from an OCT to an "outermost region" in the near future (Sutton 2012, n. 1, 92). The outermost regions are the overseas French (Martinique, Guadeloupe, French Guiana, Réunion, Saint Barthélemy, Sint Maarten), Spanish (the Canary Islands), and Portuguese (Azores and Madeira) territories that are classed as integral parts of the EU but also benefit from special measures to assist their development (Sutton 2012, n. 3, 92).

29. "European Council Is against Bosman Law," *Curaçao Chronicle*, October 16, 2013, http://curacaochronicle.com/politics/european-council-is-against-bosman-law/.

30. Anthony Deutsch, "Riots in the Netherlands after Caribbean Man Mitch Henriquez Dies in Police Custody," *HuffPost*, July 2, 2015, https://www.huffingtonpost.com/2015/07/02/netherlands-riots-police-mitch-henriquez_n_7712962.html; "Mass Arrests in Dutch Riots after Police Custody Death," *Al Jazeera*, July 4, 2015, https://www.aljazeera.com/news/2015/07/mass-arrests-dutch-riots-police-custody-death-150704052425176.html.

31. "Call for International Solidarity for the Fight against Zwarte Piet & Blackfacing," *Stop Blackface*, n.d., http://stopblackface.com/kozp/664-2/ (accessed January 28, 2018); Joe Sommerlad, "Black Pete: Who is the 'Racist' Christmas Character Sparking Clashes in the Netherlands?," *Independent*, November 19, 2018, https://www.independent.co.uk/news/world/europe/zwarte-piet-black-pete-racist-christmas-character-protest-sinterklaas-a8640611.html.

REFERENCES

Adler-Nissen, Rebecca, and Thomas Gammeltoft-Hansen, eds. 2008. *Sovereignty Games: Instrumentalizing State Sovereignty in Europe and Beyond*. New York: Palgrave Macmillan.

Adler-Nissen, Rebecca, and Ulrik Pram Gad, eds. 2013. *European Integration and Postcolonial Sovereignty Games: The EU Overseas Countries and Territories*. New York: Routledge.

Aldrich, Robert, and John Connell. 1998. *The Last Colonies*. Cambridge: Cambridge University Press.

Allen, Rose Mary. 2010. "The Complexity of National Identity Construction in Curaçao, Dutch Caribbean." *European Review of Latin American and Caribbean Studies*, no. 89 (October): 117–125.

Alofs, Luc, and Leontine Merkies. 2001. *Ken Ta Arubiano? Sociale Integratie en Nativevorming op Aruba 1924–2001*. Oranjestad, Aruba: VAD/DE Wit Stores.

Anderson, William A., and Russell R. Dynes. 1975. *Social Movements, Violence, and Change: The May Movement in Curaçao*. Columbus: The Ohio State University Press.

Aruba Central Bureau of Statistics. *2010 Census Migration Characteristics of the Population*.

Baker, Randall, ed. 1992. *Public Administration in Small and Island States*. West Hartford, CT: Kumarian Press.

Baldacchino, Godfrey. 2006. "Innovative Development Strategies from Non-sovereign Island Jurisdictions? A Global Review of Economic Policy and Governance Practices." *World Development* 34, no. 5: 852–867.

———. 2013. "The Micropolity Sovereignty Experience: Decolonizing, but Not Disengaging." In *European Integration and Postcolonial Sovereignty Games: The EU Overseas Countries and Territories*, edited by Rebecca Adler-Nissen and Ulrik Pram Gad, 53–76. New York: Routledge.

Beriss, David. 2004. *Black Skins, French Voices: Caribbean Ethnicity and Activism in Urban France*. Boulder, CO: Westview Press.

Bishop, Matthew Lewis. "The French Caribbean and the Challenge of Neoliberal Globalisation: The Silent Death of Tricolore Development." In *Governance in the Non-independent Caribbean: Challenges and Opportunities in the Twenty-First Century*, edited by Peter Clegg and Emilio Pantojas-García, 119–145. Kingston, Jamaica: Ian Randle Publishers.

Bonilla, Yarimar. 2010. "Guadeloupe Is Ours." *Interventions: International Journal of Postcolonial Studies* 12, no. 1: 123–137.

Central Bureau of Statistics. 2010. *Statistical Yearbook of the Netherlands Antilles 2010*.

Clegg, Peter, and Emilio Pantojas-Garcia. 2009. *Governance in the Non-Independent Caribbean: Challenges and Opportunities in the Twenty-First Century*. Kingston, Jamaica: Ian Randle Publishers.

Curaçao. 2010. Directed by Sara Vos and San Snoep. Zeppers Film and TV.

"Curaçao, Aruba Seek Pan-American Aid to Attain Independence." 1948. *Chicago Daily Tribune (1923–1963)*, February 4, p. 14.

Curaçao Central Bureau of Statistics. 2013. *Resultaten Arbeidkrachtenonderzoek* (AKO).

Curaçao Central Bureau of Statistics. 2014. *Demography of Curaçao Census 2011* (November).

Curconsult. 2013. "Continue Building Together: Second Follow Up Perception Study Dutch Caribbean." Curconsult, Research and Management Consultants.

de Hart, Betty. 2004. "Political Debates on Dual Nationality in the Netherlands 1990–2003." *IMIS–Beitrage* 24: 149–62.

De Jong, Lammert. 2005a. "Extended Statehood in the Caribbean: Definition and Focus." In *Extended Statehood in the Caribbean: Paradoxes of Quasi Colonialism, Local Autonomy and Extended Statehood in the USA, French, Dutch, and British Caribbean*, edited by Lammert De Jong and Dirk Kruijt, 3–19. Amsterdam: Rozenberg Publishers.

———. 2005b. "The Kingdom of the Netherlands: A Not So Perfect Union with the Netherlands Antilles and Aruba." In *Extended Statehood in the Caribbean: Paradoxes of Quasi Colonialism. Local Autonomy and Extended Statehood in the USA, French, Dutch, and British Caribbean*, edited by Lammert De Jong and Dirk Kruijt, 85–123. Amsterdam: Rozenberg Publishers.

———. 2009. "The Implosion of the Netherlands Antilles." In *Governance in the Non-Independent Caribbean: Challenges and Opportunities in the Twenty-First Century*, edited by Peter Clegg and Emilio Pantojas-Garcia, 22–44. Kingston, Jamaica: Ian Randle Publishers.

Duijf, M.A.M., and Alfred H. A. Soons. 2011. *The Right to Self-Determination and the Dissolution of the Netherlands Antilles*. Nijmejen, the Netherlands: Wolf Legal Publishers.

Eman, Mike. 2011. "Defending the Democratic Rights of EU Citizens Overseas: A Personal Story." In *EU Law of the Overseas: Outermost Regions, Associated Overseas Countries and Territories, Territories Sui Generis*, edited by Dimitry Kochenov, 433–437. Alphen aan den Rijn, The Netherlands: Kluwer Law International.

Emmer, Piet. 2007. "Van de Antillen blijf je af. Hoezo?" *NRC Handelsblad*, November 10.

Essed, Philomena. 1991. *Everyday Racism: Reports from Women of Two Cultures*, 1st ed. Alameda, CA: Hunter House.

Essed, Philomena, and Isabel Hoving. 2014. *Dutch Racism*. Amsterdam: Rodopi.

Expatica. 2009. "Suspicion and Irritation." *Expatica*, November 1. http://www.expatica.com/nl/news/news_focus/Suspicion-and-irritation_-why-all-is-not-well-in-the-Kingdom-of-the-Netherlands_13461.html.

Grosfoguel, Ramón. 2003. *Colonial Subjects: Puerto Ricans in a Global Perspective*. Berkeley: University of California Press.

Guadeloupe, Francio. 2013. "Curaçaoans on the Question of Home: The Lure of Autochthony and its Alternatives." In *Caribbean Sovereignty, Development, and Democracy in the Age of Globalization*, edited by Linden Lewis, 189–207. New York: Routledge.

Hepburn, Eve. 2014. "The Accommodation of Island Autonomies in Multinational States." In *Constitutionalism and the Politics of Accommodation in Multinational Democracies*, edited by James Lluch, 87–107. Oxford: Palgrave Macmillan.

Hillebrink, Steven. 2008. *The Right to Self-Determination and Post-Colonial Governance: The Cases of the Netherlands Antilles and Aruba*. The Hague: T.M.C. Asser Press.

Hintjens, Helen. 1995. *Alternatives to Independence: Explorations in Post-Colonial Relations*. Aldershort, England: Darmouth Publishing Company.

Jalabert, Laurent. 2010. "Les mouvements sociaux en Martinique dans les années 1960 et la réaction des pouvoirs publics." *Études Caribéennes* 17 (December). https://journals.openedition.org/etudescaribeennes/4881.

Kochenov, Dimitry, ed. 2011a. "EU Law of the Overseas: Outermost Regions, Associated Overseas Countries and Territories, Territories Sui Generis." In *EU Law of the*

Overseas: Outermost Regions, Associated Overseas Countries and Territories, Territories Sui Generis, 3–67. Alphen aan den Rijn, the Netherlands: Kluwer Law International.

———. 2011b. "EU Citizenship in the Overseas." In *EU Law of the Overseas: Outermost Regions, Associated Overseas Countries and Territories, Territories Sui Generis*, 199–220. Alphen aan den Rijn, the Netherlands: Kluwer Law International.

Koulen, Ingrid, and Gert Oostindie. 1987. *The Netherlands Antilles and Aruba: A Research Guide*. Dordrecht, the Netherlands: Foris Publications Holland.

Maas, Willem. 2014. "The Netherlands: Consensus and Contention in a Migration State." In *Controlling Immigration: A Global Perspective*, 3rd ed., edited by James F. Hollifield, Philip Martin, and Pia Orrenhuis. Stanford, CA: Stanford University Press.

Miles, William. 2001. "Fifty Years of Assimilation: Assessing Franc's Experience of Caribbean Decolonisation through Administrative Reform." In *Islands at the Crossroads: Politics in the Non-independent Caribbean*, edited by Aaron Gamaliel Ramos and Angel Israel Rivera, 45–60. Kingston, Jamaica: Ian Randle Publishers.

Milia-Marie-Luce, Monique. 2009. "Migration in the French Caribbean: People from Around Here and Over There and the Question of Visibility." In *Governance in the Non-Independent Caribbean: Challenges and Opportunities in the Twenty-First Century*, edited by Peter Clegg and Emilio Pantojas-Garcia, 203–214. Kingston, Jamaica: Ian Randle Publishers.

Murdoch, Adlai. 2008. "Introduction: Departmentalization's Continuing Conundrum: Locating the DOM-ROM between: 'Home' and 'Away.'" *International Journal of Francophone Studies* 11, nos. 1 and 2.

Oostindie, Gert. 2000. *Het Paradijs Overzee: De Nederlandse Caraiben en Nederland*. Leiden: Uitgeverij.

———. 2005. *Paradise Overseas: The Dutch Caribbean; Colonialism and its Transatlantic Legacies*. Oxford: Macmillan Caribbean.

———. 2006. "Dependence and Autonomy in Sub-national Island Jurisdictions: The Case of the Kingdom of the Netherlands." *Round Table* 95, no. 385 (September): 609–626.

———. 2009. "Migration Paradoxes of Non-sovereignty: A Comparative Perspective on the Dutch Caribbean." In *Governance in the Non-independent Caribbean: Challenges and Opportunities in the Twenty-First Century*, edited by Peter Clegg and Emilio Pantojas-Garcia, 163–181. Kingston, Jamaica: Ian Randle Publishers.

———. 2011. *Postcolonial Netherlands: Sixty Years of Forgetting, Commemorating, Silencing*. Amsterdam: Amsterdam University Press.

———. 2013. "Postcolonial Sovereignty Games with Europe at the Margins." In *European Integration and Postcolonial Sovereignty Games: The EU Overseas Countries and Territories*, edited by Rebecca Adler-Nissen and Ulrik Pram Gad, 203–216. New York: Routledge.

Oostindie, Gert, and Inge Klinkers. 2003. *Decolonising the Caribbean: Dutch Policies in a Comparative Perspective*. Amsterdam: Amsterdam University Press.

Pommer, Evert, and Rob Bijl, eds. 2015. *Five Years of the Caribbean Netherlands: Impact on the Population (Summary for the Public)*, summarized by Karolien Baig. The Hague: Netherlands Institute for Social Research.

Putnam, Robert. 1988. "Diplomacy and Domestic Politics: The Logic of Two-Level Games." *International Organization* 42, no. 3 (Summer): 427–469.

Ramos, Aaron Gamaliel, and Angel Israel Rivera. 2001. "Puerto Rico: Regional Transformations and Political Change." In *Islands at the Crossroads: Politics in the Non-independent*

Caribbean, edited by Aaron Gamaliel Ramos and Angel Israel Rivera, 1–27. Kingston, Jamaica: Ian Randle Publishers.

Rezvani, David. 2014. *Surpassing the Sovereign State: The Wealth, Self-Rule, and Security Advantages of Partially Independent Territories*. Oxford: Oxford University Press.

Rojer, Olga E., and Joseph O. Aimone. 2008. "Cola Debrot: 'My Black Sister.'" In *Founding Fictions of the Dutch Caribbean: Cola Debrot's "My Black Sister" and Boeli van Leeuwen's "A Stranger on Earth,"* translated and with an introduction by Olga E. Rojer and Joseph O. Aimone, 17–44. New York: Peter Lang.

Römer, René. 1998. "Ethnicity and Social Change in Curaçao." In *The White Minority in the Caribbean*, edited by Howard Johnson and Karl Watson, 159–167. Kingston, Jamaica: Ian Randle Publishers.

Sharpe, Michael. 2005. "Globalization and Migration: Post-Colonial Dutch Antillean and Aruban Immigrant Political Incorporation in the Netherlands." *Dialectical Anthropology* 29, nos. 3–4 (September): 291–314.

———. 2008. "Dutch Empire." In *Africa and the Americas: Culture, Politics, and History*, edited by Richard Juang and Noelle Morrissette, 385–389. Santa Barbara, CA: ABC-CLIO.

———. 2009. "Curaçaoan 1969 Uprising." In *The International Encyclopedia of Revolution and Protest: 1500 to the Present*, 942–943. Hoboken, NJ: John Wiley & Sons.

———. 2014a. *Postcolonial Citizens and Ethnic Migration: the Netherlands and Japan in the Age of Globalization*, i-xii, 1–270. London: Palgrave Macmillan.

———. 2014b. "Race, Color, and Nationalism in Aruban and Curaçaoan Political Identities." In *Dutch Racism*, edited by Philomena Essed and Isabel Hoving, 117–131. The Netherlands: Rodopi.

———. 2020. "Extending Postcolonial Sovereignty Games: The Multilevel Negotiation of Autonomy and Integration in the 2010 Dissolution of the Netherlands Antilles and Dutch Kingdom Relations." *Ethnopolitics* (April): https://doi.org/10.1080/17449057.2020.1726031.

Statistics Netherlands. 2013. *The Caribbean Netherlands in Figures, 2012*.

St. Maarten Department of Statistics. *Stat. Census 2011, Unemployment and Participation Rate by Age and Sex*.

Suksi, Markku. 2011. *Sub-state Governance though Territorial Autonomy: A Comparative Study in Constitutional Law of Powers, Procedures and Institutions*. Dordrecht: Springer.

Sutton, Paul. 2012. "The European Union and the Caribbean Region: Situating the Caribbean Overseas Countries and Territories." *European Review of Latin American and Caribbean Studies*, no. 93 (October): 79–94.

van der Pijl, Yvon, and Francio Guadeloupe. 2015. "Imagining the Nation in the Classroom: Belonging and Nationness in the Dutch Caribbean." *European Review of Latin American and Caribbean Studies*, no. 98 (April): 87–98.

van Hulst, Hans. 2000. "A Continuing Construction of Crisis: Antilleans, Especially Curaçaoans, in the Netherlands." In *Immigrant Integration: The Dutch Case*, edited by Hans Vermeulen and Rinus Penninx, 93–122. Amsterdam: Het Spinhuis.

van Niekerk, Mies. 2000. "Paradoxes in Paradise. Integration and Social Mobility of the Surinamese in the Netherlands." In *Immigrant Integration: The Dutch Case*, edited by Hans Vermeulen and Rinus Penninx, 64–93. Amsterdam: Het Spinhuis.

———. 2002. *Premigration Legacies and Immigrant Social Mobility: The Afro-Surinamese and Indo-Surinamese in the Netherlands*. Amsterdam: Het Spinhuis, 2000; translation: Lexington Books.

Veenendaal, W. P. 2015. "The Dutch Caribbean Municipalities in Comparative Perspective." *Island Studies Journal* 10, no. 1: 15–30.

Veenendaal, W., and G. Oostindie. 2018. "Head versus Heart: The Ambiguities of Nonsovereignty in the Dutch Caribbean." *Regional & Federal Studies* 28, no. 1: 25–45.

Watts, Ronald L. 2009. "Island Jurisdictions in Comparative Constitutional Perspective." In *The Case for Non-sovereignty: Lessons from Sub-national Island Jurisdictions*, edited by Geoffrey Baldacchino and David Milne, 21–39. New York: Routledge.

Acknowledgments

Neither the original concept nor the final form of this book would have come into being without the critical help of numerous people along the way.

First, I would like to thank my Martinican colleagues, Anny Dominique Curtius of the University of Iowa and Rodolphe Solbiac of the Université des Antilles, Schoelcher, Martinique, for working with me to come up with the initial idea and helping to put it into motion. Nelson Maldonado-Torres and Michelle Stephens of Rutgers University and Yolanda Martinez-San Miguel, then of Rutgers and presently of the University of Miami, evaluated the original set of essays for the Critical Caribbean Studies series and recommended the expansion of manuscript and theme to its present format. I would also like to thank the contributors who responded positively to both calls for papers.

My thanks and appreciation go to the anonymous readers who evaluated the final manuscript. My thanks also to my fellow Antiguan, Professor Paget Henry of Brown University, giant scholar and enduring friend, who responded to the call and agreed to coauthor an essay with me at relatively short notice. My thanks also to my brother, Ambassador Colin Murdoch, for permission to use the photo of Prime Minister Gaston Browne of Antigua and Barbuda and Alfred Marie-Jeanne, president of the Collectivité Territoriale de Martinique.

The appearance of this book marks the culmination of an extended period of work that also has been a labor of love. Finally, this book is a testament to the continuing resilience of the Caribbean people, and to the conviction that true sovereignty will indeed one day be a reality. *A luta continua*.

Notes on Contributors

ROSE MARY ALLEN is a visiting lecturer at the University of Curacao. She has published and copublished several books and articles on cultural heritage, migration, diaspora, gender, and cultural diversity. She is a Caribbean postgraduate research partner in the Netherlands Organization for Scientific Research projects *Traveling Caribbean Heritage* and *Gendered and Sexual Citizenship in Curacao and Bonaire.*

ALESSANDRA BENEDICTY-KOKKEN is a senior researcher/research coordinator at the Research Center for Material Culture at Wereldculturen in the Netherlands. She also teaches at Universiteit Utrecht and the City College of New York (City University of New York, or CUNY). Previously she was associate professor at the City College of New York and the Graduate Center (CUNY). She is the author of *Spirit Possession in French, Haitian, and Vodou Thought: An Intellectual History* (2015). She is coeditor of *Revisiting Marie Vieux Chauvet: Paradoxes of the Postcolonial Feminine* (2016), a special issue of *Yale French Studies*; and coeditor of *The Haiti Exception: Anthropology and the Predicament of Narrative* (2016). She is currently series editor for Brill's Caribbean Series.

MALCOM FERDINAND is a researcher at the French National Research Center (CNRS/IRISSO). His research draws on the fields of political philosophy, political ecology, and postcolonial theory with a focus on the Caribbean. He has just published a book entitled *Une écologie décoloniale, penser l'écologie depuis le monde caribéen*, which will soon be available in English.

LOUISE HARDWICK is a professor of Francophone studies and world literature at the University of Birmingham (United Kingdome) and an associate fellow of Homerton College, Cambridge. A trained linguist and translator, she is the author of two monographs, *Joseph Zobel: Négritude and the Novel*

(2018) and *Childhood, Autobiography and the Francophone Caribbean* (2013). Her wider research interests include women's writing, cinema, biopolitics, and ecocriticism.

PAGET HENRY is a professor of sociology and Africana studies at Brown University. He is the author of *Peripheral Capitalism and Underdevelopment in Antigua; Shouldering Antigua and Barbuda: The Life of V.C. Bird;* and *Caliban's Reason: Introducing Afro-Caribbean Philosophy.* He is also the editor of the *CLR James Journal.*

VINCENT JOOS is a cultural anthropologist and assistant professor in the Department of Modern Languages and Linguistics at Florida State University. He research is focused on post-earthquake urban and industrial planning in Haiti and on the environmental destruction and population displacements pro-business policies and international agencies foster in this country.

JACQUELINE LAZÚ is an associate professor of modern languages as well as a cofounder of the Criminology Program at DePaul University in Chicago. She is an affiliated faculty member in the Critical Ethnic Studies Program, African and Black Diaspora Studies, and the Latin American and Latino Studies Departments. Professor Lazú's publications and teaching focus on Latino and Caribbean literature and culture, social movements, crimes of conscience, crimes of the state, aesthetics, and political philosophy.

H. ADLAI MURDOCH is a professor of French studies and the director of Africana studies at Tufts University. He is the author of *Creole Identity in the French Caribbean Novel* and *Creolizing the Metropole: Migratory Metropolitan Caribbean Identities in Literature and Film,* and the coeditor of the essay collections *Postcolonial Theory and Francophone Literary Studies, Francophone Cultures and Geographies of Identity,* and *Metropolitan Mosaics and Melting-Pots: Paris and Montreal in Francophone Literatures,* as well as various journal special issues. He is currently completing a manuscript entitled *Seizing Black Diasporic Subjectivity in the French Caribbean: From the Haitian Revolution to the French Antilles in 2009.*

ALIX PIERRE teaches African diaspora studies and is the director of cultural orientation at Spelman College. His research focuses on the representation and visualization of black bodies, voices, thoughts, and aesthetics across media in a transnational context. In addition to published articles and book chapters, he is the author of *L'image de la femme résistante chez quatre romancières noires: Vision diasporique de la femme en résistance chez Maryse Condé, Simone Schwarz-Bart, Toni Morrison et Alice Walker* (2014).

MICHAEL SHARPE is an associate professor of political science in the Department of Behavioral Sciences at York College of the City University of New York. Dr. Sharpe's areas of expertise are comparative politics and international relations, and his research interests concern looking comparatively at the politics of migration, immigrant political incorporation, and political transnationalism in the Netherlands, Japan, and around the world. His first book, *Postcolonial Citizens and Ethnic Migration: The Netherlands and Japan in the Age of Globalization* (2014), provides a cross-regional investigation of the role of citizenship and ethnicity in migration, exploring the political realities of Dutch Antilleans in the Netherlands and Latin American Nikkeijin in Japan.

HANÉTHA VÉTÉ-CONGOLO is a professor of romance languages and literatures at Bowdoin College, where she is affiliated with the programs of Africana Studies and Latin American Studies and contributes to the Gender, Sexuality, and Women Studies program. Her research is anchored in African and Caribbean women's studies; French, African, and Caribbean thought; and literatures and cultures examined from a black existentialist lens. Her academic publications include *L'interoralité caribéenne: Le mot conté de l'identité (Vers un traité d'esthétique caribéenne)*; *Léon-Gontran Damas: Une Négritude entière*; *Le conte d'hier, aujourd'hui*; and *The Caribbean Oral Tradition*, as well as her poetry, *Avoir et Être, ce que j'Ai ce que je Suis* and *Mon parler de Guinée*. *Discours antillaise* is forthcoming.

Index

Note: Page numbers in italics indicate figures.